The Chiang Mai Chronicle

THE
CHIANG MAI CHRONICLE

Second Edition

Translated by
David K. Wyatt
and
Aroonrut Wichienkeeo

The Chiang Mai Chronicle is volume one of a three-volume set.
The second volume is the Thai translation, translated by
Aroonrut Wichienkeeo and David K. Wyatt.
The third volume contains the plates of Hans Penth's original palm leaf manuscript of the
Chiang Mai Chronicle.

The Chiang Mai Chronicle, second edition

ISBN 978-974-7100-62-4

©1998 by David K. Wyatt and Aroonrut Wichienkeeo

No part of this publication may be reproduced or transmitted in any form by any means
without permission in writing from the publisher.
All rights reserved.

First edition published in 1995, second edition published in 1998 by

Silkworm Books
430/58 M. 7, T. Mae Hia, Chiang Mai 50100, Thailand
info@silkwormbooks.com
www.silkwormbooks.com

Typeset in HP-Garamond 12 pt. by Silk Type

Printed and bound in the United States by Lightning Source

Preface to the First Edition

Without evidence, we tell our students, historical work is only idle chatter. *The Chiang Mai History* is such a piece of evidence, which we present in homage to our teachers, to encourage our students and a wider world of readers, and to honor North Thailand on the occasion of the seven-hundredth anniversary of the city of Chiang Mai in 1996.

This is as close to a work of international collaboration as one could desire. It originated in 1991 when I visited Chiang Mai in order to choose a palm-leaf manuscript on which to work, and was reminded that the septcentenary celebrations would be coming in just five years. Because of work I had been doing on *The Nan Chronicle*, in the course of which I was captivated by the work of local historians a century and more ago, I was tempted to try to make an edition of a similar text on Chiang Mai. However, I had first to ascertain whether anyone else might have similar plans; and, if not—if I decided to work on Chiang Mai's history—I would have to identify a manuscript to use; and, once found, I would have to identify a collaborator with whom to work.

The answer to the first question, in October of 1991, was that I could find no other historian then planning to produce an edition of what I then called "the Chiang Mai Chronicle."

The second problem was more difficult. There are many—probably as many as a hundred—different copies of *The Chiang Mai Chronicle* in existence, most of them quite easily accessible through the work of Sommai Premchit, Harald Hundius, M.R. Rujaya Abhakorn, and others, who have microfilmed many manuscripts scattered throughout northern Thailand. These fall naturally into three groups: short, middle-length, and long. I ruled out both of the first two groups as being too incomplete. This left only a small group of texts. Pondering this question, I called upon Dr. Hans Penth in his office in the Social Research Institute at Chiang Mai University. He heard me out; then called me back a second day and confessed that he had once entertained the idea of working on the Chiang Mai Chronicle, and had in fact gone so far as to survey the existing manuscripts and choosing the "best," which he proceeded to place in my hands (in the form of a reel of microfilm). I was humbled by the faith he thereby placed in me, in this exemplary demonstration of international collaboration and scholarly generosity; and Aroonrut Wichienkeeo and I will be forever grateful to him.

The third question was eased by something my Thai teacher, Professor R. B. Jones, had said to me many years earlier; something about good translation being impossible without a native speaker of the language being translated from. And so I shamelessly spent several weeks in Chiang Mai "interviewing" prospective collaborators. I was then finishing up work on *The Nan Chronicle*, and so it was easy and natural to take problem-passages to those I met and see what they might be able to do with them. Mrs. Aroonrut Wichienkeeo passed this "test" with flying colors, without ever realizing, of course, that she was being "examined"!

A fourth problem then intruded; the problem of finding funding to support our work together, and finding a time acceptable to both of two very busy people. Ultimately, that problem was solved by the Thailand-United States Educational Foundation (Fulbright) in Bangkok, who awarded Aroonrut the first and only grant they have ever given to a teachers' college teacher, enabling her to visit Cornell from July 1994 to January 1995. We are most grateful to the TUSEC people, especially Dr. Pathamakha Sukontamarn, Director, for their assistance. Similarly, we thank the Rajabhat Institute of Chiang Mai for granting Aroonrut leave for the period necessary.

We especially thank Victor Lieberman, of the University of Michigan, for his assistance in dealing with some Burmese aspects of the text; to Dr. Prasert na Nagara for reading the text; and to Dr. Balee Buddharaksa for assisting with the Pali-language passages.

We are grateful to two successive heads of the Department of History at Cornell, Professor Sherman Cochran and Professor Isabel Hull, for having Aroonrut appointed a Visiting Fellow at Cornell; to Judy Burkhard, the Administrative Manager of the History Department, and Helen Swank, Administrative Manager of the Cornell Southeast Asia Program, for facilitating our work; and to our spouses, children, and grandchildren for their encouragement and understanding.

From the time we began working on this project more than three years ago, we have benefited from the advice and encouragement of our publisher, Trasvin Jittidejarak, who has been everything a publisher might be hoped to be.

We are especially grateful to each other: for patience and forbearance, for wisdom and assistance; for knowledge and occasional levity. We finish our much-too-rushed work with profound respect for each other, as well as for the anonymous author of the work we have translated.

David K. Wyatt
Chiang Mai
1 May 1995

Preface to the Second Edition

The first edition of *The Chiang Mai Chronicle* was rushed in order to meet the deadline for the 700th Anniversary celebrations of the foundation of the city of Chiang Mai in 1996: it went to the publisher at the beginning of May in 1995 and was published six months later, in the same year. We promised then that we would continue to work on the volume, and issue new editions as additional research warranted it, and as our readers' comments justified.

The first and major change to this edition is in the introduction, where I have been able to introduce new information concerning the sources of the Chronicle, and concerning what I had thought might be a Burmese version of the text (but which turns out to be completely different). I have also made small changes to the translation, notes, maps, and index.

The Thai version of the Chronicle has not yet been published, but the Northern Thai version, which is a sharp photocopy of the original manuscript, appeared in 1996.

We continue to be grateful to Trasvin Jittidecharak for her support and interest.

David K. Wyatt
Ithaca
June 1997

Table of Contents

Preface to the First Edition...v
Preface to the Second Edition..ix
Maps..xx
Tables..xx
Abbreviations..xxi

Introduction..1
    The Texts of the Chiang Mai Chronicle...2
    The Hans Penth Version..6
    Date and Authorship...7
    The Sources of the CMC..9
    "Chronicle" or "History"?...12
    Mechanical Details...13
    Dates...15
    Maps...15
    Romanization...16
    Translation...16
    Imperfections...17

Chapter 1..19
    Invocation..19
    The Succession of Kings...20
    The Lord Buddha..22
    Subsequent Kings in India..22
    Kings Who Changed the Era..23
    Queen Camadevi of Haribhuñjaya...24
    The Lineage of King Lawacangkarat...25

The Descendants of Lawacangkarat	26
The Life and Career of Khun Cüang	31
The Successors of Khun Cüang	35
King Mangrai's Parents	36
The Birth of King Mangrai	36
Accession of King Mangrai	38
Mangrai's Conquests—Müang Mòp	38
Mangrai's Conquests—Müang Lai	39
Mangrai's Conquests—Chiang Kham	39
Mangrai's Conquests—Chiang Chang	39
Foundation of Chiang Rai	40
Mangrai's Conquests—Chiang Khòng	41
Mangrai's Conquests—Müang Sœng	41
Mangrai Considers the Capture of Hariphunchai	41
Revolt of Khun Khrüang	43
New Coronation for Mangrai	45
King Ngam Müang of Phayao	47
King Ngam Müang and King Ruang of Sukhothai	48
The Meeting of the Three Kings	51
Ai Fa's Plans Come to Fruition in Hariphunchai	53
Dating of This Copy	57

Chapter 2 59

Mangrai's Conquests—Lamphun	59
Construction of Wiang Kum Kam, 1283/84	62
Wat Kat Thuam	64
Expedition to Pegu	65
Visit of the Southern Ruler	67
King Mangrai's Expedition to Phukam-Ava	68
Founding of Wat Kan Thom, 1290/91	69
Foundation of Chiang Mai	71
Visit of King Ruang and King Ngam Müang	75
Spirit-Offerings and Commencement of Construction, 1296	78
Renewed Warfare with King Yi Ba, 1296/97	79
Prince Khram Comes to Assist his Father	80

    The Battle Begins 82
    Colophon to Chapter Two 83

Chapter 3 85
    War Concluded With Phraya Bœk 85
    Prince Cheyyasongkhram 87
    King Mangrai's Three Sons 88
    Illness and Death of King Mangrai, 1317/18 90
    Sæn Phu Becomes King, 1318 91
    Usurpation of Prince Khrüa, 1319 91
    Nam Thuam Exiled to Keng Tung, 1324 94
    Sæn Phu Restored to Rule Chiang Mai, 1324/25 94
    Cheyyasongkhram Dies, 1327/28 95
    Kham Fu Begins Reign in Chiang Mai, 1328/29 95
    Foundation of Chiang Sæn, 1329 95
    Watchtower Drums for the Three Cities 98
    Death of Sæn Phu, [AD 1336?] 98
    Conflict With Nan 100
    War With Phræ, 1340/41 101
    The King and the Ugly Merchant 101
    Phayu Becomes King, 1345/46 103
    Kü Na Becomes King, 1367/68 104
    Kü Na's Death and Delayed Cremation 105
    Treason of Maha Phrom 105
    The Brave Women 106
    Corpses Cannot Go Through City Gates 107
    Sæn Müang Ma Becomes King of Chiang Mai, 1400 107
    Maha Phrom Returns to the North 108
    Sæn Müang Ma Attacks Sukhothai 108
    Building of Chedi Luang 109
    Sam Fang Kæn Becomes King of Chiang Mai, 1401 111
    Wat Chedi Luang Again 111
    Yi Kum Kam Foments Renewed War With Sukhothai 112
    Colophon to Chapter Three 115

Chapter 4 — 117

- War With the Hò, 1402/03 — 117
- The Defense of Chiang Sæn — 117
- Another Hò Attack, 1405/06 — 118
- Origins of King Tilokarat — 120
- Machinations of Sam Dek Yòi — 121
- Accession of King Tilokarat, 1442 — 122
- Sam Dek Yòi Seizes the Palace, and is Punished — 122
- King Tilok Favors Mün Lok Nakhòn — 123
- Ex-King Sam Praya Fang Kæn — 123
- Mün Sœng Sam Khrai Han Invites the King of Ayudhya to Come — 125
- Battle With Ayudhya Forces, 1442/43 — 126
- War With Nan, 1443/44 — 128
- A Vietnamese Helps Subdue Phræ, 1443 — 128
- The Fall of Nan, 1448/49 — 129
- War With Luang Prabang, April 1449 — 130
- War with the Lü of Müang Yòng, 1450/51 — 130
- Yutthitsathiang of Phitsanulok, 1451 — 130
- Tilok Fetches Yutthisathiang from Sòng Khwæ, 1452 — 131
- Tilok Attacks Müang Chawa (Luang Prabang), 1454/55 — 132
- War With the Lü, 1455/56–1456/57 — 133
- Ayudhya and Chiang Mai Send Spies Against Each Other — 133
- War With the South, 1457/58 — 135
- Renewed War at Sòng Khwæ, 1460 — 137
- Warfare With the Lü domains, 1459/60 — 139
- Ayudhya Invades, 1461/62 — 139
- Trailok Abdicates and is Ordained — 142
- Colophon to Chapter Four — 143

Chapter 5 — 145

- The Burmese Ascetic in Chiang Mai, 1465–67 — 145
- The Ascetic's Machinations Defile the Country — 148
- Military Expeditions in the Shan Region, 1462–71 — 150
- Various Deaths — 151
- Building Chedi Luang, 1475–79 — 152

The Vietnamese Attack Nan, 1480	152
Diplomatic Maneuvers With the Hò	153
Tributary Relationship With the Hò	155
Fiscal Reforms, and Deaths, 1480–85	156
War With the Lawa and Chiang Rung, 1485/86	157
Diplomacy and War With the South	157
War With the South in Nan, 1486/87	157
Officials Plot Rebellion	158
Death of Tilokarat and Succession of Yòt Chiang Rai, 1487–88	159
Yòt Chiang Rai Deposed, and Succession of Kæo, 1495	159
King Kæo's Religious Patronage	160
War With the South, 1507–09	160
Shans of Müang Pong, 1509/10	161
Continued War With the South, 1510–15	161
Chiang Mai's Fortifications Improved, 1516–18	162
Trouble With the Shans, 1517–20	163
King Kæo's Domestic Actions, 1520–22	163
Warfare in Keng Tung, 1523	164
Death of King Kæo, 1526	165
Succession of King Ket Chettharat, 1526/27	166
Construction, Fires, and Royal Charity, 1527–33	166
Ominous Omens	166
The Deposing and Exile of King Ket, 1538	167
Return of King Ket and His Assassination, 1543–45	167
Interregnum	167
Ayudhya Summoned to Intervene in Chiang Mai, 1545	168
Müang Nai Invades, 1545	169
Another Ayudhya Invasion, 1545–46	170
King Setthathirat of Luang Prabang, 1546–47	172
The Dawn of the Kali Epoch, 1548	174
Invasion from Phræ, 1551	175
Abdication of Setthathirat, 1551	175
Accession of King Mæ Ku, 1551	175
Shan Intrusions in Chiang Sæn and Chiang Rai, 1552	176
Lao (Lan Chang) Defend Chiang Rai and Chiang Sæn, 1555	176

King Mæ Ku Sees Omens at Lampang, 1556 177
Invasion of the King of Pegu, 1557–58 177
Historical Retrospective 179
Pegu, Chiang Sæn, Chiang Khæng, and the Lü 180
Itinerary of King Mæ Ku's Trip to Fight the Lao, 1559 181
Rebellion of Mæ Ku and Succession of Queen Wisutthathewi, 1564 183
Death of Wisutthithewi; Succession of Tharrawaddy Prince, 1578/79 184
Colophon to Chapter Five 184

Chapter 6 ..... **185**
Death of Bayinnaung, 1581 185
Wars With Ayudhya and Luang Prabang, 1585–1603 185
Burmese Successions in Chiang Mai, 1607–1628 186
King Suddho of Pegu Appoints Phraya Thipphanet, 1631 188
Miscellaneous Events, 1675–1706 189
The Min Yè Nara Rules Chiang Mai, 1707 190
Thepphasing Throws Lan Na into Turmoil, 1727 191
Cao Ong Kham Rules Chiang Mai, 1729 193
Cao Can Rules Chiang Mai, 1759 195
Rebellion and a New Ruler 196
Abhayagamani Takes Over Chiang Mai, 1762 196
Rebellion Spreads Through Lan Na, 1765 198
Abhayagamani Takes Control of Lan Na, 1766 198
Omens and Calamities Foretell Burma's Downfall 199
The Ca Ban Bunma Rebels in Chiang Mai 201
The Chronicle's Author Intrudes 201
Revolt in Lampang 202
The Emergence of Thipphacak 203
The Raid at Wat Lampang Luang 204
Thipphacak as King of Lampang 205
Chai Kæo of Lampang Flees to Phræ 205
Burmese Intervention in Lan Na 207
Water Ordeal Absolves Chai Kæo 208
The Children of Chai Kæo 209
The Burmese Assault Ayudhya 210

The Lan Na Revolt Begins	212
Kawila Rescues His Father	214
Siam Reorganizes Government of the North	214
Burmese Attack and the Battle of Tha Din Dæng	215
Bad Omen for Cao Phraya Ca Ban	217
The Burmese Retake Chiang Mai	218
Thai Assert Control in the North	218
A Siamese Force Oppresses the North	219
The Beginnings of the Cakri Dynasty, 1782	220
Cao Kawila Given Charge of Lan Na	221
Colophon to Chapter Six	221

Chapter 7 223

Kawila as King of Lan Na, 1782	223
Policy and Action to Repopulate the North	224
Burmese Invasion, 1784/85	225
Events in Ava, 1782–84	227
Kawila Visits Bangkok, 1785	228
Religious Actions in Lamphun, 1786	228
Military Actions, 1787	229
Burmese Invasion, 1787/88	230
Fatherly Advice, 1789	231
Pious Donation at Dòi Suthep	232
Minor Burmese Invasion, 1789/90	232
A Burmese Royal Impostor	233
Tak/Lahæng and Thœn	234
Royal Merit-Making, 1791/92	235
Luang Prabang, 1791	235
Burmese at Fang, 1792	235
Sakhæng Maung Phung	236
Attack on Chiang Sæn, 1793/94	236
Royal Merit-Making, 1794/95	236
Burmese Invasion, 1797/98	238
Müang Pu, 1798/99	239
Chiang Mai Renamed; and Merit-Making Works	240

Further Attacks in the Shan Hills ... 240
Shan Lords Submit to Chiang Mai ... 241
Expedition to the Shan Hills Again ... 241
Raja Còm Hong, 1801 ... 242
Chiang Mai Suspicious of Burmese Overtures, 1802 ... 243
Keng Tung ... 244
Burma and Vietnam, 1802 ... 245
Mission to Bangkok, 1802 ... 245
Welcoming the King Back to Chiang Mai ... 246
Coronation of Kavila as King, 1802 ... 246
Expedition to Capture Chiang Sæn, 1803 ... 247
Expedition to Bangkok, 1803/04 ... 247
Capture of Chiang Sæn, 1804 ... 248
Pursuit of the Na Khwa of Chiang Sæn ... 249
About Keng Tung ... 250
Mission to Bangkok, 1804 ... 250
Wat Inthakhin, 1805 ... 251
Expedition to M. Yang and M. Ræm, 1805 ... 251
Portents of the Uparaja's Future ... 252
Expedition to M. Yòng, 1805 ... 252
Expedition to the Khœn and Lü Regions ... 253
Chiang Khang Expedition, 1805 ... 254
Müang Wa, 1805 ... 255
Sipsong Panna ... 256
Upland Peoples ... 256
Return to Chiang Mai ... 257
Pious Works, 1806 ... 257
Mission to Bangkok, 1805 ... 258
Uparaja Returns from Bangkok, 1806 ... 258
Pious Works, 1806 ... 259
Colophon to Chapter Seven ... 260

Chapter 8 ... **261**
The Revival of Lan Na from 1796/97 ... 261
King Kavila's Advice to His Brothers, 1806 ... 263

Expedition into the Shan Region, 1807 ... 264
Assistance to Chiang Rung, 1807 ... 265
Burmese Invasion, 1807/08 ... 266
Burmese Attack, 1808/09 ... 267
Wat Phra Sing, 1811/12 ... 269
Expedition in the Khœn Area, 1811/12 ... 269
Môn Refugees Sent to Bangkok, 1815 ... 271
Death of King Kavila, 1816 ... 272
Chronicle of the Reclining Buddha ... 273
The Buddha Prophesies the Future of Lan Na ... 275
The Buddha and the Lawa ... 275
Indra Recalls the Prophecy ... 277
The Buddha's Ashes Come from Pegu ... 278
Kawila and His Brothers Fulfill the Prophecy ... 279
White Elephant Captured, 1816 ... 279
Lesbians Quarrel, 1816 ... 280
Return and Re-Coronation of the King, and Pious Works, 1817 ... 280
Miraculous Events in 1817 ... 281
The Còm Thòng Reliquary ... 282
Canals Dug in Chiang Mai, 1818 ... 282
Miracles and Pious Works, 1818/19 ... 283
Attack on M. Pan, 1818 ... 283
City Moat ... 284
More Pious Works, 1819/20 ... 284
Pious Works, 1821/22 ... 285
More City Construction ... 285
Death of the King, 1822 ... 285
Bangkok Installs the New King, 1823 ... 286
Royal Dissension in Chiang Mai, 1823 ... 287
King Suphathra Ordained a Monk, 1823 ... 287
A New King is Needed, 1823 ... 288
An Age of Misfortune ... 288
News of the Death of King Rama II of Siam, 1824 ... 290
Floods in Chiang Mai, 1824 ... 291
Death of King Maha Suphathra, 1825 ... 291

Sibling Greed ... 292
Ill Omens, 1825/26 ... 292
Attempts to Ward Off Misfortune ... 293
Funerals, Further Deaths, and Missions to Bangkok ... 293
King Phutthawong of Chiang Mai ... 295
Rebellion of Cao Anu of Vientiane, 1827 ... 296
Expedition to M. Leng, 1827/28 ... 297
A New Royal Palace ... 298
Final Colophons ... 299

Index ... 300

MAPS

1. Mainland Southeast Asia ... xxiii
1a. Interior Mainland Southeast Asia ... xxiv
2. Chiang Mai Region ... xxv
3. Shan Region ... xxvi
4. Khœn Region (Keng Tung) ... xxvii
5. Lü Region (Sipsong Panna) ... xxviii
6a. The Changing Course of the Ping River ... xxix
6b. Wiang Kum Kam ... xxx
7. Chiang Mai City ... xxxi
8. Chiang Sæn City ... xxxii
9. Chiang Rai City ... xxxii
10. Lamphun City ... xxxiii
11. Lampang City ... xxxiv

TABLES

Table 1. Rulers from Lawacangkarat to Mangrai ... 30
Table 2. Rulers from Mangrai to Phutthawong ... 144

Abbreviations

AD	*Anno Domini;* the Christian or Common Era
B.	*ban*, village
BEFEO	*Bulletin de l'Ecole française d'Extrême-Orient.* Hanoi and Paris, 1901– .
CMC	Chiang Mai Chronicle
CS	Chulasakarat, the "Lesser Era;" + 638 = AD
Cushman	*The Royal Chronicles of Ayudhya*, tr. Richard D. Cushman, ed. David K. Wyatt. Bangkok.
Doi Tung	*Prawat Phrathat Dòi Tung = History of Phra Thāt Dòi Tung.* Chiang Mai, 1993.
f°, ff°	folio, folios (page, pages)
GUBSS	*Gazetteer of Upper Burma and the Shan States*, comp. J. G. Scott and J. P. Hardiman. 2 vols. in 5. Rangoon, 1900–01.
Harvey	G. E. Harvey. *History of Burma*. London, 1925; reprinted London, 1967.
HP	Hans Penth; referring to the Hans Penth manuscript of the Chiang Mai Chronicle.
Jkm.	Ratanapañña Thera, *The Sheaf of Garlands of the Epochs of the Conqueror, being a translation of* Jinakālamālîpakaranam, tr. N. A. Jayawickrama. London, 1968.
JSS	*Journal of the Siam Society.* Bangkok, 1904– .
km.	kilometer(s)
M.	*müang, möng, mœng;* town, domain
McF	George Bradley McFarland, *Thai–English Dictionary*. Stanford, 1944.
mi.	mile(s)
Notton	Camille Notton, tr., "Chronique de Xieng Mai," *Annales du Siam*, III. Paris, 1932.

NTDict	Aroonrut Wichienkeeo *et al.*, *Photcananukrom sap Lan Na chaphò kham thi prakot nai bailan = The Northern Thai Dictionary of Palm-Leaf Manuscripts*. Chiang Mai, 1996.
Oppolzer	Theodor Ritter von Oppolzer, *Canon of Eclipses (Canon der Finsternisse)*, tr. Owen Gingerich. Vienna, 1887; repr. New York, 1962. [Eclipses are referred to by their serial number.]
PP	*Prachum phongsawadan*. 79 vols. Bangkok, 1914–1965. Reprints: 14 vols., Bangkok: Samnakphim Kaona, 1963–1974; 50 vols., Bangkok: Khurusapha, 1963–1970.
PTS	*The Pali Text Society's Pali-English Dictionary*, ed. T. W. Rhys Davids and William Stede. London, 1966.
PY	*Phongsawadan yonok*, by Phraya Prachakitkòracak, var. ed.
s.	*sakkarat*, "year of the [Lesser] Era" (CS) (s. + 638 = AD)
SN	*Tamnan phün müang Chiang Mai*, ed. Sanguan Chotisukkharat. Bangkok, 1971. ["SN" refers to the sponsoring agency, the Prime Minister's Office (*Samnak Nayok Ratthamontri*).]
t.	*tambon*, Thai administrative unit, "sub-district" or "commune"
T15RW	*Tamnan sip-ha ratchawong*. 3 vols. Chiang Mai, 1981–1990.
TM	*Tamnan Mangrai Chiang Mai Chiang Tung*, ed. Thiu Wichaikhatthakha and Phaithun Dòkbuakæo. Chiang Mai, 1993.
Udom	Udom Rungrüangsi, *Photcananukrom Lan Na-Thai, chabap Mæ Fa Luang*. 2 vols.. Chiang Mai, 1991.
UR	*Tamnan phün müang Chiang Mai*, ed. Udom Rungrüangsi, Chiang Mai, 1995.
ZY	*Zimmè Yazawin*. Unpublished Burmese chronicle of Chiang Mai, purportedly dated 1762; in Rangoon.

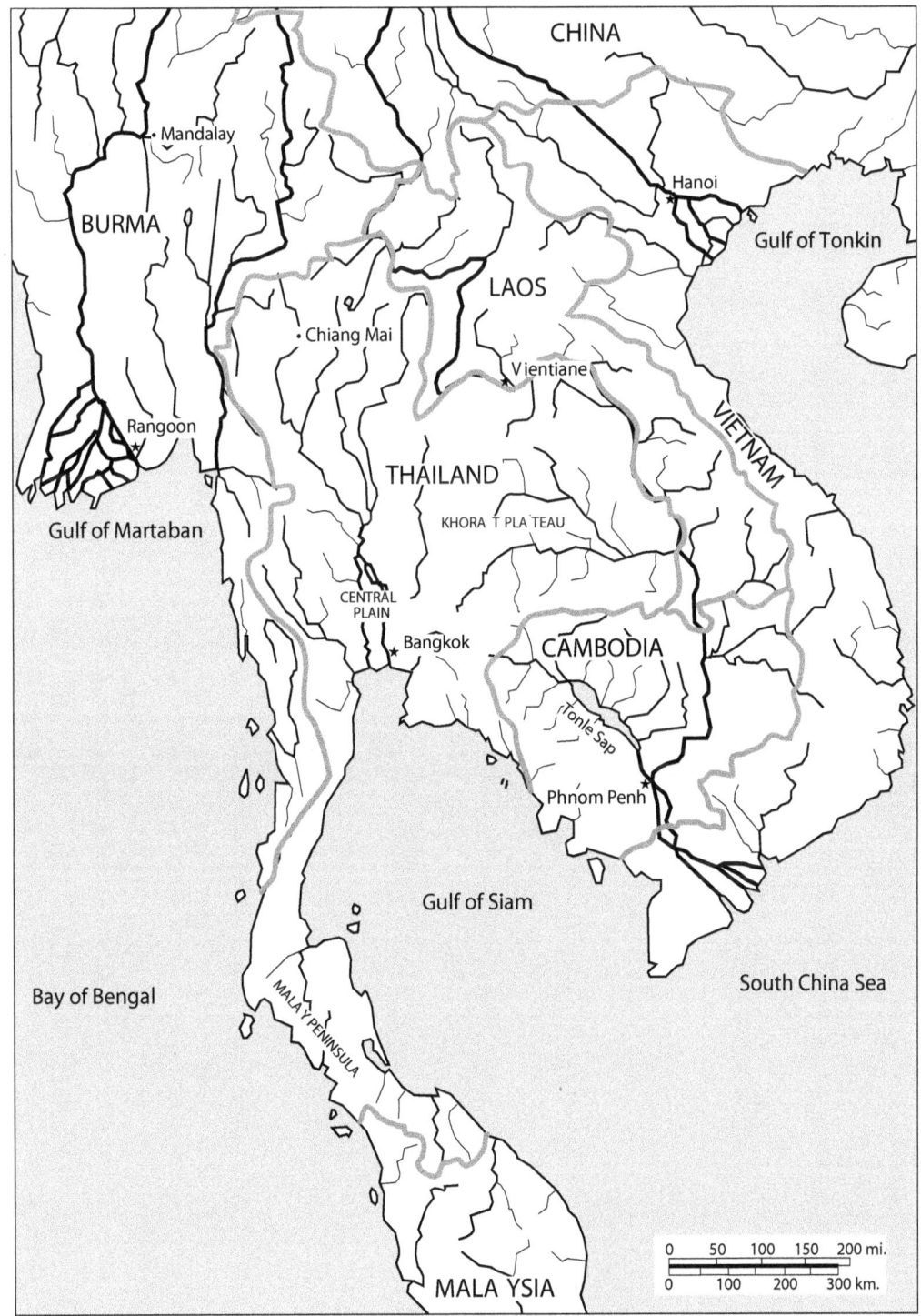

Map 1. Mainland Southeast Asia

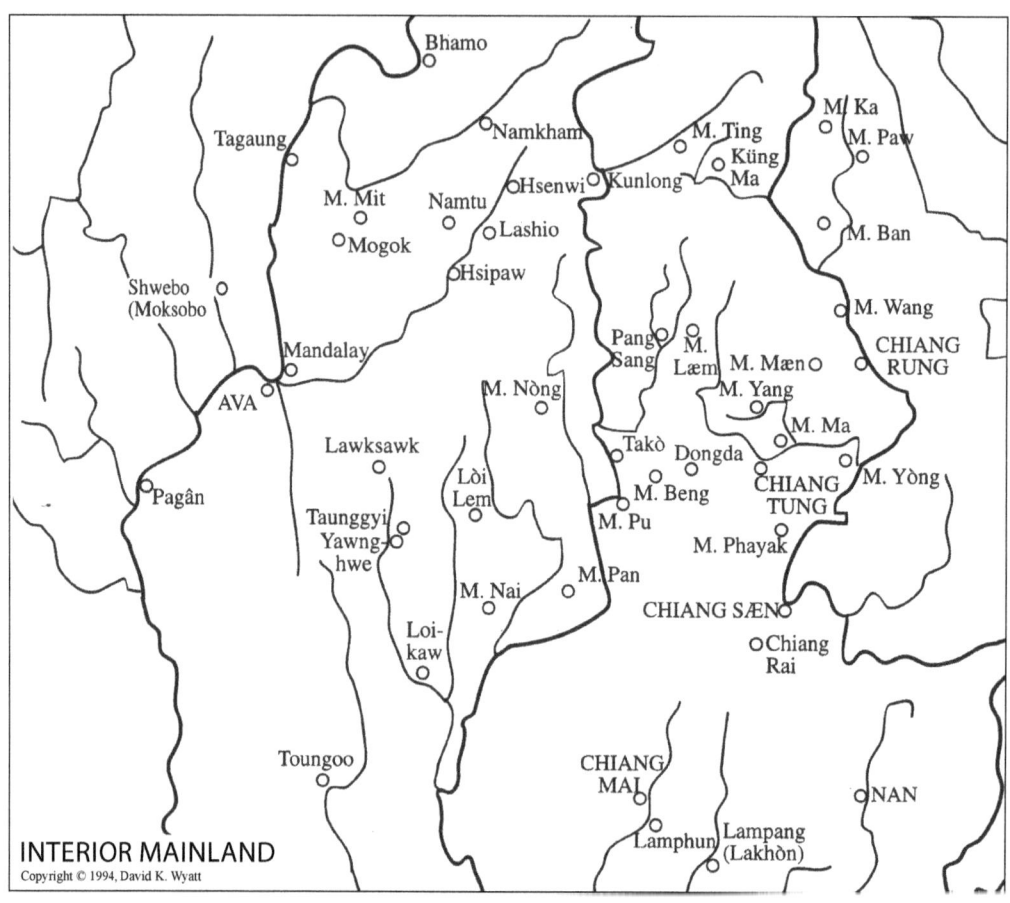

Map 1a. Interior Mainland Southeast Asia

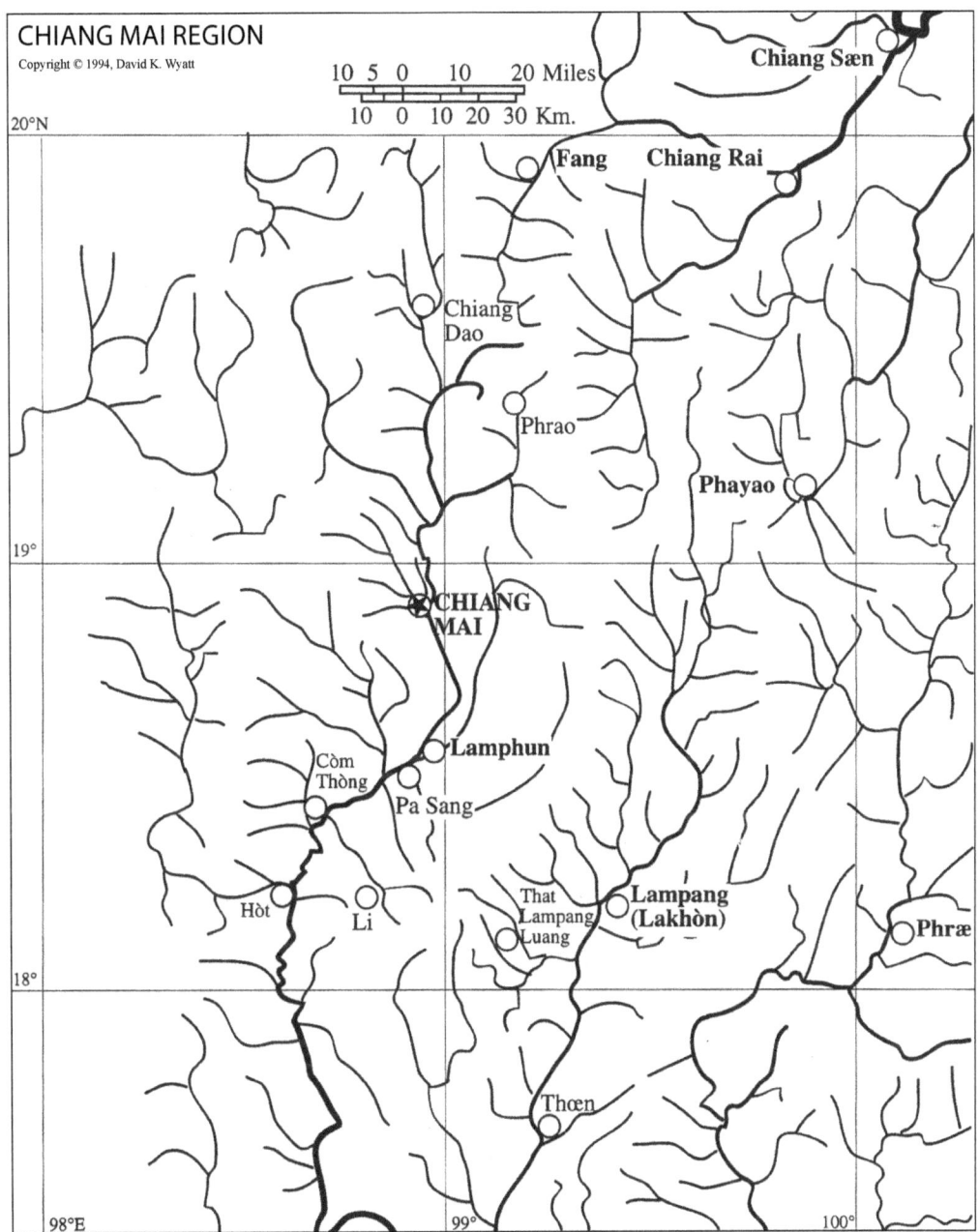

Map 2. Chiang Mai Region

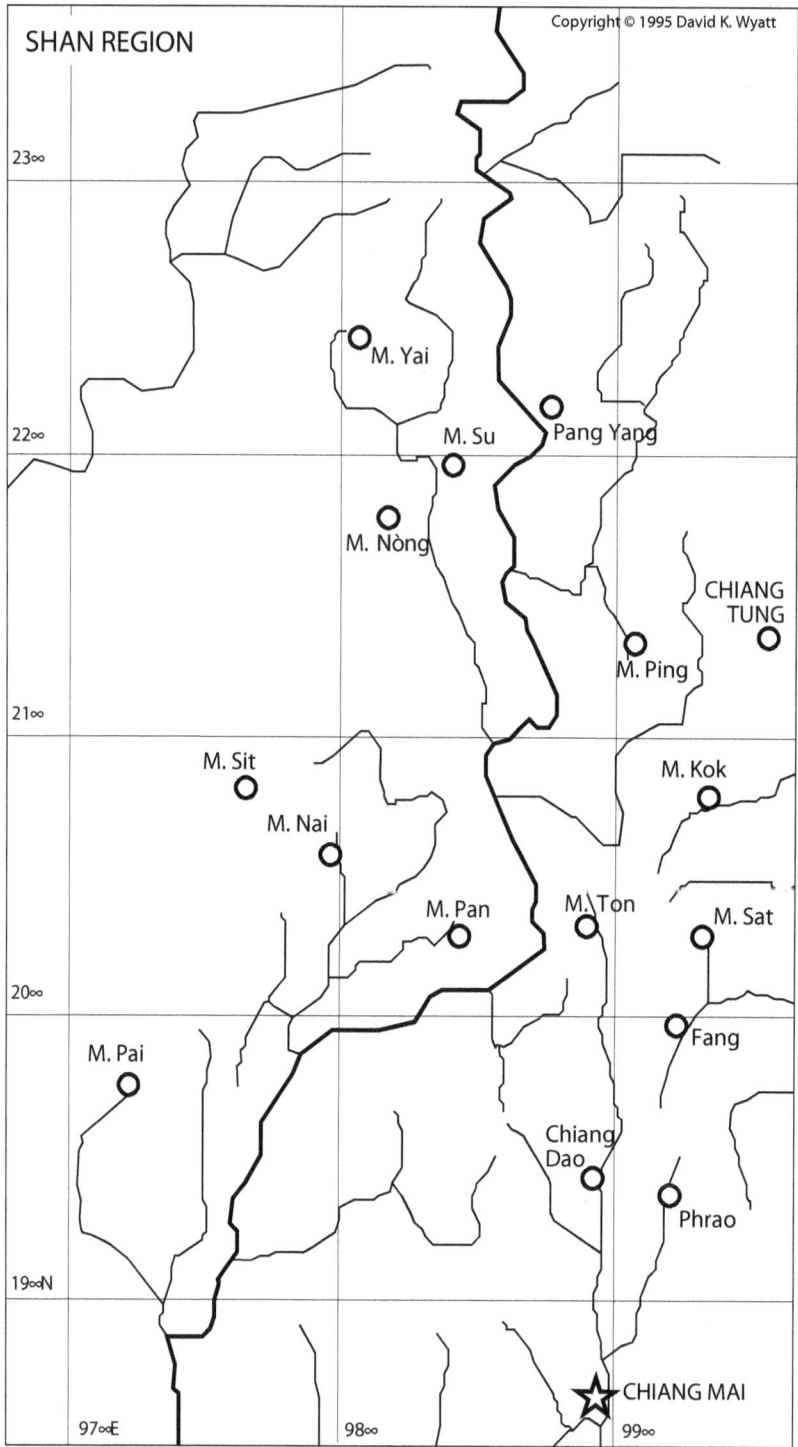

Map 3. Shan Region

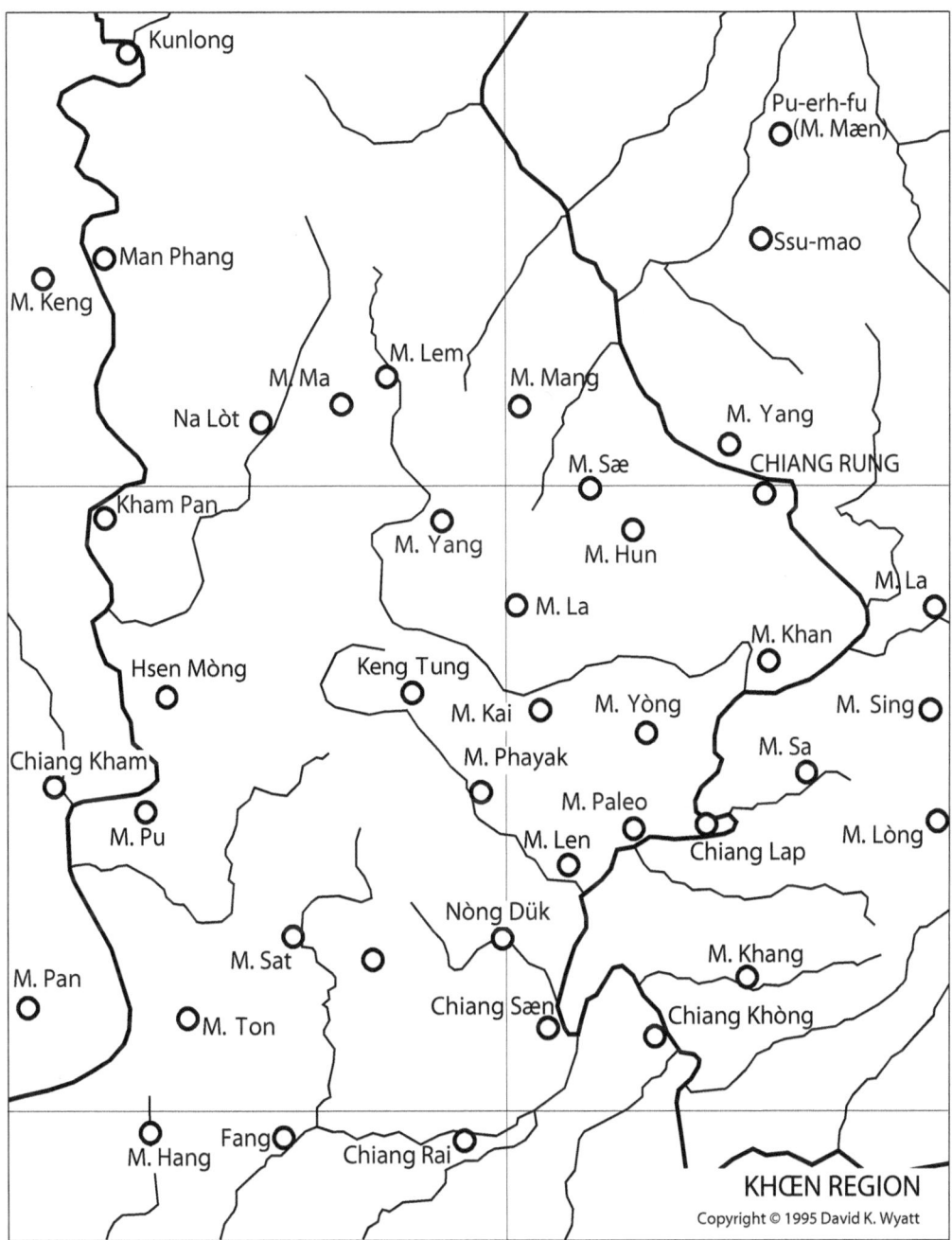

Map 4. Khœn Region (Keng Tung)

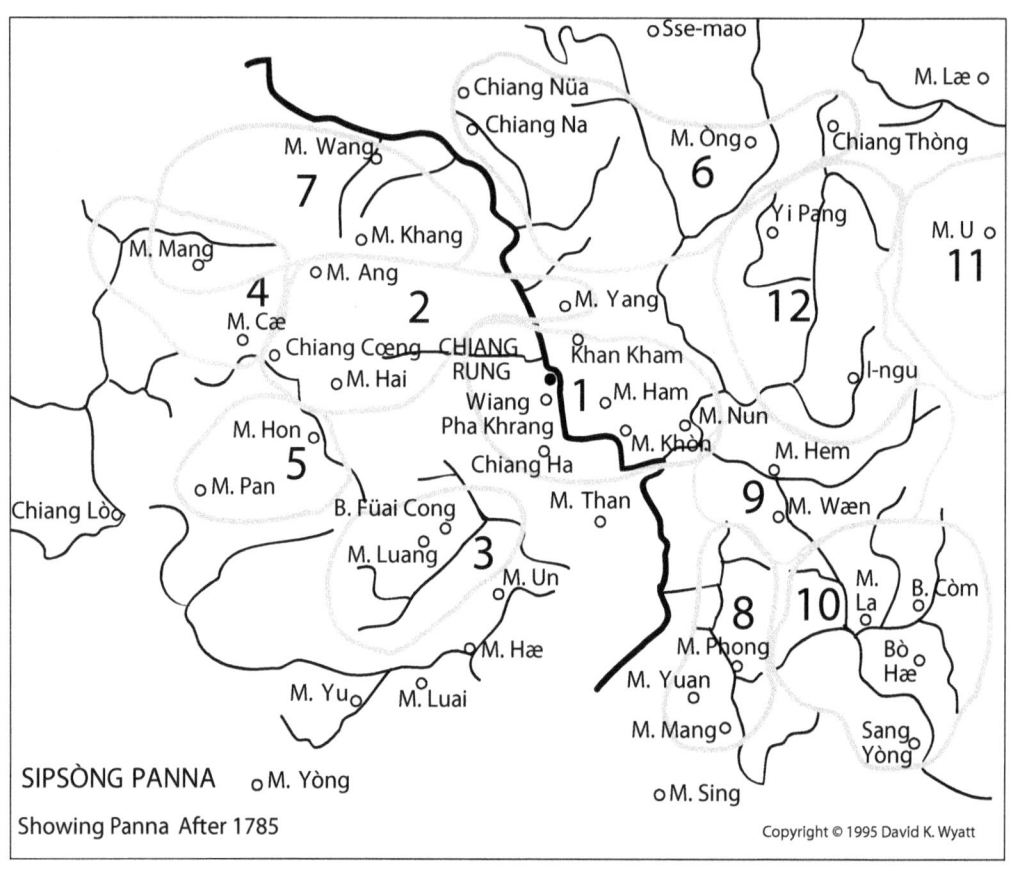

Map 5. Lü Region (Sipsong Panna)

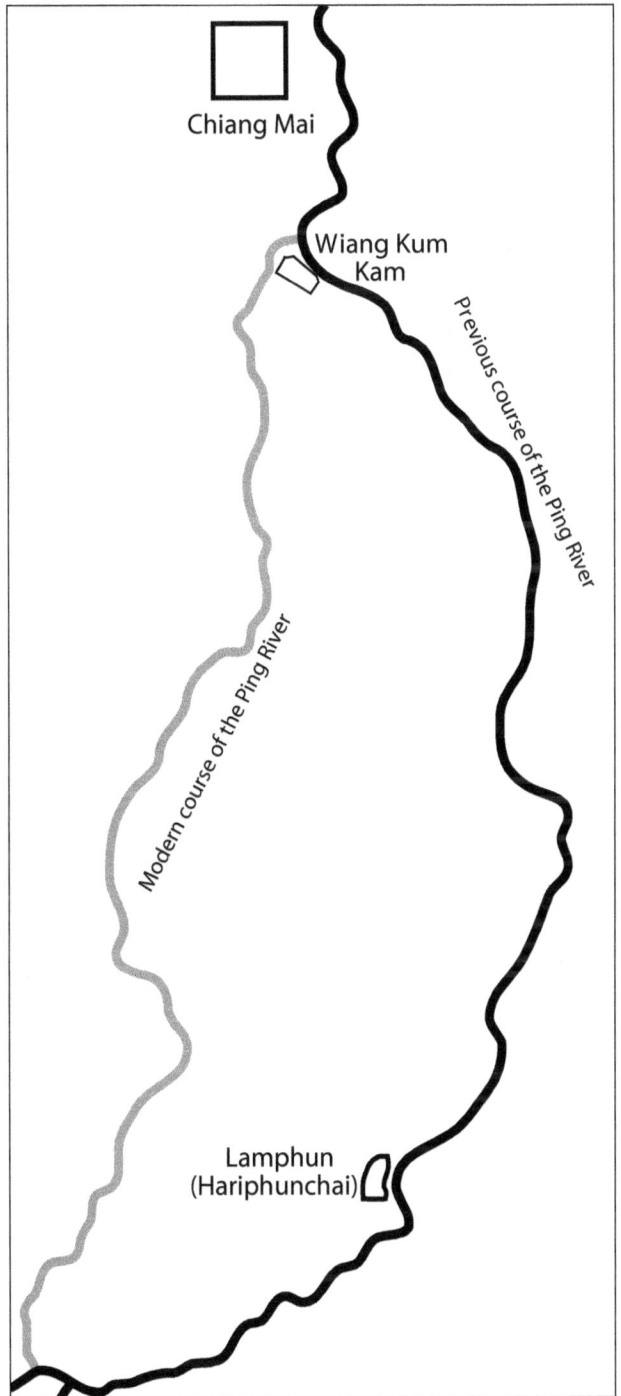

Map 6a. The Changing Course of the Ping River

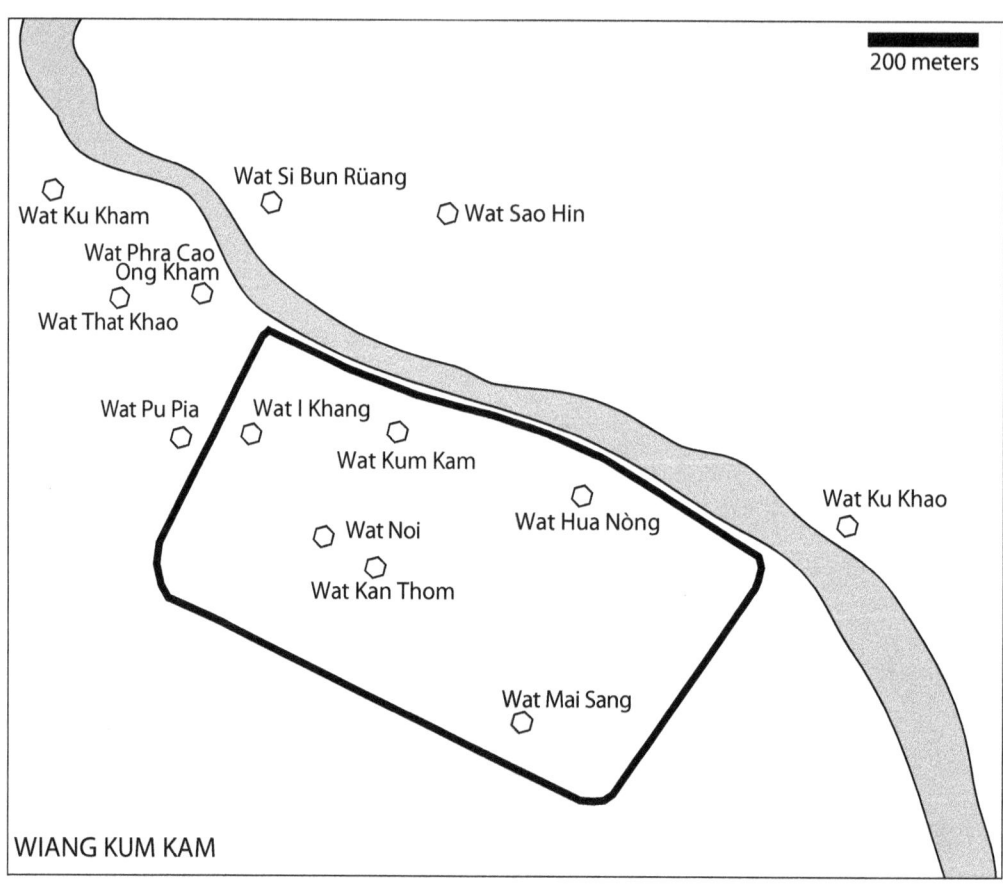

Map 6b. Wiang Kum Kam

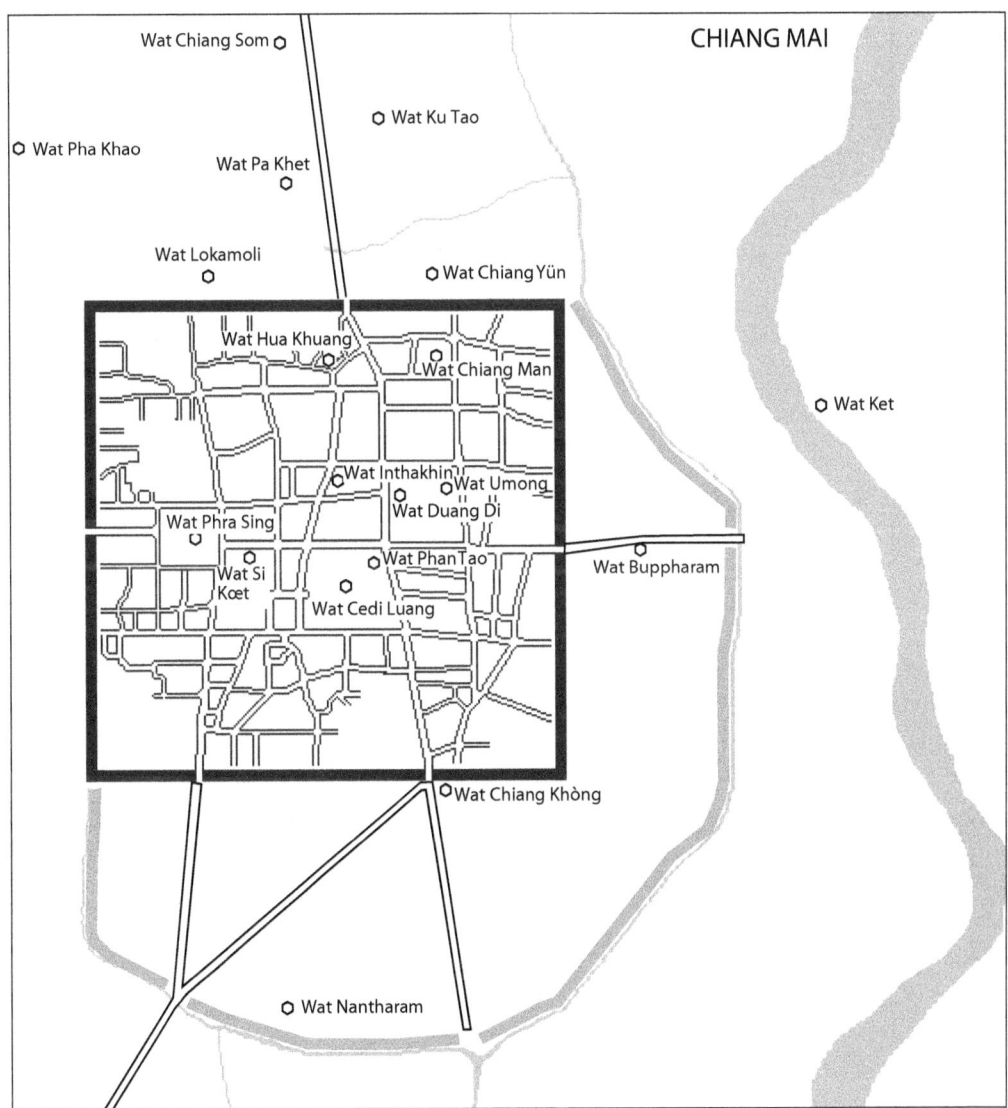

Map 7. Chiang Mai City

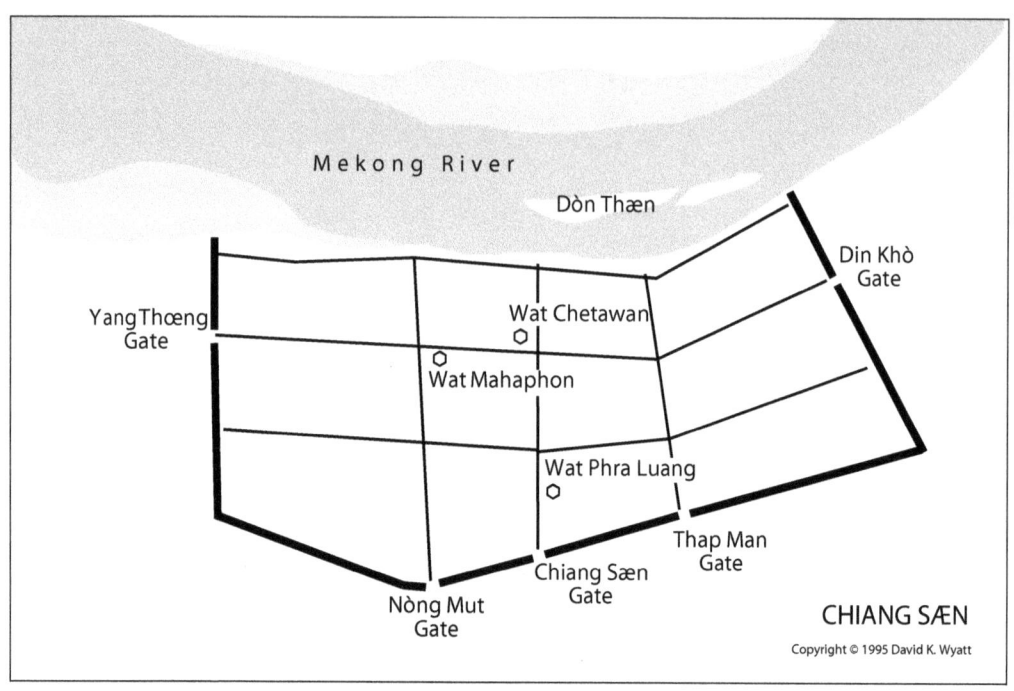

Map 8. Chiang Sæn City

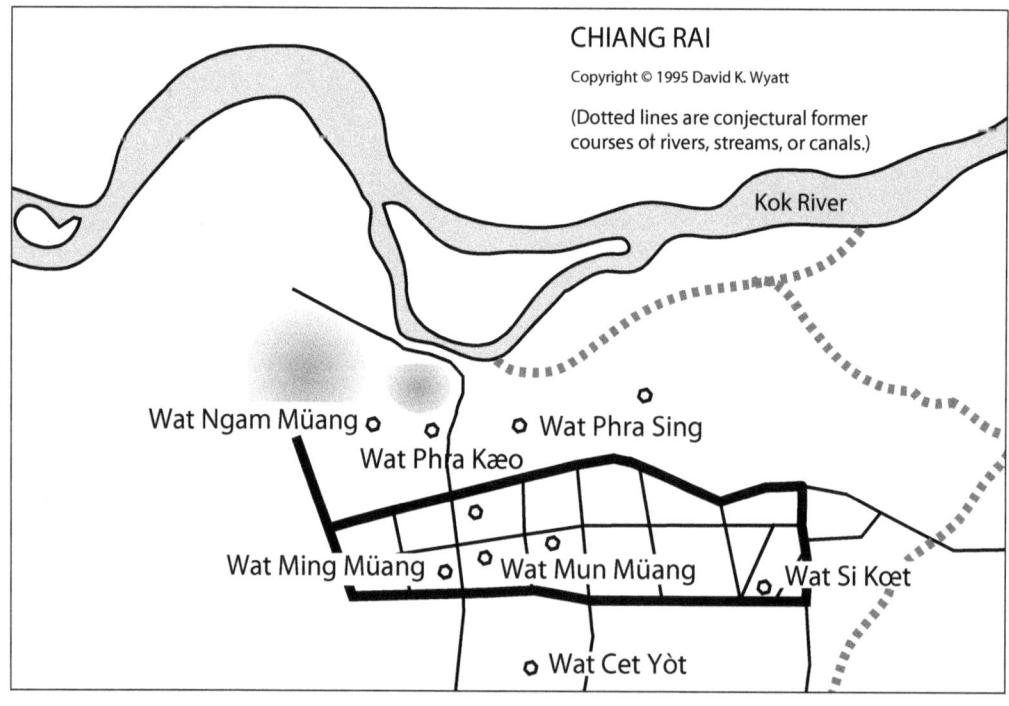

Map 9. Chiang Rai City

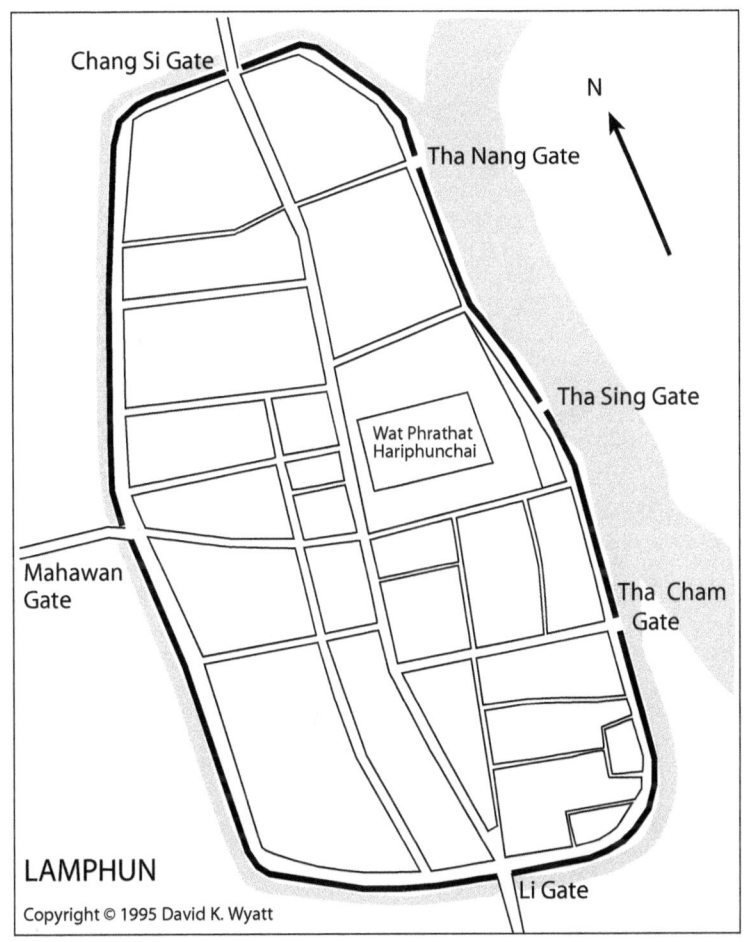

Map 10. Lamphun City

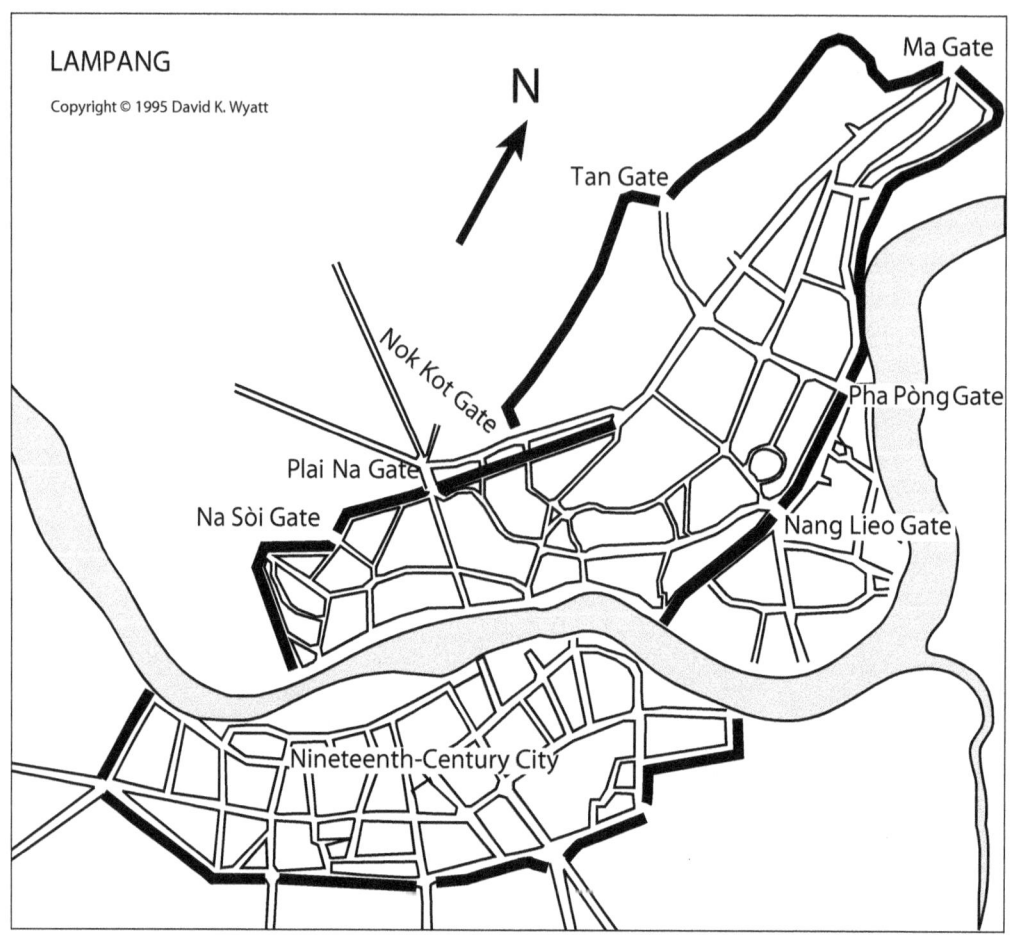

Map 11. Lampang City

Introduction

Despite the best efforts of numerous scholars over the past century, the history of Thailand has been dominated by the histories of Bangkok and its predecessor, Ayudhya. The 700th anniversary of the foundation of the city of Chiang Mai is an appropriate moment to attempt to set "the record" straight; to demonstrate that the histories of Siam and Thailand are not synonymous with the histories of Ayudhya and Bangkok. True, the old kingdoms of much of the country are barely remembered, but that is not to say that Lan Na (or Nakhon Si Thammarat, or Nakhon Phanom) should be forgotten: they once framed and ruled the lives of countless people, over many hundreds of years.

Chiang Mai, which was founded as a city in AD 1296, is often honored as a major site of Buddhist scholarship, especially in the early sixteenth century. We hope that this text might suggest that it was also a major center of historical scholarship. Over the centuries, many Northern Thai produced prodigious feats of historical work, examples of which have survived in (usually anonymous) palm-leaf manuscripts. These might have silently disappeared when nationalist governments a half-century and more ago ordered that everything written in "minority" languages and alphabets be burned. The fact that many survived in Buddhist temple libraries scattered throughout the north of what is now Thailand should attest to the tenacious hold which these written texts had in the minds and the regional identity of so many Northerners.

It is within this context that the "Chiang Mai Chronicle" should be considered. This introduction attempts to present a few salient facts about the "histories" of Chiang Mai, particularly about the text which we have translated here, and to explain how the current edition was produced.

The Texts of the Chiang Mai Chronicle

There are probably fewer than a dozen different versions of the royal chronicles of Siam known to scholars; but there are considerably more than a hundred versions of the Chiang Mai Chronicle which have come down to us. Many of the latter are known through microfilm copies preserved in various microfilm collections in Chiang Mai assembled by Sommai Premchit, Harald Hundius, M.R. Rujaya Abhakorn, and others. The importance of these microfilm collections is that they have made possible historical (and other) research into northern Thai manuscripts, work which otherwise would have necessitated visiting hundreds of Buddhist temple libraries scattered throughout the provinces of northern Thailand and neighboring areas.

The best-known versions of the Chiang Mai chronicle, however, are those which have been published. These make it possible to divide the known manuscripts into three groups, only one of which need concern us here. First is a very large group of short, or abbreviated, versions, consisting of simple king- and event-lists, running generally to twenty-five palm-leaves ("pages") or less. These often are fragmentary; and in general they may be considered to be simple abridgments of the longer versions.[1]

The second group of manuscripts might be called "middle-length" versions, ranging in length from twenty-five to one hundred pages. These also are fragmentary, but "fragmentary" in a different way than the first group. They usually confine themselves to a single period or subject—to the reign of a single king, or to a single episode, like the history of a particular set of wars, for example. We expect that these manuscripts were used as "sources" for the writing of the longer versions.

The third group of manuscripts consists of only a dozen or so texts. Of these, by far the best-known is available only in the translation made by the French Consul in Chiang Mai in the 1920s and 1930s, Camille Notton. In those years, Notton embarked upon an ambitious series of volumes of French translations of chronicles, which he called "Annales du Siam." The first three volumes of these were published in France between 1926 and 1932, with a fourth volume (in English) added in Bangkok in 1939.

---

1 The *Tamnan Mangrai Chiang Mai Chiang Tung*, ed. Thiu Wichaikhatthaka and Phaithun Dòkbuakæo (Chiang Mai, 1993) is a good example (or two examples!) of this sort.

(1) The third volume of Notton's *Annales* consists of what he called the "Chronique de Xieng Mãi" (Paris, 1932), which we refer to as Notton's *Chiang Mai Chronicle* (or "N"). This is a lengthy work of almost 300 pages, consisting of a text of seven "books" (or "chapters"), to which has been added a "History of Chiang Mai from 1805 A.D. to Our Day" from other sources. He tells us nothing of his manuscript; but we can tell with some certainty that it was a single incomplete manuscript of seven bundles or fascicles which lacked the last pages of chapter ("fascicle") seven (judging from HP, below). Notton had local assistance in reading and translating this text. The translation is, on the whole, excellent; and it is all the more credible because Notton is scrupulous in telling the reader where he could not make sense of the manuscript. (See, for example, his page 23, where he has a row of dots to indicate a long lacuna.) Local lore tells us that the original manuscript was destroyed during anti-French agitation in Chiang Mai during the Indochina War disturbances of 1940–41.

For forty years, Notton's was the only version of the Chiang Mai Chronicle known to scholars, and it was not even known to those who did not read French.

(2) In 1966, a local amateur historian and author in Chiang Mai, Sanguan Chotisukkharat, approached the Commission on the Publication of Historical Documents of the Prime Minister's Office of Thailand offering to prepare an edition of the Chiang Mai Chronicle in eight fascicles, for which purpose the Commission made him a grant of 1,200 *baht*. The Commission ultimately published that version in 138 pages in 1971.[2] Because the Prime Minister's Office published so many copies, this version (called SN for *Samnak Nayok Ratthamontri*, "Prime Minister's Office") has since become very well-known and widely-used.

Sanguan, like Notton, relied on local assistance. He tells us (p. 138) that the transcription from the manuscript, from Phra Maha Mün of Wat Cedi Luang in Chiang Mai, was done by a certain Thon Tonman, while Sanguan himself rendered the Northern Thai text into Standard (Central) Thai. Their work is dated 28 January 1967.

SN is fuller than the Notton version (N) because it has the full eight fascicles rather than N's seven. However, it is not very well done. In places, it is simply sloppy: the transcription has numerous haplographies, at least one place where an entire page (the back side of a palm-leaf) has been skipped, and a major deletion or omission in Chapter 8. Some numbers and words have either been misread, or the

---

2   Details in SN, pp. [v–viii].

transcription may have been done from a very defective copy. (And the index, which was not Sanguan's responsibility, was badly done.) On the whole, N is considerably better and more credible than SN—although, of course, N has only seven fascicles instead of SN's eight.

Sanguan seems to have used his edition in separately publishing a *Nangsü phün müang Chiang Mai* in 1972.[3] In his introduction, Dr. Hans Penth explains that this book is a translation of the chronicle, accomplished by having a monk read the palm-leaf manuscript aloud to Sanguan. He also notes that Sanguan's version is incomplete and careless.

(3) Those who know the history of Chiang Mai have long been aware of the problems of the SN version. It was probably for this reason that the Social Research Institute of Chiang Mai University in the 1980s began the full publication of yet another version of the Chiang Mai Chronicle. This version is based on a seven-fascicle manuscript from Wat Methangkharawat in Phræ which had been copied in 1889. It was published in three volumes between 1981 and 1990, under the title, *Tamnan sip-ha ratchawong* (T15RW, "History of the Fifteen Dynasties").

The T15RW is a very long manuscript of 398 pages, long mainly because it was written with only four lines on each side of each palm-leaf; the leaves being 4.5 x 55.5 cm. It is scrupulously edited, with photographs of each original palm-leaf accompanying the transcription. Its primary deficiency is that it includes only seven of the eight fascicles.

We began, thus, with three published versions known to us—Notton (N), SN, and T15RW. At least two of these, SN and T15RW, presumably were selected from a broader range of manuscripts because of their completeness, legibility, and accessibility. In particular, we may be confident that the knowledgeable staff of the Social Research Institute consulted most, if not all, of the manuscripts that would have been available to us in deciding which manuscript to use.

(4) None of us, however, was able to consult one manuscript that became known to us only in the last stages of our work, namely a Burmese manuscript known as the *Zimmè Yazawin* (ZY). We have been told that this text dates from 1762, though we know that the seventh fascicle of the Chiang Mai Chronicle ends with a date equivalent to AD 1806, and the eighth fascicle ends in 1827. (Victor Lieberman,

---

3 Sanguan Chotisukkharat, *Nangsü phün müang Chiang Mai* (Chiang Mai: Khrongkan Sun Wicai Lan Na Thai, Faculty of Social Sciences, Chiang Mai University, 1972).

who saw this text some years ago, recalls that its coverage extends only down to the 1560s.)[4]

At the Sixth International Conference on Thai Studies in Chiang Mai in October 1996, U Thaw Kaung and Daw Ni Ni Myint provided scholars with a first glimpse of the ZY in a tantalizing paper on "Sithu Gamani Thingyan's Zimme *Yazawin*, A Brief Study."[5] They explained that there seem actually to have been at least two different manuscripts by this title, neither of which seem from their description to have been based on any of the longer versions of the Chiang Mai Chronicle with which we are familiar. The ZY described by U Thaw Kaung and Daw Ni Ni Myint, which they intend to publish soon in English translation, consists of a short history of Chiang Mai, a history of the Buddhist religion, and a treatise on the revenue structure of the region. It is obviously unlike the Chiang Mai Chronicle presented in this volume

(5) Some years ago, Dr. Hans Penth of the Social Research Institute in Chiang Mai considered producing an edition and translation of the Chiang Mai Chronicle. To that end, he surveyed all the existing long (seven- and eight-fascicle) manuscripts. In the course of his investigations, he obtained a manuscript ("HP") which after lengthy investigations he determined to be the "best" manuscript. It is very similar in content and expression to the N, SN, and T15RW manuscripts, but it is more complete, more legible, and has fewer mistakes than the others. Dr. Penth's enormous kindness and goodwill have made it possible for us to use his manuscript as the basis of this edition and translation.

(6) Around the time the version in the current volume was published, another edition of the Chiang Mai Chronicle was published by a provincial commission formed in 1989 which apparently had been inactive when I was investigating the possibilities in 1991. This edition was produced under the direction of Dr. Udom Rungruangsri (below, UR). It was based upon seven manuscripts from a wide variety of sources, including HP. Based supposedly upon the oldest of these manuscripts, an 1843 manuscript from Wat Phra Ngam in Chiang Mai now held by the National Library of Thailand, Dr. Udom worked to established an "archetype" version by

---

4 Victor Lieberman (pers. comm. 3 April 1995) has seen a version of this text on microfilm, which he thinks goes only down to 1568.

5 *Proceedings of the 6th International Conference on Thai Studies, Theme VI, Chiang Mai 1296–1996: 700th Anniversary* (Chiang Mai, 1996), pp. 51–63.

"correcting" the 1843 manuscript using "better" readings from the other manuscripts and three published versions including SN, T15RW, and the *Phongsawadan Yonok* of Phraya Prachakitkòracak (a secondary work of the late nineteenth century).[6] Almost all of the footnote references to variant readings are to the HP version (cited as the CS 1288 version), thus indirectly confirming Dr. Penth's judgment that HP was the best of the various longer versions in existence, even though it was not the oldest.

The Hans Penth Version

We thus feel vindicated in our decision both to base our work upon HP, and to confine ourselves to presenting a single edition of a good manuscript rather than cluttering our work with references to lesser manuscripts (and printed works).

The manuscript consists of eight fascicles (like SN), of 23, 16, 19, 17, 24, 22, 26, and 26 palm leaves of standard size.[7] It is written in the old Northern Thai language and script. Each palm-leaf is inscribed on both sides, with five lines of writing per side. Penth numbered all the leaves with the chapter and "page" number in the left margin, together with "V" and "R" (for *Vor* and *Rück*, roughly "front" and "back" in German) to indicate the obverse and reverse of each page. To avoid confusion, and to make it easier to refer to these in the Thai version, we have renumbered the pages consecutively: thus ff° 8.1V and 8.1R have become ff° 8.01 and 8.02.

In general the handwriting is exceptionally clear, with very few insertions or deletions marked in the text. At least three scribes, judging from the handwriting, were involved in copying the text, and there are minor orthographic differences between the three. One scribe, for example, habitually left blank space between phrases or sentences, while the others did not.

The manuscript is said to have come from Chiang Sæn. It may have been copied as early as 1878, but probably dates from 1926, as Dr. Penth explains in his introduction to Sanguan's 1972 edition.

---

6 *Tamnan phün müang Chiang Mai, chabap Chiang Mai 700 pi* (Chiang Mai, 1995), p. k.

7 The UR edition reproduces the original palm-leaves of the 1843 manuscript, the eight fascicles of which number 30, 21, 23, 21, 24, 28, 33, and 30 palm leaves.

Date and Authorship

The date and authorship of HP raise extremely complex questions. Dr. Penth himself, writing about Sanguan's 1972 version—which applies equally to the HP version—opines that the manuscript was originally written in the time of King Tilok in the late fifteenth century, arguing that the manuscript is especially detailed for that period and sparse in its details for the immediately-following periods.[8] The HP manuscript itself, however, is considerably more complex than that, for even the pre-Tilok portions of the manuscript were themselves based on earlier manuscripts, written in different periods.

The essential starting-point for a discussion of the date and authorship of HP is to begin with the assumption that there was a long and rich tradition of history-writing in Lan Na and its various constituent parts. After all, we do know that a number of important historical texts were written in the region at least as early as the sixteenth century, including not only the well-known *Jinakālamālī*, *Cāmadevivaṃsa*, and *Mūlasāsana* and less-studied Buddhist chronicles such as the contemporaneous *Sihinganidāna*, but also such unstudied texts as the *Vaṃsamālinī*.[9] We know that other local historical texts were written in places like Nan well before the eighteenth century.[10]

We have to begin by asking whether the eight-fascicle version was written at a single time, or whether the eighth fascicle was added to a seven-fascicle version written no earlier than 1806 (which is the last date mentioned in that fascicle).[11]

---

8 *Ibid.*, pp. [vii–x].

9 See Balee Buddharaksa, "Vaṃsamālinī: A Critical Study of Palmleaf Texts," unpubl. Ph.D. diss., Banaras Hindu University, 1991; and Louis Finot, "Recherches sur la litterature laotienne," *BEFEO* 17, fasc. 5 (1917), esp. p. 151, which first drew my attention to this text.

10 See David K. Wyatt, "Presidential Address: Five Voices from Southeast Asia's Past," *Journal of Asian Studies* 53:4 (Nov. 1994), 1076–1091; and the same author's *The Nan Chronicle*, (Ithaca, 1994).

11 The various arguments that follow, concerning the date and authorship of the Chiang Mai Chronicle, were given in a series presented in the form of scholarly papers and lectures in the course of 1996, including: "Palm-Leaf Manuscripts and History-Writing in Premodern Northern Thailand" (Paper for Annual Meetings of the Association for Asian Studies, Honolulu, April 1996; and Paper for International Conference on Thai Studies, Chiang Mai, Oct. 1996. Published in *Proceedings*, Theme VII pp. 91–99); "Chiang Mai Chooses a King, 1824" (public lecture, Yale University Southeast Asia Studies, New Haven, 24 April 1996; and paper for International Association of the Historians of Asia, 14th Conference, Bangkok, May 1996); and "A Chiang Mai Historian, 1828" (public lecture, Siam Society, Bangkok, 12 June 1996).

We note that both of the seven-fascicle versions (N and T15RW) are incomplete: N ends mid-sentence (see HP f° 7.43); and T15RW ends without giving the reader any sense of closure. It is hard to believe that the seven-fascicle versions are complete, or were complete when their author(s) got to the end of fascicle seven. Although arguments could be offered on either side of the question, I am inclined to think that fascicles 7 and 8 were written together in 1827 or 1828 by a single author. I am inclined to believe so because there is a strange insertion in fascicle 8—a chronicle of a certain reclining Buddha image immediately north of Chiang Mai city[12]—which gives a Buddha-prophecy that serves to legitimize the actions of the final dynasty of Chiang Mai's rulers, and thus functions to structure the seventh and eighth fascicles. In the same fashion, there are three passages of the Chiang Mai chronicles in the seventh and eighth fascicles which function to provide background to later events, thus integrating the two fascicles.[13] In addition, the last two fascicles must be read, I think, as a whole to justify the author's political argument that makes sense only in the context of the First Anglo-Burmese War (1824–1826) and the "rebellion" of Cao Anu of Vientiane (1826–1827),[14] and the accession of a new king (Phutthawong) to the throne in Chiang Mai in 1825.

The author of HP does not mention the fate of Burma, and refers to the other events of these years without explicit comment; but he seems to imply that he regarded Chiang Mai's ruling line to have declined after the death of King Kavila in 1816, that subsequent kings were progressively lesser rulers, and particularly that Phutthawong had adopted a mistaken policy of distancing his state from Bangkok—by responding too slowly towards Anu's rebellion, and by taking Bangkok less seriously now that Burma in the wake of defeat at the hands of Britain was no longer a threat to Chiang Mai. The author of HP very pointedly reproduces, with approval, Cao Kavila's warning to his successors that "whoever of our descendents might revolt against the Great King of Ayutthiya [Bangkok], they will become slaves of the Burmese, Hò" etc.[15]

But who wrote this? The author never identifies him- or herself. This is not uncommon for such writings. We have to be cautious about concluding much about

---

12 Inexplicably omitted in SN. At 8.17–8.26 of HP; UR pp. 152–156.
13 An argument made most fully in "Palm-Leaf Manuscripts," as printed in *Proceedings*.
14 See note above, referring to conference papers.
15 CMC, p. 180.

the author from what he wrote, for he makes it clear that much of the text was taken, as it had to be, from other sources, almost verbatim.

What, at the least, can we tell about the author from what he writes? The author has to have been a local, Lan Na person. Throughout the text, the author displays an exceptional familiarity with local lore, local geography, and even local personalities. The author was not only literate but also well-read: he almost certainly was male, having received the traditional education in a period in a Buddhist temple. (Though for convenience we refer to the author using the male pronoun "he," the reader must remember that we cannot be certain of the author's gender.) He sprinkles Pali words liberally throughout his text, though he often mis-spells them. He had some first-hand acquaintance with the Burmese, for he sometimes uses Burmese words and phrases. He does not seem to have been a monk, for he is little interested in religious affairs: note, for example (fº 3.30) his offhanded dismissal of the *Chronicle of the Sihiṅga Buddha* image. He was not a scholar attached to the court, for at one point he expresses his hope that "the royal wise men will not find fault" with his work (fº 6.16 lines 3–4). He was well-acquainted with Bangkok and its ways; but he was most definitely *not* a Bangkok man. (See, for example, fº 7.49, line 4.) Nor was he a *cao*, a member of the ruling class, for he criticizes royal behavior (fº 8.42) and he was quite ready to see rulers deposed when necessary (fº 8.36). We might guess that he was a non-royal (non-*cao*) minor official, a clerk or someone who had been a clerk. Because he had access to documents that must have been private to the princely family of Cao Kavila, he must have had close relations within that family, and he might have been a retainer of Kavila, or perhaps was related to Kavila's family through their female relatives.

The Sources of the CMC

The question remains as to how the author of the CMC might have written his history: What were his sources, and how did he use them? Detailed answers to these questions will have to await a painstaking study of all the various manuscripts that might have been available to him. Even at this early stage of such study, however, some tentative answers can be offered.

The first four sections of the CMC (which we might call "Invocation," "Buddhist History," "Kings Who Changed the Era," and "Queen Camadevi") all are virtually identical to passages in the 1894 *Nan Chronicle* written by *Sænluang*

Ratchasomphan.¹⁶ Since the Chiang Mai author in the 1820s cannot have used a text that was not written until seventy-five years later, the best we can do is to suppose that the authors of both must have had access to the same manuscript(s) for this prefatory material. The authors of those manuscripts in turn must have had access to the canonical literature concerning the history of Buddhism such as the *Mahavaṃsa* and the *Dipavaṃsa* (which however are not identical to the tradition drawn from them and presumably other manuscripts), and to manuscripts bearing on the earliest local history of the Upper Mekong region

At the other end of the CMC, covering the period from the early eighteenth century (f° 6.05) on down to the end, the text appears to be duplicated in no other manuscripts, and for the time being we must suppose that this portion of the CMC is unique to the 1827–1828 author. Indeed, it reads like the work of a single author: the language is distinctive (being more "modern" than the language of the earlier portion). It appears to have been based on the recollections perhaps of old people living at the time the text was written, on their own memories and on their memories of the stories that had been told to them. Another possibility is that it was based upon metrical versions of the saga of King Kavila and his brothers, who were the main actors responsible for ending Burmese rule near the end of the eighteenth century. In one of his still-unpublished journals, the British traveler David Richardson mentions having been entertained in Lamphun on 5 April 1834 by

> a male and two female singers . . . sung a sort of metrical history of the exploits of the Tsoboa and his six brothers, in which the successful insurrection of Ka Weila [i.e., Kavila] the eldest brother against the Burmese 60 years ago and the carrying off the people from Kein-theu [Chiang Sæn], Kein-toung [Keng Tung] and Mein Neaung [Möng Yòng] by the present chiefs held the most conspicuous place.¹⁷

That leaves us with the last three-fourths of the first fascicle and all the rest of the CMC down part-way through fascicle six (roughly, ff° 1.08 to 6.05). It so happens that almost all this portion of the Chiang Mai Chronicle is duplicated in a specific

---

16 See David K. Wyatt, *The Nan Chronicle* (Ithaca, 1994); and "Ratchawongpakòn, phongsawadan müang Nan," *Prachum phongsawadan*, pt. 10 (Bangkok, 1918).

17 Unpublished ms., India Office Collections.

manuscript, the "History of the Lineage of the Kings of Lan Na Thai," (abbreviated "Lineage,") which was written by a certain Suriyavaṃsa Bhikkhu of Chiang Sæn in 1741. The only known copy of this manuscript is at Wat Chang Kham in Nan, where it was copied for the American anthropologist Richard Davis in 1972.[18] The existence of this particular manuscript solves one problem of the CMC, namely, that the first five folios of the sixth fascicle are centered on Chiang Sæn rather than Chiang Mai. This is understandable if we consider that this short portion was added to some earlier manuscript by Suriyavaṃsa Bhikkhu in Chiang Sæn in 1741, who added this material in order to bring his story down to 1706.[19]

If these suppositions are correct, this leaves us with four distinctive parts of the HP manuscript, based on four separate sources: (1) the unknown manuscript common to the *Nan Chronicle* and the CMC; (2) the original, un-named manuscript on which the "Lineage" text is based;[20] (3) the additions to the "Lineage" text added by Suriyavaṃsa Bhikkhu of Chiang Sæn in 1741; and (4) the original text written in Chiang Mai in 1827–1828.

We must note, however, that (2)—the manuscript upon which the monk Suriyavaṃsa based his work—is itself a composite text, composed of an unknown number of portions written probably at different times. At the least, Dr. Penth probably is correct in guessing that one such compilation was written during or shortly after the reign of King Tilokarat in the fifteenth century.[21] Another such compilation probably dates from the beginning of the period of Burmese government in the late seventeenth century. Suriyavaṃsa thus added to these, and the 1828 Chiang Mai author carried the story forward.

The 1828 author, however, did not simply copy his sources. He clearly edited them to suit his own understanding of history, to comment on what he was copying, and occasionally to take cognizance of variant traditions or to insert local legends or anecdotes. He clearly even rearranged the "Lineage" text's story of the death of

---

18 "Tamnan ratchawong phraya Lan Na Thai," Lanna Thai Manuscripts from the Richard Davis Collection, Australian National University (microfiche; Canberra, s.d.).

19 There are a few more lines here in the "Lineage" manuscript which are not duplicated in the HP. The end of the "Lineage" manuscript is equivalent to the entry for CS 1068, HP fº 6.05.

20 In a long footnote (p. 45, n. 1), Notton refers to precisely such a manuscript, from Chiang Rai, titled "History of Chiang Mai," which begins with Mangrai and continues down to the reign of King Tilok in the fifteenth century.

21 Probably something like the manuscript mentioned by Notton, above.

King Mangrai in order to make the paragraphs flow more logically: the order of two "paragraphs" is reversed.

In short, the CMC is—like many such texts, including the *Nan Chronicle* of 1894[22]—a composite text that grew by accretion over centuries. Each successive author certainly modified the earlier texts to greater or lesser extent, sometimes for stylistic reasons and sometimes to take account of varying accounts of data provided by different sources. This makes the CMC a very complex text, which cannot be understood until its sources have been fully explored so that the contributions of each successive author can be assessed. At the very least, we have to conclude that this text, like many others, is the work of real historians, working in real times and places, writing for a variety of reasons and under a variety of impulses.[23] We look forward to learning what more can be discovered of these sources as they are uncovered and studied.

"Chronicle" or "History"?

Even after several years' work on HP, we persisted in calling it the "Chiang Mai Chronicle." At some point late in our work, we realized that to call it a "chronicle" was unfair to the author, and denigrated his work. This is a work worthy, in its early nineteenth-century context, of being called a "history." (At that point we also stopped referring to it as a *tamnan*, which has similar derogatory connotations in Thai.) This is not a simple recitation of events in chronological order, nor is it uncritical. It seems to us to be a critical piece of history-writing. The author had numerous sources at his disposal, from which he selected those which, in his best judgment, told the story he wanted to tell. At numerous points in his work, our author shows us where his sources disagreed and which he chose to use. He is sufficiently objective to be independent: he is ready, on many occasions (either directly or subtly) to criticize Lan Na's rulers (and others, especially the Burmese). His work is by no means perfect or beyond reproach; but it does demand the reader's respect and, indeed, admiration.

Having reached these conclusions, then, why have we not re-titled this work the "Chiang Mai History?" At the very last minute—the day before the manuscript went

---

22 See Wyatt, *Nan Chronicle*, introduction.
23 See Annabel Patterson, *Reading Holinshed's Chronicles* (Chicago, 1994).

to the publisher—we decided that we had to stay with the "chronicle" designation. We do so advisedly, realizing that most readers would be misled by a "Chiang Mai History" title into thinking that the volume covered history down to the present, which this volume does not do. We are satisfied to associate our work with the work of Notton, which we continue to admire. We do ask the reader, however, to remember that the "Chiang Mai Chronicle" is a valid and respectable work of Lan Na *history*-writing.

Mechanical Details

The copy of this manuscript obtained from Dr. Penth was in the form of a microfilm. After having made a copy of the microfilm, the film was then used to print a photographic copy on large paper, which yielded paper copies that, if anything, were even larger and more legible than the originals. With only one exceptional page, these proved to be very clear and legible.

From the paper copy, Wyatt proceeded slowly and methodically to make a transcription into standard Thai script, which took more than two years. As he worked, he used printed copies of the SN and the T15RW versions to help him through difficult passages, and to note variations between the HP version and the others. As he finished transcribing each fascicle, he mailed a copy to Mrs. Aroonrut, who checked these against the original and worked to type them onto computer disks. Meanwhile, to vary his routine, Wyatt from time to time also tried his hand at translating easier passages, saving the more difficult ones for when Aroonrut would be present to assist.

Thus, when Mrs. Aroonrut arrived at Cornell in July 1994, they had ready for their use an enlarged paper print of the original manuscript, Wyatt's handwritten transcription as corrected by Mrs. Aroonrut, and Mrs. Aroonrut's typed Thai transcription based on Wyatt's transcription. (The Thai computerized version was in a non-standard encoding, which was mechanically converted into standard Thai encoding for use on Apple Macintosh computers.)

Mrs. Aroonrut also prepared a separate, special version of the Thai text on the computer in which all the words were separated. Wyatt was able to use these files to prepare a complete glossary of the entire eight fascicles, word-by-word, which proved to be extremely useful in tracking each use of every word in the text, and ultimately this was to form the basis for the word index for the Thai volume. This glossarial index, for example, was able to tell us that such-and-such a word occurred in fascicle 4 page 3 line 2, fascicle 5 page 21 line 3, and fascicle 6 page 13 line 1.

At first, we used our mountains of paper to prepare a rough translation of the entire text, aided on occasion by Notton's fine translation, or the SN or T15RW versions. It quickly became abundantly clear that Hans Penth was, indeed, right: that his manuscript was definitely superior to N and SN. Sanguan's version was, plainly, quite sloppy in places. Notton's manuscript included numerous passages that were garbled, and which Notton confessed that he was unable to read. Our work was based primarily upon the HP text, informed occasionally by the others.

The work of translation was very slow the first time through; but the second and third times through the manuscript were progressively easier. By late November 1994 we were going through the text yet another time, this time looking for those words or places or situations that required annotation. Both Mrs. Aroonrut and Wyatt then separately annotated the Thai and English versions, respectively, and their first annotations were compared and merged. In general, Mrs. Aroonrut's annotations were, though excellently informative and helpful, very long, and they had to be abridged drastically for the final published English version. The text, the translation, and the bulk of the annotations were completed before Mrs. Aroonrut returned to Thailand in January 1995. Considerable detailed work was completed when Wyatt traveled to Chiang Mai in April 1995.

Through the last months of 1994 and the early months of 1995, Wyatt also prepared the maps for these volumes, to which toponyms continued to be added as their locations could be ascertained. Despite our best efforts, many toponyms remain unidentified; and only those we could identify have been placed on the maps and commented on in the annotations. The reader may assume that any toponym not placed on the maps has not been identified.

Both the Thai version and the English version of the text have been paginated and numbered in such a way as to facilitate comparisons between the two. Page-divisions and line-breaks have been identically shown in both versions. In this English volume, page-breaks are shown in the form "/fº 3.11/" [indicating the eleventh page (folio) of chapter (or fascicle) 3], while line-breaks are indicated with a simple diagonal slash ("/").

In the English translation, section headings have been added so as to facilitate reading and using the text. All such italicized, centered headings are editorial insertions, and are not present in the original.

Dates

Whenever possible, all dates have been converted to the Western calendars—Julian to October 1582, Gregorian thereafter—with the assistance of J. C. Eade, and with a computer program (still in a draft version) by the Swedish physicist Lars Gislén based on Eade's work. Readers are warned that the "translation" of Thai dates is a very inexact science, owing to irregular intercalation (the addition of "leap" days and "leap" years).[24] Thus, when the text tells us that the fourth waxing of the fifth month was a Monday, but the computer tells us it was a Tuesday, it is because the computer has intercalated one extra day that year. Two days' difference usually indicates a similar problem with the intercalation of a month. ("Intercalation" means the adding of an "extra" day or month, just as the Western calendar adds a 29th day to February once every fourth year, in leap years.) Unproblematic dates have been converted in parentheses in the text, while dates posing problems have been discussed in the footnotes.

Eclipses are an excellent means of checking calendrical data. I have used the classic compendium on the subject by Oppolzer.[25]

Maps

This text includes hundreds—perhaps thousands—of place names, most of which will be unfamiliar to most readers. Take, for example, the final pages of Chapter 5, which give a royal itinerary of King Mæ Ku traveling through the region in early 1559. Passages such as this require maps, and I have tried to provide them. The maps, however, have had to be provided from scratch, as no existing maps might help us. We are not helped by the repeated refusals of the U.S. Defense Mapping Agency to allow us to consult good maps, even though Thai scholars seem to have easy access to the best of them (at a scale of 1:50,000). The best maps available to me are the 1:500,000 Tactical Pilotage Charts, which are quite handsome, but

---

24 See J. C. Eade, *The Dating System of Mainland Southeast Asia: An Overview* (Leiden: Brill, 1996).

25 Theodor Ritter von Oppolzer, *Canon of Eclipses (Canon der Finsternisse)*, tr. Owen Gingerich (Vienna, 1887; repr. New York, 1962).

unfortunately are sorely incomplete. We know, for example, roughly where Ban Yu and Müang Luai are located (see Map 5), but they appear on no map available.

In preparing the maps for this volume, I have consulted a wide variety of maps, but in each case I have re-drawn them. The regional maps for the most part are based upon tracings I made many years ago of Defense Mapping Agency maps. I found the gazetteer in *GUBSS* very useful, but the accompanying map was too poorly reproduced to be of much assistance. The city maps are mostly drawn upon the basis of 1950s maps made for the City Planning Department of the Thai Ministry of Interior, from the fine collection of the Cornell University Library. The map of Lampang is based upon a map by Sumet Jumsai, as originally re-drawn for Sarassawadi Ongsakun's admirable report on Wiang Kum Kam.

All the maps were optically scanned using Ofoto software; then traced and re-drawn using Freehand (version 4.0) software. I deliberately drew very large the "dots" marking the locations of places, in order to hide the fact that exact locations were in some cases impossible to ascertain.

Romanization

Systematic romanization of a text such as this one has proved almost impossible, for it does not make a great deal of sense to romanize systematically a text that is essentially unsystematic! I have attempted to use the standard romanization of Pali words, though the author of HP by no means wrote them correctly. I have not romanized vowel-length for Thai words. Vowels are romanized almost as expected, although the reader will need to be reminded that the æ and œ ligatures are single, not compound, vowels. The ü vowel has been widely used. The ò vowel rhymes with the English word *thaw*. Of the consonants, the only tricky one is c, as in *cao*. The general thrust of the romanization is to attempt to be at least roughly phonetic.

Translation

A few Northern Thai words and phrases were so often used that it seemed to be reasonable to be consistent in their translation. Perhaps the most frequently-used of these is the word *müang*, which I have always rendered as "domain." It can mean just a town or city, but it usually also implies the inclusion of the surrounding territory dependent upon that locality.

If the prose of the text at times seems stilted, this is a product of my effort to try to accurately reflect the original Thai. On one occasion, however, I was unable to resist the temptation to put Thai poetry into (blank) verse.

Imperfections

It is inevitable that in a work of this sort, produced as hurriedly as this one had to be, there will be numerous mistakes and imperfections. We were unable to do as much checking as we would have liked of the HP manuscript against other Chiang Mai manuscripts, nor were we able to do as much work on the footnotes as we would have liked. We hope that this volume will be sufficiently useful to readers to justify further editions, which occasion we will take to make such corrections as we can. We thank readers in advance for their indulgence, and for any suggestions they might make for improvements when we next issue this volume.

Chapter 1

Invocation

Namo tassathu. Saraṇa mahiniyaṁ Buddhaseṭṭaṁ namitvā suggatapatāmaṁ sādhu saṅghañca namitvā ahaṁ rājānurājadāyāda raṭṭhādhipatti vakkhāmi sabbadukkhā bhayarogā antarāyavināsāntu.[1] Listen, all you worthies! All the lords / [and] lord professors have created [this] as a tale and recitation and the customary lore of the succession of the royal lineages of rulers who have reigned in Nabbapurī Srī Biṅgajaiya Chiang Mai and all the fifty-seven domains[2] from the time of Lawacangkarat down to the time of King Mangrai and in / sequence to the present day. I thus reverence the Three Gems with the stanza beginning "*Saraṇa mahiniyaṁ buddhaseṭṭhaṁ.*"

Ahaṁ (I) *namitvā vandāmi* (I reverence) *Buddhaseṭṭaṁ* (the Lord Buddha), more glorious than all the Three Worlds. *Ahaṁ* (I) *namāmi* / (reverence) *dhammaṁ* (the Holy Dhamma) *sugatabhava* (who is the Light to all creatures); (I) go to the *sugatabhava*, that is, Nibbāna; *nimitvā* (I reverence) *saṅghañca* (both groups of the Holy Saṅgha—the Ariyasaṅgha and the Sammuttisaṅgha[3]—), *dakkhiṇeyyā* (worthy to receive the alms of individuals). *Ahaṁ / vakkhāmi* (I will speak of the royal lineage of kings, all the *thao* and *phraya*), *dāyādaraṭṭhādhipati* (who in succession have been the lords and masters of the domain); *sabbadukkhabhayāroga* (all the perils and physical and moral infirmities and anxieties) *vināsāntu* (may disappear), not to earn future retribution. /f° 1.02/ *Tatrāyamānupubbikathā*, as told in succession from the

---

1 A virtually identical invocation is given in *The Nan Chronicle* (Ithaca, 1994), pp. 37–38.

2 The Burmese sources invariably refer to the fifty-seven domains of Lan Na, though it is doubtful that the region ever included exactly that number of towns. Curiously, the "fifty-seven" are twice given here, first in Pali and then in Thai.

3 The Ariya monks have already attained Enlightenment; Sammutti monks are as yet unenlightened.

very beginning. The sages know the royal history and have told it from ancient times in succession, as follows.

The Succession of Kings

At the time when the Buddha Kassapa attained Nirvana, [when] Our Lord Buddha Gotama / had not yet established his Enlightenment, there was born a ruler reigning in Benares suffused with merit, with wisdom and physical and moral perfection, more than all others, whose name was Mahāsamantarāja. His long life extended for an incalculable number of years.

Thereafter, the son of Mahāsamantarāja [named Vararāja] / succeeded his father. The son of Vararāja was named Varoja [or] Kalyāṇa. The son of Kalyāṇa was named Varakalyāṇa; the son of Varakalyāṇa was named Uposatha. The son of Ubosatha was named Varābosatha; the son of Vara-ubosatha [was named] Mandhātu. The son of Mandhātu was named Varamandhātu; the son of / Varamandhātu was named Cetiya; the son of Cetiya was named Mucalin; the son of Mucalin [was] Mahāmucalin; the son of Mahāmucalin [was] Mucalinda; the son of Mucalinda was named Sāgara; the son of Sāgara was named Sāradeva; the son of Sāradeva was named Rata; the son of Rata was named Bhattiraso; the son of Bhattiraso was named Ruciya [or] Suruciya;[4] / the son of Suruciya was named Panāda; the son of Panāda was named Mahāpanāda; the son of Mahāpanāda was named Pattāpa; the son of Pattāpa was named Mahāpattāpa; the son of Mahāpattāpa was named Suddassana; the son of Suddassana was named Mahāsuddassana; the son of Mahāsuddassana was named Meru; the son of Meru was named Mahāmeru; the son of Mahāmeru was named Acsima; /f° 1.03/ and the son of Acsima was Mahā-acsimarāja. Every one of these rulers, from Mahāsamantarāja, twenty-eight in number, lived for an incalculable number of years; and they ruled in Benares, Rajagaha, Mithilā, and Kusāvatti.

Thereafter, one hundred rulers ruled in succession; then there were fifty-six rulers in succession. / Then there were eighty-four thousand rulers who continued the royal line; then there were thirty-six rulers; then there were twenty-two rulers; then there were twelve rulers; then there were eighty-four thousand rulers in succession, and after them another eighty-four thousand rulers, including for example Māghadevacakka-

---

4   This name is distinctive of the *Mahāvaṁsa* chronicle of Sri Lanka, and suggests the antecedents of the sources the author used.

vatti. Then there were sixteen including / Karādaranandārājacakapatti reigning down to Okākarāja. The son of Okākarāja was named Okākamukkha. King Okākarāja had a son by a minor wife whom he made the *uparāja*. Okākamukkha, his son by his queen, was angry with his father, and so sent one of his young retainers / off to establish a domain [for him called] Kapilavatthu. He then took his younger sister as his queen, so that his line would not be tainted by impure mixture, and thenceforth it was called the Sākyarāja [lineage]. The son of Okākamukkha was called Puṇṇa; the son of Puṇṇa was called Candama; the son of Candama was Candamukkhasivirāja; the son of Candamukkhasivirāja / was Sañjeyya; the son of Sañjeyya was Vesantara Dhammikarāja the Bodhisatva.

From Mahāsamantarāja in succession down to Lord Vesantarāja there were 276,275 in the royal lineage. The son of Vesantara was Jālī; the son [of Jālī] was called Lisisivivāhana; the son of Sivivāhana was called Sihassara. /f° 1.04/ Thereafter the sons, grandsons, great-grandsons, great-great-grandsons, and great-great-great-grandsons ruled in succession, after Jālī, down to King Jayasena, for 39,999 generations.

King Jayasena reigned in Kapilavatthu. He had a son named Sihatanu, and a daughter named Amitatā. / There was a king named Devadahasakka who, although he was a member of the same Sākya royal line, reigned in Devadahanagara. He had two sons and one daughter. The older son was named Aṇṇjanasakka, the middle daughter was named Kaccāyanā, and the [youngest] son was named Kāladevila. King Devadahasakka / sent his daughter, named Kaccāyana, to be the daughter-in-law of King Jayasena; that is, to be the queen of Sihatana; and King Jayasena sent his daughter, named Amitatā, to be the queen of Añjanasakka who was the son of King Devadahasakka. / Kāladevila was unhappy with reigning, and so went off to assume the condition of an ascetic. King Sihatanu had five sons, first Sappabuddha, then Suddhodhana, then Sukodhana, then Suttodhana, and the youngest Amittattodhana. King Añjana had / two children, the elder named Srīmahāmayā and the younger named Pajāpattīgotamī. King Añjana sent his two daughters to be the queens of Suddhodhanarāja.

At that time, King Sihatanu, King Añjana, and the ascetic Kāladevila together in concert ended the Old Era [*borānasakkarāja*], which was called /f° 1.05/ Kiṃnavasanti, and established a new era.

The Lord Buddha

In due course, in 67, a *dap sai* year, on the full-moon day of the sixth month, the *Mon* day Thursday, the Lord Bodhisatva took form in the womb of Lady Srīmahāmayā; and in 68, a *rwai sanga* year, on the full-moon day of the fourth month, a Mon Friday, he was born from the womb of / his mother in the royal line, and was named Siddhattharājakummān. From Lord Jālī in succession down to Lord Siddhattha, the line numbered more than 430,000 to the appearance of Lord Siddhattha; and counting from Mahā[sama]ntarāja in succession down to Lord Siddhattha there were 676,280. When / Lord Siddhattha was sixteen years of age his family arranged for Lady Yasodharā, the daughter of King Sappabuddha, to be his queen, and he was anointed a king. After reigning for thirteen years, when he was twenty-four years old he was ordained on a Monday, / in the midnight watch, on a sand-bar in the Nerañjarā River, and so continued for six rainy seasons, and then apperceived all with insight on the full-moon day of the eighth month, in the dawn watch, at the age of thirty-five years. He remained teaching all the world for forty-five years, and at the age of eighty years / attained Nibbāna, in the *müang sai* year, on the full-moon day of the eighth month, a Mon Tuesday, in the *kòng træ*[5] watch. The funerary pyre was ignited on a Sunday.

Subsequent Kings in India

Siddhattha was born two years before Bimbisāra. The two were good friends, because the kings who were the fathers of the two were friends. King Bimbisāra reigned in /fº 1.06 / Rājagaha for fifty-two years, and had one son named Ajātasatthu who killed his father and had ruled the principality in his stead for eight years when the Lord Buddha attained Nibbāna. King Ajātasatthu [then] ruled for [another] twenty-four years. He had one son named Upadaya, who killed his father and ruled in his stead for sixteen years. He had a son / named Anuruddha, who killed his father and ruled in his stead. The son of Anuruddha was named Mukkha. He killed his father and ruled in his stead for eight years. The son of Mukkharāja was named Nagadāsaka. He killed his father and ruled in his stead for twenty-four years.

---

5   The daily watches are given in Appendix 2 of Wyatt, *The Nan Chronicle* (Ithaca, 1994), p. 142.

The patricidal family fled [when] the people of the kingdom became angry and forced King Nāgadāsaka to leave, anointing [as king] a minister of Nāgadāsaka. / This person was Sunāga, who ruled for ten years. The son of Sunāga was Kālāsoka, who ruled for twenty-eight years. From the time of the Nibbāna of our Lord [Buddha] until Kālāsoka was one hundred years.

All the arahats convened [to edit the] Dhamma for the second time.

The eldest son of Kālasoka ruled / for twenty-two years. Then Jālanandāla was king and ruled for twenty-two years. King Candagutta was born of the Moraya[6] Line. King Cānakkhaphām killed Jālanandāla, and Candagutta was consecrated as king subduing the Jambū continent, for twenty-four years. The son of King Candagutta was Bindusāra, who was / king for twenty-eight years. King Bindusāra had one hundred sons, of whom the eldest of all was named Asoka Dhammarāja and became the *cakkavati*-king-subduing-the-Jambu-Continent. He had a son who was ordained in the religion of the Buddha, whose name appears as Mahindathera and who was head of the Sangha. From the Nibbāna of the Buddha down to Asoka Dhammarāja /f° 1.07/ was over 218 years.

One hundred arahats convened to edit the Dhamma for the third time.

The royal lineage of Rājagaha extends to here, and the lineage of Sākya kings in Kapila[va]tta.

Of the sons of King Koleyya, the one named Mittabhubabha killed him. As for Mittabhubabha, he was himself drowned and died. /

Kings Who Changed the Era

Here we will speak of all the kings who changed the era, in succession. The ascetic Devila, King Añjana, [and] King Sihatanu ended the era which was called Kīnavasanti and established a new era. Subsequently, in 67 our Lord / took form and in 68 of the Era he was born. In 148 of the era our Lord Buddha attained Nibbāna on the full-moon day of the eighth month. On the full-moon day of the twelfth month, Mahā Anandathera became an arahat, and there was the First Great Council, attended by five hundred arahats presided over by Mahākassappa. / In the secular world there was Ajātasattu who ended the Añjana era at 148 then and began

---

6   I.e., Maurya, the dynasty in which the Emperor Aśoka ruled. Candagutta is a Pali rendering of Candragupta, the founder of that line.

the first year of a new era. One hundred years later, King Kālasoka held the Second Great Council in the year 118. Then King Asoka Dhammikarāja[7] / convened the Third Great Council in the year 218 of the era.

Queen Camadevi of Haribhuñjaya

Two hundred years later, in 418 of the era, Lady Cāmadevi was born,[8] and in 456 of the era she constructed Lamphun.[9] In 458 of the era Lady Cāmadevi left Lavo[10] and ascended to rule Lamphun. The two brothers Mahantayasa and Indavara[11] were born in that year. Cāmadevi /f° 1.08/[12] ruled Haribhuñjaya for fifty years, and died at the age of ninety-two in 550 of the era. Mahantayasa subsequently ruled the principality in her stead.

In 560 of the Era, King Indavatti Dhammikarāja of Laṅka ended the Era and established a new era with the year One.

In 343 [of that new Era], King Adit became king and had ruled Haribhuñjaya for one year / when he built the Great Cetiya of Lamphun. In 346 of the New Era, equivalent to 906 of the old era, the king attained Nibbāna, succeeded by Indapatti. In 622 of the era, King Tricakkhu Anuruddha Dhammikarāja was dominant over

---

7   Many of the kings listed here are denominated "Dhammikarāja": an epithet for great, just kings.

8   Notton (p. 11, n.) guesses that these dates are in the Mahāsakarāja Era (+ 78 = AD).

9   It is interesting that Lamphun is first mentioned with its own name, and immediately afterwards is referred to as Haribhuñjaya (or Hariphunchai, the Thai pronunciation of the Pali name). A full version of the story is given in the *Cdv*. (Notton's *Annales du Siam, II* [Paris, 1930]), and it has few similarities with the story here. According to *Cdv.*, she was born in Lavo, and was summoned to rule in Lamphun, which had already been constructed, in the *pœk san* year, 1071 of the Buddhist Era (= AD 528/29). Details of the life of Camadevi also appear in Sanguan Chotisukkharat, *Prachum tamnan Lan Na Thai* (Bangkok, 1972), pp. 12–14. It is said that Camadevi was the daughter of the hermit Vasudeva, who sent her to live in Lavo.

Chinese sources speak of Haribhuñjaya and mention a princess who fled the capital [Tuan Lisœng and Utsani Thongchai, *Prawattisat Lan Na Thai samai ratchawong Mangrai cak ekkasan Cin* (Chiang Mai, 1988), p. 35].

10 Lavo is synonymous with Lop Buri, just north of Ayudhya. See also Tuan Lisœng, *op. cit.*, 58–59; and Saichon Wannarat, "Lawo kòn samai Ayudhya," *Ruam botkhwam prawattisat 2* (Jan. 1981), 84–127.

11 Some sources call him Anantayot.

12 SN completely omits this f°, skipping directly from f° 1.07 to f° 1.09.

the Jambu Continent. He ended the era in that year 622, a *pœk set* year, / and began a new era with a *kot khai* year.[13]

The Lineage of King Lawacangkarat

At that time, King Anuruddha Dhammikarāja summoned all the kings and rulers of the Jambu Continent to come together to his court. All the rulers and kings of the principalities assembled, / except those of Lan Na Thai, as they had no king. Anuruddha Dhammikarāja therefore prayed to the Lord Indra that Indra would pay attention to Lan Na Thai, because it was a place where the Teachings of the Buddha were established, and find a Great King to be / overlord of that area.

Indra accepted this commission, carefully considered the matter, and saw a son of the gods named Lawacakkradevaputta who was filled with merit and was reigning in the /f° 1.09/ Tavatiṁsa Heaven[14] and meritoriously had served [out his time in the heavens] and was of an appropriate age to leave the heaven [and return to earth]. The Lord Indra went directly to the court of that son of the gods and said, "Behold, thou who knows no suffering! Thou wilt descend to take birth in the world of men at Chiang Rao, and wilt assume the royal condition as a Great King as lord over all the rulers / in the Lan Na country, and there maintain the Great Teachings of the Buddha."

Lawacangkara, a son of the gods, consented to the words of Indra, saying, "Sadhu! Good! Fine!" He then left the heavens and descended down a bejeweled ladder from heaven with a thousand of his retainers; or, put another way, to the pinnacle of Dòi Tung[15] / to take unparented birth as a royal scion of sixteen years, finely dressed, on a fine wooden throne comported / near the Mæ Sai in Jayavaranagara—that is, Chiang Rao.[16] As for his thousand retainers, they all, men and women alike, came

---

13 The first (zero) year of the *Culasakaraja* era was indeed a *poek set* year; but the year 1 was a *kat kai* year, not a *kot kai* year. This is probably simply a mistake.

14 The thirty-third and highest heaven.

15 Dòi Tung is in Mæ Sai district of Chiang Rai province; site of Wat Phrathat Dòi Tung. See *Dòi Tung*.

16 Chiang Rao/Jayavaranagara, M. Ngœn Yang/M. Yang Ngœn: near the Mæ Sai (Sai River).

The Chronicle does not tell us that Lawacangkara descended from heaven on a silver ladder, but the local people who asked where he had come from saw a silver ladder, which then disappeared into the heavens. When others heard of this, they asked, "Is the silver ladder still there?" and from this question, the tale goes, comes the name of the principality.

to be born similarly, as princes and princesses sixteen years of age, / possessed of wondrous beauty and complexion, resplendent everywhere. When people saw them, they exclaimed among themselves, "From whence have these creatures arisen? They are like unto silver!" And so they called others to come and see them.

Having completed their journey through the air, [the heavenly retainers] exclaimed, "Is the silver [ladder] still there [*ngœn yang*]?" This is why it was called / f° 1.10/ M. Ngœn Yang. Others say that a jujube tree[17] had a bark that was white as silver [*ngœn*], standing in the midst of the *yang* trees, so it was called M. Yang Ngœn, it is said.[18] The people of the domain all saw this wonder, and so invited him to reign there, as lord and master in Jayavaranagara. It came to be that he was named Lawacangkarattharacha. This was in the *kat kai* year, the year 1 of the Lesser era. /

King Lawacakrarat took birth in that year. His renown spread in all directions—news that a godly king had descended from the heavens and had taken form as a king in Jayavaranagara. So said, everyone came bearing many gifts to present, asking to be the / subjects of King Lawacangkarat.

King Lawacangkarat then constructed a very extensive country and built farms and fields, markets and walls, for example, paddy fields, gardens, and weirs and canals, to adorn his country. / At that time, the generals and ministers together performed his consecration as their Great King, filled with majesty, to reign righteously over them.

The Descendants of Lawacangkarat

Later, the king had three sons; in sequence, the eldest was named Lao Khròp, the middle was named / Lao Chang, and the youngest was named Lao Kao Kæo

---

Note the phrase below, "Others say that . . ." This indicates the author's awareness of historiographical complexity.

17 Elsewhere referred to as a *yang* tree. The jujube has a silver-colored bark.

18 King Lawacangkarat was the first ruler in Ngœn Yang/Chiang Rao. It was not until the ninth ruler, Lao Khiang, that a new capital was built near the Mæ Sai (or Mæ Lawa) in the region of Ban Yang Sieo.

Phraya Lao Khiang constructed M. Ngœn Yang nestled between three hills—Dòi Tung, Dòi Tha, and Dòi Ya Thao; now in the vicinity of Mæ Sai district of Chiang Rai province. See Hans Penth et al., *Phrathat Dòi Tung* (Chiang Mai, 1993).

In Mæ Sai district, and along the Mæ Sai (River), there are the ruins of many large old towns. Official excavations have unearthed old city walls, and it is thought that they are the old walls of M. Ngœn Yang, or, as some old chronicles call it, Hirañá Ngœn Yang. On Ngœn Yang, see also p. 61.

Ma Müang. The youngest was the most upright and intelligent, while his two elder brothers were duller and less righteous.

One day, the three royal sons went hunting crabs in the streams. The three saw the tracks of a very large crab in the bed of the stream, which they followed along the stream until /f° 1.11/ they came to the end of the mountain range. They saw that the tracks of the crab entered there. They said, "We should track down this crab, and present it to our father. If this crab is very large, it will be very strong and will slither away into the water and we might not get it." So Lao Kao took a net and went to block its escape route, holding a / hammer to strike it. If the crab fled, it would get caught in the net and they would smash it. Lao Kao, the youngest brother, took a net and blocked the stream, holding the hammer at the head of the net, prepared to catch the crab. At that point, his two elder brothers began digging out the crab's hole, and quickly struck extensive rock, / so they could dig no further; so they blocked the crab's lair with rocks. When they had done so, they left without telling their youngest brother, Lao Kao.

Lao Kao remained there at the head of the net until the sun declined in the afternoon sky. Lao Kao called out for his two elder brothers, saying, "We can go!" but heard only his own voice echoing down the stream. It sounded as if the echo was saying not to go—to wait, / as if it were his two elder brothers replying—so he waited by the net until sunset. When the sun had set, the crab still did not emerge, so he went to seek his two elder brothers, but could not find them, only the rocks blocking the crab's hole. Lao Kao was quite angry, and lamented, "My brothers invited me to come and eat with them, and both of them tricked me into watching / without telling me, and without telling me they left, as if I were not here."

Lao Kao, the youngest, when he had reverenced his father, told him what his brothers had done, in every detail. He said to his father, "We three simply cannot live together. Please, respected Father, build for us, that each of us can be lord and master of /f° 1.12/ our own [domain]."

Hearing this, King Lao Cong said, "Lao Cakkrarat, your father, says I, your father, will build for each of you." The royal father then had one village, large and extensive, built for the eldest son, named Lao Khòp, which has been called Ban Tham to the present day; he built a village for his middle son named Lao / Chang, which was called Ban Kha; then, again, the father-king had a village built far away near [the mountain] Pha Lao, large and extensive, commodious and pleasing, for his beloved son, Lao Kao Kæo Ma Müang, the youngest, which was called

Ban Pha Rao[19] to the present day. The father-king then divided / his possessions, money, horses, elephants, slaves, and people equally among his three sons, and charged them to rule all the villages of M. Chiang Rao.[20]

King Lao Cong, that is, Lawacangkraracha, ruled in happiness over all the people. At the age of / 120 years he died and went to the next world in the *pæk set* year, 120 of the Anuruddha Era, 1302 of the Buddhist Era.[21] He was the first of the royal lineage.

Thereafter, Lao Kao Kæo Ma Müang, the youngest son, at the age of forty-one years, ruled in his father's stead. He ruled for forty-five years, and at the age of eighty-six years went to the next world. / He was the second of the royal lineage.

The two older princes, i.e., Lao Khòp [and] Lao Chang, who did not succeed their father as king, became lords [*khun*] of other countries. They had descendants to continue their lines, but these were not included in the royal lineage.

As for King Lao Kao, he had a son named Lao Sao who at the age of thirty-five years /f° 1.13/ succeeded his father in ruling the principality. He reigned for thirty-nine years, and at the age of seventy-four years went on to the next world, the third of the royal lineage.

The son of Lao Sao was called Lao Tang. At the age of thirty-five years he succeeded his father as ruler and ruled for twenty-six years, going to the next world at the age of sixty-one. He was the fourth of the royal lineage.

The son of Lao Tang was called Lao Kom. At the age of thirty-seven years he succeeded his father as ruler and ruled for eighteen years. At the age of fifty-five / he went to the next world; the fifth of the royal lineage.

His son, Lao Læ, was forty years of age when he succeeded as king. He ruled for sixteen years, and at the age of fifty-six went to the next world. He was the sixth of the royal lineage.

The son of Lao Læ was called Lao Kap. He succeeded to the throne at the age of thirty-nine years. He ruled for fifteen years, and at the age of fifty-four went to the next world. / He was the seventh of the royal lineage.

---

19   Ban Tham, Ban Kha, Pha Lao mountain, and Ban Pha Lao (or Rao): location unknown. Early settlements were very dense in certain parts of Chiang Rai province, especially north and east of the present city. See the map in *Borankhadi Chiang Rai* (Bangkok, 1990), p. 60.

20   Presumably synonymous with Ban Pha Lao/Rao. N. is defective here (III, 14).

21   This reference tells us that the reckoning of the Lesser ("Anuruddha" or CS) Era was 1182 behind the Buddhist Era (BE) at that time, not the conventional 1181.

The son of Lao Kap was called Lao Kün. At the age of forty-five years he became king. He ruled for seventeen years, and at the age of sixty-two he went to the next world; the eighth of the royal lineage.

The son of Lao Kün was called Lao Khiang. At the age of thirty-seven years he became ruler. This lord was very generous and broad-minded. He adorned the villages and governed the principality / with great intelligence. One day, he was touring the country and the jujube forests when he beheld a beauteous tree, shimmering as if with silver, which stood in Ban Yang Sieo,[22] a village which was located near the Mæ Lawa. (Today it is called Mæ Sai.[23]) This village was prospering greatly, so he had fortifications constructed and set up a / country there, taking as an omen the shimmering silvery tree standing there [amidst the silvery jujube trees]. This is the origin of Yang Ngœn. He was king for twenty-six years, and at the age of sixty-three passed on to the next world. He was the ninth of the royal lineage.

The son of Lao Khiang was called Kin; [he was] also called Lao Khriu. At the age of thirty-six years he became king. He reigned for twenty years, and at the age of fifty-six passed to the next world. /f° 1.14/ He was the tenth of the royal lineage.

The son of Lao Khriu [or] Lao Kin was called Lao Thüng. At the age of twenty-one years he became king in his father's stead. He ruled for fifteen years, and at the age of thirty-six years passed on to the next world. He was the eleventh of the royal lineage.

The son of Lao Thüng was called Lao Thœng. At the age of thirty-seven years he became king in his father's place. He ruled for twenty years. At the age of fifty-seven he passed to the next world. He was the twelfth of the royal lineage. /

The son of Lao Thœng was called Lao Ton. At the age of thirty-nine years he became king, and ruled for seventeen years. At the age of fifty-six he passed to the next world, the thirteenth of the royal lineage.

The son of Lao Ton was called Lao Som. He was very handsome. At the age of thirty years he became king in succession to his father. He ruled for twenty-one years, and at the age of fifty-one he passed to the next world. He was the fourteenth of the royal lineage. /

The son of Lao Som was called Lao Kuak. At the age of thirty-two years he assumed the rule in his father's stead. He ruled for twenty-seven years, and at the age of fifty-nine he passed to the next world. He was the fifteenth of the royal lineage.

---

22   Ban Yang Sieo: near the Mæ Sai (river), Mæ Sai district, Chiang Rai.
23   This river today forms the border between Thailand and Burma, northwest of Chiang Sæn.

Table 1 Rulers from Lawacangkarat to Mangrai

Name	Details	Born AD	Accession
Lavacaṅkaraṭṭharāja+	born CS 1 kat kai died CS 120 pœk set BE 1302	639	639
Lao Kao Kæo Ma Müang	age 41 ruled 45 yrs died age 86	673	714
Lao Sao	age 35 ruled 39 yrs died age 74	726	759
Lao Tang	age 35 ruled 26 yrs died age 61	763	798
Lao Kom	age 37 ruled 18 yrs died age 55	787	824
Lao Læ	age 40 ruled 16 yrs died age 56	802	842
Lao Kap	age 39 ruled 15 yrs died age 54	829	858
Lao Kün	age 45 ruled 17 yrs died age 62	828	873
Lao Khiang	age 37 ruled 26 yrs died age 63	853	890
Lao Kin/Khriu	age 36 ruled 20 yrs died age 56	880	916
Lao Thüng	age 21 ruled 15 yrs died age 36	915*	936
Lao Thœng	age 37 ruled 20 yrs died age 57	914*	951
Lao Ton	age 39 ruled 17 yrs died age 56	932	971
Lao Som	age 30 ruled 21 yrs died age 51	958	988
Lao Kuak	age 32 ruled 27 yrs died age 59	982	1009
Lao Kwin	age 43 ruled 15 yrs died age 58	993	1036
Lao Cong	age 43 ruled 16 yrs died age 59	1008	1051
Còm Pha Rüang	age 39 ruled 48 yrs died age 57	1038	1067
Khun Cüang	age 47/39 ruled 41 yrs died age 77	1059	1085
Lao Ngœn Rüang	age 33 ruled 26 yrs died age 59	1093	1126
Lao Chün	age 41 ruled 21 yrs died age 62	1111	1152
Lao Ming	age 25 ruled 21 yrs died age 46	1148	1173
Khun Mœng	age 35 ruled 25 yrs died age 60	1159	1194
Lao Meng	age 35 ruled 40 yrs died age 75	1184	1219
Mangrai	age 21 ruled; born CS 600	1238	1259

+ I suspect that the reigns of Lavacaṅkaraṭṭharāja and Lao Kao Kœo ma Müang have been conflated; that the first reigned 639–713 and the second 714–759, which makes him fit with the dates of Lao Sao (nexy on list)
* There is a problem here, with the son born before his father was born!

The son of Lao Kuak was Lao Kwin. At the age of forty-three he became king in his father's stead. He ruled for fifteen years, and at the age of fifty-eight he passed to the next world. He was the sixteenth / of the royal lineage.

The son of Lao Kwin was called Lao Cong. At the age of forty-three years he became king in his father's stead. He ruled for sixteen years. At the age of fifty-nine he passed to the next world. He was the seventeenth of the royal lineage.

Lao Cong had two sons. The elder was named Lao Chün, and the younger was named Còm Pha Rüang. When the latter was thirty-nine years old he became king in place of his father. He ruled for eighteen years, and at the age of / fifty-seven he passed to the next world. He was the eighteenth of the royal lineage.

The Life and Career of Khun Cüang

The son of Còm Pha Rüang was called Khun Cüang.[24] At the age of thirty-seven he became king in place of his father. King Cüang had a first son called Khun Ngœn Rüang. Lao Chün, the elder brother of King Còm Pha Rüang, and [thus] the uncle of Khun Cüang, had a daughter named Lady Ua Kham Khòn Müang. /f° 1.15/ When she grew up to be a young maiden, she was exceptionally beautiful, her many virtues a delight to the heart and eye.

The news reached the Hò[25] of M. Phrakan[26]—that is, the Kæo[27] [or Viet]—that the Lao king had a daughter who was exceptionally beautiful. The Kæo king, named Thao Kao, learned of this, and sent royal gifts to present, indicating his wish for the princess, and [repeated this] a second and third time. Khun Lao Chün, / the elder brother of Cao Còm Pha Rüang, who was the father of the lady, would not give her up; and so the Kæo king brought up an enormous army, demanding Lady Ua Kham Khòn Müang.[28] Khun Lao Chün then sent word to King Cüang, his nephew, that "Thao Kao Cha, the ruler of the Kæo, is coming to seize Lady Ua Kham Khòn

---

24 Khun Cüang probably began by ruling the Mæ Sai territory, and handed that Ngœn Yang territory over to his son Lao Ngœn Bun Rüang when he left to conquer the Kæo territory.

On Khun Cüang, the best place to start is Sila Viravong's old edition of *Thao Hung rü Cüang* (Ubon, 1943; repr. Bangkok, 1979). A Northern Thai version is given in Aroonrut Wichienkeeo and Sithon Khampæng, *Tamnan Phraya Cüang ton chabap bai lan Wat Müang Mò, amphœ müang, cangwat Phræ* (2 v.; Chiang Mai, 1981). See also Klaus Rosenberg, "A Preliminary Study in the History of Khun Chüang," in the volume titled *Historical Documents and Literary Evidence* (International Conference on Thai Studies, Bangkok, 1984; Bangkok, 1984), separately paginated; and Cit Phumisak, *Khwampenma khòng kham Sayam, Thai, Lao læ Khòm* (Bangkok, 1976).

25 Hò; variously Haw and Ho: the Thai use this term to refer to the Chinese whom they encounter by the overland, as opposed to the maritime, routes.

26 Müang Phrakan/Phakan/Pakan: M. Pakan, in northern Vietnam.

27 This always is conventionally translated as Vietnamese.

28 *Ua* is conventionally given to the second daughter, and we encounter several with names that include this element below. Note that a woman's name is changed when she marries.

Müang. / Our nephew, Cao Phraya Cüang, is a great and noble king. Do not let [Thao Kao Cha] come and look down on us in any fashion, [for] we will send forth our brave lords, our nephews." At that time, Cao Phraya Cüang was very angry, so he gathered many troops and went out to meet Thao Kao, the ruler of the Kæo domain. King Cüang was victorious, and killed Thao Kao. / Cüang then placed the domain in the care of his son, named Lao Ngœn Bun Rüang, and his uncle, named Lao Chün, the father of Lady Ua Kham Khòn Müang, for them to rule.

As for Cüang, he then took his numerous troops to take the Kæo domain, and he ascended into the Royal Palace of Thao Kao. There was a daughter of Thao / Kao named Lady Up Kæo who was exceedingly beautiful. Cao Phraya Cüang took her as his wife. Residing [there] in the Kæo domain, he made the lord of that domain submit to his power, and he ruled that domain. His great repute resounded everywhere, and all the kings residing in all the various directions heard that King Lao Cüang was endowed with great majesty and /f° 1.16/ fearless valor and intelligence and that he had defeated the ruler of the Kæo and had become ruler of the Kæo domain.

Among all those kings the king of the Hò named Cao Lum Fa Phao Phiman took the lead in assembling them at Phu Hœt,[29] which was located in the Kæo domains, that is, M. Hò Phrakan. Phu Hœt commanded an extensive plain 1,200 fathoms wide.[30] / The rulers together had a temporary palace constructed adorning Phu Hœt, and erected a pavilion there in the middle of Phu Hœt that was 135 fathoms high and 95 fathoms wide, adorned with 770 royal parasols. There was a golden ewer filled with fragrant lustral water 3 cubits[31] high and 6 cubits wide, weighing 1,400,000 units of gold.[32] With that ewer they bathed and anointed King Cüang / under 770 gold-tipped royal parasols and they used more than a hundred conch shells to anoint him.

King Cüang sat upon the bejeweled throne and was established in that royal palace. He was surrounded by 440,000 ladies, presided over by Queen Amaradevi who had come from the Lao domains / and Lady Up Kæo, the daughter of the Kæo ruler.

---

29 Phu Hœt. The name indicates a mountain. Location unknown; probably in the uplands of northwestern Vietnam, if we follow the logic of the story related here..

30 I have tried consistently to translate *wa* as "fathom." The *wa* conventionally is two meters in length, while the fathom is six feet.

31 Cubit conventionally in Old English measure is eighteen inches; the span from the tip of the nose to the fingertips of an outstretched arm.

32 Invariably, gold is measured in these unspecified units.

The rest surrounded him as his entourage; and all the various rulers, with Phraya Hò Lum Fa Phao Phiman as chief, gathered together there as witnesses with King Cüang. [Cüang] then was consecrated as the sovereign / ruler of the Kæo domain, in the *kap yi*[33] year, the ninth waxing of the fourth month, a Tuesday, in the *kòng ngai* watch, 496 of the Era (25 December AD 1134).

The king remained happily there in the pavilion for seven days, and then descended to the royal palace, surrounded by the various lords and rulers of his retinue, presided over by the Hò ruler Cao Lum Fa Phao Phiman, together with /f° 1.17/ the [various] commanders and 116,669,000 men. King Cüang then feasted all the rulers, officers, and troops for several days with rice, drink, fish, and flesh in great quantities. After five months, the lord then sent the rulers back to their own domains.

Not long afterwards, Lady Up Kæo, / the daughter of the Kæo ruler, reached the full ten-month term of her pregnancy[34] and gave birth to a son of exceeding beauty. King Cüang bestowed upon his son the name, Cao Pha Rüang Mæn Kham Kha. King Cüang remained there at Phrakan for three years and nine months. He then had / the ruler of the Hò, Cao Lum Fa Phao Phiman pay homage to him.[35] The lord then received Lady Amaradevi and all the retainers who sealed their homage to him, and he bestowed them upon his son named Lao Ngœn Rüang, who reigned as king in the Yang Ngœn domain, / Chiang Rao. The king [then] ordered his two sons, namely Cao Ngœn Rüang and Lady Üai Cai the younger, for them to remain with Lady Amaradevi.

As for Cao Phraya Cüang, he returned to the Kæo domains [where he remained for] fourteen years. He had two sons with Lady Up Kæo; the elder named Yi Kham Hao, and the younger named Thao Chum / Sæng. Not long afterwards, Cao Phraya Cüang placed the domain in the care of Thao Pha Rüang, his eldest son. He arranged

---

33 Notton (p. 17) has the *kap si* year, as does UR, p. 10. (Udom's footnote incorrectly notes that HP does not give the numeral of the year.)

34 The Thai conventionally take ten months as the normal period for human pregnancy.

35 *lai cum lai cia*. Bancop Phanthumetha (*Pai sòp kham Thai*, Bangkok, 1977, pp. 143–144) says, based on investigations in M. Yai in the Shan states of Burma, that *cum* refers to the royal seal affixed to official documents.

for his middle son, Yi Kham Hao, to go as king to the Lan Chang domain;[36] and for his youngest son, Thao Sum Sæng, to go as king of Nandapuri, that is, Nan.[37]

King Cüang /f° 1.18/ was endowed with great power, and though it is not claimed that he could fly, it is clear that he was exceptionally valorous. Cüang was proud of his bravery, and was confident enough to hand over the domain to his son, Thao Còm Pha Rüang Mæn Kham Kha, to rule, sure that he could still take the Kæo domain [of] Mæn Ta Thòk Khòk Fa Ta Yün. The Kæo lord / of Mæn Ta Thòk Khòk Fa Ta Yün brought a great many troops out to construct a stone bridge across a great river to fight King Cüang. When King Cüang saw the numerous Kæo army, he never yielded before the enemy; so he mounted his brave war elephant to engage the enemy, and took off his shirt / for a servant to take to give to Queen Amaradevi at Chiang Lao Ngœn Yang as a memento, and informed his son, Cao Khun Ngœn Rüang.

Queen Amaradevi received the coat of King Cüang, her beloved husband, and embraced it, and told her retainers, / "I was at home and saw a presaging of this. My loom was transformed into many water-buffalo and smashed the walls; the pretty crockery fell and became anteaters and scurried under the rocks; the eaves became like bees and flocked into the room and nested; heavy rains fell ceaselessly / for twenty days; the banks of the paddy-fields collapsed, as did the mountains; the rocks became fretful mermaids; deer flew into the town; frogs and toads fornicated together in the town; the black water-leeches promenaded on land and wallowed there; the royal tiger strolled /f° 1.19/ in the city; and an egg yielded forth two chicks. I took these happenings as an omen that Our Lord [Khun Cüang] would not flee the enemy; that he would mount his great elephant and rally his troops and fall into the [hands of the] enemy. We will wait until the fourth month[38] for

---

36 Lan Chang ("Million Elephants") is the conventional name of Laos, often rendered Lan Xang in French works. During this early period it should be associated with Luang Prabang.

37 Identical with the modern Thai city by that name, in the headwaters of the Nan River. It is interesting that the sons of Khun Cüang sent to rule other countries do not figure in the histories of those countries. On one of them, see below f° 1.30. On the history of Nan, see Wyatt, *Nan Chronicle*, in which, however, Khun Cüang does not figure, at least not in the Nan portion of the text.

38 The fourth month is also specified in Notton's manuscript. We can uncover no significance to the fourth month. In former times, the fourth month might have fallen around the winter solstice in December. The old Tai Lü ruling family of M. Len, who had migrated to Nan, venerated the old city and dynastic spirits in the fourth, sixth, and eighth months: see Rattanaphòn Setthakun, "Prapheni

news. I will sacrifice to the great spirits, for them to go and protect the Lord, my beloved.[39] /

At that time, all the Kæo and Mæn Ta Thòk brought up their troops and set up ready for combat. Khun Cüang brought his forces to do battle, and the Kæo and Mæn[40] surrounded and took King Cüang and killed him there on the stone bridge. When King Cüang died, his 1,005 million troops / came in and gathered up his remains and placed them on his war elephant to be returned home. The remains of the lord were given a funeral at Ngœn Yang at that time.

Khun Cüang was thirty-nine years old when he became king of the two domains. He remained at Ngœn Yang for twenty-four years, and was at Kæo Phrakan for seventeen years. He was seventy-seven / when he passed to the next world, the nineteenth of the royal lineage.

The Successors of Khun Cüang

The son of Khun Cüang named Lao Ngœn Rüang at the age of thirty-three years became king in his father's stead. He ruled for twenty-six years and at the age of fifty-nine passed to the next world. He was the twentieth of the royal lineage.

The son of King Ngœn Rüang was named Lao Chün. At the age of forty-one years he became king in place of his father. He ruled for twenty-one years, / and at the age of sixty-two passed to the next world. He was the twenty-first in the royal lineage.

The son of Lao Chün was named Lao Ming. At the age of twenty-five years he became king in his father's place. He ruled for twenty-one years, and at the age of forty-six he passed to the next world. He was the twenty-second of the royal lineage.

The son of Khun Ming was named Khun Mœng. At the age of thirty-five years he became king in his father's place. He ruled for twenty-five years, and at the age of sixty years passed to the next world, the twenty-third /f° 1.20/ of the royal lineage.

---

sakkara bucha arak ban arak müang khòng Chiang Tung," *Rüang müang Chiang Tung* (Chiang Mai, 1994), p. 55.

39 This is an extremely difficult paragraph, and we are not surprised that it also troubled Nottot (p. 19).

40 We are puzzled about who the Mæn might have been. We note that the town of Pu-erh in southern Yunnan, northeast of Chiang Rung, is sometimes referred to as M. Mæn; and we are told that there is a M. Mæn in the Black Tai region of extreme northwestern Vietnam.

King Mangrai's Parents

Lao Mœng had a son who was very handsome, named Lao Meng. Cao Lao Mœng thus had presents sent requesting the daughter of Thao Rung Kæn Chai, the ruler of Chiang Rung,[41] who was named Lady Ua Ming Còm Müang and was very beautiful in form and figure, to come as the wife of Cao Lao / Meng.[42] Thao Rung Kæn Chai was delighted, and so bestowed upon his daughter the name, Lady Theppha Kham Khrai; and then he bestowed presents, silver, gold, ivory, and luxuries, and many male and female retainers upon his daughter, who was sent to be the wife of Cao Lao Meng. Cao Lao Meng / at the age of thirty-five years became king in his father's place. He made Lady Thao Theppha Kham Khrai his primary queen, superior to all the five hundred other women.[43]

The Birth of King Mangrai

Not long afterwards, on the full-moon day of the eighth month, in the watch near dawn, the queen beheld a vision in her dreams that she was sleeping on a throne / which was glorious, and saw Venus, the morning star, hovering and descending through the air in the south, and it entered her mouth. She swallowed it, and felt great contentment. The Lady awakened in the morning, and reverenced the king and told him about the omen she had dreamed, in every detail. The king called for a soothsayer experienced in such matters, and asked / him about it. The soothsayer said, "This dream is very auspicious. The Lady will become pregnant, and will bear a

---

41 Var. Keng Hung, Chiang Hung, etc. The chief city of the Sipsong Panna region of extreme southern Yunnan. Li Fu-i, *Ch'e-li Hsüan-wei shih k'ao ting* [A Revised Study of the Genealogy of Ch'e-li Pacification Chieftaincy] (Ch'e-li, 1947), pp. 6–7, lists "Dao Rung Kian Jhai" as having ruled from 1234 to 1257. Thawi Swangpanyangkun, *Tamnan phün müang Sipsong Panna* (Chiang Mai, 1986), p. 47, gives Thao Rung the dates CS 586–609 (AD 1224–1247).

42 This passage could be said to attest to the antiquity of relations, and the primacy of Mangrai's line, between the Ngœn Yang people and Chiang Rung (standing for the Sipsong Panna) of southernmost Yunnan. The usual sociological rule is that it is preferable for a daughter to marry a man of higher rank than her father.

43 Royal polygamy: The numeral is probably not to be taken literally. Chinese records say (in the New Yuan history, ch. 149, and the Ming history ch. 315) that Chiang Rai, Chiang Sæn, and Chiang Mai were called Pa-pai-hsi-fu, the king of which had eight hundred wives. Tuan Lisœng, *Prawattisat Lan Na Thai*, pp. 1–3.

son most illustrious who will conquer the lands to the south, all the way to the sea, to be sure." The Lady was delighted, and bestowed great rewards upon the soothsayer. The Lady guarded her womb for the full ten months, /fº 1.21/ and then gave birth to a most illustrious son in the *pœk set* year—one chronicle says the *kat kai* year[44]— on the ninth waning of the first month, a Sunday, near dawn, in the eighth lunar mansion, called Pussya, in the year 601 of the Anuruddha Era.[45]

One month after the royal prince was born, his father King Lao Meng / sent word to Thao Rung Kæn Chai, the father of his queen, informing him of the birth of his grandson.[46] Thao Rung then came with a great many of his retainers. King Lao Meng exclaimed, "Thao Rung Kæn Chai has arrived!" and he announced the fact to all his ministers and generals and the city folk. They assembled to fête / the prince with the first-month's gifts, that the baby prince might be blessed with a long life. King Lao Meng and King Rung Kæn Chai, the paternal and maternal grandparents, then together bestowed a name upon the young prince, Cao Manglai [Mangrai], based upon Meng, the name of his father, and Rung,[47] from his maternal grandfather, signifying that he was the son / of Thao Meng and grandson of Thao Rung—thus, Mangrai; the son of Lady Thao Theppha Kham Khrai of Chiang Rung, [thereby] combining the names of both his grandfathers. When Thao Rung Kæn Chai had performed the ceremony for his grandson, he returned to his own domain.

---

44 The author clearly indicates that he has consulted more than one source.

45 The chronological data work out *almost* perfectly for Saturday, 2 October 1238, which was in the *poek set* year 600, not the *kat kai* year 601. The only bit that does not work out correctly is the weekday, which is only one day off. The lunar mansion is correct for the Saturday. All dates given in the text of the chronicle have been converted to AD (Julian to 1582, Gregorian from October 1582), unless the date requires comment in a footnote. Notton (p. 20, n. 2) notes that the same date is given in Jkm. (p. 111).

46 The "first-month ceremony" marks the end of the month that the new mother lies "roasting" by a fire after giving birth. We do not know exactly how the "first-month" ceremony might have been conducted when this passage was written, but presumably it included giving a formal name to the young child. The ceremony is still observed in the north of Thailand. The Lan Na people of Chiang Mai believe that a mother must lie by the fire for a month, at the conclusion of which she "comes out;" this day is considered significant, for the first non-family member to visit the home is thought to portend the future character and disposition of the child. On occasion, if the mother is unhappy with the person who comes to visit, she will return to the fire for another two or three days.

47 One would have expected Meng*rung*, not Mang*rai*. On Mangrai's name, see Hans Penth, "On the History of Chiang Rai," *JSS* 77, pt.1 (1989), esp. pp. 11–12.

Cao Lao Meng was thirty-five years of age when he became king in succession to his father. He ruled for forty years, and at the age / of seventy-five he passed to the next world. He was the twenty-fourth of the royal lineage.

Accession of King Mangrai

As for the royal prince named Mangrai, at the age of twenty-one years he succeeded his father as king in the *kat met* year, 621 of the Lesser Era (1259/60), in M. Ngœn Yang.

Mangrai's Conquests—Müang Mòp

After King Mangrai had been consecrated king, he learned that that rulers of the countries /f° 1.22/ adjoining his own were fighting over manpower and land, each claiming that they belonged to him, which was a source of great suffering to the people of the domain. The lord [Mangrai] thought, "Any land with multiple rulers is a source of great suffering to its people. Furthermore, much anxiety arises [from such situations]. All these [contending] rulers, even / though they be of the same lineage [as I]—the line of King Lawacangkarat, descendants of Lao Kòp and Lao Chang—not a single one of them has been duly consecrated a king. Only my paternal grandfather, King Lao Kao, who was the younger sibling of Cao Lao Khòp and Lao Chang, was consecrated / a king, continuing the lineage down to me today. Furthermore, the regalia of coronation—for example, the Sword of Victory, the

Spear, the Srikañjayya Dagger, and the Auspicious Gems—are things that have come down to me from Grandfather Lao Cong [Cangkaracha], and I have maintained them down to the present day, every one of them. All of those / who are my neighbor kings have not undergone coronation like me, not one of them, and they [therefore] cannot withstand me. I should attack and take those domains."

Having spoken thus, King Mangrai gathered up his troops, his elephants and horses, and his generals and troops in great numbers and attacked a domain that lay to the south / of his own domain, in order to force them to acknowledge his sovereignty. He placed one of his officers in charge of that domain, named M. Mòp[48] to the present day.

---

48 "Handed-Over" or "Delegated" City

Mangrai's Conquests—Müang Lai

Then the lord went to attack another domain, but was unsuccessful. The lord of that domain took his families and fled. Mangrai chased after [*lai*] him and killed him. He then /f° 1.23/ had one of his officers take charge [of that domain], which has been called M. Lai to the present day.

Mangrai's Conquests—Chiang Kham

Then the lord went to attack another domain, which he took at night. He placed one of his officers in charge of that domain, which has been called Chiang Kham ["Darkness"] to the present day.[49]

Mangrai's Conquests—Chiang Chang

Then the lord went to attack another domain. One in the city exclaimed that, "Since [this ruler] / is of the lineage of Paternal Grandfather Cao Lao Chang, we should present tribute welcoming King Mangrai, acknowledging him as our overlord, asking him to spare our lives. In matters of warfare, we promise to be the vanguard of his armies." King / Mangrai then considered, "He reminds me that he is of the lineage of Grandfather Lao Chang, which is true. He has shown respect for me. I should allow him to continue to rule this domain as my vassal and head of my vanguard. Furthermore, I have been victorious and defeated him." That domain got the name Chana Chang; and later / it became known as Chiang Chang, down to the present day. The term "overlord" [*cao nüa hua*] also dates from that time.

At that time King Mangrai appointed the ruler of Chiang Chang as chief to go and pursue all the domain people who had fled. / He came to an old domain of Mangrai's father, named M. Rao Phu Tao Ròi.[50] There he saw a village which delighted him, so he encamped there. He made it into a domain, which was called

---

49 Now Chiang Kham, without the first tone marker that signifies nighttime, on the Mekong in Chiang Kham district, Phayao province. It is likely to be a very ancient settlement, associated with the Ton Luang Buddha image of Wat Si Khom Kham, Phayao. See Aroonrut Wichienkeeo and Albert Lisec, *Sinlapakam Phutthasatsana nai Lan Na* (in press); and Aroonrut Wichienkeeo ed., *Thai Lü Chiang Kham* (Chiang Mai, 1983).

50 Perhaps Müang Rao/Lao [near the] Tao Ròi Mountain?: location unknown.

Tao Ròi Yam Di.⁵¹ From there, he could go to fight anywhere. There he captured not a few refugees, many thousands in number. This place has been called Tao Ròi down to the present day. /f° 1.24/

A son was born to the king in the *tao set* year, 624 of the Lesser Era (1262/63).

Foundation of Chiang Rai

Not long afterwards, the auspicious elephant of King Mangrai ran loose north of a mountain to the east. The king followed the track of the elephant and beheld a country on the banks of the Kok River, flanked by a single beauteous hill. He thought, "When Grandfather Lao Cong built a home for / my Grandfather Lao Kao, I heard that it was [founded] at the base of Mount Pha Rao. When Grandfather Lao Khriang built M. Ngœn Yang, he built it nestled between three mountains, namely Dòi Thung, Dòi Tha, and Dòi Ya Thao,⁵² which was very good, so I should likewise make [mountains] the navel of the town,⁵³ in its center. So King Mangrai / built a [fortified] city around Dòi Còm Thòng,⁵⁴ which he made the center of the city. It was built in the *tao set* year, 624 of the Era (1262/63), and was named Chiang Rai.⁵⁵

Khun Khrüang, the eldest son of King Mangrai, was also born in that *tao set* year, the year when the city of Chiang Rai was founded.⁵⁶

---

51   Or, "Tao Ròi of the Auspicious Moment": location unknown.

52   Dòi Thung, Dòi Tha, Dòi Ya Thao: see Hans Penth et al., *Phrathat Dòi Thung*.

53   The magical center of a city—variously termed the city "navel" or "heart of the city" or "city pillar" or, in Chiang Mai, the Inthakhin (pillar)—is a common feature of Tai city-building. The "heart of the city" (*cai müang*) is still found in the Shan states, e.g., in Phayak and Keng Tung, and in the Dehong Tai regions of China. Cit Phumisak supposes that Mangrai was copying the city-plan of the Khmers, who made artificial mountains the centers of their cities, and made them into the centers of their "world." (Cit, *Khwampenma khòng kham Sayam*, pp. 116–117). Chiang Mai used to have a "City-Navel Temple" (Wat Sadü Müang) in the center of the city.

54   Dòi Còm Thòng abuts the Kok River in Chiang Rai, surmounted by a reliquary. There remain traces of an old city wall at the base of the hill.

55   The modern city and provincial capital have the same name. The Chinese records (New Yuan history ch. 149 and Ming history ch. 315) say that Chiang Rai was the capital of Pa-pai-hsi-fu. The name of Chiang Rai means a city of rice-fields: see Tuan Lisœng, *Prawattisat Lan Na Thai*, p. 3. Notton has a few more details (p. 23, n.).

56   The same information is given just above (s.v. s. 624), which suggests a seam here between two separate sources.

Three years later, in the *dap pao* year, 627 of the Era (1265/66), / the king had another son, named Cao Khun Khram. Three years later, in the *pœk si* year (1268/69), King Mangrai went to live at Fang for a year.⁵⁷

Mangrai's Conquests—Chiang Khòng

In the *kat sai* year (1269/70), King Mangrai took his troops to seize M. Pha Dæng Chiang Khòng, which the descendants of Lao Khròp had built.⁵⁸ The ruler of Chiang Khòng was called Kham Ròng. / Chiang Khòng fell. [Mangrai] appointed one of his officers to govern it, and then he returned to Fang, where he took care of his many brave generals and ministers.

Mangrai's Conquests—Müang Sœng

The ruler had another son, named Cao Khun Khrüa in the *kat sai* year, 631 of the Era. Later, when Cao Khun Khrüa was six years old, in the *kap set* year (1274/75), when King Mangrai was thirty-six years old, he took /f° 1.25/ his troops to seize M. Sœng.⁵⁹ The ruler of Sœng was Khun Ròng. The city fell, [and Mangrai] appointed one of his officers to rule it. He then led his troops back to Fang, where he fêted his generals and ministers for three days and three nights. He then reigned in happiness and prosperity.

Mangrai Considers the Capture of Hariphunchai

Commerce was thriving. At that time, many parties of traders from Haribhuñjaya / came to conduct commerce in Fang. King Mangrai therefore summoned the traders and asked them, "This Haribhuñjaya where you live: How prosperous is it?" A trader replied, "The Haribhuñjaya where I live is far away, and is replete with all

---

57 Ruins of an ancient city of Fang still remain outside the modern city of that name. There are no less than the remains of six old cities, and we do not know which of them might have been the old Fang.

58 That is, the modern town of Chiang Khòng. See Charin Cæmcit, in *Warasan Chainarai* 1990. Notton's manuscript (p. 23) has a long lacuna here.

59 M. Sœng/Thœng/Phœng; in Thœng district of Chiang Rai. The ruins of an old wall remain there.

kinds of good things. Traders of all countries frequent it both by land and by / water to trade. By water, one can reach Yodhiya, and traders from there come. In trade, the people of the domain are very prosperous."

Again, the king asked, "Is the ruler [of Haribhuñjaya] richly endowed with troops, elephants and horses, and retainers? Is the country rich?" A trader replied, "The king / of my yonder domain is richly endowed with elephants and horses and retainers, and he has all kinds of wealth." King Mangrai upon hearing that Haribhuñjaya was wealthy was consumed with a desire to obtain it for his own, so he consulted with his generals thusly: "We have heard the news / that Haribhuñjaya is very rich—richer than our own domain. How can we make it our own? Consider this matter." The generals replied to the king, "Yonder Haribhuñjaya is indeed wealthy. We have heard that it is graced with very intelligent sovereignty, as the Great Reliquary of our Lord [Buddha] is located /f° 1.26/ in that city, and the guardian spirits protect it well.[60] To seize it would be really difficult. Our lord should ponder this."

At that time there was a man of rank [*khun*] named Ai Fa whom King Mangrai had maintained as a clerk and tax collector.[61] He had very good judgment and was very knowledgeable. Ai Fa respectfully addressed the king, / saying, "My lord desires to obtain Haribhuñjaya for his own. It is not difficult." The king said, "How can you say it is not difficult? The city is richly endowed with brave troops and skilled strategists, so how can you say it is not difficult?" Ai Fa replied, "We cannot attack and take it with / troops and armies. We must conquer it with military wisdom; that is, with stratagems and ruses of one sort or another, and then we can be successful."

King Mangrai replied, "You say that we can take it with stratagems. Tell me: [stratagems] of what sort?" /

Ai Fa replied, "The means I propose are very devious, and should not be explained in public. I should explain them to Your Majesty in secret."

At a time when the king was alone, Ai Fa entered and reported to the king thusly: "Concerning my / going disguised, I ask that Your Majesty state that I have broken your laws on some point or another. Your Majesty should pretend to completely strip me of my family, my wives and children, my elephants and horses, my retainers and all my valuable goods, and should exile me from Your Majesty's domain, /f°

---

60 See Mani Phayòmyong, "Prapheni bucha thewada læ süp chata müang," in *Kamphæng müang Chiang Mai* (Chiang Mai, 1986), pp. 23–26.

61 According to *TM* (f° 2), Ai Fa was a Lawa.

1.27/ leaving me with only a few things of little value and enough retainers to care for me, as appropriate. I will flee, and take refuge with King Yi Ba at Haribhuñjaya. I will display my sorrow and guilt, and state that I have been unjustifiably convicted."

King Mangrai listened to these words, and said, "You have broken our laws, / and I will confiscate your families, your wives and children, and all your goods, and banish you. You will take refuge with King [Yi Ba]. He will take pity on you and will believe you, for sure."

Ai Fa [continued:] "I will win the respect of the Haribhuñjaya people, / and they will lose respect for King Yi Ba—that I will arrange in every way. The Haribhuñjaya people will be happy with [King Mangrai]. I will do everything I can. When the Haribhuñjaya people are in my power, / I will hasten to advise you to bring up your troops to take Haribhuñjaya, and Your Majesty will be king of Haribhuñjaya, for sure. This is my plan." King Mangrai heard the strategy of Ai Fa for / seizing King Yi Ba, and said, "Good! That's appropriate for our state."

King Mangrai did accordingly. He confiscated the families, goods, and gold and silver of Ai Fa, and banished him from his domain. In the *kap set* year, 636 of the Era (AD 1274/75), Ai Fa fled and took refuge with King Yi Ba in /f° 1.28/ Hariphunchai, as planned. Ai Fa took refuge with King Yi Ba, and deceitfully told King Yi Ba as he had planned.

After Ai Fa had gone, King Mangrai had his eldest son, Cao Khun Khrüang, go and take charge of Chiang Rai, / and King Mangrai took his forces down to reign in Fang.

Revolt of Khun Khrüang

A year later, in the *dap kai* year (AD 1275/76), when Mangrai was thirty-seven years old, his son Cao Khun Khrüang was thirteen years old,[62] Khun Khram the middle son was ten years old, and the youngest Khun Khrüa was six years old. In / that *dap kai* year, Khun Khrüang, who was living at Chiang Rai, revolted against his father, saying, "My father conquered the country, and obtained two or three domains; but never said he would give me even one domain to rule."

---

62 Notton here (p. 25) notes the manuscript's confusion of the names of Khun Khüa, Khrüang, and Khuang.

There was a man named Khun Sai Riang, who was an old retainer, who joined Khun Khrüang and went with him to gather up people / in Chiang Rai, with the intention of contesting with his father to rule the domain.

At that time, Mangrai was living in Fang. He heard that Khun Khrüang and Sai Riang were plotting together to gather a force to rebel in the city of Chiang Rai. So he thought, "I, his father, have not yet gone / to the next world. I still have the power to conquer domains. Khun Khrüang has little merit, yet he would seize and rule the domain. I can craftily capture him."

So King Mangrai sought out an old retainer whom he could trust, called Khun Òng, and devised /f° 1.29/ a ruse. He said to Khun Òng, "I will have you take a message to my son Khun Khrüang in Chiang Rai. Tell him that his father dreamed he was a bird flying in the air, a friend of the hawks, and seized the corpses of ghosts. His father was quite disturbed, and feared he would be reborn in the womb of a ghost; so his father / had [Khun Òng] come to him and tie his wrists to contain his soul.[63] Tell [Khun Khrüa] to stand fast!" Khun Òng received the words of King Mangrai, and went to seek out Khun Khrüang in Chiang Rai. He told Khun Khrüang what his lord had told him to say, in every detail. Khun Khrüang heard these words, and thought, "My father / still loves me!"

Saying so, Khun Khrüang mounted an elephant and came together with Khun Òng. At that time, King Mangrai ordered a skilled archer, named Ai Phian, to take a poison arrow to lie in wait for Khun Khrüang. When Khun Òng brought Khun Khrüang there riding an elephant, Ai Phian took the arrow and shot / and killed Khun Khrüang. The place where Khun Khrüang died was very level and attractive, so a fortified city was constructed there, called M. Ying[64] to the present day.

King Mangrai then said, "Khun Khrüang consorted with a bad man, and so met his karma." King Mangrai then took his forces to gather up the remains and / conduct the funeral obsequies for Khun Khrüang at Chiang Rai, and then he reigned from Chiang Rai. From that time, reigning there the king had no further cares.

---

63 Such ceremonies are still widely performed in interior Southeast Asia. See Mani Phayòmyong, *Prapheni sipsòng düan Lan Na Thai* (Chiang Mai, 1986), pp. 203–227.

64 "Shooting City." Thought to have been a temporary town between Fang and Chiang Rai.

New Coronation for Mangrai

Tadā. At that time, a Kæo king named Thao Kæn Phongsa, the son of Thao Pha Rüang Mæ[n] Kham Kha and the grandson of King Cüang, was reigning in succession to his father in /f° 1.30/ M. Phrakan, that is, in the Kæo domain. He heard that there was a king in the yonder Lawarāja[65] domain of Chiang Rai in the same lineage as his own. Now he heard that [Mangrai] was going to give up his [home] domain and go to seize Haribhuñjaya: "I am thinking of King Mangrai, who is of the same lineage as / me, his uncle. I would like to go and visit him and ask for news of our senior relatives; and I should bring him the utensils of coronation and consecrate uncle as king, that King Mangrai may live long and well, with great majesty and power.[66] This is my good intention." His officers replied, "Your Majesty's idea is appropriate." /

King Kæn Phongsa then arranged the [coronation] utensils, all 108 items, and a conch shell turning to the right; and, putting his son in charge of his domain, he came together with his state retainers to the Lao domains, encamping his forces / on the banks of the Mekong River, at the mouth of the Chan River.[67] He then sent a minister to pay attendance upon King Mangrai, saying, "O, nephew of King Kæn Phongsa, the son of Thao Pha Rüang Mæn Kham Kha and grandson of King Cüang, and so of the same lineage as thee, he has brought the implements of coronation and the 108 requisites / and has come to perform your coronation of Your Majesty as a sovereign monarch. Right now he is encamped by the banks of the Mekong at its confluence with the Mæ Chan, and he has commissioned me to call upon Your Majesty that you may be informed."

So informed, King Mangrai was greatly pleased, and he sent numerous gifts to / f° 1.31/ welcome the Kæo king, and prepared for him a great feast of rice, drink, meat, fish, and many foods, so that no person would be wanting. Two or three days

---

65 Here, "Lawaraja," but below "the Lao domain(s)" and "Lavaraṭṭha." All have the same meaning.

66 *muddhâbhiseka*. See Ryuji Okudaira, "A Study on a Mythology of 'Kingship' Described in *Manugye Dhammathat:* Significance of *Muddha Beiktheik* or the Supreme Coronation Ceremony," *Southeast Asian Studies, Tokyo University of Foreign Studies*, no. 1, 1995, 65–83.

This episode is particularly strange because just a bit earlier (f° 1.22), Mangrai had been boasting about how he alone was a *real* consecrated king.

67 Mæ Chan: mouth of the Mæ Chan (River) where it empties into the Mekong, in Chiang Sæn district.

later, on an auspicious day, King Kæn Phongsa came to perform the coronation of King Mangrai with the implements of / 108 sorts [that he had brought]. King Kæn Phongsa presented him with the highest blessings befitting a Maharaja, that he might defeat all enemies in every direction, establishing him in a royal state, that he might reign in conformity with his every wish, / that he might be blessed with everything he wished and a long life of 120 years.

Having said this, King Kæn Phongsa conversed with King Mangrai, saying, "My great-grandfather, King Cüang, / even though he was lord of Lavaraṭṭha, then went on to conquer the Kæo domain and reigned there in the Kæo domain. He had descendants, now down to me, so we are of the same lineage. Furthermore, our lineage / includes an uncle who was my younger brother, a person named Yi Kham Hao, who went to become king of Lan Chang; another person, named Thao Chum Sæng, the younger brother, went to become king in the domain of Nandapuri, that is, Nan. I am the son of Thao Pha Rüang Mæn Kham Kha and I rule the Kæo Phrakan domain. When my father passed to the next world I became king /f° 1.32/ in his place. The Hò king, Cao Lum Fa brought all the rulers to consecrate me at Phu Hœt as Great King over the Kæo domains, just as the Hò king Cao Lum Fa Phao Phiman had consecrated my father and grandfather King Cüang. Inasmuch as I am of thy lineage, I come here / to perform the coronation of Your Majesty, that you may reign in happiness."

After saying this, King Kæn Phongsa took leave of King Mangrai, who was the head of the lineage; and when he [returned to] reign in the Kæo domain he continued the royal traditions / down to the present day. Such is the continuity of the lineage of Lao Cakkrarat.

All the rulers—of the domain of the Hò, the domain of the Kæo, the domain of Mæn Ta Thòk Khòk Fa Ta Yün—usually greatly fear the Lao kings because King Cüang went in warfare / and killed the Kæo king named Thao Kao and became king in the Kæo Phrakan domain, conquering all the Kæo domains. The martial majesty of the Lao domains continues down to the present day. The Hò, Kæo, and Mæn Ta Thòk all fear the / men of our Lao domains down to the present day. The tale of the Kæo king named Thao Kæn Phongsa coming to perform the coronation of King Mangrai is here concluded.[68]

---

68 *nidāna tamnān*: is the author using a separate source here?

King Ngam Müang of Phayao

Later, in the *rwai cai* year, 638 of the Era (1276/77), King Mangrai was still at Chiang Rai. He pondered, "I organized a stratagem /f° 1.33/ for Ai Fa to go and prepare the seizure of Haribhuñjaya through a ruse, and he has not sent me any word whatsoever that I might know [of his progress]. I should now go and capture the domain of Phayao."[69] Having so resolved, he brought up his troops and men to a place on the border between Chiang Rai and / Phayao, at a place called Ban Dai.[70]

King Ngam Müang, the ruler of Phayao, learned that King Mangrai had brought up his troops, and so he brought up his own troops, intending to fight King Mangrai at Ban Dai. There the two kings each brought up their / troops. They did not fight, but pledged friendship to each other, as they bore no enmity to each other and in a previous existence had been friends. They discussed matters of state and pledged their mutual friendship. / King Mangrai then said to King Ngam Müang that they were of a single house. Ngam Müang was delighted, and handed over to King Mangrai a part of one district with five hundred households,[71] which then came into the territory of Chiang Rai. The two / kings parted as friends, and each returned to his own country. The place where the two kings would have fought, but did not fight, has been called Rat Ban down to the present day, and will be so called in the future.

---

69 Here, Phuyao. It was called by various names: Phrayao, Phukamyao; nowadays Phayao. See Phra Ratchawisutthisophon, *Prawattisat müang Phayao, Tamnan Müang Chiang Sæn* (Bangkok: 1981) and Aroonrut Wichienkeeo, *Tamnan phün müang Phayao, chabap Hòsamut hæng Chat* (Chiang Mai, 1983).

70 Ban Dai: there is a village by this name (with this spelling) 5 km. east of Chiang Rai.

71 *pak na*: an administrative unit, or a measure of land. The word *pak* means a hundred, so 10 *pak na* total a *phan na* (*panna*). A *panna* refers to an area of rice-fields, irrespective of specific surface-area, irrigated by a single irrigation system. Probably derived from a word still used by farmers in northern Thailand, *pan na*. See Aroonrut Wichienkeeo, "Næo khit thang kanmüang: khwamsamphan rawang rabop phanna, rabob nan sip læ rabop chonlaprathan," *Ekkasan ruam botkhwam cak kanprachum sammana thang wichakan rüang Lan Na khadisüksa: Lokkathat Lan Na rawang 11-14 Sept. 1981* (Chiang Mai, 1981), pp. 1–15.

King Ngam Müang and King Ruang of Sukhothai

There was another king, named King Ruang, who was the king of Sukhothai.⁷² / f° 1.34/ This King Ruang was the son of a fierce ogress named Kangli.⁷³ The lady beheld a fisherman who was beauteous of form, and took him as her husband; and they had a son, who became King Ruang. King Ruang and King Ngam Müang were great friends, and relied upon and trusted each other. King Ruang often went to wash his hair⁷⁴ in the / Mekong [River], and brought elephants there with him passing by the domain of Phayao, along the route along which Ngam Müang brought his troops and elephants and horses. People later were to call it the Mæ Ròng Chang, down to the present day.

There was a lady consort of King Ngam Müang / called Lady Ua [of] Chiang Sæn who was very beautiful.⁷⁵ That lady harbored a grudge against King Ngam Müang for this reason: One day, at a soul-tying [*su khwan*] ceremony for Ngam Müang, Lady Ua Chiang Sæn quarreled with King Ngam Müang, who told the lady that the beef stew she had made for the ceremony was delicious but a bit too watery.⁷⁶ /

---

72 Phra Ruang; of course, King Ramkhamhæng of Sukhothai. A contemporary of Mangrai and Ngam Müang, he is usually given the regnal dates 1279–1299.

73 Notton (p. 29, fn. 2) refers us to Louis Finot, "Recherches sur la littérature laotienne," *BEFEO* 17 (1917), pp. 134, 157, which refer to the Lao tales of Buddhasen and Khun Borom.

74 Lan Na custom is to ritually wash the hair each year on one of the days at the New Year festival (*Songkran*). Villagers go to wash their hair or lustrate the head in a large stream near their homes. Obviously, Phra Ruang did not often go to wash his hair in the Mekong, as it is quite far from Sukhothai, so it is likely that he went at Songkran. Sukhothai Inscription #1 makes reference to the Mekong's clear water. See Mani Phayòmyong, *Prapheni sipsòng düan Lan Na Thai*, pp. 56–57.

75 The lady's name indicates that she was a second daughter ("*ua*"), and that she was from Chiang Sæn. We might guess that she had a dwelling at "Wiang Chiang Sum." The chronicle tells us that she performed a "soul-tying ceremony" for King Ngam Müang, and for food presented him with a special curry she had made herself. She took offense at Ngam Müang's half-hearted compliment, and acted on her desire for Phra Ruang of Sukhothai. On his way to do his (New Year's) ablutions in the Mekong, he passed by Chiang Sum. Lan Na customary law provided that a couple's marriage ended when mutual affection ceased. See Phra Ratchawisutthisophon, *Atthakhamphi hæng Phutthakhosacan* (Phayao, 1982); Surasingsamruam Chimphanao, *Khlòng cüa Phraya Kü Na* (mimeo.).

The lady is likely already to have been estranged from her husband, but Ngam Müang retained her as a concubine. Thus, in considering the case, the fault may be considered to have been Phra Ruang's alone, and not Lady Ua's, else she would have been punished as well.

76 Cf. Wyatt, *Nan Chronicle*, pp. 43–44.

The lady was upset, and feared that the king was speaking from bias against her and would no longer seek out her company.

King Ngam Müang went off to the city of Chiang Sum.[77] The lady was happy, for she had a desire for King Ruang, who was wont to come past [there] and wash his hair. She waited outside the city. King Ruang knew that / Lady Ua Chiang Sæn had a hankering for him, so he quietly seduced her many times.

Later, King Ngam Müang found out that King Ruang had cuckolded him, and tried to seize King Ruang. He deviously invited King Ruang to come to eat. King Ruang knew [of his intentions], and did not come, replying, "King Ngam Müang is of lower status than /f° 1.35/ me, and though he invites me, I will not go."

King Ngam Müang heard what King Ruang had said and was very angry, so he called for a retainer[78] named Han Bang,[79] and had [Han Bang] go and fetch a leading commoner, a nephew/grandson of King Ruang who had studied the magical arts with King Ruang and knew them well. Han Bang accordingly went and fetched / that person and presented him to his lord, King Ngam Müang.

King Ngam Müang asked that lowly person, "King Ruang and Lady Ua Kham Chiang Sæn have slept together, isn't that true?" King Ngam Müang then asked further, / "Now, has Phraya [Ruang] come yet with his elephants and horses and retainers past my domain? Which way does he come? Or has he changed form?"[80]

The commoner feared the power of Ngam Müang, and feared lying to him. / So he replied to Ngam Müang, "Phraya Ruang knew My Lord would catch him, so he did not pass by as a king, but rather as one of many passing troops with their elephants and horses. Sometimes he took on the form of a golden deer to pass by with them, and then went to wash his hair in the Mekong." /

Then Ngam Müang again sought out a clever minister, named Thao Mung, an expert in magical sciences, with Han Bang to go together to study all the magical sciences with the leading commoner. King Ngam Müang then had the two of them [Han Bang and Thao Mung] attempt to capture King Ruang.

---

77 Outside Phayao, by the Kwan Phayao (lake), where there are the remains of several old cities. See Phra Ratchawisutthisophon, Sisak Wanliphodom, Phiset Ciacanphong, and Sucit Wongthet, *Müang Phayao* (Bangkok, 1984), esp. pp. 68–69.

78 *phuak nòi:* position for a close retainer of Phra Ruang's.

79 *han* is a military rank; akin to the modern word for bravery or fearlessness.

80 Apparently it was commonly believed that one with magical powers might be able to transform him- or herself into other creatures or things.

The two /f° 1.36/ cast magical spells in order to discern if King Ruang had changed his form and to what. King Ruang had changed his form to a golden deer to match a herd passing Phayao. Thao Mung and Han Bang cast magical spells to change themselves into two dogs to chase the golden deer. The golden deer ran very fast, and the two pursuers could not catch him. /

King Ruang then changed himself into a hornet hive high in a treetop. Thao Mung and Han Bang chased him and saw this transformation. The two then transformed themselves into big hawks, in order to claw and beat and destroy the hive.

King Ruang then transformed / himself into a large mole, which went into a deep burrow beneath a mangosteen tree. Thao Mung and Han Bang pursued him. They saw the track of the large mole entering the hole under the mangosteen tree. They dug a deep trench around that tree and said, "That mole has to be in here, so we've got to have him!" / That tree then got the name Tòng tree, to the present day.

The mole scurried out of the top of its burrow. Thao Mung and Han Bang pursued it. King Ruang transformed himself into an anthill, making a high-spiked crown made of glass atop it. The two pursued, but could not see King Ruang. When / they saw that the anthill was surmounted by a glass pinnacle, they knew that King Ruang had transformed himself into an anthill. They grabbed the crown and cast a spell to destroy [King Ruang's] magical power, in order that King Ruang could not further transform himself. That place there was called Run thereafter, /f° 1.37/ to the present day.

At that time, King Ruang perceived his difficulty. He could not withstand them, and so he said, "I am King Ruang!" The two handed him over to King Ngam Müang. Ngam Müang had him put in a cage by the southeast gate of the city of Chiang Sum.[81] Ngam Müang gave him a seat and a bed, / that King Ruang might be comfortable. That gate was later called the Patu Suk Sai, changed to Patu Sop Sai to the present day.[82]

King Ngam Müang then thought, "I could kill King Ruang and my wife. However, the Southern domain[83] and my domain / would hereafter be in enmity. I shouldn't

---

81 Chiang Sum was one of a group of four cities or towns clustered around the southeast end of the great lake at Phayao. See *Müang Phayao*, ed. Phra Ratchawisutthisophon (Bangkok, 1982).

82 Apparently an old gate to the city of Phayao.

83 Or "the Southern Country." All references to the South and Southerners (capitalized) in this translation mean what we could think of as Siam.

kill them. Furthermore, my wife meant no harm. I have captured King Ruang. I should fine him: it would be proper to take from him. As for me, I am a Great King, and I should seek out my friend. King Mangrai is meritful and merciful, and he is / wise and clever. I could have him come and adjudicate the case. I should have him come and investigate and decide [concerning] King Ruang, who has offended against me. This will be fair." Having thought this, King Ngam Müang then sent gifts to be presented to King Mangrai, / asking him to come and judge the matter.

The Meeting of the Three Kings

At that time, King Mangrai, who was a just man (*uḷḷaracayasaya*), remembered the ancient practice, that lawsuits involving adultery were submitted to the judgment of experts who examined the case. "Now my two friends are at odds, and would have me come and hear their plaint. If I /f° 1.38/ do not go, it will be a great source of enmity for both of them. I should take the defendant, King Ruang, and fine him. He is a king of great power, and he will be ashamed. Furthermore, the kings of Sri Sudhammarājanagara Luang[84] and Sri Ayutthiya are relatives of King Ruang, and they will / be angry with my friend, King Ngam Müang. I should deflect that anger from my friends Ngam Müang and Ruang, that their worries will cease."

King Mangrai then went with a great number of retainers to Phayao, and encamped at an appropriate spot. / King Ngam Müang came out to greet him, happy to see his friend. King Ngam Müang presented tribute and numerous gifts to King Mangrai, his friend, and they talked at length about the matter of the offense of King Ruang. / King Mangrai said, "My friend, I am a Great King who has been duly consecrated, my head anointed. I have merit and mercy, and many subjects. As for this King Ruang, he has been consecrated king in yonder Sukhothai; yet King Ruang / has committed an offense against his friend and has now been caught. Now, my friend, bring King Ruang forth, and I will consider the merits of the case."

King Ngam Müang had King Ruang brought forth, and had him swear an oath of truthfulness before King Mangrai. King Ruang confessed that he had [indeed] taken the wife of King Ngam Müang. Thereupon /f° 1.39/ King Mangrai craftily restored the friendship of King Ruang and King Ngam Müang through a variety of

---

84 Nakhòn Si Thammarat; the Malay Peninsula city which figures so prominently in the inscription of King Ramkhamhæng (ad 1292).

means. Then King Mangrai had King Ruang ask Ngam Müang's forgiveness, and agree to pay King Ngam Müang an indemnity in cowry shells of 9 *rung* 9 *ruang*—in Thai words, 990,000 cowries.[85] Thao Ruang was pleased with the words of King / Mangrai, and arranged for the payment of the indemnity, in order to dispel the enmity. King Mangrai restored the friendship between the two kings, even greater than before—all through the mediation of King Mangrai.

Later, King Ngam Müang / called upon King Mangrai at his residence. Ngam Müang said to him, "This King Ruang is very adept in the magical arts, and can transform himself into whatever he wishes. Thereafter, even if Thao Ruang had had unkingly intentions and seduced his friend's / wife, his friend Mangrai agreed to adjudicate the case of Thao Ruang to an indemnity, in order that the two would pledge their friendship."

Having said this, King Ngam Müang arranged many offerings for King Mangrai, / and staged an entertainment on the Khun Phu beach [of Kwan Phayao?] for three days and three nights, where three thrones were set up on the edge of the Khun Phu water.[86] The three kings reclined there on the marge of the Mæ Khun Phu to watch the entertainments. King Ngam Müang paid respects to them with many royal accouterments. King Mangrai then staged /f° 1.40/ a mutual oath-taking, that hereafter these three kings would be truthful to each other throughout the rest of their lives. Whoever professed his loyalty and was unfaithful would be destroyed and lose his throne through various calamities. /

With a knife, each of the rulers then cut his own hand, and the blood was mixed and each drank it from a cup, sealing the close bond between the three. That Khun Phu River there people call the Ing River to the present day.

King Mangrai took his leave / of the [other] two kings and returned to his [own] domain and reigned in happiness at Chiang Rai. Then a retainer of King Ruang came with 9 *lung* 9 *luang* of cowries, that is, 990,000 cowries, to pay the indemnity to King Ngam Müang. King Ngam Müang and / King Ruang were friendlier than before, and King Ruang taught the magical arts to King Ngam Müang in his palace

---

85   9 rung/lung 9 ruang/luang, a measure for cowrie shells, the smallest unit of currency. Apparently these are strings of cowries; but not just any cowries that might be used in commerce: these were cowrie shells that had been used probably in a special animistic ceremony.

86   The old name of the Ing River, which flows from the Phayao Lake to the Mekong.

on the Ing River all day. That palace was called the Golden Palace, and to the present day has been called the Wang Kam.[87]

Ai Fa's Plans Come to Fruition in Hariphunchai

Here we shall tell of Ai Fa, commissioned by / King Mangrai to perform a subterfuge in Haribhuñjaya in the *kap set* year. In the *ruang sai* year, 643 of the Era (1281/82), after seven years, during which as part of his regular duties Ai Fa had been conducting that ruse for those seven years, this is what had happened.

Ai Fa had devoted himself to King Yi Ba, and that which he had /f° 1.41/ done pleased the king and generals and ministers, as well as the people. King [Yi] Ba asked Ai Fa, "When Khun Fa was in Chiang Rai, what did King Mangrai call you?" Ai Fa replied, "Mangrai made me his *khun*,[88] and had me work as a judge and supervise the collection of all sorts of / land taxes."[89] King Yi Ba then promoted Ai Fa to the status of an official judging cases and had him collect all the various sorts of land taxes.

At first, he judged cases justly and collected reasonable taxes and did not oppress / the common folk. The amounts that he collected he reduced. He did like this for two or three years. Soon he thought, "I should start my plan."

Ai Fa went to the king and said, "This domain of Hariphunchai is large, and it has much / might, majesty, and power. If I now see many commoners and slaves, villagers and townsmen, ordinary people, I should not bother my lord when people have grievances and [are accustomed to] complaining to the ruler and disturb the ruler. Furthermore, my lord's country is vast, and / its tribute and taxes are but very little. In Chiang Rai, though it be a very small country, its majesty and strength are great. Its people, great and small, would not dare to disturb King Mangrai, but they would come to me. The commands of King Mangrai /f° 1.42/ were implemented by me in every respect, and King Mangrai enjoyed the royal sovereignty in happiness.

---

87 "wang," which we can read as "palace," can also mean the deep waters at the source of a river, where fish congregate: cf. Ban Wang Lung at the head of the Ping River in Hòt district.

SN here inserts a row of asterisks, without explanation.

88 One of a group of high noble positions in the service of the king, charged with tax collection and deciding legal matters.

89 Obviously, in the time of King Yi Ba the people of Hariphunchai paid a variety of land taxes, including separate taxes on irrigated and unirrigated fields.

Furthermore, as for the tribute and land and paddy taxes, they were paid in full in great amounts."

King Yi Ba listened to the words of Ai Fa and agreed with them; and so he issued the strict order, "My country / is vast indeed, and has twice the majesty and power that Chiang Rai has, yet its taxes and tribute are very small. This should not be. Therefore, henceforth I order that Ai Fa should take care of such matters, not bothering me as to the extent to which the agricultural tribute / and land tax might be augmented and tell Khun [Ai] Fa." Then Ai Fa respectfully submitted to King [Yi] Ba, "May my lord issue an order to me [to this effect] in the midst of the public audience hall, so that it is made known to all the subjects of my lord, including all the villagers and townsmen, / that all may know. Then the king did so, issuing a royal command to Ai Fa in the midst of the royal hall that it be made known to all thenceforth.

At that time, Ai Fa gained the opportunity to carry out his stratagem. He was delighted. Ai Fa had the / ruler's palace gate locked, so that no one, not a single person, would come to audience with the king.[90] Such was the stratagem of Ai Fa, in order that the villagers and townsmen of Hariphunchai would be unhappy with King [Yi] Ba. There were many actions which he performed [to this effect], [including] collecting /f° 1.43/ heavy taxes. The villagers and townsmen of the domain were greatly distressed. Ai Fa blamed it on the king's actions. They complained, but it was the king's order. He increased the land and paddy tax and they could not resist, and had to pay / Ai Fa.

Then Ai Fa again deviously carried forth his stratagem to the king saying, "I have inspected the country of your lordship in every place and every district to see whether things were good or not. I saw that the dams and ditches in the Thuan Phukha[91] district were not good: much of the dry rice withered in the sun. I will dig another channel, north / of the east bank of the Ping River, so that it will be a river

---

90 Compare the reference in King Ramkhamhæng's inscription to answering his own "doorbell."

91 A panna, i.e., a district. It must have comprised irrigable land. It is interesting that, at least according to the chronicler, Hariphunchai in this time employed a form of administration usually associated with Tai lands to the north.

flowing out to the district of Chiang Rüa,[92] down to the Kuang River.[93] I will have the villagers and townsmen construct weirs to bring the water to the fields." King [Yi] Ba replied, "All that is good, Khun Fa!"

When it came to the hot season, the earth was dug for a dam. Ai Fa / called up all the people to come and dig the channels and dams to divert the water from the Ping River north of the mouth of the Tæng River[94] on the east side, to a length of seventeen thousand fathoms. Everyone came to dig the canal in the blazing heat, and they grumbled. Thao Fa said, "It's not / my fault: the king is having you dig. Don't blame me! If it were up to me, I would not have you dig in the hot season." All the people complained, "We have worked hard to dig the canal." This is why it is called the "Hard (*khæng*) Canal."[95]

At that time, people began to form into rotations for King [Yi] Ba. /fº 1.44/ There were eighty thousand people, with foremen[96] for each district. [Of those,] Ai Fa had fifty thousand men dig the canal every day in the four months of the hot season; and when finished the canal was called the Hard Canal. Later, in the time of King Kü Na, its name became the "Callus (*kæo*) Canal," which it has been called to the present.

Then Ai Fa slyly said to King [Yi] Ba, "Chiang Rai is a small domain, / and its king is a petty king, yet he has built a large palace. My lord is a very Great King, and he should build a great and beautiful palace. I will arrange that my lord should live in such [a palace]. Whatever your lordship pleases, I will do." King Yi Ba replied, "Whatever you do is up to you." /

---

92 Chiang Rüa panna. Administrative district. In the reign of King Mangrai, the king handed over Hariphunchai to Ai Fa to administer, and he built a new town northeast of Hariphunchai in the region of the Chiang Rüa panna. He had the river channel dug, called the Mæ Chawai. Later, it flooded heavily in the rainy season, and was discovered to be unsuitable for a city. It is thought to have been dependent upon water transport, by boat, and thus it was called the "Boat Town" (Chiang Rüa). (Cf. fº 2.05.)

93 The dam which Ai Fa proposed to build is geographically reasonable. At that time, the Kuang and Ping Rivers met north of Lamphun, not south as they do today. See map 6a.

94 The Mæ Tæng and the Ping met in the border area between Mæ Rim and San Sai districts.

95 Hard Canal: still today called the "Ai Fa Canal," from the Mæ Tæng through San Sai to Lamphun. See Sutthini Thòngsa-at, "Kansüksa ròngròi thang nam kao khòng Mænam Ping nai bòriwen thirap Chiang Mai–Lamphun," M.S. thesis (Geography), Chiang Mai Univ., 1988.

96 phò wiak: low-ranking chiefs who had the duty to call up labor from the corvéeable males for public service.

In the eleventh and twelfth months, when the rice was bursting ready to be harvested, Ai Fa called up the foremen to cut timber pillars for the palace at the Khi Ya Fa mountain in the district of Chiang Lüa.[97] Ai Fa had the pillars dragged in, and ordered them trimmed top and bottom and rolled lengthwise in, / causing much damage; and a great many townsmen perished. Farmers complained to Ai Fa and said, "Many of us have perished and will die without the rice that has been destroyed [in the process of rolling in the logs]." Ai Fa said, "It's not my fault. The king made me do it." The people were greatly upset, and said, "Formerly / our king never did such things, but now the king has violated tradition[98] to the point where we are perishing. We no longer can stand this king."

From that point, the people were alienated. All the villagers and townsmen were unhappy with King [Yi] Ba. Thao Ai Fa thus had done everything /f° 1.45/ [possible] to disturb the people and make them unhappy with King Ba, every one of them. Then, Thao [Ai] Fa dissembled, and said to the people, "King Mangrai would not dare to behave like this. He is very good-hearted and merciful to all the people. He does not oppress anyone, not one; and he is thoroughly good. / When King Mangrai hears dissatisfaction, he does not investigate and oppress the complainant."

When he often said this, there were no objections. The people, the villagers and townsmen, heard the news and said, "King Mangrai is very good." They petitioned Ai Fa, "We would like to have King Mangrai as our king." / So said all, including the generals and ministers and all the people, because those generals and ministers and people were foolish, and they spoke on the basis of what King Ba had done, not knowing that Ai Fa was carrying out a ruse to divide them from / King Ba at that time.

Thao [Ai] Fa knew that the people had been won over to King Mangrai and wished to have him as their king in Hariphunchai, and that his intentions had been fully successful. He therefore sent a message via a servant who hurried to present it to King Mangrai, saying, "Your Majesty's servant Thao Ai Fa has conducted his stratagem / over seven years, and now it has been completed in accordance with his

---

97 Mountain in the Chiang Rüa panna of Hariphunchai.

98 Note that the people of Hariphunchai had a clear sense of the limits of royal power, and they now criticized Yi Ba for his offenses against the "customs" of rulers (khòng müang). For an example, see Sommai Premchit, Khamsòn Phraya Mangrai (Chiang Mai, 1976).

intentions in every respect. I invite your lordship to raise an army and come down quickly." So said he on that day.

Dating of This Copy

Rajjavaṁsa pathama nīṭṭhitaṁ.[99] The year 1288 of the Era, 2469 of the Buddha Era, a *pæk yi* year, the first day of the first month, a Wednesday, in the noon watch.[100]

---

99 Pali. Literally, "First [fascicle] of the Royal Chronicle Here Concluded."

100 This is a very problematic date, in several respects. First, 1288 was a *rwai yi* year, not a *pæk yi* year. All *pæk* years must have zero as their final digit. The closest year that fits the data given here is CS 1240, AD 1878/79. But what is this date? Date of composition? Date of copying? I would guess the latter. Most would insist that the true date of HP is 1926.

Chapter 2

Mangrai's Conquests—Lamphun

Tadā Mangrāyarājavaccaṁ pavattiṁ sutvā pamodayanti.[1] *Tadā.* At that time, learning of the news in the letter of the *caofa* King Mangrai was delighted. He artfully had the drums beaten to quickly arrange a fourfold army[2] of numerous [troops], and said, "At this time, the *thaofa* is our enemy, and we must drive him out and [force him to] go and / take refuge with King [Yi] Ba in Lamphun. We, ourselves, will follow to capture him. If King Ba comes out, so be it, and if he does not, we will fight him."

Having said this, King Mangrai reviewed all his troops together at Fang for three days and three nights until the auspicious day arrived, and then Cao Mangrai / led his troops out from Fang by way of Chæ Sak,[3] where he built a stockade and garrisoned it with men; and then he went and stopped at Huai Hok,[4] where he [also] built a stockade which he filled with many troops. The town there was named Phrao,[5]

---

1   Pali. The meaning of this phrase is duplicated by the translated Thai that immediately follows it.

2   Notton (p. 41, n.1) explains that the fourfold army was composed of infantry, cavalry, elephantry, and chariots.

3   Chæ Sak: south of Fang. This was a fortified city (*wiang*), but its name does not begin with that word because wiang/chiang/cæ/ce/chæ all have that meaning. Bancop Phanthumetha (*Pai sòp kham Thai*, p. 187) explains that *chæ/ce/cæ* in the Shan region denotes a locality where a prince presides; and Chæ Sak seems to indicate a similar meaning.

4   Huai Hok: the name indicates a stream with bamboo, as *hok* are a large bamboo.

5   Phrao: site now called Wiang Phra Cao Lan Thòng. On a hillock about 10 km. northwest of the district town of Phrao. There are the remains of an earthen embankment (city wall). Also called M. Phrao Wang Hin. See Puangkham Tuikhieo, *Prawat müang Phrao Wang Hin* (Chiang Mai, 1981); and Thiwa Suphacanya, *Raingan kanwicai rüang chumchon boran cak phap thai thang akat* (Bangkok, 1985).

to the present day. Then he left and went by way of M. Khæn,[6] / [where he] set up for a while and had a royal dwelling constructed, adjoined by an [elephant] kraal in the middle of the town. All the people of the domain wanted to see King Mangrai [and] present tribute and gifts to him, vying with each other for his favor and climbing up on the kraal to do so. That place was called Kham Chang, / later transmuted to Khachāng to the present day.[7]

At that time, King Mangrai sent an agent to advise Ai Fa in Hariphunchai, "Now I am bringing my forces down to the vicinity of the town." Ai Fa, learning that his lord was coming to the vicinity of M. Khæn, deceitfully /f° 2.02/ went to present King Ba with the word that "King Mangrai now has brought his forces to the vicinity of Khæn. I am going to go and see the forces of Phraya Mangrai to ascertain how numerous they are. Will my Lord and Master consent?" [Yi Ba] quickly assembled his officers and men and called up and organized his forces, but no one came. / They just said that they could not help the lord, saying "We cannot help and follow you." King Yi Ba called up his forces, such as he could, and said to Ai Fa, "You should quickly collect all the elephants and horses and fight King Mangrai, as well as you can." Then Ai / Fa took the forces, in the number of thirty thousand men, out to fight. Ai Fa returned to say to King Ba, "The thirty thousand are not very many. King Mangrai's troops are two or three times as numerous. Please, my lord, add to them." / King Ba then added another thirty thousand, whom Ai Fa made his rearguard. Ai Fa then dissembled. He sent an agent to King Mangrai, telling him to arrange a party of troops to attack him from the rear. The Hariphunchai troops were / [defeated] and scattered, fleeing back to pay court to King Yi Ba, saying, "Our army which the lord arranged was ambushed by King Mangrai, destroying us. Now Ai Fa's forces still are engaged with the enemy."

Then Ai Fa sent someone to see King Yi Ba, saying, /f° 2.03/ "Now, I am still engaged with the enemy. King Mangrai's forces are many, and my forces are insufficient. I don't know what to do! My lord should gather up his family, wives,

---

6 M. Khæn, implying the *panna* of Fang Kæn. Villagers today call it M. Kæn. Traces indicate it was once a large place, with many temples including a Wat Inthakhin. In the valleys of the Mæ Kæn, the Ping, and the Mæ Ngat; in Mæ Tæng district. See *Raingan kanwicai rüang Thung Phan æk phan phüa Müang Kæn* (Chiang Mai, 1982).

7 Kham Chang/Khachang: now Ban Mæ Khacan, t. Inthakhin. This is a village moved from elsewhere which may have brought the old name with it.

children, and go to Khelang[8] to join his son, Phraya Bœk, and have him bring troops to help / me fight King Mangrai so that we can win."

King Yi Ba learned this, that Mangrai's forces were very numerous, and was sore afraid. Then Ai Fa pretended to rush into the city. King Yi Ba was now even more terrified. Ai Fa then comforted King Yi Ba, telling him, "I will send your lordship's / family on its way, and will return to the city to defend your lordship." King Yi Ba quickly gathered up his family and wives and children to flee from Lamphun and take refuge with Phraya Bœk in Khelang.

When [Yi Ba and Ai Fa] reached the ridge of the mountains, Yi Ba turned back to see his city, to see smoke / rising from the fires in the city of Lamphun. He was disconsolate, and greatly lamented the loss. Thus the mountain was called Dòi Ba Hai[9] to the present day.

Ai Fa accompanied King Yi Ba to the ridge, and then withdrew back [to Lamphun]. When King Yi Ba reached his son in Khelang, he implored him, "Help your father, and collect / your forces and bring them up and fight to regain Hariphunchai." Phraya Bœk replied, "My forces are few, insufficient to retake the town, as they have already entered it, and when they have taken it, they will hold it firmly. We can't hurry, can we? Your family, children, and wives /f° 2.04/ are already here. Whenever we have sufficient reliable allies we can raise an army, elephants, and horses and go and retake Lamphun." Phraya Bœk so restrained his father. King Yi Ba remained there with his son.

As for Ai Fa, after he had sent King Yi Ba to the mountains, he could relax and eat, / at the Sæn Khao Hò field of the Chiang Rüa[10] south subdistrict; and from a [nearby] village someone called Ai Hò offered packets of rice for travelers, which is why that place is called Sæn Khao Hò to the present day.

At that time, King Mangrai entered and plundered Lamphun, and reigned there in Lamphun, / in the *ruang sai* year, s. 643, on the fourth waxing day of the eighth month (23 April 1281), in the *kòng ngai* watch. At that time, Mangrai's age was forty-three years; and he then ruled Lamphun in peace and happiness.

---

8   Khelang: Lampang, closely connected to Lamphun since Lady Camadevi.

9   That is, "the Mountain where [Yi} Ba Lamented," or cried. Now Dòi Ti, to the east of Lamphun, just before the ascent to Dòi Khun Tan.

10   A *thung/thong* is an extensive rice-plain. Chiang Rüa/Lüa is the *panna* by that name. The text further tells us that the Sæn Khao Hò comprised the southern 500 (*na*) of Chiang Rüa.

Now we will tell of the lineage of rulers of Lamphun. From Queen Camadevi to King / [Yi] Ba there were twenty-five rulers.[11]

Itopathāya apparabhāge.[12] Thenceforward, a line of Lao rulers, including Phraya Mangrai, were lords of Hariphunchai. On taking possession of the sovereignty of Lamphun, King Mangrai bestowed children, / wives, families, and gold and silver upon Ai Fa, and then restored to him rewards of things of gold and silver, even more than before.

Construction of Wiang Kum Kam, 1283/84

Two years later, in the *ka met* year, s. 645 (1283/84), King Mangrai bestowed the town and villages of Lamphun upon Khun Fa as lord of Lamphun, and moved to build a [new] city, /f° 2.05/ declaring that he would construct a fortified city with a great many households. King Mangrai had the river dug to pass by [some] villages to give them access to the river, thereafter called Mæ Sæo, on the northeast side of Lamphun.[13] He had stayed there three years when the town was flooded in the middle of the rainy season, and the elephants, horses, cattle, and buffalo had no place to go. [That place] has been called Chiang Rüa / to the present day.

In the *rwai set* year, s. 648 (1286/87), King Mangrai moved to build Wiang Kum Kam.[14] He built a moat around the city on all four sides, channeling the flowing waters of the Mæ Raming.[15] He built a palisade on all four sides of the city, and had a great many dwellings and buildings constructed. King Mangrai built his extensive royal dwelling, palace, and hall(s), / spreading all around that site; and it has been called the New Village (Ban Mai) to the present day. Cao Mangrai ordered men to dig a pond by his palace window so that he could watch the work, and it has been

---

11 The *Cdv.* twice says there were twenty-seven rulers, so that was not our author's source. Notton, *Annales du Siam, II: Chronique de Lap'un* (Paris, 1930), pp. 43, 54.

12 Pali. "Now, thenceforward."

13 Mæ Sæo: This was the Chiang Rüa panna (district), northeast of Lamphun.

14 The remains of Wiang Kum Kam are still visible, a short distance south of Chiang Mai in Saraphi district. See Sarassawadi Ongsakun, *Wiang Kum Kam* (Chiang Mai, 1994).

15 Mæ Raming is another name for the Ping River. See Map 6a.

called the Tang ("Window") Pond to the present day. Cao Mangrai had the Kum Kam Market established / for public commerce.[16]

King Mangrai then reflected, "No one knows whether my people are happy or not," so he dressed in disguise, wearing a local leaf hat and dressed with a 100-gold-weight cloth underneath but wearing local cloth[17] on the outside, to go to the Kum Kam Market and sit on the bank of the Ping River, facing / the east, watching people entering the market. King Mangrai thought that, by sitting there, he could watch both people entering the market and people going down to bathe in the Ping River, and those who bathed first and [then] let their hair hang loose were poor; and to them he would give 100-gold-weight cloth. King Mangrai remained there watching people going to bathe and saw no one letting their hair hang loose, /f° 2.06/ not one. King Mangrai saw people of Chæ Chang[18] of Chiang Rüa district[19] riding their boats up to the market of Kum Kam, two or three boats sinking every day. Cao Mangrai decided that his subjects were dying there daily, and thereupon erected a bridge there.

King Mangrai then reflected, "I have constructed Wiang Kum Kam, which has been very satisfactory. I [now] should / build a *cetiya* for worship and veneration. In the *pœk cai* year, s. 650 (1288/89), Cao Mangrai thus had earth taken from Nòng Tang to build the Ku Kham *cetiya*.[20]

---

16 Kum Kam Market: markets were sufficiently important that they were among the first things built with a city. Located near the Ping River.

17 The cloth called *pha Thai* might be the kind of cloth ordinary people wore.

18 Chæ Chang: name of an area—probably a *panna* like Chiang Rüa. Now there is a Chæ Chang village in t. Chæ Chang, San Kamphæng district, not very far east of Lamphun. We suppose this to have been a *panna* in Mangrai's time. Ceramic artifacts found there, including of the Ming period, date from the period before Tilok, and reached their florescence in Tilok's time. See Sayan Phraichancit, *Læng tao Lan Na* (Bangkok, 1990), pp. 15–24.

19 Chæ Chang and Chiang Rüa were so close that they are sometimes referred to as Chæ Chang Chiang Rüa.

20 Now Wat Cedi Liam, built on the model of Cedi Ku Kut, Wat Camathewi (Lamphun).

Wat Kat Thuam

Here we shall tell of the building of Wat Kat Thuam.[21] After King Mangrai had built Wiang Kum Kam, / there was a large *mai düa kiang*—a Burmese word for a large *saphan* tree—in which there lived a clever *sok sawat* sylvan sprite (tree spirit)[22] who guarded over that *düa* tree and was benevolent to all the people, who took bodily form as an albino monitor-lizard living in that tree. People saw it, and all / reverenced it, and took their sons and daughters and presented various gifts to it as they wished. Not long afterwards, the *düa* tree, which was very old, died, and everyone brought candles there to worship, even including King Mangrai, the founder of Wiang Kum Kam. /

At that time there were five Mahāthera, the chief of whom was Mahākassapa,[23] who were filled with powerful goodness, who came to view the site of the dead *düa* tree, a site of great lamentation. Having come there, the five Mahāthera /fº 2.07/ meditated on the Dhamma. One day, King Mangrai went touring there and saw the venerable lords, and so asked the youngest of them who they were. The young prince reverenced the King, and said, "We here are five Mahāthera, headed by Mahākassapa." King Mangrai went to reverence the Mahāthera, and conversed / with them on many subjects. Mahākassapa told King Mangrai about King Vaṭṭhakuli; that King Vaṭṭhakuli had had the broken-off finger of an image of the Lord Buddha of great power, which allowed him to defeat the 101 kings, as if he had constructed the Buddha image himself.[24] / This he told him.

King Mangrai heard what the Mahāthera had so graciously told him, and was delighted. He took respectful leave of the Mahāthera. When he had returned to his Royal Palace, he summoned a carpenter named Kan Thom; and when [Kan Thom] came, he had him craft five images of the Lord Buddha, three seated and / two standing, the largest of which was equal to the height of King Mangrai [himself], which he had installed where the Mahāthera had been, uttering the prayer, "With the meritful power [which accrues to] me [for] having built this Buddha image, I

---

21 Namely, Wat Kan Thom. Now Wat Chang Kham in the middle of Wiang Kum Kam. See Sarassawadi Ongsakun, *Wiang Kum Kam* (Chiang Mai, 1994).

22 Notton (p. 45, n. 3) offers a long footnote on such spirits.

23 We are not told from whence these monks had come. From Haribhuñjaya?

24 See the Vaṭṭhaṁgulī-jātaka.

will raise my forces to take Ramaññadesa—Hamsavati of the Mon Country.²⁵ In the event that the / Mon ruler submits to me and to the power which accrues to me for having built these Buddha images, I will return to build a *vihāra* in which to enshrine them." Having so prayed, King Mangrai led his forces to Pegu across the Salween River down to the Asa River,²⁶ where he encamped his army. /f° 2.08/

Expedition to Pegu

At that time, the ruler of Hamsavati, Suttasoma²⁷ by name, learning that King Mangrai was coming, set up his army in the frontier region of his domain. Trembling greatly with fear, he used an envoy knowledgeable in such affairs to bear tribute and gifts to present in welcome to King Mangrai and [then] inquire / of his health and prosperity. The counselor said, "The ruler of Hamsavati has sent me to pay respects to [you, my] lord and master. Why has the Majestic Lord of Lan Na come to my country? What end is to be gained in my country? / Whatever you say, I shall [report in detail to] my master." King Mangrai replied, "We have come to see Hamsa[vati]. We desire the friendship of your Lord. If the Lord of Hamsavati would value anything above all else, / tell us, and we will ask nothing further. We wish something dear to you. Tell us what you most value."

This was a great problem for the [Mon] envoy. The envoy took leave of King Mangrai, and returned to pay court to his Lord. Hearing [his report], the ruler of Hamsavati assembled his ministers and counselors / and wise men and professors in his audience hall.²⁸ The wise men reverenced the ruler of Hamsavati and said, "The [riddle] which the ruler of Lan Na poses to us, that he desires something we value most highly: there is nothing in this world more dear to us than the royal daughter born of the flesh of our ruler. This the lord of Lan Na knows full well, /f° 2.09/ namely the princess named Lady Phai Kho, the beloved child born of the flesh of our

---

25 Ramaññadesa is the classical name of the Môn territory of coastal Burma, and Haṁsāvatī is Pegu, its capital.

26 Asa River: Notton (p. 47, n. 2) says that various manuscripts write the Saliang River, which is in Thai territory in modern Mæhòngsòn province.

27 The Môn ruler in Mangrai's time was the Shan adventurer, Wareru, who is said to have had his capital at Martaban (which probably still would have been called Haṁsāvatī). G. E. Harvey, *History of Burma* (London, 1925; repr. 1967), pp. 110, 368.

28 Notton (p. 47, n. 4) has a long footnote about this episode.

August Lord; a lady of unsurpassed beauty, and he has come to our fair city because surely he intends Lady Phai Kho, the beloved daughter of our ruler.²⁹ [Surely] our Mahāraja should not bestow his / beloved daughter upon the ruler of Lan Na, [for his] dignity is not appropriate."

The ruler of Hamsavati, Suttasomarāja, listened to those words and reflected, "I should not bestow my beloved daughter, Lady Phai Kho, upon the ruler of Lan Na, whose majesty is insufficient; [but] if I do [hand her over to him] with good will, it will redound to our friendship / and [to] to the close ties of our royal lines in the future, to our children and grandchildren." Having said this, the king of Hamsavati arranged many fine adornments, dresses, and jewels appropriate to the nuptials of his daughter. Moreover, he gave up elephants and horses and a group of five hundred men and women and their families / for the use of his beloved daughter Phai Kho, to accompany the Lady, together with many retainers to present to King Mangrai. When King Mangrai had obtained Lady Phai Kho as his royal queen, he was greatly filled with happiness and delight. The two / rulers met [there] at the Asa River, and feasted their retainers with food and drink, and staged great entertainments for three days and three nights. They pledged their undying friendship in every way. King Mangrai then took his leave and returned to his home.³⁰ /f° 2.10/

The ministers and counselors consecrated Lady Phai Kho as queen. King Mangrai [then] conferred with his ministers and counselors, saying, "I vowed to create these five Buddha images and enshrine [them] in the Mahākassapathera Temple; and, on going to the Mon Country vowed that, if I was successful, / I would construct a *vihara* in which to enshrine the images. Now I have been to the Mon domains, and fearing my great power, gained from building the Buddha images, the Mon king bestowed his beloved daughter on me as my wife. I should [therefore] build a *vihara*." / King Mangrai therefore had his craftsman Kan Thom start a *vihara*, erecting the pillars and cross-beams.

---

29 Notton (p. 48, n. 1) reminds us that the woman is named Tala Mè Sri in the *Rachathirat Mon* chronicle, and that Pai Kho is simply a rendering of the name for Pegu.

30 Notton (p. 49, notes 1 and 2) adds details from other manuscripts.

Visit of the Southern Ruler

Tasmiṁ kale.[31] At that time, the ruler of the South came as a state guest to present rattan, to a length of 1 *sen*[32] 20 fathoms, turned with lathes, for trade; thin enough to thread a needle, to King / Mangrai, in order to show off the expertise of the Southerners, which none could match. King Mangrai sought out the carpenter Kan Thom and asked him, "Can you do this?" Kan Thom replied, "Even though the Southerners can / make rattan 20 fathoms long, thin enough to thread a needle, that's not much. They're just showing off! / As for me, I could even do 100 fathoms of rattan that thin!" Kan Thom then proceeded to show him, deceitfully using 3-fathom lengths of beautiful thread, which he /f° 2.11/ soaked in the waters of the Ping River above the Kum Kam Bridge. Then he kept it in a basket to protect it from the water. He submerged it in the river there, where the water could trickle through and a small bit could be drawn through gradually, so it could be turned with a lathe. All this was done during the night.

The next morning, Kan Thom attended upon King Mangrai [in public], "I / ask permission to dive into the water for the lathed lengths I have kept there to mill for the state guest. I will drag up one piece 3 fathoms long which is unmilled, and put it into the water for the guest to see."

Kan Thom then sharpened a knife, and dove into the water and milled and turned the piece. Soon, Kan Thom emerged [from the water] and said to the ruler, / "I've finished milling the wood. My lord, may I bring it up?" King Mangrai allowed divers to fetch the milled wood for the guest to see. The guest saw the milled wood, very pretty and finished, just as straight as if it had been done on dry land. "Wonderful! Better than our craftsmen could do! / And done underwater!" he exclaimed.

The guest then issued another boast: "We shall have that craftsmen make statues of five elephants from single grains of rice to present to King Mangrai." Mangrai had five grains of rice fetched and given to / Kan Thom. Kan Thom said, "I would like to know who can do this? The guest should show me such a craftsman in the presence of King Mangrai." Kan Thom pulled that person forward and had him lie face-down. He then took a sharp ax and shaved that person's head as bare as if it

---

31 Pali. "At that time."

32 Linear measure equal to 40 meters or 20 fathoms; 25 *sen* to the km. (McF) Thus the measurement given in the text is redundant—1 *sen* equals 20 fathoms.

were done with a razor. Kan /f° 2.12/ Thom then asked, "Did that shaving hurt or not?" He replied that it did not hurt; that it was like a pat of the hand. When the guest saw that, he said, "This domain's craftsmen are very clever; better than ours." Then [the guest] took leave of King Mangrai [and returned home].

Having witnessed the demonstration of Kan Thom's skill / to the craftsmen of the South, so that they praised his domain, King Mangrai then had Kan Thom go to rule Chiang Sæn, which at that time was called M. Ròi,[33] until in the reign of Sæn Phu it was called Chiang Sæn.

King Mangrai's Expedition to Phukam-Ava

When Kan Thom was [ruling] Chiang Sæn, / he had the timbers cut for the first and second purlins of a *vihara*, as well as the cross-beams, and it was called the Kan Thom *vihara*; and he had raised the pillars but had not yet finished the building [in Kum Kam]; [and when the pieces were sent from Chiang Sæn] they all fitted perfectly. It has been called Wat Kan Thom[34] to the present day. / The structure which was the sleeping hall was not yet done. King Mangrai paid obeisance to Mahākassapathera, "*Bhante!* I have had a *vihara* completely built." Mahākassapa expressed his satisfaction, [saying] "That *vihara* is like a throne-hall, O Great King; / like a Gandhakuti; but it has no *cetiya* or sleeping-places. May the Great King [please] build a *cetiya* and a meditation cave [for us] to durably last for a long time."

King Mangrai was greatly delighted, and promised, "At this temple I will build a *vihara*, and then I will travel to /f° 2.13/ the foreign land of Phukâm-Ava.[35] If the lord of Ava does not submit to me in friendship, like the lord of Hamsa[vati], I will truly defeat him, and then I will return and build a *cetiya* at Wat Kan Thom." So vowing, King Mangrai raised an exceedingly numerous army and by stages reached / the southeastern frontier of Ava, where he encamped.

Informed [of his arrival], the ruler of Ava employed a wise counselor who knew the [Northern Thai] language to go and present tribute and gifts of welcome to King

---

33 Notton (p. 50, n. 1): M. Ralao in various other manuscripts.

34 "Southeast of Wat Chedi Liam there is a temple named Wat Chang Kham Kuat Thom," according to Notton (p. 51, n. 1).

35 That is, the central and north of the Irrawaddy valley (Burma). Ava, Lieberman reminds me, was founded only in 1365. (pers. comm., 3 April 1995).

Mangrai, whom he asked of news of fortune. The counselor respectfully said, "The King of Phukâm/Ava has sent me to reverence Your Lordship, the Lord of Lan Na of Majesty and Power, [and ask] for what reason you have come to the frontier of our country. Surely the Lord of Lan Na has come in great friendship, and we are greatly pleased. Verily, if the Lord of Lan Na desires anything / in our country, we will gladly give him everything. That being said, I have come to reverence Your Lordship."

King Mangrai replied to the counselor, "We have heard that Phukâm-Ava is replete with all kinds of horses and elephants; furthermore, we learn that the teachings of the Lord Buddha / greatly flourish [here]. Thus we have come to see the country of Phukâm-Ava. If the Lord of Phukâm-Ava would bestow anything upon us, we have heard that gemstones and precious metals are plentiful in our [own] country. We [therefore] ask for all kinds of craftsmen, for example, /f° 2.14/ goldsmiths, bronzesmiths, ironsmiths, and such." The counselor heard King Mangrai, and when he had reverenced the king of Ava, and the king of Ava had been informed, he was pleased. He consulted with his counselors and said, "I understand that the lord of Lan Na, who has great power, has come—to conquer us? or because / he wants bronzesmiths? Shouldn't we send him a clever bronzesmith? Furthermore, gold, silver, bronze, and ironsmiths; shouldn't [we also] give them [to him], for the sake of our future friendship?" / So he had his ministers and counselors take one bronzesmith, and silver-, gold-, bronze-, and ironsmiths, altogether five hundred families, to be presented to King Mangrai. King Mangrai sent the goldsmiths to Chiang Tung,[36] the bronzesmiths and their guardians / to Chiang Sæn, and the jewelers and ironsmiths to Kum Kam. And so all these craftsmen were thenceforth in the land of Lan Na, to the present day.

Founding of Wat Kan Thom, 1290/91

King Mangrai went to Phukâm-Ava in the *kot si* year, s. 652 (1290/91).[37] On his return, he had a / *cetiya* built at Wat Kan Thom, in accordance with his vow.[38] That

---

36 This is the first mention of Keng Tung (Chiang Tung), the chief city of the Tai Khœn population of extreme northeastern Burma.

37 This was a *kot yi* year. Probably a scribal error (*yi/si*).

38 Today this *cetiya* is at Wat Chang Kham. It has been renovated many times

cetiya was 6 fathoms wide at its base and 4 fathoms high, and had niches for [images of] the Lord [Buddha] on two levels. The lower level had three seated Buddhas, and on the upper level was one standing image. There were images of the Lord Sāriputta and [Lord] Mokkhalāna,[39] and images of the god Indra and Lady Dharaṇi were erected to watch over /fº 2.15/ the images of the Buddha.

At that time, there was a group of Mahāthera who brought two relics of the Lord Buddha from Siṅhala in Laṅgka[40] to present to King Mangrai. Receiving those relics of the Buddha, King Mangrai was overjoyed. He uttered the vow that, / if these were true relics of the Buddha, they should manifest a miracle and cause his doubt to be dispelled.

Mangrai lustrated the relics with fragrant water. That evening, the relics manifested a marvel in their golden casket, shedding forth colorful rays in the water in which they had been lustrated, broken / into three parts: the rays of one were yellow as gold, the second were dark-green as Indanila emeralds, and the third were white as silver thread.

King Mangrai was filled with devotion for the relics. He took one relic and enshrined it in the chief Buddha image. / King Mangrai then gave five hundred gold pieces to the Mahāthera to go and venerate the Great Bodhi tree[41] in Lanka. The four [remaining] Mahāthera accepted the five hundred gold pieces and returned to Lanka, where they venerated the Great Bodhi tree. The four / Mahāthera vowed, "We will take the teachings of the Lord Buddha and establish them in the Lan Na country. If they are not yet truly established there, may seeds of the Great Bodhi tree fall down onto our robes." Thereupon, seeds of the Great Bodhi tree fell down onto their robes. /fº 2.16/ The four Mahāthera placed the seeds of the Great Bodhi tree in their almsbowls.

The seeds of the Bodhi tree sprouted and grew in all four [almsbowls], and they brought them to King Mangrai to be planted at the rest-house by the Yang Grove in

---

39 These two are the most famous and ubiquitous of the Buddha's disciples.

40 Sri Lanka.

41 The Great Bodhi tree was believed to be grown from a sprout of the tree under which the Buddha attained Enlightenment.

Fang, at Rua Nang,[42] and at the Tha Kan district (*panna*);[43] and then King Mangrai had / his mother, named Thep Kham Khrai, and Lady Phai Kho take [the fourth] to plant in the place of the [former] *düa kiang* tree at Wat Kat Thom. King Mangrai reverenced the Great Bodhi tree with various implements. The Great Bodhi tree manifested a marvel that night, illuminating the whole city with its rays. / Angels (*devata*) took the form of a white elephant with a thousand retainers surrounding the Bodhi tree to protect it all night, that no creature might approach it; and if they came close, they would be harmed. King Mangrai arranged for all sorts of things to be / the necessaries for Wat Kan Thom. He delimited an area in which the rice-land tax (*kha na*) at the New Year of 620,000 cowry shells were funds for alms, an area in Mæ Cæm[44] of 500,000 cowries for food, and an area of Chæ Chang of 500,000 cowries for betel for the monks. Moreover, King / Mangrai and Lady Phai Kho dedicated fifty-five villages, with five hundred families—namely the Mons (Meng)[45] whom they had brought from Hamsavati—pouring the water of irrevocable donation dedicating them to the service of Wat Kan Thom.[46]

Foundation of Chiang Mai

Here we shall tell of the building of the City of Chiang Mai.

King Mangrai stayed at Kum Kam /f° 2.17/ for five years. In the *ruang mao* year, s. 653 (AD 1291/92), one day King Mangrai toured on a litter out to the north with

---

42 We guess that a full reading might be that he planted one at Wiang Rua Nang, which is not otherwise known.

43 From an examination of old city walls, ancient sites, *cetiya*, Buddha images, and ceramics, Tha Kan would appear to have been a city since Haribhuñjaya times. Nowadays it is known as San Pa Tòng district town, about 30 km. south of Chiang Mai and 20 km. west of Lamphun. It must have been an important place for Mangrai to have chosen to plant a Great Bodhi tree there.

44 Probably to be identified with Mæ Cæm today, which is on an important route to the Salween and Pegu. It was prosperous and fertile, in the valley of the Mæ Cæm. Its prosperity from both agriculture and from trade would have made it a suitable area to raise income to support the Religion. It has never been officially surveyed.

45 *Meng* is the term usually applied by the Lan Na Thai to the Môn of coastal Burma. See Aroonrut Wichienkeeo, "Meng (chat)" in *Saranukrom Thai*, 454 (Bangkok: Ratchabandit Sathan, 1992), pp. 14948–59.

46 This donation of lands and revenues to the Religion is usually termed *kalpanā*.

a great many retainers. Arriving at Ban Hæm—some say Ban Hæn⁴⁷—[they found it to be] a place suitable for building a fortified city [*wiang*]. He remained there for three nights, and in a dream he saw a vision of a person who told him that here would live a ruler of great majesty / and untold wealth. King Mangrai moved a bit [further] to the north, and saw a place suitable to build a city; so he slept there for three nights. People set up nets in the middle of that place as a fence, in order to protect King Mangrai. Thus that place was called "Net-Fence City," to the present day.⁴⁸ The king slept there three nights, but saw / no omen.

So he moved to the northeast. He saw another place suitable to build a city. He slept there to await a dream for three nights. People erected mats there to serve [as a fence] to protect King Mangrai, so it has been called "Mat City" (*Chiang Ruak*) to the present day.⁴⁹ The king slept there three nights, but saw no omen.

So [King Mangrai] traveled further / in the forest another day, and slept there for three nights. On the third night, he saw [a vision of] a lady, beauteous in form; and so that place has been called "Beauty City" (*Chiang Som*) to the present day.⁵⁰

Again the ruler moved to sleep again in the fields to seek a dream, for three nights. Again, he saw a beautiful maiden. The king would not take that place, discarding / that area. It has [since] been called "Throw-Away City" (*Chiang Thum*).

The ruler again returned to Kum Kam. He saw there a very large writing-palm (*lan*) tree, so he went under the shade of that palm, which has since been called Yang Phak, or Chiang Lan.

The king returned to Kum Kam for the cold season. King Mangrai mounted a wondrous elephant and, surrounded by numerous retainers, went to tour /f° 2.18/ around Mount Ussupabatta, that is, Dòi Suthep,⁵¹ and there had hunters pursue game in the forest around the foot of the mountain. He went around [the mountain]

---

47 Ban Hæm/Hæn: location unknown. Note the reference to conflicting sources.

48 Might this be identified with the Rua Nang mentioned above? See also Prasert na Nagara, *Khlong nirat Hariphunchai* (Chiang Mai, 1989); Aroonrut Wichienkeeo et al., *Wat Rang nai Wiang Chiang Mai* (Chiang Mai, 1986), and her *Raichü wat læ nikai Song nai Chiang Mai* (Chiang Mai, 1975).

49 Chiang Rüak, an important center in Kum Kam, was northeast of Wiang Rua Nang.

50 Chiang Som was a small town, located to the north of Chiang Mai, about 3 km. north of the White Elephant (Chang Phüak) Gate, where some *cetiya* remain. Near it was another old city, called Wiang Bua, where there are many old, abandoned temples.

51 Dòi Suthep: the large mountain which dominates Chiang Mai from the west.

to the east, on the edge of the forest, where they found a grove, a thicket of thick grass, a wondrous place outside where the thatch-grass grew. It was a peaceful place, very level and smooth. The ruler toured around it, and saw there was little thatch-grass / outside [the thicket], while within it the thatch formed a pleasant thicket, very thick and overlapping in series. In that thatch grove there was a level field of *yung muai*,[52] a Burmese word—the Thai call it *ya mung khatai* [elephant grass?]—growing thickly around there, / inducing great happiness.

At that time, hog-deer a mother and child, two of them, came out of the thatch forest in search of food. They came straight through a pack of wolves. Everyone saw and stood watching them going back and forth in front of the crowd of people. A small wolf watched them a short while, while the deer went out and then entered back into the thatch grove / as before. The wolves surrounded the grove, but they were unable to catch their prey. Then, the deer stood on a good site (*cheyyabhumi*), miraculously without fear, yet afraid to come out and face the wolves. The wolves feared this running [back and forth], as they were unable to / catch their prey.

The hunters saw this marvel, and came and reported it to King Mangrai. King Mangrai mounted his elephant and came to the spot where the wolves had entered the thatch thicket. The two hog-deer did not fear to come out and confront the wolves, and the wolves fled, having given up on catching /f° 2.19/ their two prey.

King Mangrai saw and heard that marvel and said, "Since I came touring in search of a place to found a city, in many places, I found no place until I came here that was an auspicious site, where I should build a city—a true *Jeyyanagara*, here by the thatch. Here I will found / my palace and dwelling, in which to live, where I can be truly at peace."

King Mangrai had a net set out to mark off his palace, where the two hog-deer had been caught so easily; north of the thatch thicket, near the Mæ Yuak which served as a moat surrounding [so to speak] the two hog-deer. / That place has been called "Deer City" (*Wiang Fan*) to the present day.[53] King Mangrai prophesied that, in the future, this domain will have as rulers a mother and son.

---

52 Why does the author take to using Burmese words here?

53 Wiang Fan: not identified. This is the manuscript's only mention of this place. However, there is a Mæ Yuak stream about six km. north of the Chang Phüak Gate; and in the area watered by that stream there is the Wat Phra Nòn Khòn Muang (or Phra Nòn Mæ Chayüang, or Phra Nòn Phrang). Might this be the place? Note the Chronicle of the Reclining Buddha which appears below in fascicle 8.

Then King Mangrai had the elders of the domain / assembled,[54] and told them the story of the dog chasing the hog-deer into the *kha* thicket, so that the elders could all hear it. He then asked, "Is this really a good place?" They replied to King Mangrai, "We have heard this: this place / has been called a special place, where all the rulers of yore came. At the New Year, two albino hog-deer, mother and fawn, who were lords of the deer, emerged from the great forest and came to this auspicious place. The two hog-deer were very special creatures, and were able to defeat the wolves."

King /f° 2.20/ Mangrai heard this and his pleasure was heightened, and he was determined to construct his palace on this auspicious site. King Mangrai thus moved to occupy this auspicious site on that day, the eighth waxing day of the seventh month, a Thursday, a Thai *kot cai* day, at *dithi* 8, *nathidithi* 30, the moon being in the / seventh lunar mansion named the Punnabasu and the *rasi* of Kakkattha'apo, in the watch near dawn, 3 *luknadi plai 2 bat* of water, the *Lagna* in Mina-apo *rasi*, in the new-year period on the *Phraya Wan* day[55] as the era was incrementing one year to be 654, a *tao san* year (Thursday 27 March 1292).[56]

When King Mangrai had moved to enter the royal palace on / the auspicious site, he had a great many large and small dwellings constructed—what are called low and

---

54 This statement implies that there were old people who had been living in the area for many decades. They were probably Lawa who had been living there for a long time. The oldest chronicles refer to such Lawa, who had connections with Dòi Suthep. Cf. Sanguan Chotisukkharat, "Tamnan ratchawong Mangrai khròng müang Chiang Mai," in *Kamphæng müang Chiang Mai* (Chiang Mai, 1986), Appendix, pp. 40–41; his "Tamnan Sao Inthakhin," in his *Prachum tamnan Lan Na Thai I* (Bangkok, 1982); Thiu Wichaikhatta, "Kansang müang Chiang Mai, cak Tamnan Phrabat Dòn Klang Còm Thòng," in *Kamphæng müang Chiang Mai*, p. (39), and his "Phraya Mangrai khao müang, cak Tamnan Ratchawong Mangrai khròng müang Chiang Mai," *Kamphæng müang Chiang Mai*, pp. (39–40); Kraisri Nimmanhaeminda, "Phi Lua kin mu, phi Tai kin kai," in *Kamphæng müang Chiang Mai*, pp. 192–197; and "Lua nai Lan Na," Documents of a seminar under that title at the Witthayalai Khru Chiang Mai, 1988.

55 Those who would insist that the New Year always falls on 15 April need to be reminded that the Western (Gregorian) calendar only took its present form from October of 1582. In this period, the New Year (the *Phraya Wan* Day) usually fell around 27 March.

56 Thursday, the eighth waxing of the seventh month, a *kot cai* day, indeed was the first day of the new year. Lars Gislén's Thai calendar computer program would have us off by one day: the seventh lunar mansion was on the seventh waxing/*dithi* 7, and only the eighth day of the month had the correct *kot cai* day. All probably depends on the time of day, and the difference between the two days is too small to be significant for our purposes.

high dwellings and the Burmese call *mayang churawa*.[57] King Mangrai coming to live there, the northeastern side of that auspicious site was called Chiang Man.[58] / There, on the narrow part, the king had the land cleared and leveled on the east side, which has been called Chiang Thang to the present day.[59] King Mangrai determined that he would establish the city on this spot, which would be pleasing and agreeable.

At the northeast corner was a large swamp / where elephants, horses, cattle, and buffalo could come down to bathe and drink.[60] The king then called upon all the carpenters to come and fell, trim, and shape a great many timbers and construct buildings—an elephant shed, horse shed, and a gatehouse—and to construct a large new city on the auspicious site, which would serve as the navel [of the city].[61] /f° 2.21/ He would have a moat dug and roads built all around the city, three thousand fathoms on a side.

Visit of King Ruang and King Ngam Müang

The king then thought, "I would build a truly large city, so I should invite King Ngam Müang and King Ruang, who are my friends, to come." Having decided thus, he sent to invite his friends—King Ngam / Müang and King Ruang—to come. When the two kings arrived, he sought their advice. "The field which is near the auspicious site should be our assembly spot." So King Mangrai came together with the two kings and said to them, "On this spot here there were / two albino hog-deer, mother and fawn, here at the *kha* thicket. Even dogs and people in general would be unlikely to do harm here, so this surely is an auspicious site. Thus I surely should

---

57 V. Lieberman (pers. comm., 3 April 1995) says that "the closest words I could come up with were *ma-yabin*, 'a partition reaching from the floor to the roof in a palace,' and *su-yon thodara*, 'a storehouse.' Perhaps the latter.

58 The present vicinity of Wat Chiang Man.

59 The area to the northeast of Wat Chiang Man.

60 This large swamp to the northeast of the northeast corner of the city is still a low-lying area around the Mæ Kha, called Nòng Bua Cet Kò or just Nòng Bua. It took the water overflowing from the north moat of the city, and in flood times flowed down the Mæ Kha to the Ping near Kum Kam.

61 This "city navel" was probably located in the vicinity of the present "three kings" statue, as there is a deserted Wat Sadü Müang ("City Navel") there, and the City Pillar (Sao Inthakhin) was located there before being moved to Wat Chedi Luang. Aroonrut Wichienkeeo, *Wat rang nai wiang Chiang Mai* (Chiang Mai, 1986). These are much discussed in the *Tamnan Chiang Mai pang dœm* (Chiang Mai, 1994).

build my city here, taking the auspicious site as its center, running to the north, the west, and the east / a thousand fathoms, two thousand fathoms on a side. This is what I think, and I have sought out my two friend kings to come and discuss the matter. Should I or shouldn't I? Please consult and tell me what you think."

King Ngam Müang replied, "My friend, I don't think you should establish a city here two thousand fathoms on a side." /

King Ruang said, "My friend King Ngam Müang has told you [what he thinks], and he surely is correct. What he says is perceptive, and you should take it seriously and deliberately and with a view to future dangers. In the future, wise men might look down on this and say that you did not fully consider the future and the past. /f° 2.22/ In the future, foes and enemies will besiege [the city], and no one will be found who can protect [the city] sufficiently and you will be defeated. I would like to [build] from the auspicious site to the west, east, south, and north just 500 fathoms [, i.e., 1,000 fathoms on a side]."

King Mangrai said, "What my friend King Ruang / says is good. What he says is somewhat negative, and I have to listen to the opinions of both my royal friends. What they have said is fair and just, in accordance with Dhamma." Three-fourths of the generals and ministers were satisfied with the words of King Ngam Müang, while one-fourth were very satisfied with the words of King Ruang. /

King Ruang again said, "The holy ascetics Sudorasi and Sukkadandarasi[62] were certainly endowed with great supernatural powers, and they could have constructed an enormous city 10,000 leagues or even 100,000 leagues on a side, yet with due consideration for the future they built Lamphun very small, in shell-form." /

King Mangrai listened to this example of the two holy ascetics and the founding of Lamphun, and [carefully] considered future states and fates, and said to his two royal friends, "That being so, I will measure it 1,000 fathoms long by 900 fathoms wide."[63]

The three / rulers agreed. King Mangrai then invited his two friends to come to the auspicious site, in order to inaugurate his palace and consorts' palace.

At that time there was an albino mouse the size of a cart-axle diameter, with four followers, who came out of the auspicious site to the east /f° 2.23/ and entered a

---

62 The two ascetics who, in legend, founded Lamphun; cf. the *Cdv*. But how did King Mangrai know about them?

63 The city walls therefore cannot have originally been square.

hole in a large tree or a banyan tree—in Burmese a *phin yòng* tree—not far from the auspicious site.⁶⁴ The three rulers saw the albino mouse as a marvel, and together took puffed rice and flowers to reverence the lord mouse at the foot of the banyan tree with puffed / rice and flowers on a golden tray, [praying for the longevity of the city]. That tree became the guardian spirit-tree of the city, down to the present. The three rulers had the area where the city would be built swept clean, and took a rope to measure out the ground on the west sloping to the east, which was powerfully auspicious. /

King Ngam Müang and King Ruang conversed with King Mangrai, "Our friend, we should found the city here, which we consider to have seven auspicious qualities: (1) We hear that formerly two albino deer, mother and fawn, came out of the forest to the north / to live on the auspicious site here. People customarily paid respects [to them]. (2) Two albino hog-deer, mother and fawn, lived on the auspicious site here. They confronted the wolves, and all the wolves fled without fighting. / (3) We saw an albino mouse and its four followers come out of this auspicious site here. (4) This site, on which we would build a city, slopes from west to east. (5) Here, we see that a waterfall from the Ussupabatta Dòi Suthep flows /f° 2.24/ into a stream flowing to the north and to the east, and there is another stream flowing to the south and to the west to surround Kum Kam city. This river is a city-boon (*nagaraguṇa*). (6) This stream flows from the mountain downwards: this is called the Mæ Kha. It flows / eastwards, and then southward, close to the Mæ Ping, where it has had the name Mæ Tho to the present.⁶⁵ There is a large swamp on the northeast side of the auspicious site, named Isananerajapuri, or Nòng Yai, to the northeast. Foreign rulers greatly venerate it.⁶⁶ / (7) The Mæ Raming flows from the Mahāsra [pond], which the Lord Buddha, when he was alive, came to bathe in at Bathing Bowl Mountain (Dòi Ang Song),⁶⁷ flowing out to become the Ping River—to the east of the city—as

---

64   The magically most-powerful site in the city was where the large tree grew that was the abode of the protecting, tutelary spirits of the city. See Mani Phayòmyong, "Prapheni süp chata," in his *Prapheni sipsòng düan Lan Na Thai* (3rd ed.; Chiang Mai, 1994), I, 89–102.

65   Called the Mæ Kha to the present.

66   Notton (p. 59, n. 4) has a fascinating note referring to mentions by foreign visitors to Siam such as Simon de la Loubère and Fernão Mendes Pinto.

67   The Dòi Ang Song, or Dòi Chiang Dao, is west of Chiang Dao district town and north of Chiang Mai. Atop that mountain there is a deep indentation filled with water, and the legend of Dòi Ang Song says that the Buddha visited there and bathed in it. Some believe the mountain to be

the seventh auspicious quality. King / Ngam Müang and King Ruang pointed out these seven auspicious qualities to King Mangrai.

King Mangrai thought, "My two royal friends show genuine knowledge, intelligence, and wisdom of the auspicious qualities. / Whatever wisdom there is, my two friends possess it." King Mangrai then invited his two friends to inspect the place where he would dig the [city] moat, on all four sides, and where he would build the city walls and the city gates; and the three rulers sat on the northeast [side of the city]. King /f° 2.25/ Mangrai had his two ruler friends lunch, and then went to inspect the troops of the two rulers, making sure that they were satiated with rice, water, meat, and fish, every one of them.

Spirit-Offerings and Commencement of Construction, 1296

Then the two rulers arranged implements for offerings to the guardian spirits; and they performed an offering ceremony consisting of three parts, / one for the auspicious site where they would found the city; a second one for the Lord Albino Mouse Spirit in the midst of the city; and the third one further divided into five parts for the five gates they would erect. King Mangrai had officials versed in royal business / conducting the business of the city raise a group of fifty thousand men at the auspicious site to build the royal apartments, the palace, the consorts' palace, and the throne-hall, as well as storehouses and stables for the elephants and horses.[68] All this work was done by [the first group of fifty thousand] conscripts. Another forty thousand built the fortified city and prepared the moats and other / works on all four sides of the city, as well as prepared the gates, observation towers,[69] and boat-sheds. King Mangrai organized these conscripted groups to build everything, and began the construction of the various palaces and moats and the building of the city walls / in 658 of the Era, a *rwai san* year, on the full-moon day of the eighth month, a Mon Thursday (19 April 1296), in the sixteenth lunar mansion, in the watch near

---

magical, the residence of all the guardian and tutelary spirits of Chiang Mai, headed by Cao Luang Khamdæng, who convene there on every *wan phra*. They believe that the mountain's many caves store the food of the spirits. There is a large cave at the base of the steep mountain, and a temple.

68 Notton (p. 60, n. 2) here adds details taken from other manuscripts.
69 Used to observe the enemy and direct the city's defense in times of warfare.

dawn, with the *lagna* in the Mina-apo mansion,[70] when all the construction was commenced, when the city moats were dug beginning from the northeast corner proceeding towards the south along all four sides /f° 2.26/, all simultaneously. The Chiang Mai market was begun at the same time.[71]

The three kings had the sacrifice-officiants divided into six groups to petition all the heavenly spirits [*devata*] to come and protect the city as the auspicious site in the center of the city as well as at the five gates, on that day. The three kings had the city built together with the towers as a single set, / and the consorts' palace and king's dwelling, all of them, and had them completed, all of them, in four months, complete in all respects. King Mangrai then had a great entertainment put on for three days and three nights to host the officers and men and those who built the city, satiating them with food and drink. The three rulers / then together conferred a name upon the city, "Nabbapuri Sri Nagara Chiang Mai." At the thicket of the auspicious site they had a royal palace built, which is called the Golden Palace to the present day. King Ngam Müang and King Ruang took leave of King Mangrai, / their friend, and each then returned to his own domain.

Nagara paṭisaṅkharaṇaṁ samattaṁ.[72]

Renewed Warfare with King Yi Ba, 1296/97

Here we will tell of King Yi Ba, who went to Phraya Bœk, his son, in Khelang Lakhòn [Lampang].

King / Mangrai sent an agent to ferret out the secrets of King Ba, in the *tao sanga* year, until the *rwai san* year—a span of four years.[73] The spy learned all clearly, and came to report the news to King Mangrai. "King Ba and Phraya Bœk will come to

---

70   Thursday 19 April 1296 was not the full-moon day but the next day (Thursday), first waning of the sixth month. The Gislén computer program agrees on this day, when the moon was in the sixteenth lunar mansion.

71   The market was originally in the center of the city. The MS. tells us that Mangrai died there, and that his son erected a reliquary there where he fell, which is still there. See Prasert na Nagara, *Khlong nirat Hariphunchai* (Chiang Mai, 1973), p. 15.

72   Pali: "The story of the founding of the city, here completed." This reads like the (original) end of the chapter. We might suppose that it appeared at the end of the source our historian was using.

73   A problematic date. The first is all right (*tao sanga* = s. 644 = ad 1282/83); but three/four years later takes us to the *rwai* **set** year (s. 648 = ad 1286/87), not the *rwai* **san** year.

attack and seize /f° 2.27/ Hariphunchai and Kum Kam and Chiang Mai. 'I must take them,' [King Yi Ba said]. We cannot let them! Now they are drilling their elephants and horses and practicing archery and gunnery and drilling their troops, five days at a time and then two days' rest, without interruption. My lord must quickly call up and drill his forces, elephants, and horses and get ready / to fight King Ba and Phraya Bœk. He has appointed the full moon of the fourth month (31 December 1296) for Phraya Bœk to bring up his troops. The vanguard will take your lordship's city, for sure."

When the spy came, on the tenth waning of the first month (14 October 1296), King Mangrai heard the news / and was excited: he rose up, clapped his hands as loud as a gunshot, and said, "This time we will defeat the enemy for sure!" Then King Mangrai had the assembly-drum sounded to call up all the troops and distributed rewards of cowries and silver to / them, for them to be his strength. Then, King Mangrai collected armed-men, 235,000 of them; and then the king sent full news to his son, Prince Khram, in Chiang Rai: "May my son announce / to his officers that they should prepare all the elephants, horses, and warriors. They should divide into two groups—one group to set up west of the town, adjoining Dòi Kham,[74] ready to fight the vanguard of Phraya Bœk; and a second group to come to the east of the Ping River heading down to Lamphun, ready to cut off the rear of Phraya /f° 2.28/ Bœk.

Prince Khram Comes to Assist his Father

Prince Khram heard his father's message, and quickly summoned all his forces to assemble, every village and domain. Prince Khram then assembled all his troops, including 518,000 just of Chiang Rai, plus district (*panna*[75]) men amounting to another 204,000; / altogether 725,000 men. Prince Khram divided them into two

---

74 A small hill south of Dòi Suthep and Chiang Mai. This area historically was inhabited by Lawa, and it was there that the Lawa divinity Khun Luang Wilangkha lived (who was also the soul of the Pu Sæ and Ya Sæ divinities of the Lawa). A ceremony to propitiate the Lawa spirits is held there each year in the ninth month. The legend in the *Tamnan Phrathat Dòi Kham* tells us that the mountain got its name from the fact that a shower of golden rain fell after the Lord Buddha had preached there to the Lawa.

75 *luk panna*. I have translated this as "district" throughout. It actually refers to the territories governed as part of a *panna*.

groups; one of 150,000 men commanded by the governor of Fang, to go southwest of Wiang Kum Kam by the foot of Dòi Kham, following his father's instructions; and Prince Khram himself led 572,000 troops east / of the Ping River to a place where he encamped them. In the evening, Prince Khram ascended into his reviewing tower; and he saw his men on all four sides, extending as far as he could see, without end; and that place has been called Chen Phò to the present day.

The lord / encamped there, ate his evening meal and prepared for bed, and then called in a thousand trusted volunteer warriors, whom he was to lead mounted on his own war elephant with the thousand men as his guard to rush to his side, to assist King Mangrai in Wiang Chiang Mai, saying / "My father tells me that Phraya Bœk is coming with his troops; so I have divided my forces into two groups, according to our lord's instructions in every detail—one group of 150,000 men I have had the governor of Fang command, to come down the west to set up at the foot of Dòi Kham, between the mountain and the Ping River; /f° 2.29/ and I am commanding the other group on the east bank of the river, with 572,000 men, to hold the Holy Reliquary of Hariphunchai. Now I send my blessings to my father, and pray that he will not leave the city [of Chiang Mai]: he should remain comfortably in his palace, just holding all his / forces to defend it. He should not let his forces' attention lapse [for even an instant], lest anything happen."

When King Mangrai heard his son Prince Khram's admonitions to his troops, he was pleased, and said, "My son's ideas are good; but I should / arrange a Chiang Mai force of 160,000 men to defend the three cities [Chiang Mai, Kum Kam, and Lamphun], each of fifty thousand troops, and another ten thousand men to dig the city moat around Chiang Mai down to the north of the Chiang Mai market." On the east, they used the / Ping River as a moat, thus protecting the two cities, Chiang Mai and Kum Kam. King Mangrai mounted his war elephant, named Phetchaphon [*Bejjabala*] and led a force of five hundred war elephants and eight thousand war-horses and a force of one hundred thousand troops. / "I will take this force down to attack King Ba and Phraya Bœk. As for my beloved son, he should take his troops up to fight [King Ba and Phraya Bœk] and capture them. Don't let a single one escape!"

Prince Khram replied, "I like the war-plan which my father has given. /f° 2.30/ Even if the father and son [King Ba and Phraya Bœk] flee to Khelang, or to Yodhiya, I will still capture them! There's no stopping me!" Prince Khram said this to his father, and King Mangrai was thus informed of his son's strategy. He was very pleased, so he gave auspicious amulets / for defeating the enemy and many silver and gold rewards to his son, as well as the Sri Kañjeyya sword, which was a very ancient sword of [King] Lawacangkarat, of such great power that, when drawn, it gave the power of courage to all troops, except foes, / owing to the great power of the sword. Prince Khram then took leave of his father, and rushed to assemble his troops through the night; and at dawn he marched his troops out in ranks, down to a landing [on the river]. There a party reconnoitered the enemy, and / quickly reported [back] to Prince Khram, "The father [King Ba] has not come: there is only Phraya Bœk. The son [Phraya Bœk] has a very large force. Now, their vanguard is set up at Wiang Chiang Thòng,[76] and the rear-guard is still arriving in great numbers."

Prince Khram took his forces to pursue the rear-guard, and took elephants, / horses, and troops to block the way [of the rear-guard]. Then he followed the enemy to Chiang Thòng, [blocking Bœk's retreat] that night.

Phraya Bœk slept at Chiang Khrüng, and at dawn took his forces to surround Wiang Kum Kam. Prince Khram quickly took his forces [down] /f° 2.31/ to a place south of Kum Kam around midnight, when it was very dark, and had his troops rest there; and it has been called Kham Khün to the present day.

The Battle Begins

Then Prince Khram had a cavalry force of one thousand carry word to the ruler of Fang, who was with his force at the foot of Dòi Kham, [telling him] that, "Tonight, near dawn, you / should engage the vanguard of Phraya Bœk, and not let them get to Chiang Mai. When I hear that you have engaged them, I will join you."

At dawn, the governor of Fang attacked the vanguard of Bœk. When he heard the tumult, Prince Khram / knew that the governor of Fang had engaged the enemy. In early morning, Prince Khram then took his troops to enter Kum Kam. The troops of Phraya Bœk heard the loud noise of the war-drums and dashed to Phraya Bœk to inform him of the situation thusly: / "Nearby, the tumult is fierce. King Mangrai probably has taken his troops out of the city to block us off. Another group is attacking us head-on, and this vanguard is pressing at us, intending to block our retreat." So informed, Phraya Bœk instructed a force of his vanguard, / "All of you must engage the troops who have come to attack our van and defeat them. As for me, I shall advance to fight the enemy who has attacked our rear." Then Phraya Bœk

---

76 Perhaps in the Còm Thòng region?

turned his elephant's head to the west, to engage the king's force to the southwest of Kum Kam.

Then the governors of Fang and M. Sœng /f° 2.32/ volunteered to Prince Khram, "We two want to fight Phraya Bœk, the king. Please let us try this." Then Prince Khram said, "The forces of Bœk are very numerous—whole rows of ivory! My lord's elephantry / are unequal to them. If I am to really volunteer to fight, you must give me enough forces to support me. The governor of Chiang Khòng will become our right-wing, and [the governor of] M. Sœng[77] our left-wing, and we will poll our forces for volunteers to compose the crow's-wing.[78] / May the governor of Fang push up towards me. I will myself take a force of Chiang Mai men, true warriors, to drive our elephants straight into the force of Phraya Bœk. When we have wedged our body in, we will [sandwich and] smash them in and push them into our crow's-wing. When they have been pushed down into our crow's-wing, the governor of Fang should press them [from the other side]. / Have all the cavalry volunteers fight the enemy, and all the footsoldiers' first ranks shoot arrows into the enemy," so Prince Khram instructed his troops; and then he signaled his forces to attack, using the drums and gongs to signal for all to attack Phraya Bœk, on that day. /

Colophon to Chapter Two

Dutiya nagararājavaṁsa nidānagāthā samutāparipuṇṇā.[79]

---

77 Notton (p. 65, n. 1) notes that PY here has M. Thing. Thœng is meant.

78 On ancient warfare, see H. G. Quaritch Wales, *Ancient South-East Asian Warfare* (London, 1952). Note especially Chs. 6–7 and Figure 2.

79 Pali: "Second Book of the History of the City, Tale and Recitation, Here completed."

Chapter 3

War Concluded With Phraya Bœk

Namo tassathu. At that time, Phraya Bœk became aware that Phraya Khram was bringing up an army behind him, so he turned his elephant around to face the attack. Phraya Bœk's elephant was in must, and would not be controlled. Phraya Khram saw his chance. He urged forward his elephant, Phan Pan Phon Sæn by name, to confront the elephant of Phraya / Bœk. The elephant of Phraya Khram wounded Phraya Bœk's elephant in the neck and raised the elephant up and pushed it back. Then Phraya Khram's middle guard[1] slashed Phraya Bœk with his lance on his seat. The alarmed elephant withdrew and fled. The place where the two rulers dueled on elephant-back was the later site of a village called / Ban Nœk; and when a roofed bridge later was built there to cross the Tho River, the bridge was called the Roofed Bridge.[2]

Then the regiment of the ruler of Fang withdrew back, and Mün Chiang Khòng and Mün Sœng surrounded the crow's-wing [formation] and set upon the horse and elephant troops, and many of the troops of / Nakhòn Khelang [Lampang] died, struck by the volleys like[quills from a] porcupine. People [later] built a village there, called Porcupine Village to the present day. The Khelang officers rode female elephants [in] to rescue Phraya Bœk and spirited him away, and the elephantry of Phraya Khram was not in time [to prevent them from doing so,] because / the elephants saw the female elephants of Khelang, and they would neither fight nor run; so Phraya Bœk's elephant was able to flee.

---

1   A man of rank fighting on elephant-back was accompanied by two or three (or more) men atop the beast, who joined him in fighting and controlled the elephant.

2   Now Ban Khua Mung, on the banks of the Ping west of Wiang Kum Kam. It is unknown whether the village is old, or whether an old toponym has been taken from the manuscripts and applied to a newer village.

At that time, the army saw the chance to make a good stand, when Cao Phraya Khram could easily get through to Phraya Bœk, but he was unable to do so; so Cao Phraya Khram told his councilors, /f° 3.02/ "We do not know whether Phraya Bœk is alive or dead. We should follow them." So he went to Cao Mangrai, his father, in Chiang Mai to ask whether they should pursue Phraya Bœk, and [, if so,] if his father would have some people minister to the ill and wounded. /

King Mangrai, on hearing his son's report, was greatly pleased, and bestowed rewards on his son and all his troops to encourage them. Cao Phraya Khram then had his troops pursue Phraya Bœk in the valley of the Tan River[3] in the territory of Nakhòn Khelang. / He gave rewards to the valorous who had attacked Phraya Bœk on the head of his elephant and there dispatched him. Many Nakhòn Khelang troops died there. [Then] the prince brought his forces to plunder Nakhòn Khelang.

At that time, / Phraya Yi Ba [had] fled to take refuge with Phraya Phitsanulok[4] in Sòng Khwæ,[5] and he died there. Phraya Khram cleared Nakhòn Khelang, and had his troops go and sounded the Un Müang drum[6] and took care of his forces for three days and / three nights, and bestowed lavish rewards upon every one of his troops. Then he sent a force of 500 horse cavalry back to his father, King Mangrai, in Chiang Mai, with a full report on all that had occurred, and requesting an [additional] force of 100,000 men [so that he could] go after Phraya Yi Ba in Sòng Khwæ. If the lord /f° 3.03/ offered up the city to him, so be it; and if he did not, he would fight and take him.

So informed, King Mangrai replied to his son, "Don't go after Phraya Yi Ba. My son, you have killed Phraya Bœk, and you have taken Nakhòn Khelang, / with your great power. It can be said that you have conquered and have killed the lord of the whole domain; you are victorious. You, my son, have brave and valorous troops controlling Nakhòn Khelang, who there will make trouble for / Phraya Yi Ba if ever he tries to return, and he will not easily retake the city, as Nakhòn Khelang

---

3   The Mæ Tan flows towards Lamphun from the Khun Tan mountains to the southeast.

4   Phitsanulok: city and province in central Thailand. See Sisak Wanliphodom, *Müang boran nai anacak Sukhothai* (Bangkok, 1989), pp. 68–73.

5   Major old city near Phitsanulok, on east bank of the Nan River, around Wat Mahathat. See Sisak Wanliphodom, *Müang boran nai anacak Sukhothai*, pp. 71–72.

6   Drum beaten after victory is gained. Its name is equivalent to "Heating Drum." The "heat" is to be contrasted with the city that is "cold" after deaths. The drum is beaten to signify that the domain is "warm."

is a city related to Lamphun,[7] and has been so ever since the Maharishi built it for Mahantayot, the son of Queen Camadevi." Cao Phraya Khram heeded the royal utterances / of his father forbidding him to pursue [Yi Ba]. Cao Phraya Khram then appointed a very able general, skilled in all the military arts—a *sattrujeyyasenā*[8]—to go and eat Nakhòn Khelang.

The prince then took all / his armies and generals back to Chiang Mai, where he paid all reverence to his father. King Mangrai had his son sit by the royal throne, and made him heir-presumptive (*uparaja*). The king was greatly pleased with his son and all his officers, and had the Un Müang drum sounded throughout the cities of Chiang Mai and Kum Kam /f° 3.04/ for seven days and seven nights. He fêted every one of the troops, bestowing gold and other valuables and cloth upon all of the officers, and money and presents to all the troops, without exception.

As for Cao Phraya Khram, King Mangrai / gave him Chiang Dao as a gift to be a resting place between Chiang Mai and Chiang Rai. He gave him four wives, four male and four female war elephants, four war horses and mares, each with gold trappings, as well as a golden bowl, a golden ewer, a golden betel-nut set, and an / an orchestra with victory gongs, Hò flutes, oboes, and ceremonial conch shells. King Mangrai also bestowed a new name upon his son, calling him Cao Phraya Cheyyasongkhram.[9]

Prince Cheyyasongkhram

Then Cheyyasongkhram with all his officers took / leave of King Mangrai to return to their homes. When the lord reached Chiang Rai, he fêted his officers, and then each returned to his [own] home. Cao Phraya Cheyyasongkhram then appointed a group of people as a work-party, namely carpenters, / to clear Chiang Dao city and build a small palace and dwelling and eating places and horse and elephant stables; and every year the prince dwelt at Chiang Dao when he came to pay attendance upon his father. He dwelled there from the full moon of the fifth month (late January) to the full moon of the eighth month (late April), and then

---

7   Domains that are linked by kinship are different from *luk panna* which are linked by politics and administration.

8   Sanskrit: *sattrujeyyasenā*, "victorious over enemies."

9   Jeyyasongkhram, pronounced Chaiyasongkhram, means "victorious in warfare."

returned to Chiang Rai. This he did every year. The prince then /f° 3.05/ set up many granaries in Chiang Dao, every one of them filled with rice, as food reserves for his troops, retainers, and brave warriors. While the prince was at Chiang Rai, he appointed a chamberlain (*ca ban dap rüan*) to attend upon his nobles and wives in the / royal palace in the city of Chiang Dao.

Cao Phraya Cheyyasongkhram had three sons. The eldest was named Thao Sæn Phu, so called because when his mother was about to give birth to him, the ruler took her [up the mountain] to attend an entertainment, when / the New Year was about to turn. The lady gave birth to the royal prince there on the mountain, which is why he was called Cao Sæn Phu. The middle son was named Thao Nam Thuam, because in the year he was born, severe floods engulfed the whole country, so he was called Phò Thao Nam Thuam ("Lord Flood"). / The youngest son was called Thao Ngua, because on the day he was born, the people of the town brought gifts, including many *hòi ngua*,[10] so he was called Thao Ngua. When the three princes grew up, their father, Cao Phraya Khram, had the princes schooled in the palace, / that they might attain to wisdom in the palace of King Mangrai. King Mangrai was gracious to his grandsons, and taught them all the various arts and sciences; and whenever King Mangrai ate his meals, he was pleased to have his grandsons prepare his food and eat with him, every day. *Jayasaṅgrāma paricesa tho.*[11] /f° 3.06/ *Samatto.*[12]

King Mangrai's Three Sons

Here we will tell of the three sons of King Mangrai.

Khun Khrüang, the eldest, broke the laws of his father, seizing Chiang Rai. Mangrai, who was at Fang, had Khun Khrüang fetched from Chiang Rai and shot; and the place where he was shot is called M. Ying to the / present day.

Khun Khram, the middle son, had a generous nature, and was methodical and industrious and loyal to his father, it is said. He ruled Chiang Rai, and was named Phraya Cheyyasongkhram.

---

10   Udom defines this as a kind of shellfish (*hòi*), *hòi khong*, and says that it is a Shan word. McFarland explains *hòi khong* as a freshwater snail.

11   Properly, "*Jeyyassaṅgrāma parichedda tho*," "End of Chapter Two, The Victorious War." The manuscript from which this copy was made must have had a chapter-break here.

12   Pali: "Done."

Khun Khrüa, the youngest, had an ugly nature [and his father] had him rule M. Phrao to keep him away / from the wife of his elder brother—Cao Phraya Cheyyasongkhram—who stayed at Chiang Dao awaiting Khun Khrüa; and, knowing this, Khun Khrüa remained where he was.

In the *ruang kai* year (1311/12), when King Mangrai was aged seventy-three years, he fell / ill, and went to stay at Wiang Kum Kam. Khun Khrüa then came from Phrao to attend his father at Wiang Kum Kam. King Mangrai had his favorite son, Cao Phraya Cheyyasongkhram, summoned. On arriving at Chæ Sak, he learned that Khun Khrüa was still attending their father, / so while still at Chæ Sak he sent someone to report to his father. King Mangrai, learning that Khun Khrüa was still attending upon him, and that he had seduced the wife of Cao Phraya Khram, his elder brother, pondered thusly: "Of my three sons, the only one who has pleased me has been /f° 3.07/ Cao Phraya Cheyyasongkhram. As for the others, the eldest, Khun Khrüang, has already been killed, and the youngest, Khun Khrüa, who was just as deserving of death I should have killed, but I did not, and instead I sent him away." Thinking thus, King Mangrai ordered Khun Khrüa taken, together with all his wives and children, retainers and families, / and sent to the Southern Phòng domain.[13]

The Shans[14]—all the Phòng people, e.g., at Chiang Thòng, / M. Pan, and M. Li—guarded him, not allowing him to go anywhere.[15] They then said, "King Mangrai is filled with majesty and bravery, and has pacified the whole country. He is greater than any other in the whole country. Now King Mangrai has expressed his / affection and care for us, and he has sent us his beloved son, Khun Khrüa, as our lord and master. We should make no objection, and should respect him, and have him as our lord and master. Cao Khun Khrüa was pleased, and said, "In no wise have I offended against my father, / unlike my elder brother, Cao Phraya Cheyyasongkhram, whom I have never liked; so King Mangrai had me come to stay with you." The Shan were delighted, and they built him a city, a country, a small palace, and a sleeping hall. /f° 3.08/ After [ceremonially] bathing him, they consecrated Khun Khrüa as their lord

---

13 This term is not otherwise known. We might get an indication of where it was by the next sentence, which identifies M. Nai. Thus the M. Nai–M. Pan area is indicated.

14 *Yieo, Ñieo, Ngieo.*

15 There are many toponyms in this paragraph. As best we can determine, all lie in the Shan area west of the Salween River in the vicinity of M. Pan and M. Nai. For a description of M. Nai, see Bancop Phanthumetha, *Pai sòp kham Thai*, pp. 41–42. See map 3.

CHAPTER THREE   89

and master. Then the Phòng Tai Shan built a city for Cao Khun Khrüa to live in, called M. Nai [Moné] to the present day.

When / Mangrai had Khun Khrüa exiled to go and live among the Shan, King Mangrai ordered the *ca ban* and Mün Fang Kæn[16] to take an auspicious royal elephant named Rak Samœ Cai, together with gifts, to receive his son. Delighted to hear / what his father had said, he exclaimed, "My father, King Mangrai, really loves me!" Then the prince quickly mounted the royal elephant, Rak Samœ Cai, and traveled through the night to Wiang Kum Kam, where he nursed his father. [His father's] illness gradually abated, and King Mangrai returned to Chiang Mai.

Counting / the [members of the] dynasty from Lawacangkarat to King Mangrai there had been fifteen [i.e., twenty-five kings].[17] If we speak only of the rulers who reigned in Nopburi Si Chiang Mai, which was founded as the capital, the learned teachers have decreed that King Mangrai, who was the first / to reign in the capital on the Ping [River], was the first ruler.

Illness and Death of King Mangrai, 1317/18

At that time, Cao Phraya Cheyyasongkhram came to nurse his father until his illness passed, and then he returned to Chiang Rai. As for King Mangrai, he reigned in Chiang Mai, full of pious faith in and patronage for the Teachings of the Lord Buddha, /f° 3.09 / performing meritorious acts until at the age of eighty years he passed on to the next world with the fruits of his actions, dying in the Chiang Mai market, in the middle of the city, in s. 679, a *müang sai* year (1317/18). His generals and councilors placed his remains in a golden urn / and informed Cao Phraya Cheyyasongkhram in Chiang Rai.

Informed that his father had died, Cheyyasongkhram came with a large force to Chiang Mai, and had a palatial pyre constructed for the remains of his father and made merit / for his remains, and he was cremated in the Chiang Mai market. He built a reliquary[18] for his father's bones in the market in the middle of the city, and

---

16 Many of the titles consist of a numerical ranking (*phan, mün, sæn*) followed by a place name. Here, Mün Fang Kæn must have been in charge of the Fang Kæn Panna.

17 The HP MS. clearly writes "15" but the table given in Chapter 1 clearly has 25 rulers. Probably a misreading of the author's sources.

18 *ku*, a funerary memorial to enshrine the ashes of the deceased after cremation; not called a *cetiya/chedi*. Notton (p. 74, n. 2) says that this memorial was in the Chang Phüak area of the city.

planted a banyan tree over the reliquary, in order that the site not become a public thoroughfare. /

Sæn Phu Becomes King, 1318

Cao Phraya Cheyyasongkhram organized the country, remaining there for four months, and then had his eldest son, Thao Sæn Phu, aged forty-one years, consecrated to rule in Chiang Mai in place of his grandfather, Mangrai, / in the *pœk sanga* year, s. 680, in the month of Jyestha—the Thai say the full moon of the ninth month (Monday 15 May 1318).[19] He was another in the ruling line. He then appointed his middle son, Phò Thao Nam Thuam, to go and rule M. Fang, and his youngest son, Phò Thao Ngua, to go and rule Chiang Khòng.

Usurpation of Prince Khrüa, 1319

Cao Sæn Phu had ruled Chiang Mai /f° 3.10/ for just one year when, in the *kat met* year (1319/20), Cao Khun Khrüa, his uncle who ruled M. Nai, brought in a force of more than a hundred thousand troops, Phòng Tai men, stating that he had come to pay homage to the remains of his father, King Mangrai. He encamped his forces, elephants, and horses at Wiang Kum Kam, and stationed a group to support him / on the Khao San Plain.[20] Soon, he and his bodyguard force went to pay their respects to his father [at the] Chiang Mai market. Then he deceitfully presented gifts and asked after news from Phraya Sæn Phu, his nephew, saying, "Uncle has come to pay his respects to King Mangrai. Don't be suspicious of / Uncle. Don't close the city gates to him. Uncle has come to ask for news from his nephew: is he well?" Then Phraya Khrüa arranged for armed men to go to the Chiang Mai Gate[21] and the Suan Dòk Gate,[22] intending to take Cao Sæn Phu at dawn.

Sæn Phu knew of this, and thought, / "My town will fight Uncle, and if Uncle defeats me, he will kill me; while if I defeat Uncle, my troops will kill him for sure.

---

19 In other words, the text makes an equivalence between Jyestha (which is the seventh month in the Siamese calendar) with the ninth month of the calendar of Chiang Mai.
20 Thong Khao San: location unknown.
21 The central gate of Chiang Mai on the south side: see map 7.
22 The central gate of Chiang Mai on the west side: see map 7.

I must not remain here." Thinking thus, he gathered up all his family, his wives and children, his elephants, horses, and slaves, his gold and silver, his jewelry, and all his / valuables, and took his forces and hurriedly withdrew out the North Gate[23] to Chiang Som in the middle of the night.

When he reached there, Thao Nam Thuam, his younger brother at Fang, sent his elder brother on to Chiang Rai. The prince then paid homage to his father, saying, "Cao Phraya Cheyyasongkhram tells me that his Uncle has come to /f° 3.11/ seize the domain." Phraya Khrüa came to usurp his nephew's [place] and eat Chiang Mai in the *kat met* year, s. 681 (1319/20), another generation of the ruling line.

Thus learning of this, Cao Phraya Cheyyasongkhram was overcome with anger, and roared, "Phraya Khrüa has taken my city. He thinks he can do so with / impunity. I can destroy him whenever I wish. His crimes are three. First, he has taken one of my wives; [second, he has] usurped power from my son, Cao Sæn Phu, who ruled Chiang Mai; and third, he has taken Chiang Dao, which was a gift from my father. He should be destroyed." /

In the *kot san* year, first waxing of the seventh month (Saturday 28 February 1321),[24] Cao Phraya Cheyyasongkhram organized an army for his son, Phò Thao Nam Thuam, who ruled Fang, saying, "My beloved son, take this army and go and capture your uncle, Khun Khrüa, at Chiang Mai. Don't / let him escape to the Shan domains, as he will make trouble for the country. When you take Chiang Mai, I will award that city to you to eat."[25] Cao Phò Nam Thuam paid his respects to his father, saying, "I know that my uncle, Khun Khrüa, does not respect my father / as ruler. I've wanted for a year to take him. Now I volunteer, and my father need not worry. I will take my uncle, Khun Khrüa, and I won't let him escape."

Cao Phò Thao Nam Thuam of Fang then took his father's army off to Chiang Mai city, encamping /f° 3.12/ on the Nòng Sæn Tò Plain. On the thirteenth waning

---

23 Now called the Chang Phüak ("White Elephant") Gate. (See Map 7) Here called the *pratu hua wiang*, meaning the "northern" gate. It is first called the Pratu Chang Phüak Hua Wiang at f° 5.35, and called the Pratu Chang Phüak at f° 6.06.

24 The "seventh month" (or eighth) might occur twice in a year that ran from late March to late March. In this case, it was at the end of the year.

25 In many Southeast Asian languages, a ruler is said to "eat" the domains assigned to his sustenance. That is, he governed them.

of the fifth month, a Tuesday, a Thai *rwai yi* day,²⁶ in the morning watch, he arrayed his forces in [the formation] called Rajapañña,²⁷ and employed the strategy of having some of his soldiers put their weapons in carrying-baskets, as if they had come to labor there, and go in through every city gate, / infiltrating the whole city, while the rest surrounded the entire city. Some [also] waited at the small palace. They were everywhere. When Phò Thao Nam Thuam entered the city, he had the gongs²⁸ and the Sabat Chai drum²⁹ sounded in a noisy din.

Cao Phò Thao Nam Thuam / then said, "As for my uncle, Khun Khrüa, we haven't got him yet; but we've as much as got him. If my uncle fears dying, and tries to escape, don't kill him. Just catch him and sent him to me."

So far as we know, that evening Phraya Khrüa had drunk to intoxication, / very much so. Before dawn, he had crawled away to sleep off his stupor. The gatekeeper dashed in to tell the ruler that the ruler of Fang, his nephew, had brought up an army, which had surrounded the small palace and were throughout the city, and would [soon] come to take the lord. /

Phraya Khrüa was frightened, arose from his bed, and drunkenly staggered to sound the alarm drum to summon his forces. Not a single person responded. Phraya Khrüa was scared to death. He dashed to the palace to prepare weapons, [but] not in time.

Cao Phò Thao Nam Thuam had a large piece of timber fetched /f° 3.13/ to ram open the door and catch Phraya Khrüa, and had his uncle placed in confinement, in the southwest corner of the city; and he appointed Mün Rüang³⁰ to attend upon him, and to build a dwelling there. Later, Mün Rüang built a plaza to the east of that house, / and it still appears there to this day, as the Chiang Rüang Plaza. Nam Thuam killed many of the retainers that had accompanied Phraya Khrüa. Having cleared out Chiang Mai, Cao [Nam Thuam] reported everything / to Cao

---

26 Not an exact match. The day closest to matching the data given (in the Gislén program), is Tuesday, the thirteenth waning of the sixth month, a *rwai yi* day, s. 683 = ad 1322 March 16.

27 Military formation unknown.

28 War gong sounded always in conjunction with the Sabat Chai drum, indicating that a city now was surrounded, or an army had arrived at a city. Cf. ff° 3.12, 3.20, 3.27, and 4.26.

29 Sounded in conjunction with the *yong gong*; also sounded to signal the end of a battle.

30 Mün Rüang was an official of *cao mün* rank who made his home in the southwest corner of the city of Chiang Mai. After his death, his ashes were interred in a reliquary near his old home, and that corner of the city has been called the Ku Rüang corner or fort to the present day.

Phraya Cheyyasongkhram, his father. So informed, Cao Phraya Cheyyasongkhram was delighted, and arranged the utensils of consecration for his officials to perform the consecration of Nam Thuam, then aged thirty years, as lord [*phraya*] to rule / Chiang Mai, in the *tao set* year, s. 684 (1322/23), [he being] the fourth in the royal lineage.

Nam Thuam Exiled to Keng Tung, 1324

Two years later, in the *kap cai* year (1324/25), Nam Thuam was disloyal to his father, Cheyyasongkhram, so [the latter] commissioned Cao Phò Thao Ngua, the youngest, / to take Nam Thuam away from Chiang Mai, saying, "Cao Phò Thao Nam Thuam has been disloyal to me, his father. As you two are brothers, who love one another, I cannot kill him. Take him away to M. Khem."[31] So Thao Ngua had his elder brother, Cao Phò Thao /f° 3.14/ Nam Thuam, kept at M. Khem, there provided with all comforts. Not much later, the people of M. Khem together declared that, "As Phò Thao Nam Thuam was born from the flesh of Cao Phraya Cheyyasongkhram, who has great majesty, we should make him our lord." / So in concert they consecrated Nam Thuam as ruler in M. Khemarattha.[32] As for Cao Khun Khrüa, he remained under house arrest for four years, and then died. Cao Phraya Cheyyasongkhram conducted the funerary rites for his younger brother, Cao Khun Khrüa, in Chiang Mai. /

Sæn Phu Restored to Rule Chiang Mai, 1324/25

At that time, Cheyyasongkhram reflected that, "As my son, Cao Phò Thao Sæn Phu, is well versed in the royal ways, is of good disposition, and thoroughly knows the ways of princes, it is fitting that my son, Cao Sæn Phu, be consecrated and be given a second chance to rule Chiang / Mai." The lord then went from Chiang Rai

---

31 Khemaratha was the classical name of Keng Tung (Chiang Tung). See below.

32 This reference makes it clear that Keng Tung (Chiang Tung) is meant by "Müang Khem" above. On the history of Keng Tung, see Sao Sāimöng Mangrāi, *The Padaeng Chronicle and the Jengtung State Chronicle Translated* (Ann Arbor, 1981); Thawi Swangpanyangkun, *Phongsawadan müang Chiang Tung* (Chiang Mai, 1990); *Rüang müang Chiang Tung* (Chiang Mai, 1994); and Aroonrut Wichienkeeo, "Tamnan Tungkharasi phün müang Chiang Tung (Chiang Mai, 1988).

to Chiang Mai to consecrate his son, Cao Sæn Phu, to rule over Chiang Mai. In the *kap cai* year, s. 686 (1324/25), Cao Sæn Phu returned to rule in Chiang Mai.

At that time, / there was a beloved wife of Cao Sæn Phu, named Lady Sip Kham, who was his queen. That lady was in the habit of visiting Wiang Kum Kam, which she did regularly, crossing the Mæ Tho. She therefore had a bridge built across the Tho River. It has been called the Sip Kham Bridge to the present day.

Cheyyasongkhram Dies, 1327/28

After Cao Phraya Cheyyasongkhram /f° 3.15/ had consecrated his son Cao Sæn Phu, he reigned happily in Chiang Rai. Two years later,[33] in the *müang mao* year, s. 689 (1327/28), at the age of sixty-three years, he passed to next world, in Chiang Rai. /

Kham Fu Begins Reign in Chiang Mai, 1328/29

Sæn Phu appointed his own son, Cao Thao Kham Fu, to take care of Chiang Mai, and conducted the funerary obsequies for Cheyyasongkhram, his father, in Chiang Rai, for one month, and then continued to reign in Chiang Rai. He then had his son, / Kham Fu, consecrated, at the age of twenty-six years, as ruler of Chiang Mai in the *pœk si* year, s. 690 (1328/29).

Foundation of Chiang Sæn, 1329

Not long afterwards, Sæn Phu went to build M. Ròi.[34] / He had a moat dug around the city on three sides—the moat on the eastern side being the Mekong River—and had walls built on all three sides; and Sæn Phu then reigned in that city, which has been called Chiang Sæn / to the present day. The chronicles say[35] that Chiang Sæn was built in the *müang mao* year, s. 689 (1327/28), [while other] chronicles say the

---

33 Notton (p. 78, n. 1) says PY has 3 years.

34 As we see below, this was the old name of Chiang Sæn. Notton (p. 78, n. 3) says that various manuscripts write Chiang Lao here.

35 A rare and interesting reference to the fact that the historian was working from (usually unspecified) sources. Note also the next sentence.

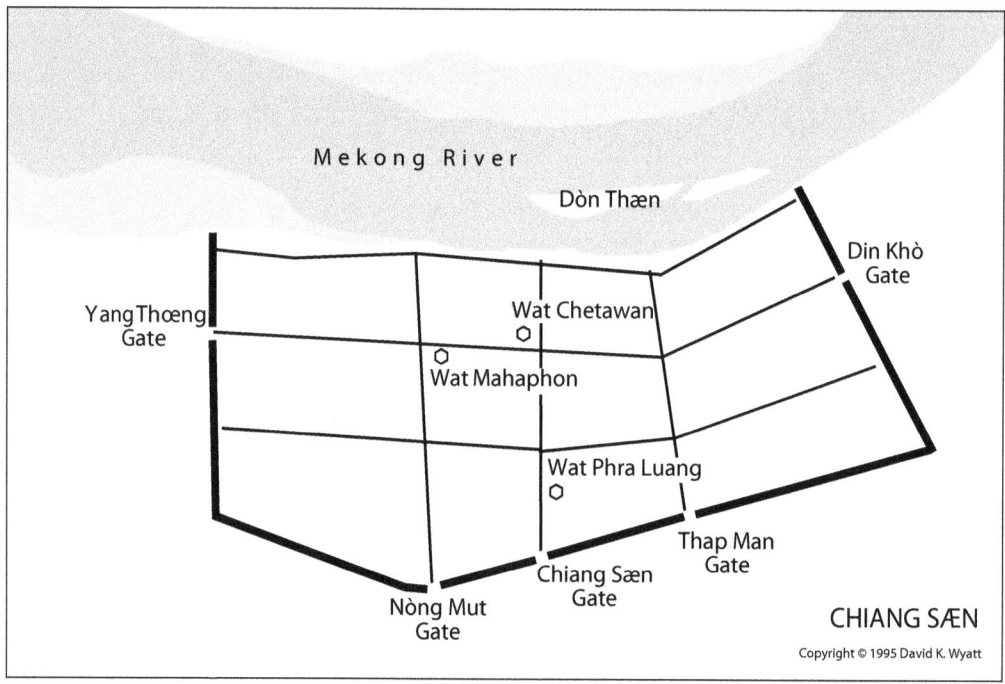

pœk si year, s. 690, on Friday the second day of the waxing moon of the seventh month, a Thai *pœk si* day (Friday 3 March 1329), in the evening watch, the *lagna* in the Libra lunar mansion,[36] the city of Chiang Sæn was built, /f° 3.16/ measuring 1500 by 700 fathoms, with five gates: the Yang Thœn Gate, the Nòng Mut Gate, the Chiang Sæn Gate, the Tha Man Gate, and the Din Khò Gate.[37]

To the south, the Mæ Tœm was the border with the territory of Chiang Rai; to the southwest, Kiu Khò Ma was the frontier with M. Fang; to the west, / Pha Ta Læo marked the border with M. Sat; to the northwest, M. Rai Dòi Chang was on the border of Chiang Tung; to the north, M. Kai Sam Thao was the border with Chiang Tung; to the northeast, M. Luang Bò Ræ marked the border / with the Hò;

---

36 Friday 3 March 1329. Thai *pœk si* day is not possible: probably a lazy misreading, taking year name also as day name.

37 A *wa* is conventionally rendered as a fathom, roughly six feet or two meters; so the old city of Chiang Saen measured 3000 x 1400 meters. There is a very good (Thai) fold-out map of old Chiang Saen at the back of Somcit Rüangkhana, *Namchom borânnawatthusathân nai 'amphoe Chiang Saen, cangwat Chiang Râi* [Guide to Antiquities in Chiang Saen district, Chiang Rai province] (Bangkok: Fine Arts Dept., 1970). There is no scale on the map, so it is not possible to check the dimensions given in the chronicle, save on the ground itself or with a better map. The five gates of the city are shown on the map of Chiang Sæn City.

to the east, Dòi Chiang Chi marked the frontier with Chiang Khòng; and to the southeast Kiu Khang Wai Nòng Ngua marked the frontier with Chiang Khòng.[38]

On the north there was the Hua Pong customs post and the Thap Phœng customs post; to the west the Thap Yang and the Thap Mak customs post; / to the south, the Tha Wang customs post; and to the east the Hat Luang customs post; and, inside, there were the Hang Dòn Mun and Tha Sai customs posts.[39]

Cao Müang Sai 9 *panna*; the left division, 7 *panna*; the right division, 8 *panna*. The Outer *panna*: M. Phayak[40] [1 *panna*], M. Rai 1,500 *panna*; M. Luang[41] 1,500 *panna*; / Phukha 1; M. Len Nüa included in the 9 *panna*; the ruler of M. Len Tai included in the 8 *panna*; Khwa Dong Phalæo 500 *na*. These people were subject to the corvée, and they had 12 judges, 1 officer as messenger for the judiciary, 1 officer in charge of the granary, 1 officer in charge of munitions, /f° 3.17/ 2 officers in charge of the royal palace, and 1 for foreign affairs. Such was the allocation of the territories of Chiang Sæn; altogether 32 *panna*.[42]

As for the allocation of territories dedicated to the Religion, those persons dedicated were to perform [their services] to the religious institutions, as specified in the instruments of dedication written on stone.[43] As for the freemen / of Chiang Sæn, they were organized in levies, in *buak*, *kò*, *khum*, and *tò*.[44] As for those skilled with gold and silver, and drum smiths, they were to present [the fruits of their labors] to whoever ruled the domain. Similarly for ivory lost when elephants died,

---

38 We can identify very few of these features that are supposed to delineate the frontiers of Chiang Sæn. In general, we can gauge its size by noting that the domain did *not* extend to Keng Tung, Chiang Khòng, and the Sipsong Panna (the "Hò"). See map.

39 The localities in this paragraph are even more difficult to place than those above. In general, the main purpose of the paragraph is to list the customs posts (*kang*) where, presumably, fees were imposed on the movement of goods.

40 M. Phayak: see map 5.

41 Probably Müang Luang Phukha? In present-day Laos.

42 Is there some way of obtaining the total of 32 *panna* mentioned here? There is a first group, presumably of "inner" *panna*, amounting to 9 + 7 + 8 = 24 *panna*. The "outer" *panna* comprise a maximum of 7.5 *panna* (assuming that those "included" within the first group are counted a second time. The 500 *na* of Khwa Dong Phalæo is one-half a *panna*. This is a fascinating paragraph for suggesting the shape of local administration.

43 This is quite unequivocal: mi tam sima carük.

44 Manpower levies of some sort. Clearly, Notton had no clearer idea of what these might have been than we do, for he also left them untranslated.

/ elephants, horses, laborers, cattle, beehives and wax, iron forges, distilleries, sweets manufactories, charcoal-burners, everything hanging from trees, lacquers, the produce of wet and dry rice fields and from orchards, and fish and game, all produced in the territory of the ruler were to be presented to the ruler. /

Watchtower Drums for the Three Cities

Cao Phraya Sæn Phu had a village built north of Dòn Thæn [island in the Mekong]. One day, Phraya Sæn Phu slept in that village. In the watch before dawn, he had a dream in which a man said to him, "I have fashioned three drums: one to keep / in Chiang Mai, one to keep in Chiang Rai, and one to keep in Chiang Sæn." Phraya Sæn Phu awoke. In the morning, he opened his eyes and looked up and saw a tree floating by the Dòn Thæn [island], so he had it fetched. He recognized it as *mai du* fine timber,[45] so cut it into three pieces. /fº 3.18/ The first he had fashioned into a watch drum for the tower in the center of Chiang Mai; [the second] was for the watch tower in the center of Chiang Rai; and the third for the watch tower in the center of Chiang Sæn, at Wat Phra Luang.[46]

Death of Sæn Phu, [AD 1336?]

Cao Sæn Phu had ruled for seven years when he fell ill,[47] and a physician was fetched to a secluded place. The physician / said that the prince's age was advanced, and would reach its end within that very year. All the councilors devised a strategy to have two very large rafts carry [a royal] dwelling to show that he was still healthy, and float it in the middle of the Mekong, / thus not revealing to anyone that the ruler was ill, for if people knew, then rulers of other countries would find out, and would invade the country. When [the palace] had been built, [the ruler] entered it on the rafts in / the middle of the Mekong, and the rafts were towed on the Mekong from

---

45 "*Pterocarpus macrocarpus* (*Leguminosæ*), a large, beautiful timber tree" (McF, 333).

46 Every town, and even temples, might have such towers to, among other things, serve as a "clock" and watchtower.

47 Notton (p. 80, n. 1) notes that PY says that Sæn Phu reigned seven years in Chiang Sæn until falling ill and dying in cs 696 [ad 1334] at the age of sixty.

the Phra Hin landing to Dòn Thæn [island] and to Tha Nang [on the other bank], not letting other boats pass.

After three days, the ruler died. His remains were placed in a golden urn, which was floated in the middle of the / Mekong for two months, while the news was communicated to Phraya Kham Fu. Kham Fu appointed his son, Cao Thao Phayu, to take charge of Chiang Mai, while [Kham Fu] took an armed force of 240,000 men of Chiang Mai, Fang, and Chiang Rai to Chiang Sæn. All the councilors /f° 3.19/ consulted a chicken-bone oracle,[48] and then decided to have the remains of the late ruler kept in the old city, north of the mouth of the Kok [River],[49] near the market landing, where a large hole was dug and a large building built to cover it. Everyone brought their boats there to moor by the market, and they brought the golden urn ashore there, so everyone knew that the ruler had died, / and they helped move the golden urn into the structure. There it was adorned with gold and silver accouterments and golden bags on each side.

Then some nobles and people were assigned to care for it, some fifty households; and later they were dedicated / as litter-bearers, twenty households for the Sangharaja[50] of Wat Phra Luang[51] and thirty to maintain the remains of Sæn Phu. Cao Sæn Phu was aged exactly sixty years when he went to the world beyond, and he was the fifth of the dynasty. At that time it was year 700 of the Era, a *pæk yi* year (1338/39).

---

48 Foretelling the future on the basis of chicken bones is well-known among Tai peoples. It is found in the Sipsong Panna in a text presented by Li Fu-i to Kraisri Nimmanhaeminda. The best description is found in Renu Wichasin, "Kanthamnai kraduk kai khòng khon Thai bang klum," in *Ekkasan prakòp kansammana rüang Khon Thai nòk prathet: phromdæn khwamru* (Bangkok, Kasetsat University, 1989), pp. 87–117. Notton (p. 80, n. 2) adds a reference to Henri Roux, "Deux tribus de la région de Phongsaly," BEFEO 24 (1924), p. 478.

49 Mouth of the Kok River: The same toponym appears in the *Nan Chronicle*. What is this "old city," north of the Kok? Perhaps Chiang Sæn Nòi or Wiang Prüksa. About 3 km. downstream from Chiang Sæn.

50 More than an abbot is indicated: probably some local ecclesiastical chief. See Yuphin Khemmuk, *Phutthasatsana nai Lan Na* (M.A. thesis, Silpakorn Univ., 1989).

51 Perhaps Wat Chedi Luang, in the middle of Chiang Sæn; built by King Sæn Phu.

Conflict With Nan

Phraya Kham / Fu had not ruled long in Chiang Sæn when he invited the Kao[52] ruler of M. Nan to join him in attacking Phraya Ngam Müang of Phayao. The two rulers took their forces to pillage both cities[53] of Phraya Ngam Müang. Ngam Müang was able to flee. The men of / Phraya Kham Fu got much good plunder, e.g., gems and rings, silver and gold, which they brought to Cao Kham Fu, and Kham Fu did not share them with the Kao ruler of Nan. The Nan people were very offended, and Khun Ngua urged the ruler of Nan to attack Kham Fu.

There were two retainers of Kham Fu named Ong Khwan Kham and Sæn Pha Nòng, who argued /f° 3.20/ that they had sufficient plunder, and urged Kham Fu to withdraw to Chiang Rai. He consulted a chicken oracle,[54] specifically the Luang Man Than,

which had been consulted since the time when King Mangrai consulted a chicken oracle when he fought and defeated Phraya Ba [of Hariphunchai].[55] This time, the Kan Thom [officiant] had someone go into the market to cause total confusion / so that the Nan Kao were unable to buy or sell food. Phraya Kham Fu withdrew his force to Chiang Sæn. The Kao ruler of Nan brought his force up to Chiang Sæn, and then withdrew it to take and plunder Fang.

[Now,] Phraya Kham Fu was angry, and mustered his forces to pursue and fight the Kao of Nan, led by Sæn Pha Nòng / riding a royally-caparisoned elephant. One of the retainers of the Kao of Nan named Nai Rong saw Sæn Pha Nòng and thought that [Pha Nòng] was Phraya Kham Fu, so he goaded his elephant closer and recognized the general Sæn Pha Nòng. Nai Rong goaded his elephant closer

---

52 The Kao were the Tai people of the Nan River valley, apparently mentioned in the famous thirteenth-century inscription (face IV, line 1) of King Ramkhamhaeng of Sukhothai. See A.B. Griswold and Prasert na Nagara, *Epigraphic and Historical Studies* (Bangkok, 1992), p. 278, fn. 115 (s.v. Kāv).

53 There is a cluster of old cities around Phayao. See Sucit Wongthet, *Müang Phayao* (Bangkok, 1984). Can this be the same Ngam Müang who was a contemporary of Mangrai?

54 Unlike the chicken-bone oracle, this is a technique of divination using a live chicken (*swai kai*). One of us (AW) has heard tell of this by Tai Lü elders in Chiang Kham district of Phayao. According to this technique, a baby chick is released on magical cloths on which there is writing, and its path spells out the desired result. See Yuphin Khemmuk et al., "Satsana khwamchüa læ prapheni khòng chao Thai Lü: Süksa muban That, Ban Yuan, Ban Wæn, amphœ Chiang Kham, cangwat Chiang Rai," in *Thai Lü: Chiang Kham* (Chiang Mai, 1986), p. 118.

55 This is *not* mentioned in fascicles 1 or 2 of this text.

to engage the elephant of Sæn Pha Nòng. Nai Rong's lance slashed / at Sæn Pha Nong's elephant by the side of the mouth, and the latter broke contact and fled. Nai Rong followed, and cut off the tail of the royal elephant. Phraya Kham Fu brought his army to rescue Sæn Pha Nòng. [Another] retainer of the Kao of Nan, named Yòn Nguak, / engaged in an elephant duel with Ong Khwan Kham. Phraya Kham Fu then had the gongs and Victory Drum sounded, rallying his forces to surround and take Ong Khwan Kham. The forces of the Kao ruler of Nan were broken and fled. Kham Fu led his forces to pursue and kill them, and many of the Kao men of Nan died. Phraya Kham Fu pursued the army of the Kao ruler /f° 3.21/ of Nan, as far as M. Ngæ, and then withdrew back to Chiang Sæn. As for the Kao ruler of Nan, he took his men by way of M. Salao and the districts of Phayao, en route [back] to Nan.

War With Phræ, 1340/41

In the *kot si* year, s. 702 (1340/41), when Phraya Kham Fu was thirty-eight years of age, he led / his forces to take and plunder M. Phræ,[56] but failed and returned by way of Nakhòn Khelang, appointing Sæn Mai to head the rear guard. The Phræ people sent an army intending to cut off the tail of the elephant of Phraya Kham Fu. Kham Fu had Sæn Ta Chuai and Sæn Mai fight the Phræ force, but / they failed and withdrew. Cao Phraya Kham Fu brought his forces back to Chiang Sæn. Thereafter, Cao Phraya Kham Fu did not lead his armies out anywhere. He enjoyed the royal sovereignty peacefully in Chiang Sæn. /

The King and the Ugly Merchant

In that era there was a merchant named Ngua Hong,[57] a good and wealthy man, but ugly in physical appearance. He had many young adolescent wives, so beautiful in every way as to excite the passions of all men. That merchant lived in / Chiang Kham, a district of Chiang Sæn. Kham Fu regarded him as his friend, [like] a member of the same household, and they loved each other dearly. Whatever the ruler wanted, Ngua Hong gave him; and whatever Ngua Hong wanted, the ruler gave it to him. The councilors and retainers of the ruler, and the elders and retainers

---

56 Phræ/Phlæ: modern town and province by that name. See map.
57 A fifth son.

of /fº 3.22/ Ngua Hong, did everything together. Whenever the ruler visited Ngua Hong in Chiang Kham district, he went to Ngua Hong's home, and Ngua Hong had his wives bathe the ruler's feet. Ngua Hong's wives considered the ruler to be very handsome, and came to be filled with carnal desire for him. Whenever Ngua Hong came to the ruler's / palace, he stayed in the royal dwelling, and the ruler had an attractive noble[woman] or wife take him away to bathe Ngua Hong's feet, [but] they considered Ngua Hong to be unattractive, and vied to avoid the task and not one of them developed any desire for Ngua Hong. The retainers of the two men liked each other, and agreed that, / as they loved each other, even to the death, they would never be disloyal to one another, and any who was disloyal would die, if on land by being eaten by wild tigers or bears or wild ogres, or if on water by being eaten by an aquatic ogress. / Agreeing so, the retainers of the two lords thus swore to each other.

Some time later, one day Phraya Kham Fu, feeling mischievous, decided he wanted to toy with his friend, namely Ngua Hong, to dispel his melancholy; and so he took an adult monkey, completely shaved, and painted skin on him with gum from gum trees, to which he stuck [white] cotton / to look like body hair. He placed him in a box, well-sealed, and he had two servants, who were comedians, sent to present the box to Ngua Hong, [with the message] that the king had a small servant who was very handsome whom he was sending to him in this box. [The king's] two messengers discussed [their mission], remarking, "For sure! /fº 3.23/ The merchant will beat us if he opens it!" They surveyed their escape routes.

At dusk, Ngua Hong opened the box and saw the monkey, which was quite ugly with the cotton stuck to it. He was angry, and slammed his gate shut, threatening to beat the messengers. They were able to escape through the floorboards.

Ngua Hong / hurriedly summoned his horse to pursue them. The groom was a friend of the two fugitives, and prepared the horse as slowly as he could. He pretended to hurry, slowly dressing the horse with bridle and saddle. Ngua Hong said, "Are you preparing / the horse?" The groom replied, "You're in a hurry, so I'm hurrying too. I'm putting on the bridle and saddle." Then he rushed to prepare the horse as usual. The merchant said, "Open the gate! I'm chasing those two malefactors who fled!" The gateman pretended / to open the gate, but slowly, fumbling with the latch. Ngua Hong had light shone on the gate, and saw that it was still shut; so he said to the gateman, "It's locked!" The gatekeeper replied, "It's very dark. I'm hurrying to open the gate. I'll hammer the bolt open to open it for you!" /

By the time it was open, the two had fled—no one knew where. The idiom, "You're hurrying, I'm hurrying, the horse is saddling" dates from that time.

Phraya Kham Fu knew his friend was offended, so he went to Chiang Kham to calm his rage, [telling him] not /f° 3.24/ to be angry. Phraya Kham Fu returned [to his friend's] home, and one of Ngua Hong's wives, a very beautiful woman, came to bathe his feet and led him into the house, and excited him carnally. The lord was smitten with lust and lost his control, and hungered to sleep with the lady. He signaled her with his hands to / signify their promise. The lust arose that night, when the lord bedded the lady for the whole night. The merchant did not know that the lord had bedded his wife.

Six or seven days later, the lord went to wash his hair in the Chiang Kham River.[58] A large water ogress / came up from under a cliff and stole away the lord back into her lair.

Everyone, including the king's councilors, diligently searched for him, but found him nowhere. After seven days, the ruler's body surfaced, and everyone knew that Phraya Kham Fu was dead. Phraya Kham Fu / was Ratchabut[59] for twenty-five years, and at the age of forty-seven years passed on to the next world. He was the sixth of the dynasty.

Phayu Becomes King, 1345/46

All the councilors took the remains of the ruler to Chiang Sæn. The great merchant was disconsolate. All the councilors and the great merchant had / the news of Kham Fu's death passed to Cao Phò Thao Phayu, his son, in Chiang Mai. Phayu then had his own son, Cao Phò Thao Kü Na, take care of Chiang Mai, and Cao Phraya Phayu went to conduct the funeral of his father, Kham Fu, in /f° 3.25/ Chiang Sæn for one month and fifteen days until completed.

The prince then took his father's bones and deposited them in the city of Chiang Mai, near the Suan Dòk Gate,[60] where he had a *cetiya* built to enshrine them; and he built a temple there for the monks to live in. At the time, everyone going to the

---

58 Mæ Chiang Kham: river, Chiang Kham district, Phayao province; flowing into the Mekong.

59 Literally, this just means a royal son; but it can also be a title in the line of succession to the rulership. In some cases it is the functional equivalent of *uparaja*.

60 Notton (p. 84, n.3) says that PY says it was 100 fathoms from the Suan Dòk Gate.

market saw the temple, which came to be called the Li Chiang Phra. / Later the Buddhasihiṅga [Image] was in that temple, and it came to be called Wat Phra Sing, to the present day.[61]

At that time, Cao Phò Thao Phayu was twenty-nine years old, and the councilors consecrated him as ruler in Chiang Mai, / in the *dap rao* year, s. 707 (1345/46).

Upon assuming his reign, the prince went to invite Mahā Abhayaculathera,[62] with ten disciples, to come from Hariphunchai to stay at Wat Li Chiang Phra [i.e., Wat Phra Sing]. Cao Phraya Phayu in ruling was faithful to the ten kingly virtues,[63] / and delighted in the Teachings of the Holy Buddha. He had two sons, the elder [of whom] was Phò Thao Kü Na, the Ratchabut, by Cintrathewi, who was the daughter of Cao Ngua Thœng, the ruler of Chiang Khòng.

This Ratchabut had several names: at birth / after a month he was named Phò Thao Phantu, then Phò Thao Vesa Phu, then Phò Thao Kü Na, because his father had him rule a hundred-million *na*; then Thao Kü Na. His younger son was named Phò Thao Maha Phrom.

When the elder son /f° 3.26/ came of age, his father Cao Phayu had him go to rule Chiang Rai.[64] Cao Phraya Phayu was Ratchabut to the age of twenty-nine years, then was ruler for twenty-eight years, and went to the next world at the age of fifty-seven years./ He was the seventh of the dynasty.

Kü Na Becomes King, 1367/68

The councilors then consecrated Phò Thao Kü Na, then aged / forty years, as ruler in Chiang Mai in the *müang met* year, s. 729 (1367/68). Cao Phraya Kü Na enjoyed the royal sovereignty with justice and deep faith in the Teachings of the

---

61 The *cetiya* in which the ashes of King Kham Fu were enshrined was at Wat Phra Sing in Chiang Mai. Earlier in the twentieth century, when the great *vihara* of Wat Phra Sing was being built under the leadership of Khruba Sriwichai, three urns filled with precious objects were found there. See the photograph in Notton, *Annales du Siam III* (Paris, 1932). The precious objects have since disappeared.

62 On early religious renovations, see Yuphin Khemmuk, *Phutthasatsana nai Lan Na*.

63 *thotsaphitratchatham*: almsgiving, observing the precepts, liberality, honesty, gentleness, asceticism, equanimity, refraining from oppression, tolerance, and even-temperedness.

64 Notton (p. 85, n. 5) follows PY in saying that Phayu founded Wat Bun Yün at Chiang Sæn in cs 729 (ad 1357).

Lord Buddha. He built temples, / *cetiya*, kuti, and *vihara*, lavishing great splendor upon them. Cao Phraya Kü Na was deeply versed in the *dharmaśāstra, rajaśāstra*, and history; he was versed in the ten arts, for example, *gajjaśāstra*—namely, the qualities / of elephants.⁶⁵ The rulers of foreign countries in great numbers presented tribute to him, and at the beginning of each year without fail envoys brought tribute to present to him. In his time, M. Ping Chiang Mai was blessed with brave generals; the country and all its people / were peaceful and happy.

Cao Thao Kü Na had one son by Lady Yasuntharathewi, who was the granddaughter of Phò Thao Ngua Thœng of M. Chiang Khòng. When a royal son was born, the rulers of many foreign countries presented tribute to him. This omen was the reason why Cao Phraya /fº 3.27/ Kü Na named his son Cao Phò Thao Sæn Müang Ma ("a hundred-thousand countries came").

Kü Na's Death and Delayed Cremation

Cao Phraya Kü Na had a village⁶⁶ built outside the city to the north, next to what was later Wat Phram. The prince had enjoyed the royal sovereignty in Chiang Mai for twenty-one years when, at the age of sixty-one years, he passed to the world beyond, the eighth of the dynasty. / Before he was cremated, the remains of Kü Na were kept on a field in a village north of the city, by Wat Phram.⁶⁷

Treason of Maha Phrom

When Phò Thao Maha Phrom, who ruled Chiang Rai, heard the news of his elder brother's, Kü Na's, death, and that he had not yet been cremated, he determined to usurp [power] / from his nephew, Cao Sæn Müang Ma, who ruled Chiang Mai. He devised a stratagem to go and attend the funerary rites of his elder brother. He brought his forces from Chiang Rai to Chæ Sak, and dismissed the officer who ruled there, and the forces of the forts, and put his own men in charge everywhere. Then

---

65   All these are Pali/Sanskrit terms for the Indic arts and sciences; together they tell us that by the standards of the day Kü Na was very well-educated.

66   PY says it was a palace, according to Notton (p. 86, n. 2).

67   Location not certain. In the area north of the Chang Phüak Gate. Kü Na seems to have preferred this area, where he lived and died.

he came to Chiang Mai, encamping his army at / Nòng Pha Chi, later called Nòng Pha Di, next to this temple. Then Cao Thao Maha Phrom reported to the Chief Minister, a man named Sæn Pha Nòng,[68] pretending that he had come to conduct the funerary ceremonies for his elder brother.

The Brave Women

Sæn Pha Nòng discerned the [real] reason, that Thao Maha Phrom had come to usurp power from his nephew; so he replied, / "I must first go and prepare, with our lord." He hurriedly assembled a force of ten thousand to defend the city and consulted a chicken oracle. He got the Khun Sæn Müang Ma and the Bòn Bang Khun Phom Sæn, so he sounded the *yong gong* and the Victory Drum in noisy alert. /fº 3.28/ Thao Maha Phrom heard it, and realized, "He is not one of us." So he went to round up the people of Wiang Kum Kam, but was able to take only all the women and valuables, and then went to sleep at the Ai Chang Market,[69] and then hurried back by the banks of the Ping. [The women's] husbands hastened to Sæn Pha Nòng. Sæn Pha Nòng had volunteers garrison the city, / namely Mün Rok Nakhòn with eighty-six thousand men.

Cao Sæn Pha Nòng took a force of seven thousand men in pursuit of the group of Thao Maha Phrom in the darkness. Cao Sæn Pha Nòng hurriedly left the city with his force in pursuit of Thao Maha Phrom in the middle of the night. The Kum Kam men stealthily rejoined their wives and children. / Their wives and children heard the sounds of their menfolk. The women took up the swords of Thao Maha Phrom's men and set upon these retainers, many of whom died; then they took up their things and sought out their menfolk. At the place where Maha Phrom's retainers died, / people later built a *cetiya* and a temple, which came to be called the Temple of the Brave Women, to the present day.

Cao Sæn Pha Nòng then had a loud huzzah sounded and his men formed up into a force to pursue Thao Maha Phrom. Thao Maha Phrom arose from his resting place and quickly dressed and mounted his elephant and / took his force and fled

---

68 Name the same as Nan ruler, fº 3.20 above.
69 Ai Chang Market: location uncertain. Perhaps the market of Wiang Kum Kam.

[south] by way of M. Fòm, going by way of Nakhòn [Lampang], fleeing to take refuge with Phraya Bòrommatraicak in M. Ayotthiya.⁷⁰

Corpses Cannot Go Through City Gates

Cao Sæn Pha Nòng then returned, and said to his officers, "We have not yet had time to do the funerary honors to the remains of our lord. Right? Cao Phò Thao Maha Phrom /f° 3.29/ is summoning the lord of the South, Bòrommatraicak, to help him seize Chiang Mai; and [we] cannot let him do so. We should hold the remains of our lord king in the city, but it's not right to enter [by way of] the gates. We'd have misfortune ever thereafter." Therefore together they cut through the [city] walls nearest to Wat Phram and brought in the corpse of King Kü Na in a / golden urn. They built a bridge across the city moat and took [the urn] to the Chiang Khwang quarter.⁷¹ Then he appointed Mün Lok to look after Nakhòn Khelang [Lampang].

Two months and twelve days after Thao Maha Phrom went to seek the protection of the ruler of the South, Phò Thao Maha Phrom, with the ruler of the South, brought an army up by way of / Nakhòn [Lampang]. Mün Lok mounted a first-class elephant to engage him by Wat Chiang Phum. The Southern people's elephants took fright and fell into a well there. Then the Southern people took their army out to seek the city on the Ping [Chiang Mai]. Sæn Pha Nòng took an army out to engage the Southerners. The Southerners were broken, and fled back to the South. /

Sæn Müang Ma Becomes King of Chiang Mai, 1400

The body of King Kü Na remained in its state for six months, and then Kü Na's body underwent the funeral ceremonies. Then the royal councilors, including Sæn Pha Nòng, consecrated Cao Sæn Müang Ma, aged fourteen years,⁷² to rule and reign

---

70 Ayudhya, capital of Siam. Usually spelled this way in this text. The Siamese king is Phra Bòrommatrailokanat (r. 1448–1488).
71 Chiang Khwang was the royal quarter of Chiang Mai, in front of Wat Chiang Man.
72 Jkm. says twenty-three years (p. 127). There he is called Lakkhapurâgama.

in / Chiang Mai, in the *kot cai* year, s. 762, on Friday the full-moon day of the eighth month, a Thai *pœk yi* day.[73]

Maha Phrom Returns to the North

At that time, Cao Thao Maha Phrom, who had taken refuge with the ruler of the South, sinned against his protector, seducing the wife of the Southern ruler. The ruler of the South distrusted him, and sent Thao Maha Phrom back [north]. The wife of the ruler /f° 3.30/ of the South stole the Sihiṅga Buddha [image] and gave it to Thao Maha Phrom, so he easily brought the image with him, as is explained in the *Chronicle of the Sihiṅga Buddha*.[74] When Thao Maha Phrom arrived, Cao Sæn Müang Ma [at first] did not believe ill of him, and sent his uncle, Cao Thao Maha Phrom, to rule / Chiang Rai as before.

Sæn Müang Ma Attacks Sukhothai

Tadā param. [Some time] thereafter, the ruler of Sukhothai offended against Phraya Bòrommatraicak of Ayotthiya. Bòrommatraicak took his principality and placed it under the protection of Cao Sæn Müang Ma. Cao Sæn Müang Ma raised an army, saying / he would go to take Sukhothai. He encamped his army outside the city. Cao Phraya Sæn Müang Ma did not go out to fight, but stayed to take the city [i.e., Sukhothai]. The lord of Sukhothai came out and communicated with a senior woman,[75] acting as an envoy who came out to talk to / the ruler of Sukhothai, who told him that he did not want to fight the ruler of the South.

At dusk, the lord of Sukhothai prepared his army to fight Cao Sæn Müang Ma. The engaging force was broken and fled, and Cao Sæn Müang Ma lost elephants, horses, and most of his men, and withdrew to Thap Salit. / On his way, they

---

73 If this is to be a *kot cai* year, this has to be either 722 or 782, but not 762. If it is kot si 762, then it could have been Wednesday, fourteenth waxing of the eighth month, a *pœk yi* day; 7 April 1400.

74 The author of the Chiang Mai history is telling the reader that, if he or she wishes to know more of the history of the Sihinga Buddha image, they can read further on the subject in the *Sihiṅgabuddhanidāna*, the Chronicle of the Sihiṅga Buddha. The author has made a clear decision to focus on political and military, not religious history.

75 Probably a daughter or wife of the ruler, who was acquainted with political affairs.

recovered two of the missing, Ai Op and Yi Ra, who carried Cao Sæn Müang Ma [on a litter] until they reached Chiang Mai. Cao Sæn Müang Ma took care of them as his Right and Left guards.[76] They lived south of Chiang Som, on the eastern side. There they fashioned two white elephant statues /f° 3.31/ which were placed to the left and right of the thoroughfare, and people have had to pass between them, ever since ancient times; and those two elephant statues have never been razed.

Then Cao Sæn Müang Ma performed works of merit; for example, he cast the Cao Sikkhi Buddha image,[77] enshrined at Wat Kan Thom[78] and donated land / as rice for the image, 100,000 cowries [worth], and 100,000 [worth] as alms for the votaries of the image.

Building of Chedi Luang

Here we will return to the story. When King Kü Na died, his soul was not at rest, and he became a tree spirit (*rukkhadevata*) in a banyan tree along the road to Pagân.[79] There was a / group of Chiang Mai merchants who went to trade at Pagân who on their return trip stopped to rest in the shade of that tree. The tree spirit Kü Na showed himself to them, and said, "I am Phraya Kü Na. I lived as ruler in Chiang / Mai, fond of the special knowledge of *Gajjaśāstra*—that is, I was a doctor of elephantry. On dying, I became a spirit in this tree. I cannot be born in the World of the Gods (*devaloka*), [so] I ask you merchants to tell my son, Cao Sæn Müang Ma, that he should build a *cetiya* in the middle of the city [of Chiang Mai] so tall that people can see it / from 2,000 fathoms away. Please [ceremonially] pour water to dedicate the merit to me so that I can be reborn in the Realm of the Gods."

Having listened to this, the merchants went to tell Cao Sæn Müang Ma as instructed. So Cao Sæn Müang Ma had an area cleared in the center of the city, south of his palace, had a stone base prepared, /f° 3.32/ and erected a [ceremonial] *Bodhi* tree, its trunk of silver and its leaves and crest of gold, as tall as the king himself. Then Cao Sæn Müang Ma cast a Buddha image of gold, and one of silver,

---

76   *phuak chang*. Perhaps military leaders.

77   The Cao Sikkhi Buddha image is named after one of the previous incarnations of the Buddha. It is carved of black stone, and is now in Lampang.

78   Notton (p. 90, n.2) here has Wat Klat Thom, glossed as Wat Kat Thom in the footnote.

79   That is, on the trade route to Burma.

and went to [place them] in the base of the *cetiya*, where the two Buddha images were placed with the *Bodhi* tree, and / placed implements of worship before the *Bodhi* tree and the Buddha images. The prince then built a *cetiya* covering them; but it was finished only to eaves-height when, after he had been building the *cetiya* for ten years, he died, at the age of thirty-nine, after a reign of twenty-five years. He was the ninth in the dynasty [of Mangrai].

Cao / Sæn Müang Ma had two sons, of different mothers. One was Thao Yi Kum Kam, so called because this prince was born in Wiang Kum Kam. The other was Thao Sam Fang Kæn. This prince was [so named] because when his mother was three months pregnant [with him], Cao Sæn Müang Ma took the lady on a tour / of his country, into the Sipsong Panna, traveling from one *panna* to the next, until in seven months they came to Fang Kæn Panna. It was in the tenth month [of her pregnancy], and she gave birth to a royal prince [there], so he was named Sam Fang Kæn for that reason.

Here we will tell of the mother of the prince Sam Fang Kæn. That lady was of a noble family, and quite beautiful. She / was a lady-in-waiting in the service of the queen mother (*mahathewi*), the mother of Cao Sæn Müang Ma.

One day, when bringing a face-towel to the queen mother, who was bathing, she saw a sparrow alight before her and walk seven steps. Later, the queen mother sent the lady to /f° 3.33/ the Mahāsvāmī Buddhañāna at Wat Chiang Yün. The lady told the monk about seeing the sparrow walking, and he said that the lady was a devotee; that she should not tell anyone, but that she would be a queen mother like the queen mother was now—but she should not tell anyone. Later, the queen mother used the lady to seek out Cao / Sæn Müang Ma, her son. Cao Sæn Müang Ma took the lady and slept with her, and soon she was three months pregnant. The queen mother was suspicious, and asked, "By whom are you pregnant?" The lady replied, "I am pregnant by our lord the king, your son." The queen mother / then gave her a lady's accouterments and sent her to be a wife of Cao Sæn Müang Ma, her son; and the king took the lady with him when he went to tour his country, as we have seen; and when they came to the *panna* of Fang Kæn, their son was born, in the *kat sai* year, / s. 750.[80]

---

80   ad 1388/89. This seems to be out of sequence. A year that would fit the *kat sai* designation would be s. 751 = ad 1389/90. Fang Kæn Panna today is t. Inthakhin, Mæ Tæng district.

As for the older son [by a different mother], Phò Cao Phò Thao Yi Kum Kam⁸¹ when he was twelve years old, Cao Phraya Sæn Müang Ma, his father, had him go and eat Chiang Rai. By the time Prince Sam Fang Kæn, the younger brother, / was thirteen years old, he was his father's delight; and when Cao Phraya Sæn Müang Ma was dying, he chose Cao Sam Fang Kæn to reign in his stead. Cao Sæn Müang Ma was thirty-nine years old when he passed to the next world.

Sam Fang Kæn Becomes King of Chiang Mai, 1401

All the royal officers consecrated Prince Sam Fang Kæn, aged /f° 3.34/ thirteen years, to rule, in the *ruang sai* year, s. 763, on the full-moon day of the eighth month, a Friday, Thai *kot sanga* day.⁸²

The prince becoming king, the lady his mother became the queen mother, named Tilokacukthewi, following the prophecy of the Mahāswāmī. The king went to build a beautiful temple where / he had been born in the Fang Kæn Panna, named Wat Phœng;⁸³ and it stands there to the present day.

Wat Chedi Luang Again

As for the *cetiya* which his father, Cao Sæn Müang Ma, had been building, it was still not finished, being only to eaves-height. His mother, the queen mother, established her residence in Ban Suan Hè, and she regularly went to supervise the building of the *cetiya*; so she opened a gate / where the king had gone for the construction of the *cetiya*, called the Suan Hè Gate.⁸⁴ Being ancient, [this gate] could not be sealed up. The great *cetiya* was called the great reliquary.⁸⁵ In the time of Cao Phraya [Ti]lok,

---

81 Phò Cao Phò Thao: probably an error; should be Phò Thao.

82 This date also does not work. 763 *was* indeed a *ruang sai* year, but there was no Friday kot *sanga* day around the middle of *any* month in that year. Perhaps Saturday twelfth waxing of the eleventh month, 23 July 1401.

83 *Jkm.* (p. 129) names the temple Puracchanna, which Dhanit Yupho in a footnote glosses as Wat Mung Muang.

84 It is not known which city gate is intended here.

85 *ku luang*. It was not called a *cetiya*, and did not enshrine the Buddha's bodily relics so it was not called a *that*. It came to be called Chedi Luang in the time of King Tilok.

the great reliquary fell down, so Cao Phraya Lok had Mün Damphra Khot[86] take / laterite to rebuild it in the *pœk set* year, s. 800, tenth waning of the second month, a Thursday, Thai *ka pao* day, *ræk* Kot 12;[87] and they built it through three years until it was completed. At its base it was 27 fathoms wide, and it was 41 fathoms high; so it has been called 'the Great Cetiya" (Chedi Luang to the present day. /

Yi Kum Kam Foments Renewed War With Sukhothai

At that time, Cao Phò Thao Yi Kum Kam, who ruled Chiang Rai, thought, "I should be king of Chiang Mai; but the nobles all agreed that Cao Sam Fang Kæn should rule there." He raised an army from Chiang Rai to seize power from his younger brother in Chiang Mai. He failed, and took /f° 3.35/ his partisans to flee and take refuge with Phraya Sai Lü[88] in M. Sukhothai.

So Phraya Sai Lü raised an army in support of Cao Phò Thao Yi Kum Kam [in his bid to] take control of Chiang Mai. The army came up by way of Phayao, intending to seize and plunder Phayao; so they set up an observation tower at Nòng Tao 12 [fathoms] high and sufficiently wide / to hold 700 men. The people of Phayao then melted off the copper covering of Wat Mahaphon[89] and cast a cannon of 6 *kamnak* units of gold, with a cannon base four fathoms wide, and they sacrificed an albino buffalo. They fired volleys at the tower. Two hundred / of the Southern men in the fort died.

Seeing the bad situation, Phraya Sai Lü had Phò Thao Yi Kum Kam lead a force up by way of Ban Chæ Phran[90] to Chiang Rai, so Cao Phò Thao Yi Kum Kam took charge of the army of Phraya Sai Lü. Cao Phò Thao Yi Kum Kam commanding the army of Phraya Sai Lü came back by way of Fang / to Chiang Mai, reaching the Chiang Ruak Market[91] on Saturday, the Thai day *ruang met*.[92] There they greatly

---

86 This man's title indicates something like an expertise in public works (construction).

87 Another date that does not work. 800 (1438/39) was a *poek sanga* year. The nearest *poek set* was 780; but again there are no Thursday *ka pao* days in that year which fit with the other data.

88 Phraya Sai Lü Thai, king of Sukhothai.

89 There was a Wat Mahaphon in Phayao.

90 Ban Chæ Phran is between Phayao and Chiang Rai.

91 Market by the Chiang Rüak Gate, which today is called the Tha Phæ Gate.

92 The only Saturday *ruang met* day in 800 is equivalent to 7 March 1439.

frightened the market. The ruler encamped his army at the *hiang* forest[93] and sent a man in to bear the message that "We will have the Phò Thao Yi Kum Kam, the elder brother, rule Chiang Mai. If you / will not agree, we will fight you." The Chiang Mai people replied, "You may wish to have Thao Yi Kum Kam eat Chiang Mai, but we will not have him; so come ahead and fight us." The Southerners said, "Then fight it is, and the winner takes Chiang Mai. Whoever is wounded in the neck is defeated." So one of the Southern men, /f° 3.36/ who was a skilled swordsman, and one Chiang Mai man, named Han Yòt Cai Phek, the most valorous swordsman, set about dueling with their swords, meeting in the Chiang Khwang [ward], each with two swords. Han Yòt Cai Phek [finally] slashed the toe of the Southerner, and it appeared that the Chiang Mai man had won the encounter.

There was / another Chiang Mai man named Phek Yot who collected people aged sixteen to thirty years, two hundred of them, and gathered at Dòi Suthep, looking for Southerners seeking fodder for elephants and horses, and assaulting stragglers [separated from the South forces] and killing them and cutting off their heads, which they then presented to King / Sam Fang Kæn every day.

King Sam Fang Kæn said, "This [Phek Yot] is just a boy, but is very brave." So he organized four groups to do the same, who presented heads to him every day, and they were thus called "boys" to this very day.[94]

One day, Phraya Sai Lü prepared to / capture Chiang Mai. He was asleep, and in his dreams he saw an elephant chasing a lion. He had invested Chiang Mai for seven days, so he moved to the foot of Mount Seven Fountains.[95] He went to wash his hair at Dòi Pha Lat Luang.[96] Then, villages of Lawa and Kachin people[97] came to dwell in the city of Chiang Rüa. Cao Sæn Pha Nòng / had them set up a fort [stretching] from Hua Lin to the foot of Mount Seven Fountains, and had about two hundred carts arranged in a line, each bearing a black, red, white, or yellow banner at the head of every cart.

---

93 A forest of a certain kind of trees, outside the walls of Chiang Mai. Notton (p. 93) simply says that "The prince encamped at Pa Hieo (cemetary) . . ."

94 In later times, these *dek chai* ("boys") came to be high-ranking military men.

95 A small hill at the (east) base of Dòi Suthep, just north of the present site of Chiang Mai University.

96 Small waterfall there above where the University is now.

97 The Kachin here are called Khang. Cf. Bancop, *Pai sòp kham Thai*, p. 61.

Phraya Sai Lü had a Chiang Mai man caught, whom he asked, "What are all those banners?" /fº 3.37/ The man replied, "The Chiang Mai men have occupied Chiang Rüa, and they've set up a fort and are using the banners to signify their groups, preparing to come and fight your forces." Phraya Sai Lü was quite afraid, and said, "This Phò Thao Yi Kum Kam: he has invited us to come [here from Sukhothai] to die! / They've rallied their forces. They've been raiding us, and we'll die for sure!" So he hurriedly readied his elephant, and announced to his forces, "Before dawn, we're withdrawing quickly, across the Mæ Ping to the mouth of the Kang to the east."[98] He posted a rear-guard / divided into three groups, assembling at Nòng An.

That night, King Sam Fang Kæn had Mün Mak Kham, Mün Sam Mak Pu, Mün Khem, and Mün Khüa go after Phraya Sai Lü, unaware that they had divided into groups there, and attacked / the Southerners, and they fought there. Many Chiang Mai and Southern men died. They fought in small groups there by the pond, which was called Nòng Sæn Thòn, later called Nòng Sæn Thòn Sòn to the present day. That night, Phraya Sai Lü went to sleep at Nòng Phai, near / Ngæ Ngao, then he went north to cross to the west side of the Mæ Ping and traveled through the forest.

Phraya Sai Lü said, "I drank the water of Seven Fountains, which was delicious. Where else might there be water as good as that?" By the aura of his majesty, water gushed out of that mountain for /fº 3.38/ Sai Lü to drink, as delicious as the water of Seven Fountains; so it got the name Mount Fountain-Water to the present day.

Cao Thao Yi Kum Kam led the army of Phraya Sai Lü by stages to Chiang Rai. They rested there for seven days. One day, Phraya Sai Lü took note of the characteristics of the city [plan] of Chiang Rai, with Dòi Chang Kum in the shape of a mouse and Dòi Tham Phra / in the shape of an elephant. The Phraya saw the two mountains shaped like an elephant and a mouse, and he said to all, "Anyone living here in this city will never be well-endowed with possessions." Phraya Sai Lü then rounded up all the Chiang Rai men and Phò Thao Yi Kum Kam and returned to Sukhothai. Phraya Sai Lü / had Cao Phò Thao Yi Kum Kam rule a town called Sak.[99] His lineage would end there in the South country.

Then, King Sam Praya Fang Kæn took it as an omen that Phraya Sai Lü had brought an army to encamp at the foot of the Seven Fountains Mountain and had

---

98 The Mæ Kang (or Mæ Klang) is in Còm Thòng district, where it has a large waterfall.

99 Notton (p. 95) has M. Suak; but a footnote says that PY has M. Sak, on the Mæ Sak, a tributary of the Yom River.

washed his hair at Pha Lat Luang to show his great fear of the Chiang Mai people. / So Cao Sam Praya Fang Kæn had Seven Fountains City[100] built there, commemorating the defeat of the enemy.

Colophon to Chapter Three

Biṅganagara fascicle 3 here completed.

---

100 Wiang Cet Rin is immediately to the north of Chiang Mai University, north of Huai Kæo Road. There are still the remains of a circular wall and moat there.

Chapter 4

War With the Hò, 1402/03

Namo tassatta. Cao Phraya Sam Praya Fang Kæn[1] had reigned from the *ruang sai* year to the *tao sanga* year (1402/03), one year, when Phraya Sai Lü came to attack. After that, the Hò lord, Cao Lum Fa, had Hò chiefs fetch tribute of rice of four thousand double-baskets. King Sam Fang Kæn said, "The four thousand double-baskets of rice have not been required since they were ceased in [the time of] grandfather King Kü Na. / I won't have it." The Hò chief reported this to the Hò ruler, Cao Lum Fa Phao Phiman. Cao Lum Fa was very offended, and told Cao Fai Fa of M. Sæ[2] to lead a large army to seize Chiang Sæn. So King Sam Praya Fang Kæn had Cao Sæn Kham Rüang / mount an elephant named Cao Sæn Chai Prap Sattru [and take] an army of fifteen thousand men of M. Phing Chiang Mai to go to help hold Chiang Sæn.

The Defense of Chiang Sæn

At that time, the person who ruled Chiang Sæn organized 30,000 people of the districts, together with twenty-two thousand men from Fang, Chiang Rai, Chiang Khòng, Sœng,[3] and Phayao, / who together went to hold Chiang Sæn, both within and without, on every side. Then the lords who headed the armies together consulted in a secluded place, and decided to make battle against the Hò north of the Chiang Sæn walls on [a field] 2,000 fathoms by 1,700 / fathoms. That night, they decided to dig a trench arm-length deep, and cut sharp bamboo stakes [with] leaves fully covering it to cover the trench and make it level all around to the width of a fathom. Then, they had trenches dug as wide as a span and a fathom deep, covered with woven rattan level with the ground, in order that the traces could not be seen. They

---

1 Notton (p. 99, n. 1) has a long and useful note about this king.
2 On Sipsong Panna map. The implication is that by this time the Chinese were controlling the Sipsong Panna region.
3 Sœng = Thœng.

had a canal dug on the north, west, and east /fº 4.02/ to block over a length of a hundred fathoms. When all this was done, they had the Chiang Rai and Fang men as their right-wing, the Chiang Khòng and Sœng men as their left-wing, and the Chiang Mai and Phayao men to be the main body; and they set up a cavalry force of five horse to decoy [the enemy into the traps].[4]

When it was near midday, the Hò brought their force up. Our men then / sounded the alarm drums to rally the wings. The body force then stood fast. To make the Hò think that our forces had defeated the Hò, they feinted to draw the Hò elephants and horses forth to fall into the traps. We organized the crow's-wing defense to catch them all, and they pursued and slashed / the Hò to death in great numbers. Our men got many elephants and horses that had fallen [into the traps]. Three days later, the Hò regrouped their forces and again besieged Chiang Sæn. Our forces sent scout forces out to pursue and slash the elephant-men and horsemen and footsoldiers, and the Hò were wounded and failed to penetrate. All the Hò wore iron and copper / and leather armor. Our men went out to capture Hò, and [brought back] one man, whom they asked, "Why don't you die when hit, slashed, shot with spears and swords and guns and arrows? How can we defeat you?" [The man replied,] "Use hot sand and pebbles hurled with iron ladles down their necklines in order to roast and burn them, / and then they'll be defeated."

So advised, our men swept up sand and pebbles to be heated as red-hot as fire, and [gathered] iron ladles to hurl them; and they heated them over fire. The Hò were defeated, and retreated back to their own country.

Another Hò Attack, 1405/06

Three years later,[5] in the *dap rao* year, s. 767 (1405/06), /fº 4.03/ the Hò king, Cao Lum Fa, again sent his troops to the frontier of Chiang Sæn, and sent a Hò [man] to inform our people, "Cao Lum Fa has had us besiege the whole country of the king of Lan Na, everywhere!"

---

4 Such methods of defense are employed to the present day. I have benefited from the advice of Major Daniel Tarter, U.S. Army, who looked over this section.

5 Notton (p. 101) inexplicably says one year later; but the date is the same.

King Sam Praya Fang Kæn was informed, and had all the astrologers and scholars assembled to investigate the horoscopes / of the cities of Chiang Mai and Chiang Sæn. They said, "The stars of the cities are very bad."⁶

At that time there was a Mahāthera, Sirivaṁso by name, at Wat Dòn Thæn in Chiang Sæn, who knew all the magical arts. King Sam Praya invited the Mahāthera to come and stay at Wat Ku [i.e., Chedi] Luang, in the center of the / city [of Chiang Mai], and had the astrologers and scholars hurriedly assembled in the Golden Palace (Rong Kham) to advise him concerning the horoscopes of Chiang Mai and Chiang Sæn. They said that the fate of the cities was very bad, as they had said before. Mahāthera Sirivaṁso conversed with the astrologers and scholars, and they said, "Together we have consulted / and agreed that the city's' fate dictates that we should lose the city. This is really true, and Indra, King Asoka, and King Kalinga all agree;⁷ but it's not absolute: we can avoid this fortune through sacrifice, if you heed our advice. We should together / worship the cities' horoscope, worship the domain's Fortune, Majesty, and Age gods; and worship the guardian spirits of the cities, in each place; and worship the four *catulokavāla* and Indra as the fifth; and then invite all the gods (*devata*) to assist in protecting the city and all the parts appertaining thereto."

Then all the astrologers and scholars /f° 4.04/ said, "Fine, in every respect that the scholars advise, that Mahāthera Sirivaṁso should arrange all the ceremonial requisites for worship, in each place, as advised." King Sam Praya⁸ so ordered the ceremonial requisites, and ordered that the Mahāthera should take them back to worship the guardian spirits in Chiang Sæn and Chiang Rai; / and worship the guardian spirits along the way.

The Mahāthera therefore worshipped the guardian spirits along the way from Chiang Mai all the way to Chiang Rai and Chiang Sæn, conducting worship of each guardian spirit and even including fully worshipping the spirit of King Mangrai and worshipping the spirits along the way from Chiang / Rai to Chiang Sæn. The

---

6   The horoscopes (*duang chata*) diagram the position of the heavenly bodies at the moment that, in this case, the city was founded. Such diagrams are frequently seen on stone inscriptions. They exist precisely because of the reason indicated here.

7   Who, and why, is the king of Kalinga included here?

8   Notton (p. 101) states that from here in the manuscript, it always refers to Sam Fang Kæn as Sam Phraya. The HP manuscript is the same, and the implication is that both are in the same ms. line.

Mahāthera chanted the *Rattanasutta* and the *Metta-āsana-natiyasutta*,[9] pouring water donating merit[10] to the guardian spirits of each place. Then the Mahāthera performed worship of the guardian spirits of Chiang Sæn / and erected sacrificial stands in four places in the middle of the city to worship the four *cattulokapāla* and the middle hall to worship Indra. Then he worshipped all the guardian spirits of the Mekong River. Before dark, in the *kòng læng* watch, there was thrice a great rainstorm with thunder and / wind; and on the seventh time there was lightning. The Hò headquarters of the Hò chief was struck, killing a great many of the Hò. The Hò thought that the domain of the Lan Na people had enormous and mysterious power, and they had sinned against the king of Lan Na, [causing] so many men to die. "Henceforth, we should never attack /f° 4.05/ the country of the lords of Lan Na, for all generations."

This is the *History of the Hò Attack*.[11]

Origins of King Tilokarat

King Sam Praya had ten children by various wives, here listed in birth order:[12] (1) Thao Ai, (2) Thao Yi, (3) Thao Sam, (4) Thao Sai, (5) Thao Ngua, (6) Thao Lok, / (7) Thao Cet, (8) Thao Pæt, (9) Thao Ao, and (10) Thao Sip. Of these ten, when Thao Ai was five years of age, his father said that he would be his successor [as king]; and he had him live in a village adjacent to Wiang Cet Lin. Fourteen years later, (Thao Ai) died when he was nineteen years old. His father then had Thao Ngua, the fifth child, go to rule / Chiang Rüa district, and called him Cao Chiang Lan. The sixth child, Thao Lok, was sent to rule M. Phrao, which was given an additional 500 na.[13] Thao Cet was sent to rule Chiang Rai, and Thao Sip, the youngest, was sent to rule Fang and was called Cao Thao Sòi. As for the five others—Thao Yi, Thao Sam, Thao Sai, Thao Pæt, and Thao Ao—he gave them no charges, but / had them report to Thao Lok.

---

9 These sutras were often chanted on such occasions.

10 This idea is deeply rooted. When an irrevocable gift is made, the usual thing is to pour water on the ground. The idea is that what is spilled (or poured) cannot be replaced.

11 This sentence is a clear indication of the author's sources. Compare the *Prawat tang müang Nan*.

12 Male children sometimes were given numbers as names: ai (1), yi (2), sam (3), sai (4), ngua (5), lok (6), cet (7), pæt (8), ao (9), sip (10). sòi indicates the last child.

13 This is, of course, an assignment of labor, not a bequest of land.

Cao [Lok] was born in the *kat pao* year, s. 733 (1409/10),[14] and ruled M. Phrao Wang Hin. He disobeyed his father, who removed him and sent him to rule [M.] Yuam Tai.[15]

Machinations of Sam Dek Yòi

There was an official of King Sam Praya named *nai* Sam Dek Yòi[16] who was a serving person / who ate after the king, and he supported Cao Thao Lok's bid to rule Chiang Mai. Sam Dek Yòi had someone go to seek Thao Lok at Yuam Tai, without anyone knowing he had gone, and secretly bring him to (Chiang Mai). King Sam Praya Fang Kæn was not in Chiang Mai that day, but at Wiang Cet Lin, as was his wont.

Soon, one day near midnight, Sam Dek Yòi /f° 4.06/ set fire to the pavilion of King Sam Praya at Wiang Cet Lin and completely destroyed it, and then fled back to the city. In the watch near dawn, King Sam Praya did not know that his son was in the city. The king mounted his horse and rushed from Wiang Cet Lin to his palace, and there learned that his son had come into the royal palace.

In the morning, the father-king / and his (royal) son were each seated on thrones in the throne-hall, on the north side. King Sam Praya, the father, then sent to invite the monkhood to assemble. The two kings did not speak [to each other]. In the late [morning], a young Mahāthera said, "Why have the two great monarchs summoned us?" / The father-king said, "Even though all of Chiang Mai is my proper heritage, now I hand over the domain to my son, Thao Lok, [for him] to be king." Saying that, he took a golden ewer to solemnly pour the water of irrevocable donation of the domain to his son.

Then he said to his son, / "As for him [Sam Dek Yòi], I was pleased to have him be my regular kitchen-servant; but he was not true to me. You are my beloved son, but if you do not favor [Sam Dek Yòi] quickly and easily, although he has helped you to become king, he will become insincere and untrue to you; so / do not raise him into

---

14 This is a very bad date. The correct date, judging from Tilok's age at death as reported below, is s. 771, a *kat pao* year; 1409/10.

15 Mae Sariang district of Mae Hong Son. The implication is that Phrao was in the core of the kingdom, while Yuam Tai was on the periphery. "Yuam Tai" indicates the southern part of the Yuam river valley.

16 Maybe something like, literally, Page Number Three.

a very high position. As for me, your father, I will be satisfied anywhere you send me to live." Thao Tilok then had his father go to M. Sat.

Accession of King Tilokarat, 1442

King Thao Tilok was then thirty-four years of age. His generals and ministers consecrated him to rule in Chiang Mai in the *tao set* year, /f° 4.07/ s. 804, on the full-moon day of the eighth month, a Mon Saturday, Thai-day *kot cai* (Saturday 19 May 1442),[17] under the name of Mahā Sri Sadhammarāja. He was the tenth ruler of the royal line.

King Tilok then ruled, and favored Sam Dek Yòi to be lord and master and ruler of Khan district; so he was called *sæn* Khan.[18]

Sam Dek Yòi Seizes the Palace, and is Punished

One month and fifteen days later, Sam Dek Yòi, / who was a *cao sæn*, nonetheless was unfaithful and decided to seize the lord of Chiang Mai, just as [the king's] father had predicted. So, he occupied the Golden Palace of King Tilok. King Tilok sent for Mün Lok of Nakhòn / and said, "Sæn Khan has occupied the Golden Palace. What can we do to get him out of there, oh uncle, without killing him?" / Mün Lok Nakhòn, Mün Ma, Mün Sim, and Mün Tam then entered into the Golden Palace first, and said to Sæn Khan, "You are *not* royal, nor are you a *thao phraya*."[19] Sæn Khan said nothing. Mün Lok [then] reported to the king, "I will kill him / to get him out of the Golden Palace, and then [I shall] flee." The king said, "Uncle, if you can remove him, fine; but don't kill him. He supported me to become king." Mün Lok then took the Nakhòn men, all eight thousand of them, to fill the Golden Palace and said, "You cannot stay here—you shouldn't." Then he led Sæn Khan /f° 4.08/ by the hand out of the Golden Palace and quickly to the banks of the Callus Canal.

---

17 The day that works out correctly is Saturday, tenth waxing, ninth month, *kot cai* day.

18 The word used here, and elsewhere in this chapter, is *panna* for district. Khan *panna* has to have been on the Khan River/watershed, presumably in San Pa Tòng district of Chiang Mai. "sæn," which is literally a hundred-thousand, is an administrative rank like *ròi, phan, mün* etc.

19 This sentence attests to the importance of descent from Mangrai in defining those eligible to rule in Chiang Mai.

Later, the king had [Sæn Khan] go to rule Thuan district, so he was called Mün Thuan. He had his home by the banks of the Callus Canal at a place called Ban Nòng Lom.[20]

Later, the king thought, "I should favor [Sam Dek Yòi] and have him go to rule a very distant domain." / So he sent him to rule Chiang Sæn.

King Tilok Favors Mün Lok Nakhòn

Then, King Tilok said to Mün Lok Nakhòn, "Uncle, come and live in Chiang Mai with me. As much as Nakhòn has to offer you, I will give you." Mün Lok replied, "If you really want me to live in Chiang / Mai, I ask for four favors. If you give them to me, I will come to live and serve my lord." King Tilok then said, "Whatever favors you ask are fine, and they're yours." Mün Lok said, "The four favors are these: (1) Swordsmen, soldiers, officials, whoever flees, / inside or out, I want to have them killed as examples. (2) Judges who consider cases, if appeals are made to the king and he finds their decisions unsatisfactory, I wish to have killed. (3) If any commoners fight or quarrel, and don't tell me first and instead seek out the king, I want to have them / killed. (4) All tax-collectors shall be placed under the full authority of the administrators. I request these four boons." King Tilokarat replied, "I grant these." Mün Lok Nakhòn then came as Mün Sam Lan to serve King Tilok in Chiang Mai, and Mün /f° 4.09/ Kæo, his son, ruled Nakhòn in his stead, as Mün Kü Han Tæ Thòng to rule M. Kü (or Khüi).

Ex-King Sam Praya Fang Kæn

Mün Lok Sam Lan called up soldiers in Ngæ district,[21] two thousand men; Chæ Chang district, two thousand; Chiang Rüa, two thousand; and Thuan [district two thousand]; altogether eight thousand men. Mün Lok Sam Lan paid court / to King Tilok and said, "I will go to take King Sam Praya Fang Kæn, your father, who lives

---

20 Following Kraisri Nimmanhaeminda, who located the "Callus" Canal in Chiang Mai's San Sai district, northeast of Chiang Mai, *panna* Thuan has to have been there, since Hariphunchai times. Ban Nòng Lom has to have been in this area.

21 Does this reference suggest that Ngæ *panna* might have been able to muster two thousand able-bodied men for warfare? Or a mün controlled two thousand men?

at M. Sat with the name of Cao Sam Praya Mæ Nai."²² Then he had Mün Kü Han Tæ Thòng head the army to fetch him. Cao Thao Sòi, ruling Fang, was told that / Cao Thao Lok had had Cao Sam Praya Mæ Nai, his father, move to Sat. Cao Thao Sòi,[the youngest brother,] then said, "He's not dead yet, and he has not sworn allegiance to anyone." So [Cao Thao Sòi] invited Cao Sam Praya Mæ Nai, his father, to come to Fang. He paid attendance upon Cao Sam Praya Mæ Nai / and said, "I will restore your lordship to rule Chiang Mai as before." Cao Sam Praya Mæ Nai said, "I poured the water of irrevocable gift to hand over the domain to Thao Lok to rule Chiang Mai. I cannot return to rule Chiang Mai a second time." Cao Thao Sòi / called his men in to defend the city of Fang in great numbers. Mün Kü Han Tæ Thòng did not succeed in seizing Cao Sam Praya Mæ Nai in Sat, and returned.

King Tilok learned this, and so spoke with Mün Lok Sam Lan, [saying] "Now Thao Sòi has had my father come to Fang. He has invited [him] to defend the city. /fº 4.10/ What shall we do?" Mün Lok Sam Lan then said to King Tilok, "I should have the retainers of Mün Kü Han Tæ Thòng go and arrest him."

[King Tilok] had Mün Kü Han Tæ Thòng command a force of ten thousand to go and seize Fang. They failed and returned. King Tilok again had Mün Lok Sam Lan take an army to go / with thirteen thousand men. This time, four officers went with Mün Lok Sam Lan—Mün Thuan, Mün Müang who ruled Tha Kan, Mün Khan who ruled Fang Kæn district, and Mün La[m]phun—with a force totaling twenty-four thousand men. They reached a place called Dòi Pha Lai. Mün Lok Sam Lan stopped to eat there. / A swordsmen leader of the *phan* rank said, "My elephants are tired: let them rest." Mün Lok Sam Lan said, "The Burmese [named] Cam Klup has only just reached me." [So Mün Lok Sam Lan] caught the swordsman and killed him, and appointed the Burmese Cam Klup to be the leader of the swordsmen in his place.

They reached Fang later that morning. Mün Lok Sam Lan then / had a group go in the evening, and they were able to take Fang. Mün Lok Sam Lan entered the city. Cao Sam Praya said, "Mün Sam Lan, don't kill me!" Then [Mün Lok Sam Lan] entered, sought out Thao Sòi the ruler of Fang, but failed. Thao Sòi fled to take refuge with Mün Sœng Sam Khrai Han. [Mün Lok Sam Lan] followed Thao / Sòi, who died at M. Sœng. Mün Lok Sam Lan then sent Governor Sam Praya

---

22 This reference might suggest that M. Sat is on the Nai River (Mæ Nai). See map 3.

back towards Chiang Mai. When Governor Sam Praya came to Chiang Mai, King Tilokarat had his father go up to live in the Golden Palace.

Mün Sœng Sam Khrai Han Invites the King of Ayudhya to Come

As for Mün Lok Sam Lan who was coming back from Fang, he had not yet reached Chiang Mai. Mün Sam Khrai Han was angry, and so sent a letter to invite King Bòrommaracha [to come]. /f° 4.11/ King Bòrommaracha brought an army to encamp at Chiang Thòng.[23]

Mün Lok Sam Lan arrived in Chiang Mai at twilight. King Tilok said, "I've only just become king, and a large army now has come. What should I do?" Mün Lok Sam Lan said respectfully, "My lord, don't get excited. It is my duty to defend Chiang Mai. / My lord need not leave the city, as we know not whether those outside are friend or foe. I will volunteer to go. The group of troops who volunteered to take Fang are just returning. They are tired and hungry, and my lord should take care of them." King Tilokarat then / bestowed silver and cloth upon all of them. At twilight, Mün Sam Lan went to await them at Tha Ngua.

The king sought out Mün Sœng Sam Khrai Han to summon him to come to Chiang Mai and see the king. The king said, "You've done well. Go follow Mün Sam Lan." Mün Sam Khrai / Han attended upon Mün Sam Lan. Mün Sam Lan said, "You've come! The ruler of the South has just brought up an army to invade our lord's city." Mün Sœng Khrai Han said, "Fine! Even if *ten* kings of the South attack, I will fight them!" Mün Sam Lan then took the letter [Mün Sœng Khrai Han] had written and showed it / to its author, and said, "The seal affixed to it is truly [Mün Sœng Khrai Han's] own seal. But I don't know who wrote the letter." Mün Sam Lan had his servant, named Mongkhon, look at it. [Mün Sœng Sam Khrai Han] could not argue with the evidence. He said, "You say you don't know?" [Khrai Han replied,] "It's my own sin." Mün Sam Lan then had Mün Sœng Sam Khrai Han taken off to be decapitated and his head put on a raft /f° 4.12/ of banana-tree-trunks to float down the river to the ruler of the South, named King Bòn [Bòrommatrailokanat].

Cao Mün Sam Lan encamped his army at Lamphun. The various provincial chiefs came, five in number, namely: Mün Mòk Lòng, governor of Phrao; Mün Khòm,

---

23 Chiang Thòng: locality in the Còm Thòng district of Chiang Mai.

governor of Chiang Rai; Mün Kham Yat of Chiang Sæn; Mün Kæo, son of Mün Sam Lan, of Nakhòn; and Mün Yi Lò of Fang. Cao Mün Lok Sam Lan organized / a force of Chiang Mai and provincial men numbering one hundred thousand men. Then he paid attendance on the king, saying, "I will drive carts of Phum, Khan, and Tha Kan districts for bamboo slats [for suspension bridges to cross over the Ping River] to oust King Bòrommaracha." Then King Tilok said, "Take carts to go to seek Mün / Sam Lan and shout [across] to him, 'I have had the head of the villainous Sam Khrai Han floated down [the river], but has it got there yet?'"

Battle With Ayudhya Forces, [1442/43]

At that time there were three Chiang Khòng men named Han Ai, Han Yi, and Han Sam, who said to the king, "We three [wish to] volunteer to fight the army of the king of the south / and defeat them." So the king had the three go to Mün Sam Lan at Lamphun.

Mün Sam Lan said, "The army of the king of the south is very numerous, and three are not enough to defeat them." Han Ai said, "It doesn't matter how many troops King Bòn has. / We three have volunteered to scatter them, and tonight we'll do it to the army of the king of the south. You [should] organize your troops to move in to support us."

As twilight fell, the three braves carried [baskets of] grass for the elephants and slipped in with the army of the king of the south, each along his separate path. Han Ai /f° 4.13/ carried his load [of elephant grass] to the elephant of the king of the south. He released his load of elephant grass and lay down nearby. He placed his head-cloth over his face and pretended to be ill. When it came time for the Southern watchmen to come and check, Han Ai thought, "I should give it a try now, as they may come and find me." He stealthily went up into the elephant-enclosure, and slit the throats of the / elephant-keepers, husband and wife.[24] Then he descended the tail of the elephant, and cut the rope tethering the elephant, releasing it, and it trumpeted and fled. Mün Sam Lan's army heard the loud commotion. [Mün Sam Lan] took his troops and attacked into the army of the South. The Southerners were defeated all night long, as our men pursued them, and many died.

---

24 The elephant-keeper brought his wife along: for help with the elephants? or in lieu of logistics support?

The forces / of the king of the south fled helter-skelter to Tha Khandai, and there regrouped near dawn. The Chiang Mai and provincial armies chased them to the foot of Dòi Pa Kò.

Mün Mòk Lòng [of] Phayao stopped to rest and eat [breakfast] beside the road. Mün Kæo Nakhòn caught up with him, and asked, "Whose army is ahead of me here?" He was told, "The force of the / governor of Phayao." Mün Kæo Nakhòn asked, "Why aren't you fighting? Why are you stopped? You're shirking your duty! I'm going to fight the king of the south." Mün Mòk Lòng of Phayao said, "As for me, I have gained [by fighting] many towns and villages for the king—I don't know how many. I'm no child. Don't impugn my bravery." /

Then [Mün Mòk Lòng] gave three pots of tonic herbs to his elephant, Meng Garuda, to consume.[25] Then he mounted his elephant, asked for his goad, and signaled him to go and fight the elephant of the governor of Chaliang-Sukhothai, named Klamphængphekphon. Mün Mòk Lòng fought him to the peak of Dòi Pa Kò, protecting against Meng Garuda's tusks breaking; and although Meng Garuda's tusk was broken off, he defeated the elephant of the Southerner. Ten elephants of the Southerners fell from the mountain top and died. /f° 4.14/

The governor of Sòng Khwæ saw the bad situation, and said to King Bòn, "You are a king, and should hurry away. I will try to hold the rear." So the ruler of Sòng Khwæ took six thousand troops to fight with Mün Mòk Lòng, who was urging forward the elephant Meng Garuda, who fell into a stream with the elephant of the ruler of Sòng Khwæ. The ruler of Sòng / Khwæ brought elephants to surround and capture Mün Mòk Lòng, and said to him, "I will take you captive." Mün Mòk Lòng said, "I'm no rice-leaf-tip." The ruler of Sòng Khwæ then cut off his head to present to the king of the south, which he placed on a gold tray, explaining that "This person was truly brave, and many of us were killed because / of him;" and he had the head of Mün Mòk Lòng floated down the river.

Mün Sam Lan brought his troops back to Chiang Mai, and paid court to King Tilokarat, [saying,] "This Han Ai was excellent, and he should be rewarded." The king then favored Han Ai to be Mün Tha, / with the title of Mün Ai Hang Chang.

---

25 We have not seen such a reference before—elephants being given (presumably) stimulants before a battle.

War With Nan, 1443/44

One year later, in the *ka khai* year (1443/44), the ruler of Nan, Phraya Kæn Thao,[26] had refused to be a vassal of the king, and was disloyal and plotted to destroy the king: he deviously had the king informed that the Vietnamese were invading / the city [of Nan], and asked for troops to help defend the city. King Tilokarat was unaware of his trickery, and sent forty thousand men there, commanded by Mün Phæng [of] Phayao with elephantry, plus provincial contingents [of] Mün Sœng Ta Ngam, Mün Yi Lok the ruler of Lò,[27] Mün Òi, Mün Chæ Phran, and Mün Ngao Kao. /f° 4.15/

They encamped on the east bank of the [Nan] River, with twenty-three thousand men. Not long afterwards, Phraya Kæn Thao determined to capture Mün Phæng [of] Phayao. He deceitfully stole the troops of the king to go and harvest rice. Mün Phæng of Phayao was unaware of this, and left, leaving only Mün Sœng ['s contingent]. In the late afternoon, Phraya Kæn Thao invited Mün Phæng / of Phayao and his elephantry and troops to come and dine with him at his palace; and ordered his royal troops to go. [?] Mün Phæng and all died.

A Vietnamese Helps Subdue Phræ, 1443

The king was furious, and sent a force to attack and take the city of Phraya Kæn Thao of Nan. In the *ka [khai]* year, on the / thirteenth day of the waxing moon of the second month (Tuesday 5 November 1443), they reached Phræ. The ruler of Phræ was Thao Mæn Khun. He organized his forces to hold the city of Phræ, and did not come out.

The king [Tilokarat] reached Nan, and sent a force headed by the queen mother, to take Phræ.[28] So the queen mother / had her army surround the city of Phræ on all sides. Thao Mæn Khun did not come out to pay homage to the queen. The queen then said, "This Thao Mæn Kham has not submitted to us: What shall we do?" The

---

26 Cao Intakæn ruled Nan for sixteen years from 1434. Wyatt, *Nan Chronicle*, pp. 52–53.

27 M. Lò: in Cun district of Phayao. Notton (p. 110 and n. 2) has M. Lòng, in which case Long, west of Phræ, is indicated.

28 One of many cases in Tai history when women took a leading role in warfare.

officers then said to the queen, / "We should fire the *pu cao* cannon[29] [into his city] if he does not surrender." The queen then asked, "Who knows how to [so] use the *pu cao* cannon?" There was a Vietnamese named Pan Songkhram, who was a chief of a thousand,[30] who said to the queen, "I know how to use a *pu cao*." Phan Lam Na[31] Pan Songkhram continued, "You have to arrange offerings for me."

The queen /f° 4.16/ then arranged for offerings for Pan Songkhram, consisting of an albino buffalo, thirteen albino chickens, thirteen thousand units of ducks, and a [set consisting of] a cushion and mats, betel-nut tray, water ewer, new pots, new bowls, new mats—the full set. Then Phan Lam Pan Songkhram arranged the full set, and the next day he said, "I will shoot the top off a sugar-palm tree close to the / city gate. When [the king] sees this, he will be terrified, and will submit, owing to the power of the *pu cao* cannon." Then Pan Songkhram actually shot off the crown of the sugar-palm tree. Thao Mæn Khun [still] did not surrender. Then Pan Songkhram said, "I'll fire the *pu cao* [cannon] and shoot the trunk of the sugar-palm tree so that it splits from crown to root." So Pan Songkhram shot / the *pu cao* cannon at the sugar-palm tree as he had said. Thao Mæn Khun saw that and was sore afraid, and surrendered, and presented tribute of delicacies and milled rice and buffalo to the queen. The queen then had Thao Mæn Khun rule M. Phræ as before.

The Fall of Nan, 1448/49

As for King Tilok, / he was preoccupied with King Kæn Thao [of Nan] for six years, from the *ka khai* year (1443/44) to the *pœk si* year (1448/49), until he succeeded in taking Nan. King Kæn Thao fled to take refuge with the king of the south. The king [Tilok] then had Thao Pha Sæng, younger brother of King Kæn Thao, take the waters of allegiance and rule Nan in place of King Kæn Thao in that *pœk si* year.[32] / King [Tilok] then took his troops over to M. Phræ in the *kat sai* year (1449/50).

---

29 There is a hint here of the novelty of gunpowder artillery. Note, however, that this is almost a century before the arrival of the Portuguese in Southeast Asia.
30 He had the rank of *phan*.
31 This title seems to imply expertise in agriculture.
32 Cao Pha Sæng also is named in Wyatt, *Nan Chronicle*, p.54.

War With Luang Prabang, April 1449

In the eighth month (April) [of that year] the queen died in Chiang Mai. King [Tilok] left his troops and returned to Chiang Mai. Just as he was arriving, the king of Chawa [i.e., Luang Prabang],[33] seeing that Nan was weak and unstable, brought his armies to attack Nan, encamping his troops at Thap Som Pòi[34], with ten thousand troops. /fº 4.17/ The king [Tilok] then had Mün Ngœn, the ruler of M. Phrao, together with men of other domains, go to set up his troops at a place near Thap Som Pòi, where they fought with the Chawa and contested without issue. Mün Ngœn of Phrao then sent word to the king. The king then had another one hundred thousand Chiang Mai troops / sent to fight the Chawa at Thap Som Pòi, and defeated them. The Chawa fled.

War with the Lü of Müang Yòng, 1450/51

One year later, in the *kot sanga* year (1450/51), the king took his armies to fight the Lü of Ban Phung[35] and M. Yòng,[36] and defeated them.

Yutthitsathiang of Phitsanulok, 1451

One year later, in the *ruang met* year (1451/52), Phraya Yutthisathiang,[37] who ruled Sòng Khwæ, submitted to be a vassal of the king. / The background of this occurrence is like this. King Bòrommatrailok [of Ayudhya] and Phraya Yutthisathiang had been boyhood friends. Yutthisathiang had said to Bòrommatrailok, "When you are a lord, make me great[, too]!" / Trailok replied, "When I become king, I will make you *uparaja* of half the domain." When Trailok became king, he had Yutthisathiang rule just Sòng Khwæ, but not become *uparaja* as he had promised. / Yutthisathiang

---

33 Or Swa. The conventional, traditional name of Luang Prabang.
34 Notton (p. 112, n. 1) says that Thap Sompòi is a locality five or six km. north of Nan.
35 Village near M. Yòng.
36 M. Yòng: chief city in the Lü-speaking area east of Keng Tung in Burma.
37 Yudhiṣṭhira in A.B. Griswold and Prasert na Nagara, "A Fifteenth-Century Siamese Historical Poem," in *Southeast Asian History and Historiography: Essays Presented to D.G.E. Hall*, ed. C.D. Cowan and O.W. Wolters (Ithaca, 1976), pp. 123–163, which is an admirable summary of the events of this period and an analysis of the poem *Yuan Phai*.

was angry with Trailok, and sent a person to attend upon King [Tilokarat of Lan Na] and tell him, "I will be happy to come under Your Lordship." Tilok replied, "Fine! Come!" Yutthisathiang had [his retainer] ask, "When I come, what shall I be called?" /f° 4.18/ Tilok replied, "I shall call him 'son.'" The servant then asked Tilok to escort him up [to Chiang Mai].

Tilok Fetches Yutthisathiang from Sòng Khwæ, 1452

In the *ruang met* year (1452), on Tuesday the thirteenth day of the waxing moon of the fifth month,[38] an auspicious day, the king [Tilokarat] brought his troops to receive Yutthisathiang of Sòng Khwæ, encamping his armies at the Thung Yang of M. Fang.[39] He organized / his forces numbering twenty-five thousand, [plus] forty thousand Chiang Mai men and eighty thousand men of other domains. He encamped his forces beside the Ping River in Sòng Khwæ for twenty days. The lord of Sòng Khwæ invited the king to go and capture M. Pak Yom.[40] He captured the governor of Pak Yom, a very handsome man. The king would have him come along, [but] / the ruler of Sòng Khwæ said, "If the king will take this person, the ruler of Pak Yom, back [with him], then you might as well kill me." King [Tilok] reconsidered, and then had the governor of Pak Yom killed; and then he returned to Sòng Khwæ. The ruler of Sòng Khwæ fêted the king at his home, / and then the ruler of Sòng Khwæ had a group of elephants and horses and men and weapons completely assembled, and moved out with king [Tilok].

The Sòng Khwæ people, men and women, numbering more than ten thousand persons, were led by Mün Han Nakhòn[41] in procession to a place called Nam Lüm. There, all the *khruba* and *Mahāthera* came to say / that "You should not rest here. There are very many Chaliang people here, who are likely to harm you." Mün Yi Thara replied, "You needn't fret. We are quite numerous. Pay no mind." The

---

38 A difficult year for calculation, owing to probable mis-intercalation. Perhaps Thursday 3 February 1452.

39 Located by the Nan River in Uttaradit province, 18 km. north of Müang Thung Yang; also known as Sawangkhaburi. See Sisak Wanliphodom, *Müang boran nai anacak Sukhothai*, p. 216.

40 Pak Yom: location uncertain. Appears in Sukhothai inscriptions as Bang Yom. Probably on the Yom Canal between the Yom and Nan rivers in Uttaradit province. See *ibid.*, pp. 22–23.

41 Notton (p. 113) takes this as a descriptive term, "the braves of Nakhòn [Lampang];" but with the prefixing *mün* it would seem to have to be a personal title.

Chaliang people attacked the forward group of Mün Nakhòn, many of whom were killed; and more than a thousand Sòng Khwæ people were captured. Mün Nakhòn fell back. /f° 4.19/ Mün Kœng Tin Chiang stood fast, and the Southerners pursued up to Mün Kœng Tin Chiang['s position]. They saw the white parasol [of royalty][42] and realized that this was a group of the king [Tilok], and stopped. Our people then reported to the king. The king then had Mün Ma Kham Wæng and Mün Phran Dong take about a thousand cavalry and about a thousand archers / to go after the Southerners and engage them, shooting their poisoned arrows simultaneously [in volleys at them]. The elephantry and cavalry officers exactly carried out the king's instructions. The Southerners [then] withdrew, and many Southerners were killed and fled.

When they came to a deep place along the river, / a man of our forces reported, "The Chakhrao[43] folks will attack us." The king was angry, and had Mün Yi Thara and all the officers lead the Sòng Khwæ people in procession. The king stopped [to rest] by the deep place to fight the Chakhrao people, and defeated them. / The king reached Chiang Mai, and had Phraya Yutthisathiang of Sòng Khwæ rule the Phukha district, and then rule Phayao. Phraya Sòng Khwæ said, "The king of the south is just a minor person, not really a king. In future I will pay homage [only] to King [Tilok] as a king; and thereafter he was called "king." /

Tilok Attacks Miiang Chawa (Luang Prabang), 1454/55

In the *kap set* year (1454/55), the king went to M. Chawa and obtained Chiang Tin Khròng Nòi Khròng Luang.[44] Reaching Kæt Læng, he had Mün Kœng Tin Chiang and all the Chiang Mai men and all the various domains' men go by way of M. Lüak and Nun[45] [on the] Mekong. When the king reached [M. Chawa], he sent Mün Kœng Tin Chiang to Nun, and then /f° 4.20/ returned.

The king of Chawa had Mün Khwa Sük command a force to ascend the Mekong. Mün Phran Dong reported that the Chawa people were advancing on the king's

---

42 The white parasol is the traditional Indic symbol of royalty, preserved until recently in Laos.
43 Is this related to the city Chakangrao in the Luang Prasœt Chronicle?
44 Notton, SN, and *T15RW* all have the same. This might, however, instead mean that "the king ... obtained the large and small localities dependent upon Chiang Tin, which was under Lan Chang.
45 Notton (p. 114, n. 3) thinks this might be Tha Nun, a locality on the banks of the Mekong.

forces. He volunteered to fight the Chawa and push them into the Mekong, killing many of them. The king [Tilok] replied, "That Mün Phran has volunteered is very good, as you have said." So Mün Phran took troops, elephants, and horses, and hid / at a place in the forest. [There] he pretended to beat a horse and break his leg, and led it across the sand [riverbank] with the cavalrymen following it behind. The Chawa men saw the horse on the strand. Mün Phran Dong then set his troops to attack the Chawa along the river, and killed many of them. The Chawa realized their bad situation, and fled / back.

War With the Lü, 1455/56–1456/57

One year later, in the *dap khai* year (1455/56), King Tilokarat organized his forces to go to Chiang Rung to take M. Tun and M. Lòng, but they failed to take Ban Chæ.

In the *rwai cai* year (1456/57), the king again went to Chiang Rung [to take] Ban Chæ Lao, which he took, together with M. Ing and Ban Chæ.[46] /

Ayudhya and Chiang Mai Send Spies Against Each Other

At that time, the ruler of the South, Bòrommatrailok, knew that Chiang Mai had much power—that King Tilokarat had extended his domains, had much power, and had very-skilled officers and commanders—and that he had conquered all the domains he had attempted to take. / The king of the south wondered why Chiang Mai had so successfully augmented its power, and so investigated its causes. He had a spy named Han Phrom Sathan stealthily enter Chiang Mai in order to learn its secrets.

At that time, King Tilokarat [also] had a spy /f° 4.21/ named Han Sai Sung[47] arrange his hair and clothing like a Southerner and secretly go to learn the secrets of the South Country. Han Sai Sung lived in and saw the secrets of the South Country. As for Han Phrom Sathan, he stealthily entered the city of Chiang Mai. He surveyed the city of Chiang Mai on every side, and noticed a large and tall banyan tree that cast a very large shadow / on the northeast outside the city moat, which is now the

---

46 Ban Chæ Lao = Ban Chæ? M. Ing: locations unknown.
47 The *han* (rank) number four (sai) named Sung.

auspicious site where everyone enjoys the shade. He thus noted that this was a great glory of the city of Chiang Mai and a source of its power.

One day, near dusk, when people were going to / market, he stole through the Chiang Rüak Gate. The gatekeeper was suspicious, so he grabbed his wrist and told Mün Cæm, the *ca ban*,[48] to beat and interrogate him. [Phrom Sathan] told him, "King Thao Bòrommaracha intended for me to come and seek out all the secrets of M. Phing Chiang Mai, [asking] why / the king of the north [Chiang Mai] continued to reign so prosperously and happily in his country, and why his troops took every country they attacked. When he learned why, he would bring his troops up to Chiang Mai and capture it. Thus has he commissioned me."

Mün Cæm, the headman, on learning this reported it to King / Tilokarat. King Tilok instructed the headman to keep the prisoner, and tomorrow before breakfast he would have two of the headman's retainers take Han Phrom Sathan to be presented to King Tilok. King Tilok then devised a strategy to have an escort [for the prisoner] not come. As for the king, /f° 4.22/ when he came out to sit on his throne, he saw his cook(s) in the royal kitchens on the north side. Then he had the headman bring Han Phrom Sathan out. King Tilok again had his men beat and interrogate Han Phrom Sathan, making him tell all that the ruler of the South had had him do. [Phrom Sathan] begged for his life from King Tilokarat. [Tilok] asked him to drink the / water of allegiance to become his royal vassal, and then King Tilok granted him his life, and said, "You are a dog who bites [others] at your master's bidding[, without provocation]. I will not kill you. Furthermore, my servants are numerous. I don't want you as my servant. I want you in the / South as before." He spoke duplicitously.

[King Tilok] then had his officers and ministers called up for the conquest of all the far north, as far as the banks of the Salween and everything in between. Then he had Phrom Sathan's head shaved and dressed him and had him given a hundred *pæng*[49] of silver, / and ordered him to go and report to the ruler of the South, his lord, on what he had seen, in every detail. He cleverly had Han Phrom Sathan go out via the north gate [Chang Phüak] and stay in a sala in the middle of the market. Then he pretended to organize armed troops / to come from the west and east to meet at the north gate and go out by way of Chiang Som, as if they were going to meet

---

48   The ca ban was in charge of the city's public order; the gatekeeper presumably was responsible to him.

49   Ancient measure of money. Unknown.

their commander. He staged all of this so that Phrom Sathan would see it, and then he had a page (*han dek chai*) escort him to the frontier of the South. King Tilokarat staged all this so that the ruler of the South would call up his troops /f° 4.23/ and [King Tilok] would have his forces ready to fight them; and the king of the south fell for it all. [King Tilok] had shaved the head of Han Phrom Sathan to this end.

When [King Tilok] had sent Han Phom Sathan off, he summoned all his officers to receive their orders, [that] whenever there was war, they would be ready. As for Han Phom Sathan, he reported everything to King / Bòrommatrailok. King Bòrommatrailok was convinced that King Tilok had gone with all his forces to the north.

War With the South, 1457/58

In the *müang pao* year (1457/58), the king of the south, with his son Intharacha,[50] came up with his troops to take Chiang Mai. They came by way of Lakhòn / and encamped on the other bank of the Ratchathani River.[51] King Tilok took his Chiang Mai men and men of the other domains and encamped at the foot of Mount Ba.[52] At that time, all the officers and ministers came along, presided over by King Tilokarat and Cao Phò / Thao Bun Hüang who governed Chiang Rai; Cao Yòt Müang, [the king's] grandson, who ruled M. Chæ Sak; Mün Kœng Tin Chiang; Mün Dam Phra Han Tæ Thòng; and all the officers of other domains, including Cao Phraya Sòng Khwæ. They encamped at a place / where the ruler of Sòng Khwæ had a camp gate flanked by two ponds with bamboo thickets around them. At that time, King Bòrommaracha employed a spy to reconnoiter the encampment of Phraya Sòng Khwæ, as King Bòrommaracha considered Phraya Sòng Khwæ to be the cause of this war; and he asked for volunteers to breach the enemy's lines. /f° 4.24/

At that time, the king's son, Intharacha; Khun Phek Chot, the governor of Kamphængphet; and Khun Ratcha-asa, the governor of Sukhothai, volunteered to attack the armies of that leprous dog. When they had volunteered, in the middle of the night they launched their attack on the army of / Phraya Sòng Khwæ. Those three went ahead, but when they were 8,000 fathoms from the army of Phraya Sòng

---

50 Prince Intharacha: also mentioned in the Ayudhya chronicles.
51 The Wang River.
52 Dòi Ba: perhaps Dòi Ba Hai, see above. Notton (p. 117 n. 4) makes the same connection.

Khwæ, [they found that] Phraya Sòng Khwæ had hung lamps from the tree branches. Learning that the invaders were quietly stealing towards the army of Phraya Sòng Khwæ, Phraya Sòng Khwæ summoned the elephant Phet Maha Phinai to come up to the camp entrance to engage the elephant of / Intharacha. Intharacha moved his elephant to engage [in battle] the elephant of Phraya Sòng Khwæ at midnight. Phraya Sòng Khwæ said [to Intharacha], "You'd fight me, eh?" Intharacha replied, "*I* am Intharacha!" Phraya Sòng Khwæ then urged Khun Phek Chot on towards the ponds, and did the same with all three of the invaders. / The elephant of Phraya Sòng Khwæ gored at the elephant of Khun Phek Chot, who was thrust into the pond. Khun Ratcha-asa then tried the same, and Phraya Sòng Khwæ and his elephant Phek Maha Phinai fought him and drove back Khun Ratcha-asa's elephant. The elephant Phek / Maha Phinai of Phraya Sòng Khwæ attacked beneath the eyes of the elephant of Khun Ratcha-asa and pushed him into the pond.

At that time there was much bedlam and din. The king had four *phan* of Kum Kam and *phum tasæng* of the vanguard drummers sound the attack drum signal to rally the troops. Cao Chæ Sak mounted his elephant Mongkhon; Mün Ca Sòi mounted his elephant Khwan Phek, /f° 4.25/ Phuak Cet Chang Phu Sena mounted his elephant Phuban, and Mün Dong Nakhòn mounted his elephant Chai Songkhram. En masse, they pursued the group of Intharacha. All together, they fired at the Southerners, who died in great numbers. Intharacha was hit in the forehead, and halted. Mün Dong [Nakhòn] then attacked and split the Southerners. The Southerners formed a crow's-wing [formation] to surround Mün Dong. His men turned their shirts inside-out, to red, / like the Southerners. The Southerners wondered who was whom. Mün Dong was able to escape. While it was still dark, there was a heavy thunderstorm, and he saw Sæ Lo, a page, whom he took to be a Southerner, and the page joined in shooting at Mün Dong, who shouted, "Don't shoot! I am Mün Dong!" Then Phraya Sòng Khwæ and Mün / Dong pursued the Southerners, and the Southerners withdrew back on King Bòrommaracha.

The men of Bòrommaracha saw their plight, lowered their royal parasol, and withdrew by the light of the lanterns. At that time, Thao Bun Hüang and Phraya / Chæ Sak paid court upon King Tilokarat and asked for wild elephants, named Ko Thao and Pan Chomphu, [upon which] to mount and chase King Trailok. King Tilok said, "You two are my son and grandson, and you are never to be / warriors. Since you hold the rank of a *thao phraya*, nowhere can you ever be secure. If you two would pursue the group of King Bòrommatrailok in the dark, don't do it. He will try to take you by stealth. Now the Southern army has come in great numbers. It's not easy /f° 4.26/ to take them."

Mün Dong then organized a force of four thousand men of the rear-guard to feign [a much larger force] going by using branches to make clouds of dust; and he also had them take elephant-bells and trappings to hide in the bush. Mün Dong had gongs and drums sounded and horns blown to sound in the bush the assembly of the forces, and there he had the elephant-bells and / trappings sounded. The forces then were pushed forward in numbers. Mün Dong shouted out, "Hey! Hey! You Southerners! Why haven't you fled yet? The main force of the King [Tilok] is coming! You'll all die!" When the Southerners heard this, they started to withdraw. The main force of the king of the south broke off and all retreated. / Mün Dong then pressed forward against them, pushing them across Ping Mountain.[53] Mün Dong pursued them across the Ping, and then descended from his elephant mount and cut off the heads and feet of the Southerners, and many elephantry and cavalry died. All the Southerners withdrew.

Renewed War at Sòng Khwæ, 1460

In the fourth month of the *kat mao* year (January 1460), the king went to Sòng Khwæ. The king of the south / was living in the city of Sòng Khwæ. King [Tilok] invested [the city] for a time. King [Trailok] said, "The troops of the king of the north have long surrounded us. We are tired! What'll we do?" The mother of King Trailokanat said, "Don't leave the city! It's our safe haven!" / Phek Chot then volunteered to the king of the south, "I volunteer to attack the king of the north tonight. Give me six thousand men to accompany me." The King of the South replied, "Fine! Go and attack them!" Then the senior Khun Ram, informed of this, told the king, "The king will /f° 4.27/ really have Khun Phek Chot go and attack the king of the north?" The king replied, "Yes, really!" Then the senior Khun Ram said, "This Phek Chot is courageous, but only in words. If the king has him command a force of six thousand to go out, he won't be available to help defend Sòng Khwæ city. He'll just take his men [back] to / Ayotthiya, for sure." The king of the south answered, "Formerly, you did not admonish me. I've already had him go,

---

53 Ping Mountain: location unknown (probably near Phræ).

but now you forbid me. I can't keep him here." The king appreciated the advice, so he rewarded the senior Khun Ram with a golden bowl.

In the middle of that night, Khun Phek Chot got into a boat to float down to the army of Tilokarat, / when he beat a drum sounding like the main force of the king of the south and Intharacha. In the morning, King [Tilok] had Mün Dong fetched. He said to him, "Who have you ordered to be on guard? Why have the Southerners fled away? Have [the guards'] eyes put out!" Mün Dong said / to the king, "I ordered Mün Ma, Mün Tan, Mün Sœm, Mün Phuak Han, and Müang Wiang Din to stand guard. When the Southerners went past, it was very dark, as dark as when your eyes are shut. The Southerners didn't even paddle[, but floated noiselessly by]—they just floated past the king's army. / Only [when they had passed] did they make loud noise. If Your Lordship would have their eyes put out, then begin with me!" The king could make no answer to this. /f° 4.28/

At that time, Thao Bun Hüang and the governor of Chæ Sak, the two of them, both brave, volunteered to their father and grandfather, "When you'd not allow us to go, we were very offended, as we had both volunteered and you would not allow us to go, as if it were better for us to remain at home sleeping with our wives." /

The king of the south havingescaped, King Tilokarat called up his forces to pursue them. Our men killed many Southerners. In the morning, Mün Dong Nakhòn paid court on King Tilokarat, saying, "Now the king of the south has fled away and is encamped on the marge of the Ratchathani River." / There were still four thousand healthy troops, apart from the many who were ill. Mün Dong said, "I ordered all the cavalry to encircle and watch. I ask [to be permitted] to thrust on down the Ratchathani River to catch the ruler of the South, so much as we are able." King Tilokarat replied, "He's a king. We are a king. We have / defeated them, and they are ashamed. You shouldn't go." King Tilokarat withdrew his forces back to Chiang Mai, where he feasted his forces and gave rewards to all the village and domain chiefs. As for the prince-governor of Sòng Khwæ, he was given M. Ngao Kao[54] and M. Phræ, in their entireties, / land and water [revenues] alike, as a reward for having thrice engaged [the enemy] in combat on elephant.

---

54 M. Ngao is a large old city, on the Ngao River (one of the tributaries of the Yom). See Sisak Wanliphodom, *Müang boran nai anacak Sukhothai*, p. 12. Kao here is spelled with the long a-vowel, indicating the Tai ethnic group of the Nan valley.

Then, Intharacha, son of the king of the south, looked in the mirror and saw the scar on his forehead, which angered him greatly. He said, "As long as I live, I will not fight or engage the Chiang Mai army without defeating them." /f° 4.29/

Warfare With the Lü domains, 1459/60

In the *pæk yi* year, King Tilokarat had Mün Nòi and Dam Phra Sai Na . . . [text defective][55] . . . in the *kat mao* year (1459/60) King Tilokarat called up his armies to move against M. Phrong.[56] At that time, when the King would go, he asked Mün Dong Nakhòn, "I will go to fight the Lü domains. If the Southerners invade our frontiers, can you defend them?" Mün Dong replied, / "Your Majesty need not worry if the Southerners come: I will do my duty to defend My Lord's frontiers." So King Tilokarat took his forces up to attack the Lü domains. He was unable to take M. Phrong, and withdrew.

Ayudhya Invades, 1461/62

Before [Tilok] returned to the city, the king of the south, / Bòrommaracha, learned that King Tilokarat had gone to attack the Lü domains, and so he brought his forces up to attack Phræ, and crossed the Ping Mountains in force. Mün Dong Nakhòn learned of this, and gathered up troops to combat them. He said, "We should not hurry. We should prepare carefully, and then fight them and defeat them / with our wisdom."

Then, having withdrawn from the Lü domains, King Tilokarat arrived back. He learned that the king of the south was invading his domains, and that Mün Dong Nakhòn had gone to fight them. The king reassembled his forces to follow and support Mün Dong Nakhòn / and fight the king of the south.

The king of the south, Bòrommaracha, saw that the armies of King Tilokarat were exceedingly numerous, and that he was not likely to be able to withstand them, and so he withdrew back [to Ayudhya]. King Tilokarat pursued them, but he was too

---

55 This fragment of a line, including a date, is the first line on the page; and it reads like a mistake which is corrected by the date which follows.

56 M. Phrong: in the Sipsong Panna. Probably M. Phong, in the southeast.

late. He reached Chaliang[57] and said, "We will take and plunder Chaliang. /f° 4.30/ The governor of Chaliang was afraid of the king's armies, and sent out an emissary to ask to become a vassal of the king. The king was unable to take and plunder M. Sòng Khwæ.

The governor of Chaliang said to the king, "The people of M. Plang Phon are holding the city of Sòng Khwæ, so the king should be able to take M. Plang Phon."[58] The king sought / out [one of] his sons, named Phò Thao Chiang Rai, and said to him, "Now the governor of Chaliang-Sukhothai has invited us to take M. Plang Phon. You should assist us in leading all the men to go." The son of the king replied, "Your Majesty's soldiers are quite ill. I have toured their billets, and have seen their covered heads, / all of them, and they're not stirring." The king retorted, "You're too indulgent, unsuited to rule." The king ordered swordsmen to stir all the slackers from their billets; and all who stirred, fearing the king's wrath, were sent to attend upon the king. Few were unable / to go to Plang Phon.

Two people of Plang Phon, a man and a woman, were out washing their hair. Our troops caught them, and presented them to the king to be questioned. "How many people are there in Plang Phon?" They replied to the king, "There are fewer than a thousand." The king hurried there. The / Plang Phon people shot guns, arrows, and lances in flurries. Our men were unable to penetrate [the city]. So the king encamped north of the city for three days, and then he withdrew back to Chaliang. He appointed the governor of Chaliang to rule Chaliang as before. Then the king withdrew his forces back to Chiang Mai, leaving Mün Dong and officers there [in Chaliang].

In the *luang* /f° 4.31/ *sai* year (1461/62), the governor of Chaliang was unfaithful to the king, and had people invite Mün Dong to come to a cockfight. Mün Dong said to the king, "The governor of Chaliang has invited me to come to a cockfight in Chaliang. Should I go?" The king knew that the governor of Chaliang was untrue, and so he forbade Mün Dong [to go], saying, "Don't go. He'll seize you, / just like King Kæn Thao of Nan seized Mün Phæng Phayao and killed him."[59] Then the

---

57 Chaliang: Satchanalai. See Griswold and Prasert, "Fifteenth-Century Historical Poem," p. 128, and maps, pp. 124–125.

58 Now Kamphængphet. See Prasert na Nagara and Puangkham Tuikhieo, *Tamnan Munlasatsana Chiang Mai Chiang Tung* (Bangkok, 1994), pp. 12–13.

59 See Wyatt, *Nan Chronicle*, pp. 51–52; and above, f° 4.15.

governor of Chaliang again invited him, a second time. The king did not allow him to go. He invited him a third time. Mün Dong paid court upon the king in Chiang Mai. The king said to him, "He'll seize you and kill you." / Mün Dong said to the king, "[Yes,] he'll seize me and kill me, but I won't allow that. I will go and kill **him**!" The king said, "If you want to go, go!"

Mün Dong gathered up more than a thousand men and took them to Chaliang; and he had the military officers, / Mün Wiang Din, Mün Ma, Mün Sœm, and Mün Tan all carry swords into the city of Chaliang, with fire-flints and tinder, and ordered them that, at the sound of any loud commotion from the house of the governor of Chaliang, they should—whomever, wherever—burn everything. Mün Dong / then organized five hundred people to go into the palace of the governor of Chaliang. There was hardly sufficient room for the retainers of the governor of Chaliang to remain. At that time, the governor of Chaliang was seated on his bench in the middle of his palace. Mün [Dong] Nakhòn stood conversing with the governor of Chaliang, [saying] "King [Tilok] tells me that you /f° 4.32/ often have said that you would like to pay your respects to the king [in Chiang Mai]. Now the king has sent me here to escort you [there]." The governor of Chaliang feared Mün Dong, so he said, "I will go with you to pay my respects to the king. Let me prepare my things inside."

Mün Dong replied, "Don't. I'll kill you. / Have your wives prepare your things." Mün Dong then had Mün Ma and Mün Sœm close all the gates throughout the city. The governor of Chaliang announced to all the people of Chaliang, male and female, that whoever wished to go to the king with him could go, and whoever wished / to stay could stay."

Mün Dong then took the governor of Chaliang to Chiang Mai. The king then had Mün Dong rule M. Chaliang; so in that year, Mün Dong ruled two domains, namely, Nakhòn [Lampang] and Chaliang.

The governor / of Chaliang was [now] a vassal of the king, but the king said that he was unfaithful, and had the governor of Chaliang kept in M. Hang;[60] and he later died there.

---

60 Now in Burma, near the frontier with Chiang Dao district of Chiang Mai.

Trailok Abdicates and is Ordained

Then, the king of the south, Bòrommaracha, thought, "King Tilok rules in Chiang Mai, / endowed with much power and majesty. He has generals blessed with many brave warriors. As long as I live, I will take troops to combat King Tilokarat. I should have envoys bid for his friendship, and I should renounce the world and be ordained and hand rule over to my son, Intharacha. /f° 4.33/ He accordingly sent envoys. Mün Dong refused to accept the bid of the king of the south, Bòrommaracha; and instead sent to King Tilokarat the envoys requesting [monastic] requisites and senior monks to go ordain [the king] in the South. King Tilokarat then / arranged for monastic requisites and twelve senior monks of the Araññavasi Sect,[61] e.g., Thera Devakula, and a translator, to go and ordain the king of the south. That done, the King of the South bestowed rewards on the translator and the senior monks and sent them back to Chiang Mai. /

Not long afterwards, King Bòrommaracha the ordinand had a senior monk (*Mahāthera*) named Bodhisambhāra go as a royal envoy to go to ask for Chaliang as [his] alms. King Tilok pondered, "These are the words of a monk? / Address them not to me but to Mahāthera Rattanaprāsāda." He then assembled all the Araññavasi monks, and invited the Mahāthera Bodhisambhāra to go and confer with the monks of the South, e.g., Mahāthera / Sudhammarattana. King Tilok then had all the domain's leaders, for example Mün Kœng Tin Chiang and Mün Nang Hæng, join with the Sangha, and had Mahāthera Bodhisamphāra confer on all the business raised by the ordinand king of the south who had asked for Chaliang /f° 4.34/ as his alms.

Informed, the Mahāthera said to the monk Bodhisambhāra, "Formerly, when kings renounced their rule and were ordained into the religion, or were ordained as [white-robed] ascetics, they had to forswear [their claim to] being maintained by the realm. / Now, a king has been ordained, and has asked for the realm, which he should not do. The [monastic] elders should go back and tell the ordinand king all this." Having said this, they bestowed alms upon the monk Bodhisambhāra, and /

---

61 The so-called "forest-dwelling" monks of the Araññavāsī Sect are in this period best known as the "Red Forest" (Pa Dæng) Sect of the *Mulasasana* chronicle. See Sommai Premchit and Donald K. Swearer, "*Mūlasāsanā Wat Pā Dæng*: The Chronicle of the Founding of Buddhism of the Wat Pā Dæng Tradition," JSS 65:2 (July 1977), 73–110.

sent him with the translator to tell all this to the king who had been ordained. The royal ordinand received this message and was inwardly displeased.

Not long afterwards, [the king of the south] learned that a Burmese white-robed ascetic who had a deep knowledge of the magical arts had gone from Pagân to Tenasserim. / The royal ordinand invited him to come to him. Feasting him, he conversed with that white-robed ascetic. He learned that the white-robed one knew black magic, and told him all about how Chiang Mai had great power and / majesty, and he had been unable to capture it.

Colophon to Chapter Four

Rajavaṁsa cattutha kamtam nittitaṁ.[62] This is the fourth fascicle.

---

62 Pali: "The Fourth Fascicle of the History, Here Completed."

Table 2 Rulers from Mangrai to Phutthawong

Name	Details	Born AD	Accession
Mangrai	age 21 ruled; born cs 600; king in 621	1238	1259
Sæn Phu	age 41 ruled		1318
Khrüʃa	usurpation		1319
Nam Thuam	age 30 ruled		1322
Sæn Phu (second reign)			1324
Kham Fu	age 26 ruled; died at age 47 years		1328
Phayu	age 29 ruled; died at age 57 years		1345
Kü Na	age 40 ruled; ruled 21 years, died age 61		
Sæn Müang Ma	age 14 years		1400?
Sam Praya Fang Kæn	aged 13 years ruled		1401
Tilokarat	age 34 ruled; age 78 at death	1409	1442
Yòt Chiang Rai	age 32 ruled	1456	1487
Phraya Kæo	age 14 ruled; ruled 30 years; 44 at death		1495
Ket Chettarat	age 19 ruled; coronation age 30	1497	1526
Thao Chai	replaces deposed father; killed 1543		1538
Ket Chettarat (second)	assassinated		1543
—Interregnum—			1545
Queen Chiraprapha			1545
Setthathirat of Lan Chang	ultimately abdicated		1546
Mæ Ku	of M. Nai; descendant of Mangrai		1551
Queen Wisutthathewi			1564
Tharrawaddy Prince (Burmese)	ruled 28 years		1578
Thado Khòi (Burmese)	ruled 1 year and 1 month		1607
[son of previous]	ruled 5 years		1608
[younger brother of previous]	ruled 13 years		1613
Phraya Thipphanet	father of ruler of Chiang Sæn		1631
ruler of Phræ			1659
Einsheimin (Burmese)			1672
son of King Phutrai			1675
Min Yè Nara (Burmese)			1707
Cao Ong Kham of Lan Chang	ruled 32 years		1727
Cao Can son of previous			
Cao Pat son of previous	rebels but does not rule		
Abhayagamani (Burmese)			1762
Kawila	established by Siamese	1742	1775
Setthahattiraja younger brother of Kavila			
Maha Suphathrarat younger brother of Kavila	died 1825		
Phutthawong			1826

Chapter 5

The Burmese Ascetic in Chiang Mai, 1465–67

Tato thero pañca santi.[1] At that time, the Burmese ascetic asked, "How is the city of Chiang Mai laid out?" So the royal ordinand [King Trailok] had Han Phrom Sathan fetched and had him instruct the Burmese ascetic. Han Phrom Sathan said, "There is a banyan tree which is the glory of the city, lying / to the northeast of the city." The ascetic said, "So, if that tree remains, Chiang Mai will remain powerful?" Han Phrom Sathan replied, "Give me a thousand of gold as my fee and I will go and get / rid of that tree, agreed?" The ascetic said, "I would like to get rid of that tree!" Han Phrom Sathan / then said to the royal ordinand, "Then give the Burmese ascetic a thousand of gold and three hundred of silver and two sets[, inner and outer,] of robes as fee, and he will go."

The ascetic took his fee and returned to Pagân, and then went by way of Pegu to M. Thrang,[2] gradually proceeding up / by stages until he reached Chiang Mai, where he lodged at Wat Nantharam.[3]

At that time, [there was an official named] Phan Khrao Ai who habitually went to give alms and to perform his obligations and hear the Dhamma at Wat Nantharam, where he learned that there was a Burmese ascetic of Pagân who was very learned. He so reported to King Tilokarat in every detail. So King Tilokarat /f° 5.02/ had all the royal scholars and astrologers interrogate him in writing on all the learning of that Burmese ascetic. The ascetic answered all their written queries and demonstrated the merits of his teachings convincingly, in every detail. The scholars

---

1 Pali: "The Monk. Fifth." This seems to make more sense than the *Tatotheropucasanti* with which the fifth chapter of Notton begins.
2 M. Thrang now is Papun, on the west bank of the Salween in Burma.
3 Wat Nantharam is in t. Hai Ya, Müang district, Chiang Mai.

and astrologers then submitted these to King Tilokarat, / and King Tilokarat said, "He really knows well all the arts and sciences," so he had Phan Khrao Ai have a small kuti built there, just south of the way to the Great Bodhi tree, where the Burmese ascetic could dwell. /

Thereafter, whenever anything occurred in the country, [the king] had the Burmese ascetic consulted, and he told them what to do in every respect. Thenceforward, everything that happened in the country flourished more than before. The ascetic did everything from that temple, / which thereafter came to be known as the

Pagân Temple, to the present day. The Burmese ascetic lived in Chiang Mai and came to be known as the Pagân monk Mang Lung Lwang. King Tilokarat then had [three persons,] Mün Chang Kum Kam, Phan Thepphakhun, and an interpreter / go and interrogate the Pagân monk Mang Lung Lwang, "Your knowledge, which you know [so thoroughly] and you have demonstrated in this our country, I have practiced in every way; but are there other such arts which would make Chiang Mai flourish? As for We ourself, We have ruled Chiang Mai /f° 5.03/ so that its power and majesty are known throughout the Jambu Continent. Furthermore, are there ceremonies which could be performed that would make our life longer and more happy and complete? Please, O great Pagân monk, tell us in every detail." Mün Chang Kum Kam, / Phan Thepphakhun, and the interpreter interrogated the Pagân monk in this fashion.

The Pagân monk Mang Lung Lwang replied, "The magical arts which conduce to the flourishing of the country, and cause the Great Lord / who rules the country to have majesty and power to subdue all the Jambu Continent, are verily like those of King Asoka, who had a long and happy life, and I have studied them fully. Those life-extending techniques are difficult of attainment. If / the Great king really wants them, he can attain them. We will explain them all, in every detail. If they are too difficult for him, then tell me and I will not so teach him."

Mün Chang Kum Kam, Phan Thepphakhun, and the interpreter then reported to King / Tilokarat in every detail. King Tilokarat said, "However difficult these actions may be, it is no matter. I really want to learn." Then Mün Chang Kum Kam and the interpreter went to tell the Pagân monk Mang Lung Lwang, "The king is anxious to do it /f° 5.04/ in all ways. Thus you should tell him the techniques which he should study, in every detail." The Pagân monk Mang Lung Lwang then explicated the ceremonies, as follows. "As for M. Ping Chiang Mai, its glory is in the northeast quadrant. You should build a house there, [so you can] cross the moat and city wall

/ to the inside, and tap into the lion characteristics. Furthermore, you should clear [the adjacent areas] both inside and outside [the city] so they are completely flat and clear. If there is a large tree there—coconut or sugar-palm—cut it down and dig out its roots, so that it's completely extirpated. Erect your royal palace / there, and use *ngæ* and *du* trees for the [central] pillars [of the palace].[4] Otherwise, you may use whatever wood you like in your palace and sleeping quarters, the living-quarters for your private dwelling, sleeping quarters, and elephant / and horse stables. I will go and point out the auspicious place." Then, Mün Chang Kum Kam, Phan Thepphakhun, and the interpreter went to tell King Tilokarat what the Pagân monk Mang Lung Lwang had told them, in every detail.

King Tilokarat / heard all this, and was very pleased. He had them go to invite the Pagân monk Mang Lung Lwang to come and dwell at Wat Phram, where he could oversee the new construction. Then King Tilokarat sought out all the high dignitaries, for example Mün Kœng Tin Chiang, Mün Dam Phra Han Tæ Thòng, and /f° 5.05/ the Mün Lam and all the foremen to come with all their laborers to raze the city wall which King Mangrai had built, and to fill the moat and level it. Then he had them cut down the banyan tree which was the glory of the city of Chiang Mai, / with its wide and beautiful shaded canopy, from its crown down to its roots, and clear the area to be completely flat. Then the Pagân monk Mang Lung Lwang went to delineate the living quarters and palace and sleeping quarters and the horse and elephant stables and various rooms. He then announced its name, "Si Phum." Then he opened up the gate to the earthen city and named it the Si Phum Gate.[5] / He also had the Si Phum Bridge built.

In that year, the Pagân monk Mang Lung Lwang said, "We have finished building Si Phum in all respects. In what month and day shall we perform the coronation of the king who subdues the Jambu Continent? Also, the Si Phum [quarter] is filled with magical power; and / sleeping quarters are auspicious. Whenever we hear that an enemy is attacking, from whatever direction, [you are to] arrange flowers and perfumed water and set them up above the royal throne in the sleeping hall, and

---

4   When a dwelling is built, these pillars are raised first. See Mani Phayòmyong, *Prapheni sipsòng düan Lan Na*, pp. 170-178. Notton (p. 131, n. 1-2) gives Latin names for these two: *Shorea obtusa* and *Pterocarpus macrocarpus*.

5   The Si Phum Gate was eliminated, probably when King Müang Kæo renovated the city walls. See Hans Penth, "Prawat kamphæng müang Chiang Mai nai adit doi sangkhep," in *Kamphæng müang Chiang Mai*, p. 14.

knock on the [magical] pillar in that direction; / and the enemy will flee from the majesty power of that magical pillar."

The construction of the Si Phum Ward was accomplished in one year between the *dap rao* year (1465/66) and the *rwai set* year (1466/67), being finished in s. 828, on the full moon day of [the month of] Vaisakha (29 April 1466). Then the Pagân monk Mang Lung Lwang and /f° 5.06/ all the officials, high and low, together consecrated King Tilokarat to have the royal power to subdue continents, like King Asoka. Then they had the king mount the Sivakaya golden palanquin, named Prap Traicak, dressed with [the raiments of] a raja, and donning / the jeweled crown named Brahmadesa, and wearing beautiful jewels. He entered the [new] royal palace in the Si Phum Ward, like Indadhipatiraja entering the Suvejeyyanta Palace.

The Ascetic's Machinations Defile the Country

Ever since the Burmese ascetic entered the service of the king of / the south and destroyed the glory of the city, and built the Si Phum Ward, [Chiang Mai] became a defiled place, as if the glory of the city had been sullied with urine and defecation. Harmful things befell the country, the ruling family, and all the high officials.

Not / long afterwards, Cao Mæ Thao Hò Muk made accusations against Cao Phò Thao Bun Rüang, saying that he was evil. King Tilokarat had him exiled to M. Nòi.[6] Later, she deceived King Tilokarat into killing / Phò Thao Bun Rüang. Subsequently it became known that he was not guilty.

Later, [there was the case of] Mün Ma, a very brave warrior, who was guiltless. He quarreled with a man named Ròi Ngua. Ngua wrote a letter saying that Mün Ma was disloyal, and was revolting against the king. Then Ròi Ngua ordered minor officials to steal the seal of Mün Ma to stamp the letter. /f° 5.07/ He then took the letter and left it in the palace, north of the Pæn Gate. A group of swordsmen found it and presented it to King Tilokarat. The king had the letter read, demonstrating that Mün Ma was disloyal, so he had Mün Ma taken off to be killed. Only later did he learn that he was blameless. King / Tilokarat was very contrite, and issued the order that henceforth anonymous letters would not be read, which is still the rule.

---

6   In t. Wiang Nüa, Pai district, Mae Hong Son province. See Wiwan Sængcan, "Müang Nòi khòmun cak tamnan læ lakthan borannakhadi," *Müang Boran* 10:1 (Jan–Mar 1994), 64–67.

Not much later, the ruler of the South, King Bòrommaracha, sent a son to bring tributary presents, in order to learn news of the Burmese ascetic, Phukâm / Mang Lung Lwang, who was to destroy the tree which was the glory of Chiang Mai. Furthermore, the Southern King Bòrommaracha also hired a Chinese Muslim (*pha si*)[7] named Thipphalòng to cast a spell on King Tilokarat. He had poisons secreted at all the gates of the city.

Now, / King Tilok ordinarily accorded honors to all state guests who attended upon him [in audience], and respected the Southerners because they recognized his dignity. Thus King Tilokarat had [the three sorcerers] Mò Khæn, Mò Ban Lòng, and / Mò Chuang Na come to tell him what was happening. When it came time for the state guests to have audience with him, he deviously had straw archways erected over every gate; he used a piece of wood remaining from a coffin, a piece of a water-buffalo bridle, joists from a verandah, pieces from a pig-sty, a bottom step from a staircase, and the lintel from a doorway, each of them decorated with red cloth to cover it and hide the defilement. /f° 5.08/ Then they had the guests enter through the [bewitched] gate on the north. At that point, the Chinese Muslim and the Southerner were unable to enter the arched entrance. King Tilok had the two of them beaten and interrogated. The Chinese Muslim told him, "The king of the south hired me to plant poisons. Also, the King of the South hired / a Burmese ascetic named Mang Lung Lwang for one thousand units of gold to cleverly destroy the tree which is the glory of Chiang Mai. Then he pretended to send an ambassador, who in fact was to check on these activities. If the Burmese ascetic could not destroy the tree which is the glory of the city, I was to obtain the return of the one thousand units of gold." / King Tilokarat had the Southerner go to confirm [the story] with the Burmese ascetic; and he replied that he could not deny anything that had been said. So the Burmese ascetic was beaten.

The next day, the Southern guests came to present their tribute and open / the royal letter. The guests were then feasted at an evening meal. The deputy ambassador became covetous to possess a golden bowl, which he put in his bag, and then all the guests paid their respects to King Tilokarat and carried the bag out when leaving the hall.

---

7   This is the usual reference for a Chinese Muslim (from Yunnan); probably better termed "White Turban."

At this time, there was a brahman Laka, / a cook who helped the head cook prepare meals. He saw the diplomat conceal the golden bowl in his bag, so he had some swordsmen and drummers follow and seize the golden bowl and the deputy ambassador. The deputy ambassador was brought to King Tilok. King /f° 5.09/ Tilok then had an interpreter and the *hasip ca* La take the thief and show him to the ambassador. [The thief] said, "I was overcome with greed and stole [the golden bowl]." King Tilok sent the Southerner guests back, according to ancient custom. As for the Burmese ascetic and the Chinese Muslim, they were placed in the cangue and / were thrown into the river by the Pòk Rapids. As for the deputy ambassador who had stolen the golden cup, Mün Dam Phra Ai had him sent to the *Phan* Cæm,[8] to be taken to be killed. When the state guest reached the border, Mün Dam Phra Ai was told by King Tilokarat / to give a signal to a *han dek chai* to take two hundred men to wait by the road where the guest would pass, and then the *han dek chai* was to attack and kill the guests there, all of them without exception. Then King Tilokarat dug by / three of the city gates and dug up six jugs, and another in the middle of the city, making seven jugs altogether. He had them burned up north of the Sip Kham Bridge, and had the ashes thrown into the Mæ Tho.

The history of the insincere friendship of Chiang Mai and the / South.[9]

Military Expeditions in the Shan Region, 1462–1471

Here we will tell of King Tilok leading his armies to the Shan domains.

In the *tao sanga* year, s. 824 (1462/63), Kham Lòt, the ruler of M. Tuk Tu [and] Müang Kham Phuak, the ruler of Chiang Thòng,[10] came to ask King /f° 5.10/ Tilokarat to take M. Nai.[11] The king had Thao Yòt Chiang Rai—his grandson, namely the son of Thao Bun Rüang—and Mün Bun Tin Chiang and various provincial chiefs take troops to attack Nai. They reached a place called Dòi Ma Thao. There, / Cao Phò Thao Yòt Chiang Rai would have Shans meet them and take them to Nai. King Tilokarat hurriedly brought up a force to join them. The

---

8   Notton (p. 134, n.1) explains that these were rapids on the Ping River, at the frontier between the lands of Chiang Mai and Rahæng (Tak).

9   Again, this sentence reads like an archaic footnote, where the author indicates his source.

10 M. Tuk Tu and M. Chiang Thòng are domains in the Shan states of Burma.

11 M. Nai: see map 3.

king took his troops and entered Nai. The ruler of M. Nai, named Ngœn Pòng Fa, / stole away to hide at M. Nòng Bòn. The king went and encamped his army north of the market at Nai. He had the rulers of Tuk Tu and Chiang Thòng fetched and brought to him. When the ruler of Tuk / Tu and the ruler of Chiang Thòng attended upon him, the king expressed his great pleasure. Then the king had the princes of all the various domains assembled, in order; for example, the ruler of Tuk Tu, the ruler of Chiang Thòng, and the rulers of the various domains. With them sitting there, he delivered / royal advice and instruction to the various Shan rulers. Then the king again led his forces to M. Nòng Bòn [in order] to capture the ruler of Nai. The ruler of Nai feared the [royal] majesty, and came out to pay homage to the king. The king had the ruler of Nai rule Nai, /f° 5.11/ the ruler of Tuk Tu rule M. Tuk Tu, and the ruler of Chiang Thòng rule Chiang Thòng, as before. The king gave each of them two cannon and two hundred matchlocks. The king [then] returned, stopping overnight at Pang Chang, Bang Thok, Nam Ram, and Chiang Thòng / in succession on his way back to Chiang Mai.

When the king went to the Shan [domains] on that occasion, he acquired eleven Shan domains: M. Su, M. Lai Kha, M. Cit, M. Cang, M. King, M. Lòk Còk, M. Cam Kha, M. Kup, M. Yòng Hui, / M. Nòng Bòn, and M. Si Phò; altogether eleven domains.

King Tilokarat acquired Shans as his subjects, both male and female, numbering 12,328 persons. He took the various Shans so acquired and distributed them to / the districts (*panna*), some to Tha Kan, some to Kao Chòng, some at M. Phrao, and some as *dang sip*, to the present day.

In the *kot yi* year, s. 832 (1470/71), the king and Mæ Thao Hò Muk went to M. Pan[12] and M. Nai. The ruler of Nai, named Ngœn Pòng Fa, presented his son / to the king and offered tribute. Mün Bun Rüang, the ruler of Chiang Rai, died in the Shan domains at that time.

Various Deaths

In the next year, a *ruang mao* year (1471/72), Mæ Thao Hò Muk died. *Tao si* year (1472/73) and *ka sai* year (1473/74): nothing.

---

12 M. Pan: see map.

In the *kap sanga* year, s. 836 (1474/75), Mün Dong, the /f° 5.12/ ruler of Chiang Chün,[13] died, and the ruler had Mün Khwæn, the ruler of Chæ Hom,[14] go and rule Chiang Chün in his stead; and he had Mün Kòng, the ruler of Chiang Rüa, go and rule Nakhòn.

In that year, the ruler of Sukhothai attacked Chiang Chün and killed Mün Khwæn, the ruler of Chiang Chün. Chiang Chün was recaptured. / At that time, the Mün who was ruler of Nakhòn and acting as ruler of Chiang Chün fled away.

Building Chedi Luang, 1475–1479

In s. 837, a *dap met* year (1475/76), and in the *rwai san*, *müang rao*, and *pœk set* (1478/79) years, these four years, Mün Dam Phra Khot constructed the Maha Chedi Luang in the middle of the city, until s. 841, a *kat khai* year, / in the eighth month (21 April–20 May 1479), when King Tilokarat went in state procession to Phra Rom Prang,[15] for twenty-seven days, and then returned to the city.

The Vietnamese Attack Nan, 1480

In the same year, in the waxing moon of the fourth month (11–25 February 1480), an army was assembled to go to the Shan domains. They went to M. Hang. The Vietnamese attacked M. Chawa (Luang Prabang). The Chawa fought the / Viet. The Viet then crossed [the river] at M. Chawa and advanced to the frontiers of M. Nan. Thao Kha Kan, the ruler of Nan, took up forty thousand troops to fight the Viet and defeated them, killing many Viet. He had their heads cut off and sent to be presented to King Tilokarat. The Viet were furious, / and did not withdraw. King Tilok consulted with his officers, saying "The Viet have entered our frontiers. What should we do??

All the officers, high and low, consulted together. [One urged,] "We should take leather leads and tie them to the tails of the elephants, and attach fathom-long

---

13 Chaliang, Si Satchanalai.

14 Chæ Hom: old city in Chæ Hom district, Lampang province. See the *Tamnan Chæ Hom*; and Aroonrut Wichienkeeo, "Chiang rü müang: khòsangket bang prakan," in *Ekkasan prakòp kansammana rüang sinlapawatthanatham*, Chiang Rai, March 1994.

15 Notton says he went to Lampang.

wooden logs to the tethers and /f° 5.13/ release the elephants into the concentrations of Viet. When the elephants run loose, they will swing their tails, and the logs will strike the heads of the Viet [soldiers] and they will die, and they won't be able to organize." [Another suggested,] "We should tie them between the breasts of pairs of elephants and release those pairs so that their [suspended] logs will strike the Viet heads and / kill them.

At that time there was an archer, named Mün Thum, who knew how to make 3-fathom arrows and blunderbusses. Mün Thum said to the king that he had not yet finished making the arrows. Then / two brothers, Hò retainers, said to the king, "The Viet have not withdrawn. We and the Viet speak the same language. We two brothers can induce the Viet to withdraw [just] by the force of the royal majesty." King Tilokarat said, "If so, fine! You / two brothers should go and converse with the Viet in their language." He offered those two a reward of a thousand of silver, and had the two Hò paddle boats down to speak with the Viet, following this strategy. [They said to the Viet,] "The rulers living to the west will bring up troops in great numbers to assist us. / Thao Kha Kan will be in command, and take our Viets, and cause innumerable Viet to die, so not a single one will be left. The preparations made have been quite immense. Furthermore, your commander, Cao Bua Sam, has died. You like fighting, don't you? It's too bad that you have not withdrawn."

The Viet heard this, /f° 5.14/ and were quite afraid, so they withdrew. Then the king brought his forces back to Chiang Mai. When he arrived there, he transferred Thao Kha Kan to rule Chiang Rai, and had Mün Kha Thap go to rule Nan in his place.[16]

Diplomatic Maneuvers With the Hò

Then King Tilokarat thought, "I should take the Viet captives and present / them to the Cao Lum Fa." So he arranged to take the captives to be presented to the Cao Lum Fa, with the message that "The Viet brought their troops to attack Lan Chang, two hundred thousand strong, fought and defeated the Lan Chang people, and then crossed the river to invade the frontiers of M. Nan, one of / our districts. The king of Lan Na then had Thao Kha Kan, the ruler of Nan, with an army of

---

16 On these events, there is a different version in Wyatt, *Nan Chronicle*, p. 57. Here, the new ruler was Thao Ai Yuam.

forty thousand, go out and fight the Viet, many of whom died. Thao Kha Kan cut off many of their heads and presented them to the king of Lan Na. Many [Viet] were taken prisoner. The king of Lan Na then had me / present them to Cao Lum Fa, who is his superior."

Cao Lum Fa exclaimed, "Unbelievable!"

Cao Fai Fa of M. Sæ said to the Cao Lum Fa, "As to whether what he says is true or not, ask the prisoners."

So the Cao / Lum Fa had the prisoners asked. They said, "Our Vietnamese lord sent three million warriors to attack Lan Chang, and appointed Cao Bua Sam to command them. They attacked Lan Chang. As for Cao Bua Sam, Thao Kha Kan killed him. Of the three million troops, Thao Kha Kan killed /f° 5.15/ many, so that not even a million men were remaining. Furthermore, many of us were taken prisoner, and were brought to be presented to the Cao Lum Fa."

Cao Lum Fa slapped his biceps and exclaimed, "Ah! Ah! Hey! In this world, / I'm just one man, with the power to conquer all domains. The king of Lan Na is verily the man with the second-best power and bravery. Also, the king of Lan Na has much wisdom, and many troops. / But when he says he has few, he's just modest. In reality, he has many; he has lots of Viet warriors as captives. Saying that he has few when in fact he has many is the mark of a wise man."

So he / issued a command that, "Henceforth, do not let the king of Lan Na have [just] the rank of a lord of one hundred thousand. Give him the status of a lord of a million. He is a great man, and do not seat [his envoys] like the envoys of other kings." Then he issued an / order, a sealed rescript, kept in the [archives of the] Golden Pavilion (*hò cia kham lüang*) saying, "Henceforth, in all the west consider the king of Lan Na to be the greatest. Advise all rulers in the west to heed the words of the king of Lan Na. In all the east, /f° 5.16/ I [of course] remain the greatest, and will advise accordingly."

Cao Lum Fa then had two high-ranking Hò carry the sealed rescript as special envoys to Chiang Mai, and to celebrate the glory of King Tilokarat. "Whatever enemies of Cao / Lum Fa might arise, the kings of Lan Na should have all local rulers take their troops and subdue them." Then the two high-ranking Hò took the sealed rescript as envoys to Chiang Mai.

On an auspicious day, King Tilokarat / had the Hò envoys presented. The two high-ranking Hò were to take their seats on a throne when attending King Tilokarat, just as high-ranking Hò going abroad were seated on thrones equal in stature to those of other rulers. King Tilokarat then had an interpreter go and say to the two high-ranking Hò, "Coming [to us] as envoys now is more serious and greater / than on previous occasions, because the Cao Lum Fa has had you two high-ranking Hò deliver a sealed rescript celebrating my honor as the [preeminent] ruler in the west, promoting me to this honor, and having me announce so to all [other] rulers. All the regions to the east are retained to the Cao Lum Fa / to superintend. That the Cao Lum Fa has raised me up to his level is a great honor. Furthermore, I have had my envoy attend upon Cao Lum Fa, and he has had my envoy seated at the level of a lord of a million, as if I were personally attending upon him in M. Videha and he had seated me equally with him. Have the two Hò [envoys] consider /f° 5.17/ how I, sitting on an equal plane with them, can give orders to all the rulers in the west? If the two high-ranking Hò [envoys] bring me the Cao Lum Fa's command celebrating my glory as a Great King, won't the two Hò thereby contravene the command of the Cao Lum Fa? /

The two high-ranking Hò listened to the serious words of King Tilokarat. They felt guilty at sitting at the same level as King Tilokarat, so they looked up at the king and said, in the Hò language, "*si lam cing plan,*" which is to say, "The Lan Na king is very astute, / exceeded only by the Cao Lum Fa. No other foreign king can compare with him." The two high-ranking Hò then said, "The king of Lan Na should arrange seats for us however it suits him." King Tilokarat / then had a mattress brought out 1 *khüp* and 4 *niu* high for the two high-ranking Hò to recline on in the throne hall of King Tilokarat. After one month and fifteen days, the two high-ranking Hò took leave of King Tilokarat.

Shortly thereafter, Cao Lum Fa was thinking how Thao Kha / Kan was reported to be brave, and he wondered what he looked like. So he had a skilled painter go to paint Thao Kha Kan in the four poses (sitting, standing, walking, and reclining) and displayed it in the Golden Pavilion, where it remains to the present day.

Tributary Relationship With the Hò

Not long afterwards, Cao Lum Fa had the two high-ranking Hò come to request /f° 5.18/ tribute [from Lan Na]. King Tilokarat refused to give it, saying, "Previously the Cao Lum Fa granted permission in a sealed rescript delivered to me saying that I was to supervise the western regions, and that if there were any enemies of the Cao Lum Fa arising, I would have my warriors go / and suppress them. Therefore, any tribute due the Cao Lum Fa I will render by maintaining my elephantry and cavalry and infantry, who are volunteers [in the service] of the Cao Lum Fa. If the lord really wants tribute, I will send it; but if any enemies of the / Cao Lum Fa arise, I won't send [my troops] to suppress them. The two high-ranking Hò should go back to tell this to the Cao Lum Fa for him to consider."

The two high-ranking Hò reported to the Cao Lum Fa, telling him all the circumstances of King Tilokarat, in every detail. / The Cao Lum Fa said, "Over all the earth, none is braver than the king of Lan Na. None must look down on the king of Lan Na as [lord of] a small country. Don't think like that. Whatever tribute Lan Na sends is up to the kings / of Lan Na, who maintain their brave troops for us." King Tilok thought, "The Cao Lum Fa will require no tribute from us. We should send tribute to him." So he sent four kinds of tribute: nine tusks of elephant ivory, / f° 5.19/ nine pieces of Burmese cloth, nine pieces of Thai cloth, and nine rhinoceros horns.

Fiscal Reforms, and Deaths, 1480–1485

In the *kot cai* year, s. 842 (1480/81), Chiang Mai flourished in every way. King Tilokarat had Mün Dam Phra Khot reform the tax collections of the Phing [River Basin] domains and the other domains, to collect the various taxes in gold, silver, and cowries, / which accrued to the royal treasury in great amounts.

In the *ruang pao* year, s. 843 (1481/82), the Maha Chedi Luang was inaugurated.

In the *tao yi* year (1482/83), Mün Dam Phra Khot died, and [his remains were] interred at Yuam Tai.

In the *ka mao* year, on the second waning of the seventh month,[17] Mün Ca, the judge, died. In the same year, in the first month, / the minister Mün Tin Chiang died.

In the *kap si* year (1484/85), it was all right [i.e., no one died].

In the *dap sai* year (1485/86), King Tilokarat had the leading officials, Mün Luang Chiang, Mün Dam Phra Ai, and Mün Ca Kham Nòi, decorate the north face of the Maha Chedi Luang.

---

17 Either Tuesday 25 March 1483 (beginning of year) or Sunday 14 March 1484 (end of year); probably the latter.

War With the Lawa and Chiang Rung, 1485/86

In the same year, the Lawa brought a force to attack and take / M. Yòng. The king had Mün Ca Kham Nòi go and chase out the Lawa, who fled to Chiang Rung. Mün Ca Kham Nòi went and was unable to take Chiang Rung. The king had Mün Dam Phra Ai go to assist him. The Lawa released a mad elephant to attack the group of Mün Dam Phra Ai. Mün Dam Phra Ai / had them work in concert to shoot the elephant, who died. Mün Dam Phra Ai then entered and plundered and took Chiang Rung, and then returned.

Diplomacy and War With the South

In the same year, a *dap sai* year, Phraya Yotsarat sent envoys to further royal friendship; [the diplomats comprising] an ambassador and his deputy. King Tilokarat refused to see them, and they returned [home] after twenty-three days. Mün Dam Phra Ai /f° 5.20/ ordered his men to wait at the landing and seize and kill them there.

The king ordered Phan Phuang Tu Ma, the nephew of Mün Dam Phra Ai, go to inspect the frontiers of T(r)ün,[18] and to climb the [palm] trees there for [writing] leaves. The Southerners also came to inspect the frontiers and met our men there climbing the palms, and fought them there. The king again had Mün Ai Nakhòn / go down to help Phan Phuang Tu Ma fight the Southerners at M. Tœn. The Southerners were beaten and fled.

War With the South in Nan, 1486/87

In the *rwai sanga* year, s. 848 (1486/87), the Southerners brought up an army to M. Kip and M. Hin,[19] districts (*luk panna*) of M. Nan. The Southerners killed Mün Kip and Mün Hin. King Tilokarat / went in procession to Mæ Th(r)a.[20] The ruler

---

18 Note the end of the paragraph, which has Müang Tœn: we would guess M. Thœn, pronounced Tœn in northern Thai. To the south of Lampang, on the frontiers with Tak.

19 M. Kip, M. Hin: in the far south of Nan province. See Wyatt, *Nan Chronicle*, p. 34 (map).

20 Probably the Mæ Tha, southeast of Lamphun.

of Nan sent a messenger to attend upon the king, to tell him that the invading force had withdrawn. The king then returned to Chiang Mai in that *rwai sanga* year.

Officials Plot Rebellion

When the king had returned, he had six officials go and take charge of Nakhòn: Mün Dam Phra Ai, / Mün Ca Kham Nòi, Mün Cet Chang the ruler of Chiang Sæn, Mün Mon the ruler of Chiang Rai, Mün Mahin of Fang, and Mün Phrao, who assembled together at the mouth of the Tui.[21] [Four of them—]Mün Chiang Rai, Mün Phrao, Mün Chiang Lü, and Mün Ca Kham Nòi—met secretly together, / and agreed to support Mün Wiang Din to become ruler, and sounded out the intentions of Mün Dam Phra Ai, who would not join them; so they tried to kill him. Mün Wòng, the son-in-law of Mün Phrao, learned of this, so he had the city garrison have elephants barricade the city gates, every one of them. Mün Ca Kham Nòi felt uncomfortable with this, and fled off to the /f° 5.21/ Mahāthera of the Red Forest [Sect]. The king then had them all assemble at the Red Forest [Temple],[22] with three royal pundits and Phan Lam Khæk Kassapa, Phan Chœng Upali, Mün Sumongkhon, Phan Ca Kæo, and Pundit Nòi who went to investigate, and they reported that [the accused] were guilty. The king then had Phan Lam Khæk take Mün Mon Chiang / Rai to be executed, and had the Phan Lam Khæk rule Chiang Rai instead; had Lam Bun take Mün Phrao off to be executed and had Lam Bun rule M. Phrao instead; and had Lam Kham Nòi take Mün Chiang Lüa off to be executed and had Lam Kham Nòi rule Chiang Lüa instead. Mün Ca Kham Nòi was [considered] less guilty, and had taken refuge with Mahā / Ñānathera, the patriarch of the Red Forest [Sect]. The cleric asked that he not be executed.

Death of Tilokarat and Succession of Yòt Chiang Rai, 1487–1488

In the *müang met* year, s. 849, on the third waxing of the ninth month, a Sunday,[23] near dawn, King Tilokarat passed to the world beyond. King Tilokarat had ruled the

---

21 On the railway line between Lamphun and Lampang; place called Sop Tui. Notton (p. 143, n. 2) says 3 or 4 km from Lampang.
22 Temple, now deserted, at the foot of Dòi Suthep.
23 Friday (third waxing) 25 May 1487; or, more likely, Sunday 27 May 1487.

country for forty-four years. The age of the lord was seventy-eight. Counting from / King Mangrai to King Tilokarat, he was the tenth in the ruling lineage.

As for King Tilokarat, he had a son named Phò Thao Si Bun Rüang. His father had him rule Chiang Rai. He had offended against his father's will, so he was exiled.

Cao Phò Thao Bun Rüang had / a son, named Phò Thao Yòt Chiang Rai. This prince was born in the *rwai cai* year, s. 818 (1456/57). At the age of thirty-two years he became ruler in place of King Tilokarat, his royal paternal grandfather, in the *müang met* year, s. 849, on the full-moon day of the tenth month, a Mon Monday, Thai day *rwai sanga*.[24]

King Yòt appointed Sæn Cu to be Cao Sæn;[25] Klang Chiang /f° 5.22/ to be Mün Sam Lan, the military commander; and Mün Ca to be Mün At, ruling Nakhòn. King Yòt had a queen named Nang Pong Nòi, who was very beautiful. By her, King Yòt had a royal son, born in the *tao yi* year, s. 844 (1482/83), named Cao Rattana. King Yòt did not like that son very much: he loved [best] the son of a Hò / named Phrao Salang, whom he raised to be his son, and then had go to rule M. Phrao.

Yòt Chiang Rai Deposed, and Succession of Kæo, 1495

King Yòt Chiang Rai underwent coronation on a Monday, which was inauspicious (*kalakini*) for the country's fortune. King Yòt was very like the Hò towards the generals and ministers, who tried to dissuade him, but he would not listen, / and he acted against the customs of rulers and did not heed the ten royal precepts.[26] The generals and ministers were dissatisfied with him, and together deposed King Yòt, and together crowned Cao Rattana, the royal son, who was fourteen years of age, as king in the *dap mao* year, s. 857, on the full-moon day of the seventh / month, a Sunday, a Thai *pæk yi* day,[27] under the name of Phutadhipatiraja, also called Phraya

---

24 There were four *rwai sanga* days that year, only one of which was on a Monday, at the end of the year: the twelfth waxing of the seventh month, 24 March 1488.

25 This is the first mention of this rank, higher than a *sæn*. This phenomenon is sometimes referred to as "title inflation."

26 There is a good statement of these rules of kings in *Khamsòn Phraya Mangrai* (Chiang Mai, 1976), pp. 1–12.

27 The best option might be the *pæk yi* day, Saturday eleventh waning of the second tenth month, 18 July 1495.

Kæo. His father, Thao Yòt Chiang Rai, had ruled for nine years, and was exiled to M. Samat.[28]

King Kæo's Religious Patronage

King Kæo Phutadipatiraja was then king, and performed various acts of merit; for example, building / the Buppharam, and then inviting the Mahā Sangharaja Pussadeva to be Supreme Patriarch and take care of the monks in that temple. At the time he donated that temple, there was a miraculous earthquake. He had a silver Buddha image enshrined in the Buppharam. Later, the king built a temple for the [town-dwelling monks[29] living] in the direction of the Rose Garden (Suan Dòk) / f° 5.23/ and in the city, and for religious ceremonies in which the royal folk floated ordination rafts[30] on the Ping River. Then the king built Wat Phra Sing and Wat Mahā Chedi Luang, and unfailingly made merit and donations.

As for his father, King Yòt, at the age of forty years he had been exiled to Samat. After ten years, / at the age of fifty he died, in the *dap pao* year (1505/06). King Kæo went to conduct the funerary obsequies for his father for a month, having him lie in state at the Great Bodhi tree, and then he built an *uposatha* over his ashes there.

In the *rwai yi* year, s. 868 (1506/07), Thao Müang Kham Khai Fa[31] brought / in a great many people, men and women, to be subjects of the king. The king had Thao Müang Kham Khai Fa go to rule Phræ, and then go to rule Sœng.

War With the South, 1507–1509

In the *müang mao* year, s. 869 (1507/08), King Kæo took an army to go and attack Sukhothai, / but he was unable to take the city, and withdrew back. The Southerners [pursued them and] cut off the rearguard at Mæ Chok. Mün At, the ruler of Nakhòn, fought the Southerners [there], and killed many of them.

---

28 Probably near M. Nòi, with whose name it is often joined

29 Intended for Gāmavāsī (town-dwelling) monks, in contrast to Araññavāsī (forest-dwelling) monks.

30 Particularly at this time of great religious controversy, ordinations of monks often were held on rafts on the water, in order to avoid uncertainties over the official boundaries of consecrated lands.

31 A footnote to Notton (p. 146) says possibly Ai Fa, chief of M. Kham, according to a variant.

In the [pœk] si year, s. 870 (1508/09), a Southerner named Khalaho[32] brought an army up to attack Phræ. Mün Cit, the ruler / of Nan,[33] took an army to fight them, and they were defeated by the Southerners and threw their arms away. The Mün Sai and Mün Khwa and many men died there.

Shans of Müang Pong, 1509/10

In the *kat sai* year, s. 871 (1509/10), the Ca Ban Ròng, who was a Mün, took an army to attack the Shans of M. Pong,[34] but they were unable to take the city, being defeated by the Shans.

Continued War With the South, 1510–1515

In the *kot sanga* year, s. 872 (1510/11), /f° 5.24/ the Southerner named Khalaho [again] brought an army up to attack Phræ. Mün Sam Lan and Mün Dam Phra Ai went out to battle the Southerners, but were beaten and withdrew, and encamped at Bò Thòng. The Southerners then fled and withdrew. Mün Kham Khai, the ruler of Nakhòn, engaged in single elephant combat with a Southerner, and won. The Southerners retreated. Both we and the Southerners had many troops killed / there.

In the *ka rao* year, s. 875 (1513/14), Mün Phing Yi went to seize Southerners, and took more than forty captives.

In the *kap set* year, s. 876 (1514/15), in the eighth month (April), Mün Phing Yi and Mün Li went to seize Sukhothai and Chaliang people, and brought back more than twenty / people, and the Chaliang people became subjects. In that same year, in the fourth month (15 December–15 January) King Kæo went to Chiang Sæn and took royal folk to be ordained on a raft in the Mekong River. Many died of smallpox. He remained there for four months, and then returned to Chiang Mai.

In the *dap khai* / year, s. 877 (1515/16), Mün Phing Yi went to seize Sukhothai, but failed. Mün Mala, ruler of Hua Khian, took troops to seize Kamphængphet

---

32 Clearly the Kalahom.
33 Cf. Wyatt, *Nan Chronicle*, p. 59.
34 M. Pong/Phong: see the Phong Tai Shans in Chapter 2.

people, and obtained three elephants and eighty captives. They returned to Chiang Mai, and Mün Mala was sent to rule Nakhòn.

In the first month (September 1515), Mün Mala took men / of Nakhòn and went to round up Kamphængphet people, but was unsuccessful.

At that time, Mün Phing Yi took a force down to take Sukhothai, saying that he would not accept failure. The horse cavalry entered the city and caused great disorder. The Southerners defended the city, and some of our cavalry officers were lost. The main Southern force /f° 5.25/ followed up. There were two sons of the Southern ruler, named Phra Ok and Phra Athit;[35] and four ministers, Yuttha, Seyya, Eyyara, and Sahatsachai, who headed their force of three hundred thousand. On the seventh day of the waxing moon of the second month (14 October 1515) they captured Thap Muang Khan, and we lost six officers, including Cao Sam / Kham Chiang Rai and others not listed. On the thirteenth waxing of the second month (20 October), our forces crossed the Wang [River] to fight the Southerners at Nam Bò Kæng Hòi, and there we lost two elephantry officers.

At that time, Mün Dang Tao Kham met the Southerners in elephant-combat and won. Lam Mün Sai Udom dashed [in] to engage the Southerners' elephants, and many were presented / [to the king]. Thus Lam Mün Sai Phrao was named Mün Phek Chai.

On the full-moon day of the second month, a Mon Tuesday (23 October 1515), in the mid-morning, the Southerners brought troops to take Nakhòn, first taking the Tha Nang Gate.[36] At that time, we lost three elephantry officers. Mün Tham Nòng Khwang and many of our men / died in the city.

Chiang Mai's Fortifications Improved, 1516–1518

In the *rwai cai* year, s. 878 (1516/17), men of Chiang Mai and the other domains made bricks for the city walls of Chiang Mai.

In the *müang pao* year, s. 879 (1517/18), King Kæo had Mün Phing Yi build up the city walls of Chiang Mai.

---

35 Phra Athit became *uparaja* in 1516 and succeeded his father as King Bòrommaracha IV in 1529.

36 Tha Nang Gate: gate of Lampang? Lamphun makes sense, as it has a gate by that name and Lampang does not.

Trouble With the Shans, 1517–1520

In the same year, on the seventh waxing of the eleventh month, a Mon Friday (24 July 1517), the ruler of / Chiang Thòng named Phraya Kai and the ruler of M. Nai brought elephants, horses, and men to become vassals of King Kæo, both male and female, young and old, totaling 23,220 persons. King Kæo had Mün Phing Yi and Mün Dang Tao Kham receive the Nai people, obtaining thirty-eight elephants and 250 horses.

The king had /f° 5.26/ the ruler of Chiang Thòng go and rule Fang and [newly titled him] Sæn Fang; and he had Phraya Kan, a Shan, go with him to take care of twelve hundred men and women; and he also put in his charge the Tha Kan district and the Kao Chòng [Nine Passes] district[37] of Phrao. As for the chief of Nai, the king had him go to rule M. Khròng,[38] and had him receive the border imposts.

Three years later, in the / kat mao year, s. 881, on the full moon day of the sixth month (3 March 1520), a raft ordination was held for the Flower Garden [Suan Dòk] monks, but it was not completed. Then the king had Mün Dang Tao Kham be their supervisor, but he persuaded all the Shans, such as the rulers of M. Nai and M. Khròng, to flee to the Shan domains. King Kæo had Sæn Yi and Mün Sòi Nakhòn take charge of a force / to go after Mün Dang Tao Kham to M. Sawat Thaman. Cao Müang Mahin, the ruler of Chiang Sæn, quickly joined them and they fought; and Cao Müang Mahin was killed there. His remains were rendered funeral obsequies at the Red Forest Temple at M. Hang. Also, many officers were lost. The provincial chiefs / pursued the Shans and killed some, while the rest crossed the Salween [River] to the Shan domains.

King Kæo's Domestic Actions, 1520–1522

When they returned, King Kæo promoted Mün Sam Lan Kham Lòm to be Mün Luang Ca Ban, and Mün Sòi Nakhòn to be the Sam Lan.

In the *kot si* year, s. 882 (1520/21), King Kæo underwent another coronation/ at Ban Mahā Mongkhon.[39] There were entertainments at the Royal Plaza (Khuang

---

37 This place must have been close to Phrao, with whose name it is often linked.
38 M. Khròng: now Ban Müang Khròng, in Chiang Dao district of Chiang Mai.
39 Ban Maha Mongkhon: This is not a village, but rather the name of the king's new palace.

Luang).⁴⁰ An observation tower and a Sappanwood Pavilion were built at the Southern Court.

In the *ruang sai* year, s. 883 (1521/22), drum towers were built at the Royal Plaza, and on the plaza in front of the Yòt Nakhòn Tower.

In the *tao sanga* year, s. 884 (1522/23), King Athit,⁴¹ the ruler of the South, sent an embassy to cement the royal friendship. /f° 5.27/ The royal letter of friendship was read at Wat Mün San.⁴²

Warfare in Keng Tung, 1523

In the *ka met* year, s. 885 (1523/24), Phò Thao Chiang Khong and Phraya Hin fought over the succession to rule Khemarattha [Keng Tung]. Phraya Hin took refuge with [the ruler of M. Nai,] Fa Kham Læp. Phò Thao Chiang Khong fled to take refuge with King Kæo. Phraya Tœk, his uncle, held the city [of Keng Tung] for him. King Kæo had Mün Yi Ai / hold Chiang Mai, and had Sam Yi Phing Chai take an army of more than twenty thousand men to accompany Phò Thao Chiang Khong to go and rule M. Khem, going by way of Chiang Sæn. Mün Sòi Sam Lan took an army of more than twenty thousand men by way of M. Sat.

Sæn Yi Phing Chai, on arriving at M. Khem, sent word in / to Phraya Tœk, who was holding the city, that he should come out and welcome Phò Thao Chiang Khong. Phraya Tœk would not do so. Sæn Yi Phing Chai entered and took the city, emptying it completely. Phraya Tœk fled, and persuaded the force of Fa Kham Læp to fight Yi Phing Chai at M. / Khem. Sæn Yi Phing Chai took his army out of M. Khem to Dòi Ma Ho. The Shan army and the Khem people pursued and fought them. The Shans and the Khem people died in great numbers. Our people died, too, and we lost five elephantry officers—Cao Nakhòn Khun Luang, / Mün Kæo of Chiang Khòng; Mün Sri, the ruler of Sœn; Mün Kham Pha, ruler of Chiang Rai; and Mün Chiang Khwa of Chiang Rai. The ruler of Nai, Kham Yòt Fa, was grievously wounded. Sæn Yi Phing Chai took Phò Thao Chiang Khong back to Chiang Sæn.

---

40 Most large towns had such a plaza, termed *khuang*; and north of the plaza there was usually a temple called Wat Hua Khuang ("the temple north of the plaza"); e.g., Chiang Mai, Lampang, Nan, Phayao, Keng Tung, and M. Yòng.

41 See note above on this king, Bòrommaracha IV.

42 Wat Mün San: in t. Hai Ya, Müang district, Chiang Mai.

King Kæo was angry that Mün Yi Phing Chai was guilty, in three ways: [1] he fled /f° 5.28/ in the face of the enemy; [2] he gratuitously killed innocents; and [3] when he took the domain he did not have Phò Thao Chiang Khong rule it. Furthermore, he did not have the garrisoning force drill in fighting the enemy. He was in the city for three months, and let the enemy greatly augment its forces. So [King Kæo] had Mün Ai, Phan Dap Nòi, and Sam Chang go / with Mün Sòi Sam Lan and get Yi Phing Chai and Mün Sat Kæo Khang Mum at Wat Mahaphon of Chiang Sæn[43] and kill them. Then he had Thao Chiang Khong come to rule M. Phrao, in that *ka met* year, s. 885. Phraya Hin fought Phraya Tœk over the rule of M. Khem in that same year. Later, / Phraya Tœk was killed.

In the *kap san* year, s. 886 (1524/25), the Nam Khan flooded Chiang Rüak. The people who had come to the market at Si Phum were drowned, and many died.

Death of King Kæo, 1526

In the *dap rao* year, s. 887, on the tenth waning of the fifth month (7 February 1526), King Kæo died. King Kæo / had ruled from the *dap mao* year to the *dap rao* year, thirty years altogether. King Kæo was forty-four years of age. He died of eating spoiled horsemeat and vomiting.

Succession of King Ket Chettharat, 1526/27

All the generals and ministers then chose the younger brother of King Kæo—a son of King Yòt Chiang Rai/ who [went to] live at M. Nòi—to sit on the bejeweled throne, in the *dap rao* year, on the eighth waning of the fifth month (5 February 1526).[44] He was born in the *müang sai* year, s. 859 (1497/98), and was nineteen years old when he began to rule, in the *rwai set* year s. 888 (1526/27), [but] he was thirty when he underwent coronation on the royal plaza and took the [regnal] name of King Ket.

---

43 Wat Mahaphon (deserted), Chiang Sæn. See city map.
44 I.e., two days before his predecessor on the throne died!

Construction, Fires, and Royal Charity, 1527–1533

In the *müang khai* year /f° 5.29/, s. 889 (1527/28), the Hua Wiang quarter was made into a temple and named Wat Lokamoli;[45] and Wat Bun Kian[46] and a *vihara* were built.

In the *pœk cai* year, s. 890 (1528/29), a *cetiya* and a *vihara* were built at Wat Lokamoli.

In the *kat pao* year (1529/30) there was nothing.

In the *kot yi* year, s. 892 (1530/31), there was a fire in the palace built by King Phra Müang Kæo./

In the *ruang mao* year, s. 893, in the sixth month (February 1532), there was a fire in the Tha Phæ neighborhood, and many lost all their property. King Ket, his mother, his paternal grandmother, and his grandchildren donated twenty thousand units of silver to the Tha Phæ people.

In the *tao si* year, s. 894 (1532/33), the royal palace was rebuilt. /

In the *ka sai* year, s. 895 (1533/34), King Ket led Southern envoys to the Great Reliquary of Lamphun.

Ominous Omens

On the eighth waxing of the second month, a Mon Thursday, a Thai *kap yi* day,[47] in the *khrat* watch, in the heavens there appeared shooting stars in all directions, brighter than all the other stars. In / the third month, a betel-nut tree in M. Nòng Khwang, which was large and about to burst forth with its fruit, was seen to move in all directions—[including] 11 fathoms to the north.

In the *kap sanga* year, s. 896, in the first month (September 1534), came the death of the younger sister of the queen mother of King Ket.

In the *dap met* year, s. 897, in the first / month,[48] all the generals, e.g., Mün Sam Lan, the ruler of Nakhòn; Mün Luang Chan Nòk, the son of Mün Sam Lan; and

---

45 Wat Lokamoli, Chiang Mai: outside the north wall of the city. See map 2.
46 Wat Bun Kian, Chiang Mai: present name unknown.
47 The fifteenth waxing of the second month was a Thursday *kap yi* day; 30 November 1533.
48 27 September–25 October 1535.

Mün Yi Ai conspired against King Ket. The king learned of this, and had Mün Sòi Sam Lan go and kill them.

In this reign, the king had Mün Mahin go to rule Chiang Sæn.

The Deposing and Exile of King Ket, 1538

In the *pœk set* year, s. 900 (1538/39), /f° 5.30/ all the generals and ministers were dissatisfied with King Ket, and deposed and exiled him; and they had Cao Phò Thao Chai, his son, sit on the bejeweled throne in that *pœk set* year.

In this reign, [the king] had Phraya Sutthasana go to rule Chiang Sæn.

Return of King Ket and His Assassination, 1543–1545

Cao Phò Thao Chai did not rule in conformity with the ten royal precepts. The generals and ministers / together killed Thao Chai in the *ka rao* year, s. 905 (1543/44). Then they again had Phra Müang Ket Chettharat, who was at M. Nòi, return to rule the domain again. Phra Müang Ket Chettharat ruled the domain twice. [This time] he ruled for two years.

In the *dap sai* year, s. 907 (1545/46), King Ket / Chettharat[49] made merit and had the Red Forest monks ordained at the Mahāthan Landing,[50] proceeding by the northern gate in the evening. Sæn Khrao ordered Mün Trœn, son of Phò Thao Chiang Khong; the son of Mün Ai of the palace elephant corps; and Mün Sœm, the son of Sæn Khrao; to / assassinate King Chettharat Phra Müang Ket north of the royal plaza. He was cremated at Wat Sæn Phòk,[51] and his bones were interred at Wat Lokamoli, north of and outside the north city walls.

Interregnum

Sæn Khrao then invited the ruler / of Khemarattha to come to rule Chiang Mai, but he did not accept and was undecided whether to come. Then Sæn Khrao had

---

49 Notton (p. 153, n. 1) here cites the PY to say that in 907, the king "lost his senses and caused all sorts of troubles."
50 Mahathan Landing: landing on Ping River; location unknown.
51 Wat Sæn Phòk: deserted; location unknown.

Phan Dang go to invite the ruler of M. Nai to come to rule Chiang Mai. The ruler of M. Nai had not yet come. Mün Sam Lan Ai, the ruler of Nakhòn; Mün Kæo, the ruler of Chiang Rai; Mün Mano, /f° 5.31/ the ruler of Chiang Sæn; Mün Yi, the ruler of Phran; Mün Nangsü Luang; and all the leading men together met at Chiang Sæn and had Mün Ta Sæng Phò Nòi go and invite the king of Lan Chang to rule Chiang Mai. But he had not yet come when Mün Hua Khian [of] Sæn Wi[52] brought up an army, saying that he would take Sæn Khrao. / Sæn Khrao then announced to all the men of all the districts (*panna*)—Khan, Tha Kan, M. Kü, Lamphun, Thum Tum, Ta Sæng, Chæ Chang, Chiang Lüa, Phu Kha, and Fang Kæn—that they should come and join their forces at the six gates of the city.[53] They fought for three days and three nights, until the fourth day, when Mün Hua Khian of Sæn Wi withdrew and fled to / Lamphun.

Ayudhya Summoned to Intervene in Chiang Mai, 1545

There he gathered all the Southerners who had come as envoys, all eleven of them, to Chiang Rüak, and had them go and tell the ruler of the South to quickly come to take Chiang Mai. When they reached and informed him, the Southern ruler sent his army up, but not all the way [to Chiang Mai]. At that time, all the [five conspirators] / left Chiang Sæn and came to Chiang Mai. They took Sam Khrao; Mün Trœn, the son of Phò Thao Chiang Khong; the son of Mün Ai of the palace elephantry; and Mün Sœm, the son of Sæn Khrao; the four who had killed King Ket Chettharat, and had them all killed. Then they / together raised Queen Chiraprapha to be ruler in that *dap sai* year, s. 907, on the second waning of the tenth month, a Mon Thursday, a Thai *pœk yi* day.[54]

Then King Bòrommatraicak and his army reached Chiang Mai and encamped at the Nòng Pha Tæp field,[55] east of Suan Lan. Queen Mahā Chiraprapha then ordered officers to take /f° 5.32/ gifts to present [to the Southern ruler]. On Saturday, the fourth waning of the tenth month, a Thai *kot si* day,[56] [her] army encamped at

---

52 Sæn Wi, i.e., Hsenwi; Burma. (See map 5.)

53 Now the city has five gates—Chang Phüak, Tha Phæ, Chiang Mai, Suan Dòk, and Suan Prung. The sixth was mentioned above, Sri Phum.

54 Thursday (first waning of the tenth month), 25 June 1545.

55 Nòng Pha Tæp field: probably outside Chiang Mai.

56 Saturday (third waning of the tenth month) 27 June 1545.

Wiang Rua Nang. On the sixth waning, she performed merit-making ceremonies in memory of King Ket Chettharat at Wat Lokamoli. King Bòrommatraicak of the South donated five thousand units of silver to build a funerary monument for him, and for pieces of cloth and rewards to all the officers / who had come to receive him. On the seventh waning of the tenth month (1 July 1545), the Southern king bathed at the Seven Fountains. On Sunday, the twelfth waning (5 July 1545), in the morning, the king of the south slept at Sop Khuang,[57] and then he gradually proceeded back to Yotthiya.

Müang Nai Invades, 1545

In the same year, on Saturday the third waning of the eleventh month, a Thai *kap sanga* day,[58] / the ruler of M. Nai, Fa Yòng Hui, brought troops to Phu Phiang, and on the third waning of the eleventh month (27 July 1545) they came and plundered the Chiang Som precinct [on the north side of Chiang Mai].

On the fourth waning, at dusk, there was a very loud earthquake. The finial of the Mahā Chedi Luang and that of the reliquary of Wat Phra Sing broke off / and nine other reliquaries also were destroyed.

At the end of the eleventh month (early August 1545), the ruler of M. Nai, Fa Yòng Hui, brought his troops in and encamped at Wiang Suan Dòk,[59] and he sent troops to fight at Wat Pa Khet[60] and Wat Chiang Khòm;[61] then they encamped at Wat Pa Tan,[62] and they built a bamboo bridge to cross the city moat north of the Ku Rüang Fort.[63] / The Chiang Mai people divided [to man] bunkers to fight them, and they removed the earth with which the Shans had filled in the city moat. The Shans put sharpened sugar-palm-trees into the moat, and the Chiang Mai people removed

---

57 Sop Khuang: mouth of the Kuang River, where the Kuang (which passes through Lamphun) meets the Ping River.

58 Saturday (second waxing of the eleventh month) 11 July 1545.

59 Wat Suan Dòk is the center of an old city, the walls of which are still partially visible.

60 Wat Pa Khet: location unknown.

61 Wat Chiang Khòm: location unknown.

62 Wat Pa Than (now deserted): outside the city to the southwest.

63 The Ku Rüang fort is the southwest corner of the city walls.

them. The Shans filled in the moat for a month and twenty-five days, but they were unable to fill it; and they burned up the bunkers.

On the tenth waning of the first month (1 October 1545), the Suan Dòk encampment was burned. [The Shans] then went to /f° 5.33/ Mæ Ta for seven days; and then on Thursday, the fourth waxing of the second month, a Thai *ka khai* day,[64] they withdrew back to their own domain.

On Thursday, the ninth waxing of the third month, a Thai *kat sai* day,[65] Phraya Klang and Phraya Sura came from Lan Chang and arrived at Chiang Mai to take charge of the country.

Another Ayudhya Invasion, 1545–1546

At that time, Bòrommatraicak, the king of the south, had Mün Sukhothai take / boats filled with weapons and come up by water to Lamphun. On the Mon Thursday, twelfth waning of the third month, a Thai *dap mao* day,[66] they began negotiations with Rajamuli. The officials—/ Cao Mün Nangsü Luang Mit, Mün Khrai Mòng Yian, Mün Lamphun, Mün Mahā That, Mün Dang, Mün Patu Hò, and Mün Khao Khæn Lan—agreed to negotiate; [but] Mün Phrao, Mün Dang Lan, and Phuak Na Rüan, these three, would not agree to negotiate, and would fight.

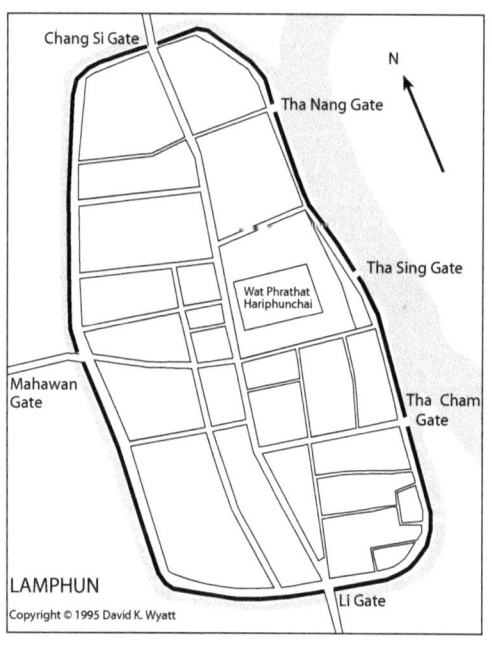

On the first waxing of the fourth month (4 December 1545), Rajamoli / and all the nobles took the proposals to Mün Sukhothai and [Mün] Lawo, [who said,] "We have not come in enmity, nor with the desire to be the single legitimate

---

64 Thursday (third waxing of the second month) 8 October 1545.
65 Wednesday (ninth waxing of the second month) 14 October 1545.
66 Thursday (eleventh waning, fifth month) 28 January 1546.

sovereignty. Let us all enter and leave freely: it's not necessary to maintain the fortified state of the city."

At midnight, Mün Sukhothai rode elephants in through the Li Gate [of Lamphun] and entered / the home of Mün Nangsü and seized the lances and swords and all the possessions; and took all the princes, nobles, and people of the town, and burned everything down from the Tha Nang Gate to the Mahawan Gate. Mün Dang Lan and Mün Phrao escaped. The king of the south left Lamphun and encamped at the Ton Rai Ton Luang [area] north of the Ku Kham [area] /f° 5.34/ of Kum Kam.

On Friday, the first waxing of the fifth month (3 January 1546), the king of the south [had] Mün Sri Mahā Thet [and] Phan Thep Monthian take tribute to present to the Queen and her two children. On Saturday the second waning (19 January 1546) there were no negotiations; [so] in the morning the king of the south had Mün Sukhothai command an army to fight on the west side [of the city of Chiang Mai]. They were defeated and fled. Cao Mün Sam Lan Ai / appointed all the nobles to go out and fight them at the Hua Rin.[67] Many Southerners died, and they dispersed to the east. The king of the south had Mün Kamphængphet command a force to fight at the Nòng Ya and Nòng Muan fields.[68] Cao Sæn Phing Chai Kæo had nobles go out to fight them, and many Southern men died, / and they withdrew across the Ping River to its east bank.

That same day, in the evening, the Southerners unsuccessfully attacked the Sæng Phung [i.e., Suan Prung] Gate.[69] Being unsuccessful again on the eighth and the ninth waxing (8–9 February 1546), they burned down Wat Sæn Thòng[70] and the neighborhood.

On the ninth waxing, at midnight, the king of the south withdrew, leaving a force behind. / On the eleventh waxing (11 February 1546) they all withdrew. The royal officers, including the commanders, pursued them to Chiang Khrœng, and captured thirty horses, killed a great many men, and obtained / many captives. The king of the south fled by way of M. Li[71] and M. Pòm to the Huai Hat. The ruler of Nan,

---

67 Hua Rin: northwest corner of the Chiang Mai city walls.

68 Nòng Ya and Nòng Muan fields: location uncertain.

69 Sæn Phung Gate: Suan Prung Gate of Chiang Mai city. In the south wall, near the Ku Rüang corner (southwest). Being in the most inauspicious portion of the city walls, it was through this gate that the dead were conveyed to cremations, like the Pratu Phi ("Spirit Gate") of Keng Tung and Phræ, or the Pratu Mara ("Devil's Gate") of Sukhothai and Kamphængphet.

70 Wat Sæn Thòng: location unknown.

71 Müang Li: at the mouth of the Mæ Li; in Thœn district, Lampang province.

named Yi Mongkhon;⁷² Mün Khruan and the Nakhòn force; and Mün Nòi Chiang Rüak pursued them and fought them, and many Southerners fell dead into the Huai Hat. They captured four elephants. Mün Kamphængphet Mün Cit and many Southerners died. About thirty thousand Southerners /fº 5.35/ went away by water. Mün Dan Patu Hò and Mün Sæ Nò Kham and their soldiers pursued them, and they caught and killed Khun Phuripañña Thao and Khun Còm Ratchamonthianban and ten thousand infantry and three thousand war boats were taken.

King Setthathirat of Luang Prabang, 1546–1547

In the *rwai sanga* year, s. 908, on Saturday the tenth waxing of the ninth month, a Thai *rwai / set* day,⁷³ King Uppayo⁷⁴ left Lan Chang and came to Chiang Sæn. At Chiang Sæn he had monks descend down onto a raft to undergo ordination. He remained in Chiang Sæn for twenty-one days.

On the seventh waning of the ninth month (11 May 1546), he reached Chiang Rai, where he remained for nine days. On the fifth waning of the tenth month, a Wednesday, a Thai *dap khai* day,⁷⁵ / he arrived at Mün Khròm and M. Kæo. On Friday, the sixth waning, a Thai *rwai cai* day,⁷⁶ Cao Sæn Phing Chai Kæo, Cao Mün Sam Lan Ai, Cao Sæn Khrao Nanthakhiri, Cao Mün Luang Phran, Cao Mün Luang Ca Ban, Cao Mün Luang Phuttha, Cao Mün Luang Lam Khæk Ñanakitti, / and all the junior officers, inner and outer, together took up the royal utensils, the parasol and fan, palanquins, elephants, horses, lances and swords, and all the processional implements, and all came out together in procession to welcome the Uppayo and invite him to enter through the / arched gateway to Wat Chiang Yün.⁷⁷ The king doffed his garments and donned a white suit, and held a bowl and flowers and puffed rice and gold and silver candles and entered and paid reverence to the Buddha image of Wat Chiang Yün. A bit before noon, he entered the White Elephant Gate⁷⁸ north

---

72 The Nan ruler, Yi Mongkhon: cf. Wyatt, *Nan Chronicle*, p. 62.
73 Perhaps Friday (first waxing twelfth month) 27 August 1546.
74 This is King Setthathirat of Lan Chang.
75 Thursday (fourth waning, first tenth month) 17 June 1546.
76 Friday 18 June 1546.
77 Wat Chiang Yün. See city map
78 The Chang Phüak Gate, on the north side of the city.

of the city to enter the palace and sit upon the bejeweled throne at noon. In the evening, he went to /f° 5.36/ reverence the Emerald Buddha[79] at its pavilion. On the seventh waning,[80] in the evening watch, he reverenced the Chedi Luang, walking on mats from the palace to the temple.

On the fourth waxing of the eleventh month, a Wednesday, a Thai *müang khai* day, in the 26th *ræk kot*,[81] at noon, the counselors and ministers together performed the rite of royal coronation of / the Phra Ratcha-uppayo as king of the domain of Chiang Mai in the Bejeweled Throne Hall in the royal palace, accompanied by his two royal daughters [and] Phra Ton Thip, who was the first royal queen, and Phra Ton Kham, her younger sister.

On the fifth waning of the eleventh month,[82] King Uppayowarat went to pay homage / to the Holy Reliquary of Suthep.[83] On the tenth waning of the eleventh month, a Wednesday, King Uppayo bestowed titles upon the counselors and ministers: Sæn Phing Chai Kæo became the Phraya Sæn Luang Sitthiratchaprakian; Mün Sam Lan Lü Chai became the minister ruling Chiang Rai; / Mün Kæo Mano became Phraya Sathira-amat; Mün Luang Phran became Phraya Watchare-amat; and Mün Phing Yi became Phraya Sutthasana-amat; all five of these being *phraya* of the golden-bowl rank.[84] Mün Luang Lam Khæk became Sæn Khæk Cheyyamongkhon; / and Sæn Khrao Pheri was named to rule Lamphun with the name of Sæn Lamphun: these two *khun* were given silver bowls and raiments. [Further,] Phraya Sutthasana was named to rule Chiang Sæn; Phraya Wachira-amat was named to rule M. Phran; and Phraya Lü Chai [was named] to rule Chiang Rai.

---

79 The Emerald Buddha was enshrined at Wat Chedi Luang.

80 Sunday 20 June 1546.

81 This (because it has a *ræk* of 26) has to be Saturday (fourth waning of the second tenth month) 17 July 1546.

82 Wednesday (fifth waning of the eleventh month in the year) 15 September 1546. Most of the problems with dates in this year are due to the fact that the chronologers in Chiang Mai should have intercalated (a second tenth month) in that year but did not.

83 On Dòi Suthep.

84 In Bangkok, the highest-ranking *phraya* had their titles engraved on golden plates. Something similar is involved here, with precious bowls involved with the conferral of ranks.

In s. 909, a *pœk san* year, on the fifth waxing of the twelfth month,[85] King /fº 5.37/ Uppayowarat returned to Lan Chang.

The Dawn of the Kali Epoch, 1548

Thereafter, the country was unstable, and had truly entered a Kali Epoch.

In the *pœk san* year, s. 910, in the latter half of the second month (late October 1548), Phraya Sutthasana said that he would depose Sæn Phing Chai. Sæn Phing Chai learned of this, but was determined not to be taken, and he stayed. In the fourth month, on the second waning (28 December 1548), / Sæn Dang Patu Hò donned his sword and buckler and took three of his men and went to Chao Phraya Lü Chai in the deep of the night. Cao Phraya Sæn Chai and Mün Khòk Müang Hò Kham went to seek out Mün Khun Luang Nakhòn at the Chiang Rüak Gate.[86] There they met with Sæn Dang Patu Hò and Mün Khòk Müang Nò Kham, / and [together] they came to Cao Phraya Sæn Luang and said, "Sæn Dang has donned his sword and buckler, and awaits a secret meeting." Cao Phraya Sæn Luang then reflected,

"Sæn Dang Nung Khrai has donned sword and buckler, and is conspiring. Surely together they are coming to take me." So he / announced to his many partisans, and called up a large number of his men, saying, "Phraya Sutthasana and his nobles have mobilized. We will set up an encampment in the city of Chiang Mai."

On the ninth waning of the fourth month (25 December 1548), in the noontime watch, Sæn Dang and Mün Thra and their soldiers fought Mün Khrai and Mün Khun Luang Nakhòn south of the royal plaza. / Mün Khrai and Mün Khun Luang led their elephants in to fight them in the middle of the city. On the fifth waxing of the fifth month, a Thursday, a Thai *rwai sanga* day (3 January 1549), in the evening watch, Phraya Sutthasana and all the nobles took their forces, including groups of elephants and horses and warriors, and fought Phraya Sæn and Phraya Wachira-amat, Mün Khrai, and the Mün Khun Luang. In the *phat* watch, they took their groups /fº 5.38/ of elephants, horses, and families and broke off fighting and fled

---

85 A year with the *pœk* cyclical element must end in a zero. Note that, just below, the year number and cyclical number are given correctly. Saturday (fifth waxing, twelfth month) 20 August 1547.

86 Chiang Rüak Gate: now the Tha Phæ Gate.

the city out the northern gate, and went to Nakhòn Lampang in the middle of the night.

Invasion from Phræ, 1551

In the *kot set* year, s. 912, on the sixth waning of the sixth month (26 February 1551), the ruler of Phræ, in his rank as Phraya Sam Lan, came to Chiang Mai with the Phraya Nakhòn of Lan Chang and the Phraya Hua Wiang of Lan Chang; and the three together intended to do ill to the country; but they failed / and fled. On the sixth waning of the seventh month (28 March 1551), the nobles gathered a force of soldiers to follow and fight them at the Chiang Mai market, and they were broken and fled back to Phræ. They had been in Chiang Mai for two months and twenty-five days.

Abdication of Setthathirat, 1551

In the *ruang khai* year, s. 913, in the eighth month (April 1551), King Uppayowarat / brought incense and candles, puffed rice, flowers, and gold and silver candles to beg pardon before the Sangha, and said that he was not coming, and that he was handing all the country of Chiang Mai over to the queen.

Accession of King Mæ Ku, 1551

So informed that the Uppayo would not be returning, the counselors and ministers / together invited Cao Thao Mæ Ku,[87] of the royal lineage descending from Cao Khun Khrüa, a son of King Mangrai, who was living in M. Nai[, to come as king.] Cao Thao Mæ Ku accepted the invitation and came.[88]

In the *ruang khai* year, s. 913, / on the fourth waxing of the ninth month (9 May 1551), King Mæ Ku entered the city of Chiang Mai and was enthroned in the royal palace on the bejeweled throne in the morning. On the tenth waning of the fourth month (22 December 1551), the counselors and ministers poured the waters of royal

---

87 Not a female ruler. His full name was Phra Mekutawisutthiwong, and he was the last king of Mangrai's dynasty. His name (Mæ Ku) refers to the Mæ Ku river of M. Nai.

88 Akiko Iijima is working on a manuscript version of a chronicle of Mæ Ku's reign.

consecration and blessings, over seven days, and then circumambulated the city, going out through the Sri Phum /f° 5.39/ Gate.

Shan Intrusions in Chiang Sæn and Chiang Rai, 1552

In the *tao cai* year, s. 914, on the tenth waxing of the ninth month (3 May 1552), the two brother princes of M. Nai and Chiang Thòng came to Chiang Rai. On the second waning of the ninth month, they went to Chiang Sæn and encamped at Dòi Kæo Kling at the mouth of the Kok [River].[89] On the eighth waning of the ninth month (16 May 1552), they fought and killed the Khwa Yan and seized his golden sword, and more than twenty infantry were killed. / On the tenth waxing of the tenth month (1 June 1552), the princely brothers and all their nobles left Chiang Sæn and went to Chiang Rai. On the tenth waxing of the eleventh month (1 July), the two princely brothers entered and tried to take Phraya Lü Chai the ruler of Chiang Rai at Dòi Pathum, but they failed. On the ninth waxing of the eleventh month (30 July),[90] the two princely brothers and the ruler of Fang / left Chiang Rai.

In that same year, a *tao cai* year (1552/53),[91] Phraya Lü Chai Sena left Chiang Rai to go and pay attendance upon King Mæ Ku in Chiang Mai. He remained there for five months and eight days.

Lao (Lan Chang) Defend Chiang Rai and Chiang Sæn, 1555

In the *dap mao* year, s. 917, on the full-moon day of the eighth month (5 May 1555), / the prince of M. Nai again invaded Chiang Rai and fought the Chawa at Thap Tao Pun and Thap Pa Khia, at the plaza. The Mün Ma of Chiang Rai and Chang Kò Kham Cet Yòi Nüa mounted elephants to combat the Chawa. The Chawa mounted six elephants to meet them. The Chawa could not win, and fled to Thap Pa Khia. / Four Chawa nobles were killed—Mün Kæ, Mün Khap Phræ, Mün Kwa, and Mün Luang.

---

89 Dòi Kæo Kling, at the mouth of the Kok River.
90 Mistake here: waxing should be waning.
91 These and the dates below, V. Lieberman tells me (pers. comm. 3 April 1995) agree with those in U Kala's *Mahayazawin gyi*, II (Rangoon, 1932), pp. 312 ff.

On the eleventh waning of the eighth month (16 May 1555), Phraya Nakhòn Si Fa and all the Chawa nobles fled to Chiang Sæn. On the thirteenth waning of the eighth month (18 May), the prince of M. Nai left Chiang Rai.

King Mæ Ku Sees Omens at Lampang, 1556

In the *rwai yi* year, s. 918, in the second month (October 1556), King /f° 5.40/ Mæ Ku went to Nakhòn to make merit at the Great Lampang Reliquary at M. Tan.[92] He saw two marvels: [1] He saw a cloud shaped like a Naga [serpent] slithering [across the sky] with its head in the west, tail in the east, spine to the north, and belly to the south, which was more than seven fathoms long. [2] He saw [the planet] Jupiter [like a] comet, / with its tail [inclined] to the north, which could be seen for a month before disappearing.

Invasion of the King of Pegu, 1557–1558

In the *müang sai* year, s. 919 (1557/58), the prince of M. Nai [sent an envoy] to tell King Mæ Ku, "Now, the king of Pegu is coming to take over M. Si Phlan Sai and / the ruler of M. Sum Sai, but we ourselves should [instead] do so. We, the elder, should expel the ruler of M. Sum Sai. Now, the king of Pegu says that he will bring up an army to do this. If this is true, please, O my younger brother the king / of Phing Chiang Mai, raise an army to assist me, your senior." This was in a letter brought by Mün Nòi Kæo and Phan Mòn.

Later, the prince of M. Nai sent a Mün Lam Khæk to report that, "Now, a vanguard of four thousand men of the king of Pegu has come to this place. / Please, O junior ruler the king of Phing Chiang Mai, send an army from your side of the Salween River, with lots of arrows and people expert at laying snares; and have Sæn Chiang Dao bring me a good army."

Then the king of Pegu, the Min Taya,[93] sent Atura and a suite of officials /f° 5.41/ to Chiang Mai. They attended upon King Mæ Ku, [with the message that,] "The king of Pegu, the Min Taya, has long enjoyed a good royal friendship with the king

---

92 Phra That Lampang Luang reliquary is southwest of Lampang. This reference tells us where M. Tan (or Wiang Tan) was. See *Sammana prawattisat Lampang* (Lampang, 1991).

93 *min taya*, of course, is a stock Burmese epithet for a king.

of Chiang Mai. We have received the envoys of the king of Chiang Mai at our court, that they might know well and see for themselves conditions in Ava, Si Phan, M. Mit, Bò Sæng [Mogok], Fa Yieo, / M. Thòn, and M. Yang,[94] all of them, and we have dispelled their false illusions. We have built many *cetiya* and *vihara*, and the merit we have earned we have given [in part] to the king of Chiang Mai. The prince of M. Nai has taken an oath of loyalty to us, and has [received] the gold and / silver plates. Now, he has violated that oath and bond with us, and he has killed the ruler of M. Sum Sai. We will take an army with elephants and horses and correct [the ruler of] M. Nai. He will not withstand us, and will seek refuge with the king of M. Phing Chiang / Mai. When he comes, quickly send him to us and [thus] cement the ties of friendship between us, even more than before."

Later, the king of Pegu, the Min Taya, sent another envoy to Chiang Mai, with Surayotha as ambassador, / Kam Mæng Phrom as his deputy, Si Phra Mun as the third envoy, and Yi Kham Müang as *tala* [secretary], who called upon the *ca ban* to present a message in accordance with ancient usage and customs. The royal letter said, "Formerly, the prince of M. Nai was very loyal to us, as on gold and silver plates. Now he has violated his oath. /f° 5.42/ He has offended against M. Sum Sai, without telling us. Thus we have sent an army to correct M. Nai. If the prince of M. Nai has put himself under the protection of Chiang Mai, send him quickly to us."

When the king of Pegu, the Min Taya, reached M. Pan, he again sent Ban Klang as a royal ambassador, and Prap Kamlang as / secretary, to tell King Mæ Ku, "The prince of M. Nai has come out to present himself and his wives and children and country completely to us as our vassals. The king of M. Phing [Chiang Mai] should quickly come to talk with us on the banks of the Salween River." / King Mæ Ku then had his counselors and envoys reply, sending Mün Khæk Sai as ambassador, Phan Rattana Prai as deputy ambassador, Yi Ca Ban Lam Khæk as third ambassador, and Yanasakhòn and Sisota as secretaries to go and reply / to Surayotha and the group of envoys. King Mæ Ku did not [himself] go.

King Pœng Phawa Min Taya, the king of Pegu, reached the Salween, and sent the prince of Chiang Thòng, Thamong Plik Sai, and Rattana Panya to call upon the king of M. Phing Chiang Mai. / The envoys of the king of Chiang Mai met the

---

94 Ava;, Si Phan, Müang Mit, Bò Sæng [Mogok], Fa Yieo, M. Thòn, and M. Yang: some of these have been placed on the relevant map.

prince of Chiang Thòng at Chiang Dao. When they arrived, they presented the letter of the king to the king of Pegu [to the envoys] at Hang Ruang.[95] The king of Pegu had Nanthachit and Kam Mæng Khrüa accompany the envoys of Chiang Mai to come out to /f° 5.43/ receive [the king of Pegu]. The king of Pegu advanced his army [following] behind the envoys to Chiang Mai. On the ninth waxing of the seventh month (28 March 1558) they encamped at Yang Phrak at the Kannika Well.[96] King Mæ Ku then invited Somdet Cao Sri Nantha [of Wat] Phra Sing, Supreme Patriarch Chai Prakian Rattanapañña [of Wat] Mæ Ki, Mahā Phutthima, Mün Mahā Mæ / Mak Lœk; and Cao Phraya Khæk Phuttima, Cao Sæn Thuan Ñanasathian, Mün Lam Khæk Sai, and Wachirapraya to go and pay homage to the king of Pegu.

The king of Pegu said, "Have the king of M. Phing Chiang Mai come out and sit enthroned with us. If you do so, / all your country and your people will be contented."

The next day, the king of Pegu toured [around] the city. On the twelfth waxing of the seventh month, the day of the New Year beginning the *pœk sanga* year, s. 920 (31 March 1558),[97] the king of Pegu moved his army to encamp on the Chang Phap, and he besieged the city / for three days and three nights, until Saturday, the full-moon day of the seventh month, a Thai *tao set* day (2 April 1558), in the morning, when he took the city of Chiang Mai.[98]

Historical Retrospective

King Mangrai built M. Chiang Mai in the *rwai san* year, Thursday the full-moon day of the seventh month, in the 8th *rœk kot*, at dawn, entering the Tula *lagna*, s. / 658. From then, it was 262 years to the loss of the city in the *pœk sanga* year, s. 920, Saturday the full-moon day of the seventh month, a Thai *tao set* day, in *rœk kot* 13 (2 April 1558), in the morning.

---

95 Or Hang Luang.

96 Yang Phrak at the Kannika [Water] Well: in Fang. See Yuphin Khemmuk, "Lao rüang prawattisat cak khlong Mangthra rop Chiang Mai," *Ruam botkhwam Lan Na khadi sancòn tam ròi Khlong Mangthra Rop Chiang Mai* (Chiang Mai, 1990), p. 96.

97 The New Year began on the previous day.

98 The "date of Chiang Mai's capture is a more specific version of dates presented in U Kala, II, 322–27, and generally agrees with the Burmese chronology." (Lieberman, pers. comm., 3 April 1995).

Pegu, Chiang Sæn, Chiang Khæng, and the Lü

In the reign of King Mæ Ku, he had Phraya Kamphon go and rule Chiang Sæn.[99]

When King Pœng Phawa Min Taya, /f° 5.44/ king of Pegu, took Chiang Mai, he took all of Lan Na Thai. He was pleased to order as follows: "The princes, governors, and the chiefs (*kæsan*) of all the mountain folk, all have submitted to us, completely. As for the ruler of Chiang Sæn, does he not fear our power and majesty? Where is he?"

The ruler of / Chiang Khæng[100] replied, "I, your lowly servant, have heard that he has gone to the [Sip] Sòng Panna of the Lü, at M. U.[101]" When he said this, the king of Pegu, the Min Taya, ordered the ruler of Chiang Khæng to go to call him to come to his court. / The ruler of Chiang Khæng said, "I am not clever; not accomplished: I'm just a mountain boy, who does government work, [but I am not an envoy]. I would go by way of M. Yòng, Chiang Lap, Ban Yu, and M. Luai[102] and have them augment my forces." / At this advice, the king of Pegu, the Min Taya ordered that the ruler of Chiang Khæng should go and take M. Yòng, Chiang Lap, Ban Yu, and M. Luai to augment his forces and [then] go to M. U, and bring in Phraya Kamphon, the ruler of Chiang Sæn, [back] to Pœng / Phawa Min Taya. Then the king was pleased to have Phraya Kamphon rule Chiang Sæn as before.

King Pœng Phawa Min Taya then handed over rule of all the country of Chiang Mai to King Mæ Ku to be king in Lan Na Thai as before. Then he ordered golden plates[103] /f° 5.45/ be given to all the officials to serve him, [he who was] junior to him. The king of M. Phing Chiang Mai, a descendent of the line of King Mangrai, and appropriate to be a king upon earth, was then consecrated a king to dwell in the royal / palace, on the Mon Thursday, fifth waning of the seventh month (7 April 1558).

---

99 It would appear that it was here that Sirivamso Bhikkhu of Chiang Sæn began his continuation of the Chiang Mai Chronicle.

100 This has always been a very difficult place to identify. In the nineteenth century it moved to near M. Sing; and it generally is in that section of the Middle Mekong, west of M. Sing. See the foldout map in H. Warington Smyth, *Five Years in Siam* (London, 1898; repr. Bangkok, 1994).

101 Now in northern Laos, but traditionally one of the Sipsong (12) Panna of Chiang Rung.

102 These are places in the vicinity of M. Yòng and M. Luai.

103 The Burmese, like the kings of Ayudhya and Bangkok, conferred titles by issuing titles written on golden plates for the highest ranks. Chiang Mai gave gifts of gold and silver bowls.

King Min Taya appointed Surayotha, ruling M. Mò Yi, to be a royal commissioner [*yokkrabat*]; Phraya Pukkawut, ruling M. Sang Yiap, as his deputy; and ten thousand troops and their officers to serve / King Mæ Ku.

On the fourth waning of the eighth month (6 May 1558), the King Min Taya took his army and returned to Pegu. He had been in Chiang Mai for a month and twelve days.

Later, the officers who had / served the king of Chiang Mai did not respect the king who was holy, so King Min Taya had Aphintha Luk Khrüa Khròng, bear an edict of the king Min Taya ordering the officers to respect the king, who was / holy.

Itinerary of King Mæ Ku's Trip to Fight the Lao, 1559

In the *pæk sanga* year, the same year, sixth waxing of the fifth month, a Mon Friday, Thai *pæk san* (13 January 1559), King Mæ Ku, the Holy, went in procession to fight the Chawa enemy and those provincial lords who were Chawa.[104]

On the sixth, he proceeded from Chiang Mai, and rested at Phœng Müang, having gone 10,000 fathoms.[105] /f° 5.46/ He stayed there one day.
From Phœng Müang, he went to sleep at Pa Yai, 12,000 fathoms.
From Pa Yai, he went to sleep in a royal hut at Pha Phœng, 8,000 fathoms.
From there he went to sleep at Phao Nòi, 8,000 fathoms.
From Phlao Nòi he went to sleep at Chæ Sak, 10,000 fathoms.
From Chæ Sak, he went to sleep at Fœi Rai, 12,000 fathoms.
From Fœi Rai he went 10,000 fathoms to sleep / at Chæ Hæng.
From Chæ Hæng he went 10,000 fathoms to sleep at Tha Kham Mæ Khrao.
From Tha Kham he went to sleep at M. Ngao, 7,000 fathoms.
From M. Ngao, he went 6,000 fathoms to sleep at Ban Yian.
From Ban Yian, he went to sleep at Klai Rüang, 10,000 fathoms.
From Klai Rüang, he went to sleep at Chiang Rai, / 6,000 fathoms

---

104 See the map of this very detailed itinerary. By no means can all of the toponyms mentioned be identified; but enough of them can be placed so that the itinerary is relatively complete.

105 Remember that a fathom is about two meters, and so 10,000 fathoms is about 20,000 meters or 20 km.

CHAPTER FIVE   181

There he organized the arming of the Chiang Mai men and all the provincial contingents, 48,000 troops, 270 elephants, 12,000 horses. He stayed at Chiang Rai for five days.

From Chiang Rai he went to sleep at Nòng Bòn, more than 11,000 fathoms.

From Nòng Bòn he went to sleep at / the Yang Field on the Mæ Phlao, 10,000 fathoms.

From the Yang Field he went to sleep at Tha Than, 10,000 fathoms.

From Tha Than, he went to Ban Rai north of Wiang Sœng 12,000 fathoms.

On the thirteenth waning of the fifth month (5 February 1559), he got the ruler of Sœng [i.e., Thœng].

On the sixth waxing of the sixth month (12 February 1559), in the *phat* watch, after dusk, the Uppayo of Lan Chang left M. Chiang Sæn for / Lan Chang.

On the thirteenth waxing of the sixth month (19 February 1559), he ordered Phraya Kamphon to go to rule Chiang Sæn.

The king who was Holy then went from M. Sœng to sleep at Kat Du, 6,000 fathoms.

From Kat Du he went to Wiang Lò,[106] 6,000 fathoms.

From Wiang Lò he went to the Chawa Bridge, 10,000 fathoms.

From the Chawa Bridge he went to sleep at Phayao, 12,000 fathoms.

From Phayao he went to sleep /f° 5.47/ at Chæ Ta, 8,000 fathoms.

From Chæ Ta he went to sleep at Thap Phui, 6,000 fathoms.

From Thap Phui he went to sleep at Nam Yang, 12,000 fathoms.

From Nam Yang he went to sleep at Nam Un, 6,000 fathoms.

From Nam Un he went to sleep at the Rapids, 10,000 fathoms.

He stayed at the rapids for two days. On the fifth waxing of the seventh month (13 March 1559), he left the rapids and went to sleep at Yang Khun Sayiap, 8,000 fathoms.

From Yang Khun he went / to sleep at Pa Lao, 12,000 fathoms.

From Pa Lao he went to sleep at M. Sòng,[107] 10,000 fathoms.

From M. Sòng he went to sleep at Wang Kham, 5,000 fathoms.

From Wang Kham he went to sleep at Pa Sieo, 12,000 fathoms.

---

106 Or M. Lò; Ban Wiang Lò, in Cun district, Phayao province.

107 M. Sòng: in Sòng district, Phræ province. See Sisak Wanliphodom, *Müang boran nai khet Sukhothai*, p. 12.

From Pa Sieo he went to Phræ, 12,000 fathoms, and he stayed in Phræ for 12 days.

On the 4th waning of the seventh month (27 March 1559), he installed / Phraya Chiang Lüak to rule Phræ.

From Phræ, he went to sleep at Khrao Ton Hua, 5,000 fathoms.

From Khrao Ton Hua, he came to sleep at the Nam Ta,[108] 9,000 fathoms.

He stayed at the Nam Ta for one day.

From the Nam Ta he went to sleep at Huai Som, 9,300 fathoms.

From Huai Som he came to sleep at Nam Mò,[109] 9,200 fathoms. /

From the Nam Mò he reached Nakhòn [Lampang] in 13,500 fathoms.

On the tenth waning of the seventh month (2 April 1559), he conducted Catupari Nò Kham to rule Nakhòn. He remained at Nakhòn for five days.

From Nakhòn he went 12,000 fathoms to M. Tan.

From M. Tan he went to sleep at Thap Puai,[110] 6,500 fathoms.

From Thap Puai he came / to sleep at Lamphun, 12,000 fathoms. He stayed at Lamphun for one day.

From Lamphun he reached Chiang Mai in 10,000 fathoms.

The king, he who was Holy, traveled on that occasion for a distance of 367,500 fathoms. He had thirty-nine temporary royal huts. He was gone for a total of two months and twenty-nine days.

Rebellion of Mæ Ku and Succession of Queen Wisutthathewi, 1564

After that, /f° 5.48/ six years later, in the *kap cai* year, s. 926 (1564/65), King Mæ Ku rebelled against the Cao Pœng Phawa Min Taya, king of Pegu.[111] The king of Pegu brought up an army and took Chiang Mai, and captured Cao Thao Mæ Ku

---

108 Nam Ta: now a village, Wiang Ta, in Phræ province. See Withi Phanitchaphan, *Cittakam Wiang Ta* = *Wiang Ta Murals* (Chiang Mai, s.d.).

109 Now Mæ Mò in Lampang province; site of a major lignite mining and electric generation operation. See Phisit Carœnwong et al., "Müang Mæ Mò, Òp Luang, læ Ban Yang Tai," in *Borankhadi phak nüa* (Bangkok, 1988), p. 21.

110 Thap Puai: village on the railway between Lampang and Lamphun.

111 King Bayinnaung, r. 1551–1581.

and brought him back to Pegu, leaving Lady Wisutthathewi[112] to rule the domain in his place.

After that, / two years later, in the *rwai yi* year, s. 928 (1566/67), the Shans came down to attack Chiang Mai. Rice was expensive, 10,000 weight for 50 units of silver. Three years later, it was again cheap.

In s. 930, a *pœk si* year (1568/69), Prince Min Taya went to take Ayutthiya and succeeded in that year.[113]

In s. 934, / a *tao san* year (1572/73), [the Min Taya] went to war at Nòng Ram.

Death of Wisutthithewi; Succession of Tharrawaddy Prince, 1578/79

In s. 940, a *pœk yi* year (1578/79), Lady Wisutthithewi died. In this reign, Kham Mu went to rule Chiang Sæn. In this same year, the Prince Min Taya had his son, named Prince Tharrawaddy Nòratha Min Khòi[114] come to rule the domain of Chiang Mai. / In this reign, the ruler of Lamphun went to rule Chiang Sæn.

Colophon to Chapter Five

Rājavaṁsa pañca kantho nitthito completed.[115]

---

112 Yuphin ("Lao rüang prawattisat cak khlong Mangthra rop Chiang Mai," p. 98) tells us that she may have been a queen of Bayinnaung, and was a younger daughter of King Ket.

113 The royal chronicles of Ayudhya say that Ayudhya fell to the Burmese on 8 August 1569. "The date corresponds to that given at U Kala, II, 431." (Lieberman, pers. comm., 3 April 1995).

114 Variously written Min Nòratha Chò etc.

115 Pali: "The Fifth Fascicle of the Royal Chronicle is Completed."

Chapter 6

Death of Bayinnaung, 1581

Phraya Lamphun did not rule Chiang Sæn for very long.¹ He left Lamphun for his wife to rule for three years; then he moved to rule M. Pai. The Min Taya had Phraya Hua Khian rule Chiang Mai, while he returned to Pegu. In s. 943, a *luang sai* year, on the second waning of the second month (12 November 1581), the Min Taya / died. His son, the Nòng Phak Wun Min Taya, ascended the throne in his stead in Pegu.²

Wars With Ayudhya and Luang Prabang, 1585–1603

In s. 947, a *dap rao* year (1585/86), the Chiang Mai army was sent to fight the South, unsuccessfully, and Nantha Kòi Tò was lost.

In s. 954, a *tao si* year (1592/93), the Uparaja took an armed force to the South to fight King Naret / with 700,000 men.³ In this reign, the Tha[rra]waddy prince went to rule Chiang Sæn.

In s. 957, a *dap met* year (1595/96), the king of Lan Chang came to support the governor of Nan as the king of Lan Na,⁴ but unsuccessfully; and he returned to Lan Chang.

---

1 Curiously, this chapter does not begin with a Pali phrase.
2 Note the switch from Julian to Gregorian calendar in October 1582. According to Harvey (*History of Burma*, p. 179), Bayinnaung was succeeded by his son Nandabayin (r. 1581–1599).
3 King Naresuan.
4 Cf. Wyatt, *Nan Chronicle*, p. 67 and fn. 7.

In s. 960, a *pæk set* year (1598/99), the Lao retreated from Pegu to Chiang Mai, / and [then] fled back to Lan Chang. The people of the South attacked Chiang Mai in that year.[5]

In s. 962, a *kot cai* year (1600/01), Chiang Rai rebelled against the Burmese, and the Burmese came to Chiang Rai.

In s. 963, a *luang pao* year (1601/02), Òkya Ram Techo[6] went as governor of Chiang Sæn. Lan Chang came up to take Lan Na, with the exception of Phayao, Fang, and Chiang Mai, / which they did not capture. Òkya Ram Techo fled Chiang Sæn in that year.

In s. 965, a *ka mao* year (1603/04), M. Sat rebelled against the Burmese, and the Burmese came and swept up many captives.

Burmese Successions in Chiang Mai, 1607–1628

In s. 969, a *müang met* year (1607/08), Prince Tharrawaddy Nòratha Min Khòi died. He had ruled Chiang Mai for twenty-eight years. His son, Thado Khòi, ruled in his stead /f° 6.02/ for a year and a month and died.[7] His middle son then ruled in his stead for five years. In the *ka pao* year, s. 975 (1613/14), he died. His youngest brother ruled in his stead for thirteen years, to the *rwai yi* year, s. 988 (1616/17), when he died.[8] In this reign, Phraya Ca Ban ruled Chiang Sæn.

In s. 976, a *kap yi* year (1614/15), Nakhòn rebelled against King Nòng Phak Wun Min Taya, the son. The Burmese came to take him; / and they took the son of the Phraya Chiang Sæn and made him a *wun*,[9] and they took elephants and gave them to him and gave him Lampang. Prince Phawa Min Taya thus was pleased with the Phraya Chiang Sæn and made him the "Albino Crow" Prince and gave him a golden

---

5 Notton (p. 172) shows us that the copy from which he worked was defective.

6 Clearly and obviously an Ayudhya title.

7 "U Kala, III (Rangoon, 1961), 50–51, refers to the new Chiang Mai ruler as Naw-rahta-zaw; and p. 175 refers to him as Anaw-rahta-min-zaw. (Lieberman, pers. comm., 3 April 1995.)

8 Harvey (*History of Burma*, p. 185) gives a confusing picture of this period in Burma. See Victor Lieberman, *Burmese Administrative Cycles: Anarchy and Conquest c. 1580-1760* (Princeton, 1984), especially his chart of rulers on page 293, which I have used. According to it, Nandabayin (r. 1581–99) was succeeded first by Nyaungyan Min (r. 1597–1606) and then by Anaukhpetlun (r. 1606–1628).

9 The Burmese *wun* had ministerial rank, and often functioned as governors or viceroys.

howdah with a red roof, gilt with gold. Thenceforth, all official business had to be / submitted first to the King of Pegu.

In s. 977, a *dap mao* year (1615/16), the youngest adoptive son of the king of Chiang Mai had Phraya Nan[10] come up to be governor of Chiang Mai.

In s. 981, a *kat met* year (1619/20), the Albino Crow Prince died and his wife ruled the domain [of Chiang Sæn] in his stead.[11]

In s. 986, a *kap cai* year (1624/25), Chiang Khòng rebelled, and / King Nòng Phak Wun Min Taya had King Suddhodhammaraja Min Ræ Cò Swa bring an army up to Chiang Mai, which then took Chiang Khòng on the ninth waxing of the twelfth month (22 August 1624).

In s. 987, a *dap pao* year (1625/26), Nan rebelled,[12] and King Suddho[13] went and took Nan.

In / s. 988, a *rwai yi* year (1626/27), King Suddho went and took Chiang Rung. King Nòng Phak Wun Min Taya died in Pegu in that same year, and Min Ræ Thippha[net] ascended to rule in his stead in that year.[14]

In s. 990, a *pæk si* year (1628/29), [he] returned to establish [himself] in Chiang Sæn. The two brother kings did not get along with each other, and the elder brother entered into the city and dwelt /fº 6.03/ in the palace of the White Crow Prince and had the Nò Kham Fa, the son of Phraya Thipphanet, rule Chiang Sæn, and then he made a royal progress back to Pegu. The ruler of Chiang Sæn went with him to send him off, as far as Fang. The governor of Chiang Mai then went up and took Chiang Sæn, and imprisoned the two, father and son, in the city of Chiang Mai. When King Suddho had reached Pegu, he took / and deposed Min Ræ Thip, and King Suddho then ascended the jeweled throne in his stead.

The governor of Lampang[15] volunteered to the king of Chiang Mai to take Chiang Sæn, and [the king] made him the governor of Lampang as Phraya "Glory of Two

---

10 Cf. Wyatt, *Nan Chronicle*, p. 70.

11 She is sometimes referred to as Nang Fa Ka Phüak.

12 Cf. Wyatt, *Nan Chronicle*, p. 71 and fn. 2.

13 "Suddho is certainly Thado-[dhamma-raja], i.e., Tha-lun." Lieberman, pers. comm., 3 April 1995.

14 Here is a faint echo of the demise of Anaukhpetlun in 1628. He was succeeded by Thalun, r. 1629–1648.

15 Usually referred to as Nakhòn or Lakhòn.

Cities" (Phraya Sri Sòng Müang), and sent / Sæn Atya to be the Wun of Chiang Sæn, and appointed a force of three thousand men to go and hold the city.

King Suddho of Pegu Appoints Phraya Thipphanet, 1631

Three years later, in the *luang met* year, s. 993 (1631/32), Prince Phawa Min Taya Suddhodhammaraja again took Chiang Mai, capturing the king of Chiang Mai to imprison in Pegu, and appointed Phraya Thipphanet, the father of Phraya Chiang Sæn, / to eat the three million rice-fields of Chiang Mai,[16] and appointed Phraya Chiang Sæn to rule Chiang Sæn as before.

In s. 994, a *tao san* year (1632/33), King Suddhodhammaraja came to take Fang, and after three years he took it.[17]

In s. 998, a *rwai cai* year (1636/37), King Suddhodhammaraja Min Taya had three thousand novices ordained, / and moved to establish [the city of] Ava. He issued an order to build Wat Chetawan at Chiang Sæn[18] at the palace of Lady Princess White Crow, as a royal establishment; and he had Maha Pa Dòn Thæn[19] come up to care for Wat Chetawan, and raised him to the rank of *somdet*.

In s. 1000, a *pæk yi* year (1638/39), Lady Princess White Crow /f° 6.04/ died.

In s. 1010, a *pæk cai* year (1648/49), King Min Taya Suddhodhammaraja died in Ava, and Phra Wanañjeyya ascended the Emerald Throne in Ava in his stead in that year.[20]

In s. 1012, a *kot si* year (1650/51), the ruler of Chiang Sæn died.

In s. 1017, a *dap met* year (1655/56), Phra Sæng Müang was appointed the ruler of Chiang Sæn / in his stead for three years and then was sent to confinement in Ava.

The ruler of Phræ rules Chiang Mai, 1659

---

16 This is a curious reference to the "three million rice-fields (na)."

17 Notton (p. 175, n. 4) says that the Burmese encampment is still visible today (1932), and called Wiang Suttho.

18 Some chronicles call this Wat Ka Phüak ("Albino Crow"). Now deserted. See Krom Sinlapakòn, *Raingan kansamruat boransathan müang Chiang Sæn* (Bangkok, 1987), p. 115.

19 From one of two temples on the Dòn Thæn island opposite Chiang Sæn, concerning which see Bunchuai Sisawat, *Chiang Mai læ phak nüa* (Bangkok, 1961), p. 549.

20 The reference is to the succession of King Pindale (r. 1648–1661). "Thalun died 1010 taw-thalin 10 wan., i.e., 1648." (Lieberman, pers. comm., 3 April 1995.)

In s. 1021, a *kat khai* year (1659/60), the lord ruler of Phræ ascended the emerald throne of Chiang Mai.

In s. 1022, a *kot cai* year (1660/61), the Southerners brought an army up to attack Chiang Mai, but failed: Chiang Sæn fell to the Southerners in that year. /

In s. 1023, a *luang pao* year (1661/62), the town [of Chiang Sæn] was [re-]established.

In s. 1025, a *ka mao* year (1663/64), Fa Sang Kung came to Chiang Sæn.[21]

In s. 1034, a *tao cai* year (1672/73), King Ing Sæ Min died in Ava.[22] The son of King Cephutrai Müang was appointed ruler of Chiang Sæn / in that year. He remained for five years and died. Phra Salœm Müang ruled Chiang Sæn in his place. The Lord ruler of Phræ who ruled Chiang Mai died, and King Ingsæ ascended the emerald throne in his stead in Chiang Mai in that year.

Miscellaneous Events, 1675–1706

In s. 1037, a *dap mao* year (1675/76), King Ingsæ / died, and the son of King Phutrai ascended to sit in his stead in that year.[23]

In s. 1040, a *pœk sanga* year (1678/79), Phra Salœm Müang died, and Rot Sang Lam was made Wun in his stead to rule Chiang Sæn.

In s. 1044, a *tao set* year (1682/83), Rot Sang Lam oppressed, and Min Sa came to arrest him and sent him to Ava.

In s. /f° 6.05/ 1054, a *tao san* year (1692/93), the prince of M. Luang came to rule Chiang Sæn.

In s. 1057, a *dap khai* year (1695/96), the ruler of Chiang Sæn died.

In s. 1061, a *kat mao* year (1699/1700), Mahadhamma Phukam died.

---

21 Notton here (pp. 176–177) has a very long footnote, giving an alternate account of the same period from the PY.

22 After Pindale, King Pyè reigned 1661–1672; then Nayawaya (r. 1672–1673). "Ing Sæ Min must be 'ein-shei min,' i.e., the [former] lord of the Eastern Palace or Heir-Apparent, Naya-waya, who died in 1673. Although Pye also died in 1034 (1672), the Ing Sæ Min epithet makes him the less probable referrent." (Lieberman, pers. comm., 3 April 1995.)

23 That is, in Chiang Mai.

In s. 1062, a *kot si* year (1700/01), Nò Sai became Wun of Chiang Sæn, and Rammasen became *Sitkè*.²⁴

In s. 1063, a *ruang / sai* year (1701/02), Mahadhamma freed Chiang Sæn from dependence on Chiang Mai.

In s. 1064, a *tao sanga* year (1702/03), Lao came seeking refuge, and were taken away to Ava.

In s. 1065, a *ka met* year (1703/04), the Lao attacked Lan Na, setting themselves up at Chiang Khòng, and then fled [back] by [way of] Nan in that year.²⁵ /

In s. 1066, a *kap san* year (1704/05), the Ni Wun who ruled Chiang Sæn was brought to Chiang Mai and executed. Rak Phaya Cesu became Wun in his stead, and Phala E became *Sitkè*.

In s. 1068, a *rwai set* year, on the fourth waxing of the eleventh month (2 August 1706), a pig gave birth to an elephant [i.e., a tusked piglet]²⁶ in Chiang Sæn.²⁷

The Min Yè Nara Rules Chiang Mai, 1707

In s. / 1069, a *muang khai* year (1707/08), the Min Ræ Nara who ruled M. Leng²⁸ came to take charge of Chiang Mai. On the sixth waning of the eighth month (22 May 1707) he appointed the man who ruled M. Rai to come to rule Chiang Rai, and Cao Nò Müang to go as Wun of Nan.²⁹

In s. 1070, a / *pæk cai* year (1708/09), the Khœn³⁰ [named] Ai Sam Pi rebelled. King Min Sala came up by way of Chiang Mai, and Ai Sam Pi went off to the Hò. The Hò captured him and sent him back to be imprisoned and [then] incinerated, together with his whole family.

---

24 I take *chakhai* as the Burmese title *Sitkè*, a police and military commander who assisted the governor. On Burmese administration, see John F. Cady, *A History of Modern Burma* (Ithaca, 1958), ch. 1.

25 Cf. Wyatt, *Nan Chronicle*, p. 73 and fn. 12.

26 This piglet either had tusks, or a very long snout!

27 It is at this point where the "Lineage" text of Suriyavaṃsa Bhikkhu ends, and here that the focus of the text shifts back from Chiang Sæn to Chiang Mai.

28 M. Leng: location unknown. Not to be confused with M. Len.

29 Cf. Wyatt, *Nan Chronicle*, p. 74 and fn. 10–12.

30 The Khœn are the Tai-speaking population of the Keng Tung area. "Khün" or "Khœn" comes from the name of the river in Keng Tung.

In s. 1077, a *dap met* year (1715/16), Sang Kòi La Khya Saphæk of Chiang Sæn went /f° 6.06/ to consult with the king of Ava and brought back a royal order (*ameindaw*) stating that, since Cao In Müang who had been appointed to rule Nan had died, Chiang Mai and Chiang Sæn concurred in sending Phraya Tün to go and rule Nan.[31] The king of Ava [also] issued a royal order [commanding] that, of the two brothers ruling the principality[, the elder,] named Khattiyawong, should be the new / Na Khwa and Phutthawongsa, the younger brother, should be the Na Sai; and that M. Kai, M. Rai, M. Len, Phayak, Phalæo, Chiang Lap, and M. Luang Phukha[32] should form military units to defend Chiang Sæn, and the Myo Wun, Na Sai, and Na Khwa should command these / henceforth.

Thepphasing Throws Lan Na in Turmoil, 1727

In s. 1089, a *müang met* year (1727/28), Thepphasing appeared in M. Yuam (Mæ Sariang). Min Ræ Nara, the ruler of Chiang Mai, appointed people to go and summon him, once and a second time, but he did not come; so he had five hundred men go to summon him to come. He came to Wat Sangkhan,[33] just outside the White Elephant Gate. / Min Læ Nara said to the four chief city ministers, "Fill the whole royal plaza with water and summon the meritful Thepphasing there. If the 'meritful' man can walk on the water, we will all reverence him." That night, his believers said to / Thepphasing secretly that he should flee. Not long afterwards, Thepphasing brought up a force to enter the city through the Rai Ya Gate.[34]

At that time, Min Ræ Nara remained at the plaza, and all the Burmese and Mon advised him that the enemy had taken the Rai Ya Gate, and the Thai people of the city fired guns but without bullets: /f° 6.07/ there were only the Burmese and Mon who would combat him, they advised.

---

31 Cf. Wyatt, *Nan Chronicle*, pp. 75–77 and fn. 7.

32 Müang Kai, Müang Rai, Müang Len, Phayak, Phalæo, Chiang Lap, and Müang Luang Phukha: all but the last are in the Keng Tung region (see map) northwest of Chiang Sæn; while Müang Luang Phukha is in Laos, due north of Nan.

33 Wat Sangkhan: now deserted; behind the market outside the Chang Phüak Gate.

34 Rai Ya Gate, or Hai Ya: city gate in the outer, earthen wall beyond the moated walls; now called the Hai Ya Gate.

There was a prince named Ong Nok, of the lineage of the lords of Lan Chang,[35] who had a force of three hundred who came to the banks of the Raming at the Wat Ket Landing[36] and volunteered to join Min Ræ Nara, saying / "Take us! I will lead my force out to fight." Min Ræ Nara forbade him, saying, "You have no children; no wives. Why should you volunteer to do this? Cao Ong Nok should stop talking about this. Thepphasing's men are now entering the city. My men are dying at the royal plaza." / Thepphasing entered the city for about a month, and ordered the area inspected to see how many Burmese and Mon were left, and to have them rounded up and incarcerated and incinerated. All the ward and district chiefs told the Burmese and Mon to flee, / as, if they did not, they would be taken into the city. All the Burmese and Mon, headed by *Care* Ne Thæk and Grandfather Ya the blacksmith, together with three hundred good soldiers, called upon Cao Ong Nok at Wat Buppha[37] asking that they [be allowed to] take charge of a group to fight Thepphasing. Cao Ong Nok asked, / "How many men have you?" They replied, "Three hundred." Cao Ong Nok then said, "Keep quiet—they'll find out! On the fifth waxing,[38] come to me at Wat Ket."[39] Cao Ong Nok then moved to stay at Wat Ket.

On the fifth waxing, they came to Wat Ket. The group of Thepphasing /f° 6.08/ saw that the group of Cao Ong Nok was very numerous, more than they could withstand, so they sent fifty men to reconnoiter the Tha Phæ Bridge[40] and south from there. In the evening, the Burmese and Mon of *Care* Ne Thæk stealthily came up to the Sri Phum corner[41] and crossed the moat and slashed their way from the head of the Tha Phæ Bridge into the city, pursuing the / group of Thepphasing, which, defeated, fled out of the city to the south. [The Burmese and Mon] then invited Cao Ong Nok to come in and rule on the sixth; and he then was called Cao Ong Kham.

---

35 Notton (p. 180, n. 2) gives more details about his background.
36 Landing by Wat Ketkaram, Chiang Mai.
37 Wat Buppha: still standing, on Tha Phæ Road, Chiang Mai.
38 No month is specified, so the date cannot be converted.
39 Wat Ket: see city map. Notton (p. 181) gives the full name of this temple: Wat Si Saket.
40 Tha Phæ Bridge: bridge crossing the Ping River from the Tha Phæ Gate, which was a gate in the outer, earthen walls of Chiang Mai, by what is now Wat Sæn Fang by the Mæ Kha (Mæ Tho) stream.
41 The northeast corner of the city.

Not much later, Thepphasing invited Dhammapaño of Nan[42] to come. Cao Ong Kham called up men to fight him / at Wiang Pa Sang.[43] Dhammapaño died at the Kai Dam banyan tree in that year.

Cao Ong Kham Rules Chiang Mai, 1729

In s. 1090, a *pœk san* year, on the fifth waxing of the fourth month (4 January 1729), Sakhæng[44] Phaya led an army from Ava across the Salween to come [to Chiang Mai]. Cao Ong Kham took twenty Thai Chiang Mai-men, twenty Tho,[45] and twenty Burmese, altogether sixty, to welcome them. / Sakhæng Phaya said he would take the Thai group, twenty of the sixty who had come to receive him, and kill them; but knowing this they fled. There remained only the forty Burmese and Tho [of the sixty] who did not flee.

Cao Ong Kham returned to the city, and the leading officials together said to him, "If you are to become a Burmese, we will leave you. If / you do that, all of us will die. The twenty who went to receive the Burmese they would have killed. We would rather fight." They said this once, and then again. Cao Ong Kham then said, "Okay!" At that time, the Burmese came to Nòng Muan, and prepared to fight. They parried [with the defenders] for two months. The Burmese /f° 6.09/ were starving, and were defeated, and fled back by way of M. Wang, Nòng Khwang, and Fœi Rai.[46] They encamped at Phayao.

In s. 1094, a *tao cai* year, on the eighth waning of the fourth month (8 January 1733), Cao Ong Kham followed up the Burmese force of Sakhæng Phaya to Phayao. The Burmese general, Sakhæng Phaya, then fled to Chiang Sæn. Cao Ong Kham

---

42 The *Nan Chronicle* seems silent on these events.

43 Wiang Pa Sang: at the mouth of the Mæ Tha in Lamphun. Since the city was built when Kavila abandoned Chiang Mai, is this reference an anachronism?

44 Thakin? ("Mr."). Lieberman says, "I don't know who Sakhæng is. The *Hman-nan-maha-yazawin-daw-gyi*, vol. III (Mandalay, 1908), 372, refers to an Avan punitive expedition sent against Chiang Mai in 1089 [1727] led by Min-yei-yanda-thu." (Lieberman, pers. comm., 3 April 1995.)

45 Neither we nor Notton have any idea who these might have been. They are sometimes called Thai Tho or Tai Tho.

46 Fœi Rai is on the itinerary at the end of Chapter 5. Lieberman states, "The *Hman-nan*, p. 373, refers to another expedition sent out in 1093." (Lieberman, pers. comm., 3 April 1995.)

took the Lawa⁴⁷ temple slaves of / the Thong Iang⁴⁸ to Chiang Mai, and named them as Phraya Phran and Phraya Wat and had them care for the Buddha Image of the Thong Iang, as before.

As for Chiang Sæn, the king of Ava issued a royal order appointing Sakhæng Phia as the Myo Wun named Phia Saphæk, / putting him in charge of Phræ, Nan, Lampang, Fang, M. Sat, Chiang Khòng, and Thœng, putting all these under Chiang Sæn.

In s. 1095, a *ka pao* year (1733/34), the Mon *Sitkè* Nòi Phung was the head of an army of ten thousand men / who came to take charge of Chiang Mai and tried to scale the walls at the Hua Rin and Ku Rüang [corners], but failed, and withdrew in defeat.

In s. 1099, a *müang sai* year (1737/38), a white-robed ascetic left Lamphun and came up as a spy to Chiang Mai, and was caught and killed. /

In s. 1102, a *kot san* year (1740/41), the *Myo Wun*⁴⁹ *Phia Saphæk of Chiang Sæn died.*

In s. 1105, a *ka khai* year (1743/44), the king of Ava was pleased to bestow a new name on the son of Phia Saphæk, Chinnawong, as *Myo Wun* in Chiang Sæn, named Phia Sarak.

In s. 1107, a *dap pao* year (1745/46), Cao Kuai of Pegu /f° 6.10/ came to receive Lady Ong Thip, the daughter of Cao Ong Kham, and bring her back to Pegu.⁵⁰

In s. 1108, a *rwai yi* year (1746/47), Cao Kuai was defeated and expelled from Pegu and accompanied Lady Ong Thip [back] to Chiang Mai.

In s. 1113, a *luang met* year (1751/52), the Lü, Khœn, and Mæn⁵¹ together rebelled against Phia Narak. Phia Narak could not defeat them, and withdrew / from the

---

47 A curious reference to the Lawa people, who in this case were dedicated as temple-slaves.

48 The Buddha image enshrined in the chief *vihara* of Wat Si Khom Kham, Phayao. Also called Phracao Thung Iang or Phracao Ton Luang.

49 Thai sources invariably write this "moi wan"; but clearly the Burmese *myo-wun* is intended; literally, the minister of a domain/province/city; hence a governor.

50 The references to Pegu here (s. 1107 and 1108) seem to be oblique references to the Pegu revolt of the 1740s. See V. Lieberman, *Administrative Cycles*, pp. 221–222 for discussion and references. (Lieberman, pers. comm., 3 April 1995.)

51 We have already met the Lü and the Khœn; but who are the Mæn? Presumably a Tai group. There are M. Mæn at Pu-erh-fu in Yunnan, and in the Black Tai region of Vietnam.

town, taking his wives and children and encamping at the mouth of the Tha;[52] and the Lü and Mæn took over Chiang Sæn.

In s. 1117, a *dap khai* year (1755/56), Phia Narak moved his Shan, Kæo, and Lao and brought them up to attack the Lü and Mæn, who were defeated and fled. Phia Narak then ruled Chiang Sæn as before.

In s. 1119, a *müang pao* year (1757/58), / the Lao brought an army up to attack and kill Phia Narak at Dòn Thæn, and he died. The son of Phia Narak named Cao Ton Thip and the son of the Cao Na Khwa named Bòwòn went down to the king of Ava, who was pleased to name Bòwòn as the *Myo Wun* of Chiang Sæn and Ton Thip to rule Chiang Rai, and *Khanan* Atthika, the foster-father of the Cao Na Khwa / to rule Chiang Lap.[53]

Cao Can Rules Chiang Mai, 1759

In s. 1121, a *kat mao* year, in the waning half of the first month (7–20 October 1759), Cao Ong Kham died. He had ruled the domain for thirty-two years. In the same year, in the third month (20 November–18 December), Cao Can, the son of Cao Ong Kham, succeeded to rule Chiang Mai in his stead.

In the same year, on the seventh waxing of the fourth month (25 December 1759), the Burmese Mæng Rong Po / brought an army up to Kòng Lom, and the Mon and Burmese fought, many people dying. The Mon did not have all that many men, but defeated and scattered the Burmese. The Mon Talaban[54] took his men and their chattels and came up to Chiang Mai. In the sixth month (16 February–16 March 1760), the Burmese and Mon generals went down to attack Ayotthiya, going by way of Tavoy and capturing it and killing /fº 6.11/ the governor of Tavoy, then continuing on to Ayotthiya.

In the same year, Nòi Wisut of Lamphun took his group up to kill Myo Wun Bòwòn of Chiang Sæn, and Nòi Wisut [ruled] in his stead.

In s. 1122, a *kot yi* [i.e., *si*] year (1760/61), Cao Duang of Lamphun took his group up to kill Nòi Wisut at Chiang Sæn, and then Cao Duang / returned to Lamphun as before.

---

52 Mouth of the Mæ Tha, where it meets the Ping in Pa Sang district, Lamphun.

53 Chiang Lap is on the Burma side of the Mekong, roughly half-way between the present Thai and Chinese borders.

54 Talaban is a Mon title.

In the same year, on the eighth waxing of the eighth month (22 April 1760), Burmese messengers came to Lamphun. On the seventh waning of the eighth month (3 May 1760), Phraya Òng Cheyya returned from Ayotthiya and came up to the Mæ Phra, where he died.

In that same year, on Monday, the second waning of the fifth month (11 February 1761), in / the morning watch, there was a solar eclipse.[55] Athura rebelled in Ava on that same day.[56]

Rebellion and a New Ruler

In s. 1123, a *luang sai* year, on the eighth waning of the fourth month (27 April 1761), Cao Pat, the younger brother of Cao Can, came from the Pa Mòk together with Phraya Tün and rebelled against Cao Can. Cao Can fled to the ruler of Thakan. The Mon Talaban / came down to Ban San, and Cao Pat took the principality. He did not, however, rule the principality: he invited the monk Cao Khi Hut of Wat Duang Di[57] to leave the monkhood and rule the principality.

On the seventh waning of the seventh month of that same year (12 April 1762), the governor of Lamphun died.

In s. 1124, a *tao sanga* year, on the first waxing of the second month, / a Sunday (17 October 1762), near midday, there was a solar eclipse.[58]

On the thirteenth waxing of the third month (29 November 1762), Lamphun and Wang Phrao fought Pa Sang.

Abhayagamani Takes Over Chiang Mai, 1762

In the fourth month (16 December–14 January 1762/63), the Burmese Generalissimo Abhayagamani with his nine divisions and nine armies came from

---

55 According to Oppolzer (*Canon*, 284) there were four solar eclipses in 1761, but the first was only in May.

56 "Athura is a garbled reference to the general-rebel Min-gaung-naw-rahta. See Koenig, *Burmese Polity*, 195." (Lieberman, pers. comm., 3 April 1995.)

57 Wat Duang Di: in Chiang Mai: originally called Wat Phanthanu Duang Di. In the center of Chiang Mai, across from the Three Kings Monument.

58 Oppolzer (*Canon*, 284) lists a solar eclipse on this day (no. 7069).

Ava to encamp at Wat Weluwan Ku Tao,[59] and then besieged Chiang Mai on /f° 6.12/ Saturday, the first waxing of the fourth month (18 December 1762). In the face of the advancing Burmese armies the Talaban commander and Phraya Kuai fled out from Chiang Mai to go to Klük Kla on the Salween.

In s. 1125, a *ka met* year, on the eighth waning of the eleventh month (1 September 1763), the Burmese captured Chiang Mai. Two or three days later, Lamphun and Ban Santhakan fell to the Burmese, who rounded up Cao Can, the son / of Cao Ong Kham, as well as all the slaves and freemen and people of Chiang Mai, all of whom they sent to Ava.

In the twelfth month of that same year (September 1763), the Burmese caught the Talaban at Klük Kla on the Salween and sent him to Ava.

In Ava in the fourth month of that *ka met* year (January 1764), the son of Phraya Òng Cheyya Nòng Tò died. In Moksobo[myo],[60] the younger brother / of the king of Ava ascended the throne.[61] His allies captured the Talaban, and took him in to Ayotthiya in that year.

After the Burmese took Chiang Mai, Abhayagamani ruled in Chiang Mai. In this *ka met* year, Sæn Khwan of the Elephant Stables got on his elephant and took his group up to raid the three groups of Burmese who guarded valuables at the Tha Òi encampment, / and escaped to set up on the Dòn Mun[62] [Island at] Chiang Sæn. General Abhayagamani appointed *Sitkè* Intha a commander to take a group of Chiang Mai people to go and fight Sæn Khwan of the Elephant Stables at Dòn Mun. The group of Sæn Khwan was thoroughly defeated and fled, and many died.

In s. 1126, a *kap san* year, / in the waxing half of the twelfth month (early September 1764), the Lao sent a royal missive to Moksobo and on the sixth waning of the twelfth month (16 September) someone killed the Talaban. On the eighth waning of the fourth month (14 January 1765), the King of Moksobo fought and defeated the Kasæ, killing the king of the Kasæ.[63]

---

59 Wat Ku Tao, outside the walls of Chiang Mai, about 1 km. north of the Chang Phüak Gate.
60 Shwebo, in Burma, northwest of Mandalay.
61 A reference to the death of Naungdawgyi (r. 1760–1763) and the accession of Hsinbyuhsin (r. 1763–1776).
62 Island in the Mekong River at Chiang Sæn.
63 Kasæ ethnic group (Manipuri).

On the ninth waxing of the fifth month (30 January 1765) there was a heavy earthquake, and people were unable even to stand up.

On the first waxing of the sixth month (20 February 1765), /f° 6.13/ there was a solar eclipse.[64]

Rebellion Spreads Through Lan Na, 1765

In s. 1127, a *dap rao* year (1765/66), Phra Müang Chai of Lamphun rebelled against General Abhayagamani at Chiang Mai, and all of Lan Na Thai east of the Salween was engaged. General Abhayagamani was defeated and withdrew to Ava. Prince (*chaofa*) Chai Kæo[65] of Lampang also fled with General Abhayagamani. / So the king of Ava ordered the Asæ Wun to take command of an army of one hundred thousand to go up and subdue all of Lan Na Thai. Abhayagamani thus returned, and Prince Chai Kæo returned with him. The king of Ava renovated his Lacquer Palace and redecorated it in that / year. Ava [also] fought with the Hò in that year.[66] The planet Jupiter approached the moon.

Abhayagamani Takes Control of Lan Na, 1766

In that year, the Asæ Wun came up and fought and regained Lan Na Thai, and he had Abhayagamani remain and take charge of Chiang Mai as before, and he had Sing Khòi Thang rule Chiang Sæn with the Shan chief of Lai Hka[67] and an army.

In s. 1128, a *rwai / set* year (1766/67), all the generals and Abhayagamani had Phra Müang Chai take charge of Lamphun on the full-moon day of the third month (16 December 1766). Lamphun fell on that day. Sing Khòi Thang of Chiang Sæn went down to Ava and placed *Sitkè* Plan Thæng Cò Swa in charge of Chiang Sæn.

In that year, a great windstorm swept Burma, breaking off the spire of the palace of the king of Ava / and destroying a gold elephant-howdah. Ava was flooded in this year.

---

64 Oppolzer (*Canon*, p. 284) lists solar eclipse no. 7074 on 19 February.

65 The Burmese "made" him a prince.

66 The Chinese invasions of Burma in the 1760s are well known. See William J. Koenig, The *Burmese Polity, 1752–1819* (Ann Arbor, 1990), pp. 17–19.

67 Shan state. GUBSS, II, pt. 2, pp. 2–12. 21°15' N, 97°45' E.

In s. 1129, a *müang khai* year, in the fourth month (December 1767–January 1768), the Hò attacked Ava penetrating all the way down to the Sungsi Mountain and took it and withdrew. The Burmese nine generals and nine armies took the capital Sri Ayutthiya in the seventh month of that year (early April 1767). /f° 6.14/

In s. 1130, a *pœk cai* year (1768/69), Abhayagamani died.

The Hò stated that they would come to attack Ava again. The king of Ava summoned all the provincial towns, including Martaban, Dagon, and Saliang,[68] in the first month (October 1768) to raise armies to go up to Ava. By the sixth month (March 1769), the Hò had not come, so the [armies] were released to return to their villages and towns.

Omens and Calamities Foretell Burma's Downfall

On the second waxing / of the eighth month (18 April 1768), the finial of the Müang Chæ Nòng Reliquary broke off and fell down. On the sixth waning of the ninth month (22 May 1768) a finial was erected at the Lamphun Reliquary.

[After] Abhayagamani died, Prince Nemyo Khamani came to replace him in Chiang Mai, in this same year.

In s. 1131, a *kat pao* year, on Sunday, the fourth waxing of the eleventh month (6 August 1769), a / comet [appeared] in the east. On the sixth waning of the first month (21 October 1769) another comet appeared, going towards the west.

In the fourth month (January 1770), *Sitkè* Nòi Phom rebelled against Prince Nemyo General White Head at Chiang Mai, but he failed, and *Sitkè* Nòi Phom died in that year. General Khuppasiha and all the generals went to attack / the Pha Khao *panna*[69] and obtained three-complexioned ladies[70] whom they brought to present to the king of Ava in that year. Lightning struck the granary of the king of Ava in that

---

68 Martaban, Rangoon, and (Thalun?). "Saliang must be Salin or Sagaing." (Lieberman, pers. comm., 3 April 1995.)

69 Pha Khao *panna*: literally, the white-cloth district. Perhaps "White Turbans?"

70 Local legend in Fang says that a Burmese King Suddho surrounded Fang in 1632, and built a city complete with walls and moat and one *cetiya*, which the local people still call Wiang Suttho. The Burmese fought with Phraya Udomsin, the ruler of Fang, whose wife was a "three-complexioned lady," pale in the morning, pink at midday, and rosy in the evening. See Bunchuai Sisawat, *Chiang Mai læ phak nüa*, pp. 317–319.

year. The finial of the Reliquary of Dagon[71] leaned down, and so it was taken to Ava in that year. The Burmese required all to have their ears pierced and gold earlobe-plugs inserted in that year.

In s. 1132, a *kot yi* year (1770/71), Mars / was in conjunction with Venus, an ill omen, [and that event] afflicted many four-legged and two-legged creatures, many of whom died. A rabbit was born with one head for three bodies, at Chiang Phlu Island.

On Monday, the third waxing of the seventh month (18 March 1771), the Southern armies, headed by Phra Kosa (Pan),[72] with a force of 7,000, came to attack Chiang Mai. They encamped at the Lai Khæng Gate[73] for nine days; then on Tuesday, / f° 6.15/ the eleventh waxing of the seventh month (26 March 1771), they were defeated and withdrew. On the eighth waning of the seventh month (7 April 1771), a great fire broke out in Ava, burning from the northeast to the north and then to the west, all the way to the temple of the Reclining Buddha before it was quenched. As for the army of the Southerners, it failed. On the eleventh waxing of the seventh month (26 March 1771), in the twilight watch, the Southerners were defeated and fled. The Chiang Mai city forces / pursued them, fighting, to the Phrabat Plain,[74] where the firearms of the Southerners hit *Sitkè* Sai, who died.

In s. 1133, a *luang mao* year, on the tenth waning of the seventh month (9 April 1771), in the morning watch, there was an earthquake coming from the north that was most fearsome.

On the seventh waxing of the ninth month (20 May 1771) someone seized the younger [brother] of the king of Ava. The / king's mother intervened, but too late: he was killed.

On the twelfth waning of the second month (18 November 1771), the king of Ava appointed Ratchasing Khòi Thang to come up to rule Chiang Sæn as before.

---

71 The Shwe Dagon in Rangoon. The finial was brought to Ava probably because it was very valuable.

72 This reference to Phra Kosa (Pan) is quite anachronistic: Kosa (Pan) is a late-seventeenth century figure.

73 Gate in the outer earthen walls of Chiang Mai to the southeast. Now called the Lakæng Gate.

74 Thung Phrabat: probably the plain near the Buddha Footprint in Pa Sang district, Lamphun.

The Ca Ban Bunma Rebels in Chiang Mai

As for Chiang Mai, Cao Phraya Ca Ban Bunma rebelled against the Burmese Commander White Head in the midst of the city, and Nai Maung[75] / was shot dead. Cao Ca Ban had a force of three hundred to fight the Burmese without even guns or swords, using only clubs and cudgels, and he himself only bore a long sword to engage the Burmese force. Commander White Head quickly entered the palace and slammed shut the gate; and Cao Phraya Ca Ban left with his group and went to Lampang and made / an alliance with Cao Kawila, who was the eldest son of Prince Chai Kæo. The seven brother princes swore an oath to be steadfast and strong to each other. Cao Ca Ban then followed up General Khuppha Thihapate at Wiang Can.[76]

General White Head was infuriating the country, /f° 6.16/ and [Ca Ban] just angered him [further]. General Khuppha Thihapate then returned to Chiang Mai. Cao Ca Ban encamped in front of Wat Buppha. The Burmese General Khuppha Thihapate and General White Head together went down to fight against Ayotthiya. [Ca Ban] organized a force of warriors. Cao Phraya Ca Ban volunteered that, / since the waterways for boats would render their passage difficult, he would go down and harass and clear out the Burmese. So he pulled together a force of seventy Burmese and fifty Thai which Cao Ca Ban would command to go ahead. After that, the Burmese said that they would take the wives and children of Cao Ca Ban and send them to Ava. Cao Ca Ban learned of this, and secretly sent word for his wives and children / and had them steal away. Cao Ca Ban then fell upon the Burmese at M. Hòt,[77] and they were broken and scattered, and [the Burmese] went to press their campaign against Ayotthiya.

The Chronicle's Author Intrudes

Here we will tell of the branch of the family of Prince Chai Kæo in Lampang. The story may be repetitious, / but it is complicated, and [many] listeners may not fully

---

75 Notton (p. 189, n.) reminds us that Phraya Ca Ban had a younger brother, Nè-maung.
76 The Lao capital conventionally written Vientiane (and so written hereafter).
77 M. Hòt: in Hòt district, Chiang Mai, about 100 km. south of Chiang Mai on the Ping River.

understand it, so [I will] make of it a separate tale here. I hope that the royal wise men will not find fault with it.[78] I will first go back to the beginning.

Revolt in Lampang

In CS 1091, a *kat rao* year (1729/30), when the Burmese / Min Ræ Nara was ruling Chiang Mai and Thep Sing came to conquer it, Cao Ong Kham came to suppress him, as related already. At that time, all of Lan Na Thai everywhere erupted in warfare. At that time there was a certain abbot of Wat Na Yang[79] who cultivated the *phum* and *phai* spirits[80] and presented himself as a "Man of /f° 6.17/ Merit,"[81] and he garnered many adherents. The abbot of Wat Sam Kha[82] and the abbot of Wat Ban Fòn[83] defrocked and became disciples of the Abbot of [Wat] Na Yang. In Lampang, there was no Cao, but only five town elders who ruled cooperatively, and none dared brook their authority. /

Word reached Lamphun that this Man of Merit had arisen at Na Yang, and the lord of Lamphun appointed Cao Mahayot Luang to take a force to Lampang. They fought at Pa Than Khum Müang,[84] and the Lampang people were broken and scattered. The Na Yang Man of Merit fled to Wat Luang Lampang,[85] and the Lamphun / men surrounded the place. When it was near dawn, they approached the walls, and the Na Yang Man of Merit fled. The Lamphun force followed. The Na Yang Man of Merit and his right and left disciples were angry, and grabbed their clubs and wooden farm tools and jousted with them. The / Lamphun men were

---

78 Here the author at least tells us who he was not (a "royal wise man").

79 Wat Na Yang: now deserted; in Mæ Tha district, Lampang. See Sak Rattanachai, *Prawat Wat Pa Tan Kum Müang* (Lampang, 1986), p. 1.

80 Some sort of black magic is indicated here, involving spirits of places (*phum*) and other malevolent spirits (*phai*).

81 *phu mi bun*; here, a *cao ton bun*. Such men were believed to be able to walk on water, and they arose especially in times of crisis.

82 Wat Sam Kha: now deserted; Mæ Tha district, Lampang.

83 Wat Ban Fòn: Müang district, Lampang.

84 Pa Than Khum Müang: Müang district, Lampang. In 1986, villagers there built a memorial to this battle. Sak Rattanachai, *Prawat Wat Pa Tan Kum Müang*, p. 18.

85 Wat Phrathat Lampang Luang: Kò Kha district, Lampang; about 15 km. southwest of Lampang. See also Bunchuai Sisawat, *Chiang Mai læ phak nüa*, pp. 453–454.

about to be defeated and flee, when by fate a musket ball struck in the forehead and felled the Man of Merit. The two disciples came to rescue him and took bullets in the head and died on the spot.[86] / Thao Mahayot of Lamphun then withdrew back to Wat Luang Lampang, and sent out his town and country men to collect all the money and fines and household taxes. Any who refused were killed or flogged, and they confiscated whatever they wanted.

As for those who administered /f°6.18/ the domain, there were Sæn Nangsü, Sæn Thep, Nai Rüan, and *Care* Nòi who resisted submission to Thao Mahayot of Lamphun. So he appointed Han Fa Ngam, Han Fa Mæp, and Han Fa Fün to go to consult with the dignitaries of the Sanam. The three envoys made a signal of winking / to begin fighting at the Sanam. There was tumult, and in the confusion the people fled to the hills. The officers of the domain—the Chare Nòi, Thao Lin Kan, and Nai Nòi Tham—and the people all fled their homes to seek refuge at / M. Ta, M. Lòng, M. Mò, and M. Cang,[87]—everywhere.

The Emergence of Thipphacak

At that time, the abbot of Wat Chumphu[88] sympathized with the people, and appealed to the dignitaries—Thao Lin Kan and Chare Nòi—to come, and he advised them, "Now there is no able person [to lead resistance]: people see anyone die, and they all / abandon their homes. I myself would defrock to save the country if I could mobilize them. All but the women I would lead to go and fight the Lamphun people. If I were unable to win, I would slit my throat and float down the river. I'll defrock today!" The dignitaries consulted together, and / asked the abbot not to leave the monkhood. The abbot was then kind enough to say, "If you won't have me defrock, then at least listen to me! How can we save our domain? We've got to think about that!" The dignitaries heeded him.

The abbot then decided to send for Thipphacak, who was a wise man and clever /f° 6.19/ at firing guns and arrows, who might be good as a military leader in combating

---

86 A bullet hole at Wat Lampang Luang commemorates this event.

87 Müang Ta (or Wiang Ta; in Lòng district, Phræ), Müang Lòng (now Ban Mæ Rang, t. Hua Thung, Lòng district, Phræ), Müang Mò (now Ban Mæ Mò, Mæ Mò district, Lampang; site of lignite mine), and Müang Cang (now Ban Mæ Cang, on Cang river, Mæ Mò district, Lampang).

88 Wat Chumphu: now in Müang district, Lampang, south of Wat Ban Fòn.

the enemy. The abbot thus sought out Thipphacak, and said to him, "O faithful one, the situation of the country is dire. We don't have a strong leader to combat the enemy. We can think only of you to / be our leader to fight the enemy, to defend the country." Thipphacak then said, "The Lamphun enemy walks and eats the same as we do. Don't be afraid in the slightest, not so much as a sesame seed, unless they can move underground or fly through the air. / Even I, though not of royal blood, can be the strong and brave leader to save the country and restore it to us.[89] I will think quickly and not disgrace Lakhòn."

The abbot then went to tell Thao Lin Kan and / Chare Nòi and the dignitaries and all the people, who were delighted, and they vowed to each other that, when they were victorious over the enemy and he had fled, they would hand the country over to Thipphacak to be its lord and ruler. They so promised.

Thipphacak / said, "If so, give me three hundred good men." The dignitaries did so.

The Raid at Wat Lampang Luang

At an auspicious moment, they set out. Thipphacak the Vagabond selected as his trusted [aides] three men—Mün Yot, Mün Chit, and Nòi Tha. In the middle of the night, when some were asleep and some not, they surrounded /fº 6.20/ Wat Lampang and placed guards on all the gates, whom he instructed, "When there is noise within and the enemy exits, attack them!"

Thipphacak the Vagabond took Mün Yot, Mün Chit, and Nòi Tha and they stole through a water conduit into [the temple], not knowing who Thao Mahayot was; so he called out, / "Which one is the lord? I'm a servant of a Lamphun man." Thao Mahayot was then playing chess, and called out in reply, "Here I am!" So he knew for sure. Thipphacak the Vagabond raised his gun and shot Thao Mahayot, and they entered slashing and fighting, and it was a noisy tumult as all joined in, even / fighting among themselves [in the confusion].

They fled out the gates, and the three hundred men outside slashed and killed many, scattering them and pursuing them to the road and cut large trees to block it, and then they returned to Rang Sat,[90] and made offerings to the guardian spirits /

---

89 "save the country and restore it to us": some very interesting political theory here!

90 Rang Sat: now Ban Hang Chat, Hang Chat district, Lampang, at the foot of the Khun Tan mountain on the Lampang side.

of Cao Khun Tan.[91] Then they returned and rested at Pa Kæo. They announced to the people, high and low, lords and ladies, monks and brahmans, that they should return to their houses and huts and homes and tend their fields. The country was peaceful and happy and commerce again could resume, for some / time.

Thipphacak as King of Lampang

At that time, the divinities, guardian spirits, notables, and people all together consecrated Thipphacak to rule as lord in Nakhòn. His [regnal] name was King Sulva Lü Chai, and his queen was named Phimmara. He ruled /f° 6.21/ and governed the country, and established the fortified city of Khròk Ngua.[92]

Then, Queen Phimmara, after a full pregnancy, gave birth to a beautiful son to whom his father gave the name, Nai Ai Ratchakuman. Then [there were additional children, namely] a son Kæo, / a daughter Lady Kham, a son Kham Pha, a son Nai Phò Rüan, and a daughter Lady Kom; altogether six children.

King Sulva Lü Chai pondered: "In all the world, there is no one accepted by all whom the population has raised / up to be king" so he had tribute and gifts, and flowers, in submission, presented to the Burmese general Maung Myo at Keng Tung, asking that they be forwarded on to the king in Ava. The Burmese general Maung Myo went himself to do as requested before the Burmese king / in Ava. The king accepted, handing over the rule of Lakhòn [Lampang] to him, and gave him a new name, Phraya Chaiyasongkhram.

Chai Kæo of Lampang Flees to Phræ

Aparabhāge.[93] Thereafter, the people of Lamphun, who had never overcome their resentment, had good men sent in the dark of night to steal into / the compound of Cao Phraya Chaiyasongkhram and surrounded it. They took guns and raked the home with fire, in order to hit Cao Phraya Chaiyasongkhram. That night it was

---

91 Cao Khun Tan: the spirit of the Khun Tan mountain is the spirit of Phraya Bœk who was killed in war with Mangrai's son, Phraya Khram.

92 Wiang Khròk Ngua: built to combine three cities at Lampang founded in the time of Queen Camadevi. Modern Lampang was built only in 1808. See Sak Rattanachai, "Müang boran nai Nakhòn Lampang," in *Khòng di Nakhòn Lampang* (Lampang, 1970), pp. 79–85.

93 Pali: "Thereafter."

owing to his good fortune and to the guardian spirits that had led him to sleep not there but in the southern building. /f° 6.22/ Thus they did not see him, and they burnt the building down.

At that time, Cao Phraya Chaiyasongkhram awakened from a sound sleep and grabbed a gun and ax and ran to a place near the enemy. He looked for a stick to grab, but found none. The assailants fled. The lord returned / and found a cudgel at the south building and hurried after them, and caught up with the assailants at Thong San in the middle of the rice-fields, and raised his gun and shot at them; and in that single field felled three men. The enemy was scattered and fell into the Khi Lek [Stream][94] and died in disarray there.

Later, the Lamphun people came to fear the power of the lord, / and sent envoys to bid to be subordinate domains in peaceful commerce [with Lampang]. Thereafter, Cao Phraya Sulva Lü Chaiyasongkhram lived practicing the virtues and heeding the Dhamma, for the rest of his life. When he passed to the next world, the generals / and ministers carried out his funeral obsequies, and then handed over the domain to Cao Chai Kæo to rule in his stead.

At that time, the whole country was in turmoil, and all the domains were fighting each other for preeminence, and chaos reigned everywhere— / Lamphun and Chiang Mai, Ban San and Wang Phrao, Tha Kan and Nòng Lòng, Ròng Lü and Còm Thòng, Sapung and Pa Sang;[95] northern villages fought with southern villages, and the southern with northern, [all becoming] slivers of constant sores. In Lakhòn, for instance, the Sæn Phün, Nòi Tham, Thao Lin Kan, and all the dignitaries together tried to kill Cao Chai Kæo and Nai Phò Rüan, /f° 6.23/ and then they took their families and fled to take refuge with the ruler of Phræ, and asked for temporary assistance, promising eternal friendship. They asked for an army of the ruler of Phræ, and with them they / returned back [to Lakhòn] with a force of 250 men. They went along the east bank of the Wang River, while Sæn Phün and Achap Nòi Tha were on their side [of the river] with their troops. / The armies met at Lampang and fought. Nai Phò Rüan met his fate with a gunshot there which ended his life. Thus they withdrew back to Phræ as before.

---

94 Khi Lek stream: location unknown. Is this Thakhilek, across from Mæ Sai?

95 This list consists of five pairs of rival localities

Burmese Intervention in Lan Na

At that time, Lan Na Thai was completely in / chaos. The Burmese general Khamani and Lan Sapo brought an army down from Ava to take control of Chiang Mai. As for the lords and dignitaries of Chiang Mai, they were in such disarray that none could be found to organize resistance, and the destiny of the town was brought to an end. / The domain disintegrated in the face of the Burmese. The Burmese took it, and swept up Nang Thep (the daughter of Cao Ong Kham) and townsmen and villagers to take [back to Ava], while some remained there. Of those who remained, there was Cao Phraya Ca Ban Bunma.

When General Khamani had taken the domain, he stayed at Chiang Mai. /f° 6.24/ He appointed commanders and leaders to attack all the towns and villages. He had General Black Back[96] take charge of troops to go to Lakhòn. All of Lakhòn presented the flowers of submission, puffed rice, flowers, gifts, silver, and gold to present to the Burmese. The Burmese did no ill or oppression of any sort. From there, they went from Lakhòn / to Phræ. Phræ did the same. The Burmese commander knew that Cao Chai Kæo had fled to Phræ in fear, so he sought out Cao Chai Kæo to interview him. Cao Chai Kæo began by referring to the generation of his father taking the domain, down to / [the story of] Sæn Phün, Nòi Tham, and Thao Lin Kan trying to do him ill, forcing him to flee to the ruler of Phræ. All this he told to the Burmese general.

The Burmese General Black Back then returned with Cao Fa Chai Kæo to Lakhòn, where he questioned / Sæn Phün, Nòi Tham, and Thao Lin Kan; and they did not corroborate each other. The Burmese general then accompanied [Chai Kæo] to Ava and called on the king, relating all to him, from beginning to end. The king of Ava was grateful, and said that Prince Chai Kæo was a good man and should be supported, and he elevated Prince Chai Kæo to be Cao Fa Singharatchathani. / Prince Chai Kæo then was sent back to rule Lakhòn, and he had Thao Lin Kan and Sæn Phün be generals. He took leave of the king and returned to Lakhòn.

---

96 General Black Back: translation of the Thai name for him (Lang Dam).

Water Ordeal Absolves Chai Kæo

Not long afterwards, Chaptha, with Thao Lin Kan and Sæn Phün, together plotted to seize Prince Chai Kæo and rule. Later, they quarreled and argued. /f° 6.25/ Prince Chai Kæo, Thao Lin Kan, Sæn Phün, and Chaptha often quarreled among themselves, and finally decided to submit to an ordeal by water, and the survivor would take the lives of the others. The Burmese generals, the *care*,[97] the *Sitkè*, and the commanders authorized the contest between Prince Chai Kæo and Thao Lin Kan. Thao Lin Kan dove into the water, but not even deeply enough to get his hair wet. / Prince Chai Kæo, on the other hand, dove right in and sat placidly under the water. Thao Phet Fa of Chiang Rai [finally] had to [be sent to] bid him to surface. The Burmese general had Thao Lin Kan and Chaptha fettered and beaten and their property confiscated, and then taken off to be executed. As for Sæn Phün, he was not killed, and he stole away that day. /

Not long afterwards, the Burmese general raised an army of all able-bodied men to go to the Lao domain. Sæn Phün induced those who had fled to the forests and hills, and Phraya Nòi Mano and Kuei Siang Muk, [to join him]. The Burmese commander Min Ræ and general Siri together collected men / at Yang Khok,[98] with Khanan Langka and Thap Mu Kam. Together they surrounded Ban Kiang and fought in the middle of the night until near dawn. As for Sæn Phün and the Burmese Min Ræ, they were defeated and [with] their men all fled to the jungle. Kuei Siang mounted a horse and / fled to the Lao domain, leaving behind the Min Ræ, Sæn Phün, Khanan Langka, and Thap Mu Kham.

At that time, the [Burmese] commander who had gone to the Lao domain returned and rested his army at Lampang Luang. Prince Chai Kæo went out to welcome the commander. The formalities concluded, the commander fully explained [what had happened], and then ordered /f° 6.26/ that the Burmese take Min Ræ, Sæn Phün, Thap Siri, and Khanan Lingka off and kill them, excepting [only] Phraya Mano [of] Ban San, Nòng Lòng, and Ròng Li, who had gone off to the jungle. The Burmese pursued them there, arrested them, and bound them at Lampang, and executed them, ten or twenty per day. They took / their wives and children to be slaves, to be

---

97 "*care* is certainly sa-yei, i.e., secretary, who along with a *sit-ke* was attached to each military unit." (Lieberman, pers. comm., 3 April 1995.)

98 Yang Khok: now Ban Pong Yang Khok, Kò Kha district, Lampang.

servants, to be wives and children, as they wished. As for Phraya Mano [of] Ban San, the Burmese took him to Ava. They later had the Shans kill him. Thereafter, the Burmese commander took a force of men—four armies and four commanders—to go down / to attack Sri Ayutthiya.

The Children of Chai Kæo

Here we will tell of the children born to Prince Chai Kæo.[99] When Chai Kæo was ruling and governing the domain of Lakhòn, he had children by the royal queen Canthra, as follows:

In s. 1104, / a *tao set* year (1742/43), the first child of Prince Chai Kæo was born. He was ordained in the Religion, and the reverend teachers conferred on him the name of Cao Khanan Kawila, the first-born. In s. 1106, a *kap cai* year (1744/45), the second son was born, named Cao Kham Som. In s. 1108, / a *rwai yi* year (1746/47), the third son was born. He was ordained in the Religion, and the reverend teachers conferred on him the name of Cao Nòi Thammalangka. In s. 1110, a *pæk si* year (1748/49), a son was born named Cao Duang Thip. In s. 1112, a *kot sanga* year (1750/51), a daughter was born, named Sri Anocha. After that, in s. 1114, /f° 6.27/ a *tao san* year (1752/53), a second daughter was born, named Lady Sri Wanna. In s. 1116, a *kap set* year (1754/55), another son was born, named Cao Mu La; the fifth son. In s. 1118, a *rwai cai* year (1756/57), another son was born, named Cao Kham Fan; the sixth son. In s. 1120, a *pæk yi* year (1758/59), another daughter was born, named / Sri Bun Than; the third daughter. In s. 1122, a *kot si* year (1760/61), another son was born, named Cao Bun Ma; the seventh and youngest son, and the last of all the children. It happened that Lady Sri Wanna and Sri Bun Than were not raised to maturity: those who survived to maturity to when he / ruled were seven sons and one daughter.

Nai Kham Pha, the younger brother of Prince Chai Kæo, had three children: one named Nai Nanthasen, one named Nai Cumpa, and one named Nai Kòn Kæo.

Lady Kham had two sons; one named Nai Khattiya and one named Nai Kham Sòn.

---

99 The descendents of Kavila sponsored a lavish volume for the 700th anniversary of the founding of Chiang Mai: *Cao luang Chiang Mai* (Chiang Mai, 1996), in which the family tree is discussed in detail.

Lady Kom / had one son, named Nai Cantharacha, and one daughter, named Lady Ta Dam ("Black Eyes").

Nai Phò Rüan had five sons and one daughter. The eldest was [a son] named Nai Wongsa; the second was Nai Phutthawongsa; third Nai Kham Mun; fourth Nai Nòi Kawila; fifth Nai Kham Lü; and / the daughter was Lady Santha.

The Burmese Assault Ayudhya

Here we will tell first of the Burmese commander of four armies and four generals who went to attack Ayotthiya.

In Lakhòn he had Cao Kham Som take command of a force to go with the commander. After the commander had set off for the South Country with his forces, /fº 6.28/ all the Burmese remaining oppressed the country with fines and extortion. Townsmen and villagers everywhere were troubled, and even the princely class and the monks were distressed.

As for Prince Chai Kæo, he saw the suffering of the people, and he handed over the domain to his wives, children, generals, and ministers to administer. / As for the prince, he attended upon Commander Khamani in Chiang Mai in the hope of helping the good ones and preventing the oppression of the country.

At that time, Phra Müang Chai and Nai Ai of Lamphun rebelled against the Burmese General Khamani in Chiang Mai. General Abhayagamani / was defeated and fled, and Prince Chai Kæo accompanied his army. General Abhayagamani went to Ava, and Phra Müang Chai and Nai Ai were victorious. They sent warriors to oppress Lakhòn, extorting cowries and silver. The wives / of the Burmese and Mons, wherever, were all taken and punished.

Cao Kawila was chief among all the royal family, who took charge of the domain, not really submitting or resisting, but trying to maintain stability. Soon, General Abhayagamani raised an army in Ava / and came to invest Lamphun, [the men of which were] scattered and dispersed; and Phra Müang Chai fled to the Hò domain, where he remains to the present day.[100]

Abhayagamani came to be the *myowun* in Chiang Mai. At that time, Phraya Can [of] Nòng Lòng had been defeated and had fled to the Lao domain. When he heard that the Burmese army had been withdrawn and fled from /fº 6.29/ Lamphun,

---

100 This reference implies that the source cannot have been written later than the 1820s.

Phraya Can returned to attack Ban Hua Süa, Dòn Fai, and Ban Kòm; but he was defeated and returned to the Lao domain.

Then, *Sitkè* Suriya of Thœn[101] and Sæn Suthon and the Mon Kòng Cò, with Nai Nòi Cumphu, brought up an army and encamped at Sop Pap [rapids].[102] Prince Chai Kæo then ordered Cao Kawila, his eldest son, to command an / army of Thai, Shan, and Burmese to go down to Sop Pap. In the morning, he drove his troops to surround the Thœn troops, but leaving the bank of the Wang River uncovered. *Sitkè* Suya, Sæn Suthon, the Mon Kòng Cò, and Nai Nòi Chumphu were defeated and, to save themselves, dove into the Wang River and fled, escaping to the area of / M. Lòng.

Soon thereafter, Commander Abhayagamani died. The king of Ava appointed General White Head to replace him in Chiang Mai. *Sitkè* Nòi Phom [of] Nòng Lòng then revolted against General White Head, but failed, and many of his partisans died.

At that time, the Generalissimo / of the main army which had taken Sri Ayutthiya brought King Dòk Düa, the king of Ayotthiya,[103] and then the Generalissimo returned to our Lan Na Thai and ordered the Lan Na / people to attack Lan Chang [and] the Pha Khao ("White Turban") *panna*. Phraya Ca Ban and General White Head fought each other in the middle of the city of Chiang Mai. Ca Ban could not defeat the Burmese because his forces were too few. Nai Mòng suffered a gunshot and died, so [Ca Ban] took his men /f° 6.30/ and fled to join the Generalissimo at the Pha Khao *panna*. He told him what had happened with General White Head's oppression, and that they had fought. The Generalissimo then returned from the Pha Khao *panna* with Phraya Ca Ban to Chiang Mai, where he stayed by the Tha Phæ Gate.

At that time, in Ayutthiya, / Cao Phraya Taksin[104] became the new king, collecting a great many followers; and he moved to set up a new capital, named Rattana Krung Sri Ayutthiya. The Generalissimo left the Lao domain and came to Chiang Mai, and said that he would go down to re-take Ayutthiya; so / he had a great many boats built.

---

101 Thœn, not to be confused with Thœng

102 Sop Pap: now Ban Sop Prap, Sop Prap district, Lampang. Notton (p. 198, n.) locates Sop P[r]ap at the mouth of the Mè Prap, a day's march from Lampang.

103 The last king of Ayudhya, King Uthumphòn.

104 King Taksin of Thon Buri (r. 1767–1782) is rarely if ever referred to as a caophraya.

The Lan Na Revolt Begins

Phraya Ca Ban then sent a man to go and tell Cao Kawila at Lakhòn that he was planning to revolt against the Burmese. Kawila was pleased. It was agreed that the plan would wait on Phraya Ca Ban, the elder, to go down to persuade the Southern army [to help them]. Phraya Ca / Ban was informed of Kawila's promise. So he craftily volunteered to go and clear the way as the vanguard [of the Burmese army proceeding south]. The Generalissimo was pleased, and commanded that seventy Burmese and Shan, and fifty Thai [be assembled] and he had Phraya Ca Ban build boats and float down ahead.

When they reached M. Hòt, in / the middle of the night, before dawn, in the watch the Burmese call *La-hta*,[105] when the men were all spread out, Phraya Ca Ban got into a boat and paddled by night and day to Ayotthiya. When he got there, he reported to King Taksin, asking that King Taksin help him with an army. [King Taksin] then ordered /fº 6.31/ his chief generals to organize a fourfold army, and when it was ready, he told his commanders, Caophraya Cakri and Phraya Surasi, to go up quickly.

In twenty-one days they reached Thœn, and then divided off a group of five thousand men to go by way of M. Li,[106] commanded by Phraya Surasi. Phraya Ca Ban led a force to Tha Wang Tan.[107] The Burmese General White Head led a force out / to fight them. The main Southern army was not in time, and the Southern force was defeated. The Burmese pursued and defeated them, forcing them into the Ping River; and then they returned. As for the army of Caophraya Cakri [and] Phraya Surasi, they came up by way of Lakhòn. At that time, Prince Chai Kæo was attending upon General White Head in Chiang Mai.

Cao Kawila / consulted with his seven sibling princes, "What should we do? If we are to be Southerners, our father will be stuck in Chiang Mai. If we are slaves to the Burmese, we'll be disgusted!" So they decided to take their father's fate as primary, / and their own fate as secondary. So they schemed to have Cao Kham Som command a force of Thai, Shan, and Burmese to pretend to go down and fight the Southerners,

---

105 We could not seem to find any Burmese word that worked here.
106 Müang Li: southeast of Thœn, on the way to Tak.
107 Tha Wang Tan: now Ban Tha Wang Tan, Saraphi district, Chiang Mai.; a large landing or port close to Chiang Mai.

not leaving many Burmese and Shan in the domain, leaving only *Sitkè* Siri Cò Su with just a few men. Cao Kham Som went down as commander / to carry out the scheme and engage the Southerners and await [the word] to retreat, so that the Burmese would trust him.

Then, Cao Kawila rebelled against the Burmese, attacking the Burmese *Sitkè* Siri Cò Su[108] who had remained in the town. Siri died, and many Burmese and Shan with him. Of the Burmese who survived, some were ill and wounded and scattered; while /f° 6.32/ some with their entrails in their hands went to join the army that had gone to fight the Southerners. When the army saw them, they were thrown into great confusion, crying out, "Now Cao Kawila has revolted against the Burmese!" Cao Kham Som retorted, "Cao Kawila has revolted? Impossible! Sometimes Cao Kawila is crazy and sometimes / not. His circulation has gone bad! Then he's wild! He doesn't mean to act like that! Though Kawila may have revolted, we his younger siblings have not joined him." The Burmese only half-believed him.

In the middle of the night, three thousand Burmese / hurried by night and day to Chiang Mai, and they reported to General White Head on all that Cao Kawila had done. General White Head had Prince Chai Kæo jailed: he would have killed him, but later felt sorry for him. /

Siam Invited to Rescue the North, 1775

At that time, Cao Kham Som returned back to his country and thought of his father; so [the siblings] all sent tribute and gifts [to General White Head]—gold and silver objects, things gilt with gold and silver, good cloth and clothes, and they wrote / a respectful letter to him, saying, "Cao Kawila must be crazy or drunk to have beaten and killed *Sitkè* Siri Cò Su. We six siblings did not know of this. We ask that you reconsider and judge carefully [the case] and not kill or beat him or do ill to him." Then they had released Burmese prisoners /f° 6.33/ carry the letter and bear the tribute and gifts to present them to General White Head in Chiang Mai. General White Head saw the letter and presents and was mollified, and he did not kill or beat Prince Chai Kæo, but the prince remained imprisoned.

---

108 "The *sitke* must be Thir-ri-kyaw-thu according to the system of transcription I have been recommending throughout this letter." (Lieberman, pers. comm., 3 April 1995.)

Then, Cao Kawila sent a letter / asking Cao Duang Thip, his younger brother, to go down and meet the Southern army and throw them all on the mercy of the king of the south. Caophraya Cakri and Phraya Surasi the commander, together led by King Taksin, were pleased, and raised / an army and sent it up to Lampang, and encamped it there. Cao Kawila presented tribute, gifts, rice, drinks, and food to greet the great commanders and led the vanguard and the army to Chiang Mai.

Kawila Rescues His Father

At that time, Phraya Kamphængphet / was the commander; and Caophraya Ca Ban, who had been defeated by the Burmese in his rebellion, when he learned that the [Southern] force had arrived, volunteered in order to repair his fault. At that time, General White Head organized his forces to go fight the Southerners at Tha Wang Tan, expecting [as usual] to defeat the Southerners there. / The Southerners organized muskets and large and small cannon arranged in rows to fire simultaneous salvos, and many Burmese died, unable to withstand them. Defeated, they fled back to the city. Cao Kawila remembered his father, and took some brave soldiers /f° 6.34/ and pursued the Burmese right into the city. The frightened Burmese were in a confused state. General White Head fled out of the city to the north by way of the White Elephant Gate, leaving Prince Chai Kæo still in the prison. Cao Kawila entered into the city.

Nai Nòi Withun and Nòi Somtamit, Chiang Mai men / who had been with the Burmese in the city, said of Prince Chai Kæo, "He is still alive in the prison, and the Burmese have not killed or beaten him." Cao Kawila rushed to the prison and had his men force open the prison and release his father. / When the Cao saw his father, he was overjoyed. He paid homage to his father with the five-point gesture (*beñcangapradiṣṭha*[109]), and then had his father mount the howdah of an auspicious elephant, in front of the main army, and then leave. King Taksin / defeated the evil enemy (*mārapakkha*) and took Chiang Mai in s. 1136, a *kap sanga* year, on Sunday, the full-moon day of the fifth month (Wednesday 15 February 1775).

---

109 The five-fold gesture of obeisance, particularly to a parent; the five points deriving from two feet, two hands, and the head touching the floor.

Siam Reorganizes Government of the North

When King Taksin took the city, he appointed Phraya Ca Ban to be the ruler of Chiang Mai; Nai Nòi Kòn Kæo, his nephew, to be the *uparaja*; / *Sitkè* Khæng to be the ruler of Lamphun with Nai Nòi Tòn Tò, his younger brother, as his *uparaja*; Nai Nòi Khòn Thòng as Phraya Surawong to defend the borders of the domain; and then he proceeded to return via Lakhòn. He rested his force at Ban Lampang, where he reverenced /f° 6.35/ the Venerable Reliquary there.[110]

When Cao Kawila had returned his father to Lakhòn, he was very happy, and he had his six younger siblings come to pay attendance upon the king at Lampang. The king appointed Cao Kawila to be the ruler of Lakhòn, with / Cao Thammalangka, the third brother, as *uparaja*; and he put the whole domain in the charge of Kawila. King Taksin and Caophraya Cakri then led all the generals and troops down via Thœn, floating along the current / of the Mæ Laming. As for Caophraya Surasi, he developed a liking for Lady Sri Anocha, the younger sister of Cao Kawila; so he had a knowledgeable retainer come to ask [for her] from the seven princely siblings, headed by Prince Chai Kæo the father. / Considering the [anticipated] closeness of the royal friendship in the future, they agreed to have Lady Sri Anocha be presented as queen of Caophraya Süa, that is, Phraya Surasi. When Caophraya Surasi obtained Lady Sri Anocha as his queen, he went / away by way of Sawankhalok.

At that time, war was everywhere.

Burmese Attack and the Battle of Tha Din Dæng

When the king of Ava learned that the king of the south had come up and attacked the Burmese General White Head at Chiang Mai, he ordered General Black Back to take a force of one hundred thousand to go down to Tha Din Dæng[111] to attack the South, and he encamped at /f° 6.36/ Mæ Saklit [or Salit].[112] There was a Mak San tree, whose leaves were like the horns of hog-deer, red-deer, and roebuck, and whose fruits sprouted from its base to its peak, on every branch, which grew in Bang Kòk.[113]

---

110 Phra That Lampang Luang seems to be indicated.
111 Tha Din Dæng: now a neighborhood of Bangkok.
112 Notton (p. 203, n. 1) gives a variant from PY, Mæ Salit.
113 Bangkok.

Phraya Yai Thala Siang revolted and fought Phraya Sakkanüng, who fled to Martaban. On Saturday, the tenth waxing of the twelfth month (17 September 1774) they fought at Martaban. Phraya Sakkanüng was defeated. / Phraya Yai Thala Siang pursued him to Rangoon. The Burmese Phraya Sakkanüng raised additional troops and fought with Phraya Yai Thala Siang at the Nam Mæ Phathang. Phraya Yai was beaten and withdrew to Martaban.

As for King Taksin, when he reached Kamphæng[phet], the Burmese Asæ Wungyi came with one hundred thousand men— / fifty thousand came by way of Moulmein to attack Lahæng,[114] Kamphæng[phet], Sawankhalok, and Sukhothai, and all were crushed. Then the Burmese surrounded Phitsanulok and fought for six months. As for King Taksin and Caophraya Cakri, they could not return to restore the situation in / these domains, because the Burmese had come to Bang Kòk; so they rushed to Bang Kòk. They rushed out to fight General Black Back at Tha Din Dæng. Caophraya Surasi had gone down to Bang Kòk, but went to join the king and fight the Burmese with / the great merit of the king. The Burmese could not withstand that, and had completely to flee.

As for General White Head, defeated he fled to Chiang Mai and was very angry. Two months and four days later, he led a force of eighty thousand[115] to surround Chiang Mai again. The Burmese arrived on Tuesday, the fourth waning of the seventh month in s. 1137, /f° 6.37/ a *dap met* year (4 April 1775). Cao Phraya Ca Ban had a force of 1,900 able young men to defend the city. The inhabitants were very starved and thirsty, having eaten all their elephants, horses, cattle, buffalo, ducks, chickens, pigs, dogs, tubers, and bananas. Cao Phraya Ca Ban sent someone secretly to ask for a Southern army and armies / from Lakhòn. Cao Kawila called up a thousand men, and led them in to defend the city, which was starving, with nothing to eat, even lizards, crickets, or grasshoppers. One day, the Burmese climbed into the city by the Si Phum fort. /

Ca Ban mobilized to fight the Burmese, who withdrew. Seven of the Burmese who entered were killed and completely eaten. The Burmese remained for eight months. When the South army arrived with thirty thousand men, on the fourth waning of the second month (11 November 1775), the Burmese could not withstand them and

---

114 Lahæng: Tak, or Rahæng. Upstream from the modern city of Tak.

115 Notton (p. 204) says eight hundred thousand and gives ten thousand in a footnote as a variant from PY.

were scattered. When the Burmese / had been defeated, the South army withdrew back down.

At that time, all were starving and emaciated and weak, and some went north while others went to the south. As for Cao Phraya Ca Ban and the *uparaja*, uncle and nephew, they accompanied their families and children and wives to Lakhòn to rest / there for a time. Then they soon returned to set up at Tha Wang Phrao,[116] and soon they returned to Chiang Mai.

Bad Omen for Cao Phraya Ca Ban

At that time, Chiang Mai was abandoned, and overgrown with weeds, bushes, and vines. It was a place for rhinoceros and elephants and tigers and bears, and there were few people. They collected together and cleared space around their homes and thoroughfares /f° 6.38/ on which to travel, as there was no opportunity to clear the whole area.

At that time, there was a man who caught two tiger cubs and presented them to Cao Phraya Ca Ban, who put them in a cage. In the middle of the night, the mother [tiger] cried [for them] along the roads in the middle of the town, as if to say,

> Lord Elephant is in the north;
> Lord Tiger's in the / south;
> a lord has seized my cubs.
> Let them quickly go!
> If you don't loose my children dear,
> I'll eat each one of you—
> all of you, from palaces and huts,
> male and female, large and small,
> every thumb and finger and your palms;
> I'll even eat your / jewelry.[117]

---

116 Tha Wang Phrao: Landing on the Ping River near Wiang Kum Kam.

117 The text is still remembered as a classical Northern Thai folk song. I have tried to keep the poetic form.

Such was the tiger's cry, voicing its plight. The seven princes (including Kawila) were Lord Elephant; Lord Tiger was Cao Phraya Surasi, the Front Palace king of the south.

The Burmese Retake Chiang Mai

Cao Phraya Ca Ban came to live in / Chiang Mai. The population was so small they could not live there, and they had to flee together to Wang Phrao again in s. 1136, the *kap sanga* year (1774/75), until s. 1137, the *dap met* year (1775/76), when Cao Phraya Ca Ban decided that he would attack Chiang Sæn. He took [his troops] up to stay at Mæ Khua Dæng. The Burmese and / Thò Po had an army of ninety-nine thousand men who left Ava and went down to Chiang Mai and bombarded it [with cannon]. Cao Phraya Ca Ban heard the sound of the guns and returned. The Burmese came out and fought them at San Tawan. His forces were small, insufficient to defeat them, and he was defeated and retreated to M. Lahæng. The Po Læ Thò Khabæhuan /f° 6.39/ reached Lakhòn. The seven princely brothers fought the Burmese, with ten Thai for every hundred Burmese: the Burmese vanguard of seven thousand with seven generals and seven armies against seven hundred Lakhòn Thai. They struggled for seven days and could not withstand them, and so with their families and belongings fled Lakhòn and went down to Sawankhalok, where they encamped / for a while. The Burmese army left to return.

Cao Phraya Ca Ban then appointed Cao Uparaja Kòn Kæo, his nephew, to go up to Wang Phrao and requisition food from the Lawa and the mountain people and hold it for him, and then Cao Phraya Ca Ban went there. Later, the / Uparaja did not give him his share of the food which had been collected, for one reason or another. Cao Phraya Ca Ban was angry and killed the Uparaja, in the year s. 1138 (1776/77). In that year, Jupiter was eclipsed by the moon, and Ava starved. /

Thai Assert Control in the North

As for the seven princes, headed by Prince Chai Kæo they left Sawankhalok to return home and re-established themselves at Lakhòn.

In the *müang rao* year, s. 1139 (1777/78), Cao Phraya Ca Ban left Wang Phrao and came down to Nòng Lòng.[118] / At that time, there was a *lan* palm at Nòng Lòng which grew forth seven shoots from its peak. Cao Phraya Ca Ban invited the Sangha to make merit through chanting [to avert misfortune], and then they cut down that palm.

In s. 1140, a *pœk set* year (1778/79), Phraya Ca Ban moved to establish the city. / f° 6.40/ Soon, in the same year, Phraya Ca Ban floated down to the South country. In s. 1141, a *kat khai* year (1779/80), Lady Bun Som, his wife, went floating down after him. Phraya Ca Ban left the South country and returned, but before he reached Lamphun, his generals and ministers—Phraya Chai and Phraya Phran—fled away to the north, / leaving only Phraya Sam Lan, Phraya Ammat, and half the men. Phraya Ca Ban reached Lamphun. Soon he went to attack Chiang Sæn, but the town was empty, and he returned. Not long afterwards, the party of Phraya Chai of Chiang Sæn–Chiang Rai came down to attack / Lamphun. Some were able to escape, while others were caught by the invaders. Phraya Ca Ban gathered people and went down to encamp at Wang Sakhæng at the mouth of the Mæ Li.

A Siamese Force Oppresses the North

In s. 1140, a *pœk set* year (1778/79), [King Taksin] ordered Cao Phraya Cakri and Cao Phraya Surasi as generals to / attack Lom Phu Nòng Bua[119] and then to attack M. Phan Phrao [and] Vientiane, which they took. In s. 1141, a *kat khai* year (1779/80), the two commanders sent a force of three hundred men as royal commissioners to leave Vientiane and come and inspect all the provinces of Phræ, / Nan, and Lakhòn. Those commissioners came and oppressed [the people], confiscating goods, gold, silver, and cloth. They grabbed the young, the unprotected infants and widows, to serve them. Cao Kawila, the eldest, the ruler of Lakhòn, was angry, and slashed and killed /f° 6.41/ the commissioners in great numbers at Wang Kœng. A group of the Southerners who were not killed sought out King Taksin. The king sent orders twice and thrice by a commissioner for Cao Kawila to come, but he did not go down. He knew he was at fault by ignoring a royal command, and so he took an army to attack

---

118 Now Ban Nòng Lòng, Pa Sang district, Lamphun province.
119 Nong Bua Lamphu; now a separate province in Northeast Thailand.

M. Lò and M. Thœng, obtaining / families there to be presented to King Taksin. Phraya Ca Ban also was summoned by the king.

The king judged Phraya Ca Ban guilty for killing the Uparaja, his nephew; and Cao Kawila guilty for having killed the Southerners, / and for having failed to heed repeated summons to pay attendance; and [he ordered] a lashing of a hundred strokes for each, and for a small earlobe cutting on Cao Kawila. For having failed to come when summoned, he was imprisoned. Cao Kavila asked that he be allowed to atone for his sins by undertaking public service, by attacking Chiang Sæn. / The king was pleased to release Cao Kawila to do so. Phraya Ca Ban was not released, and was kept there.

Cao Kawila returned to Lakhòn, and took three hundred men and went up [to Chiang Sæn]. At that time they were starving, so each man got three *khæng*,[120] plus rice gruel and betel and tubers.

As for Phraya Ca Ban, / he fell ill and died in the South.

The Beginnings of the Cakri Dynasty, 1782

Here we will tell of Cao Phraya Cakri and Phraya Surasi, the Thai commanders. After they had taken Vientiane, they left their armies and returned home. Thereupon civil war broke out in Cambodia.[121] Cao Phraya Cakri and Surasi took an army to attack /f° 6.42/ Cambodia.

In s. 1143, a *luang pao* year (1781/82), Phraya Sing and Phraya San killed King Taksin, and became kings. Cao Khòk Si Anocha then secretly sought out the men of Pak Phieo,[122] and told them, "If you volunteer to take Phraya Sing and Phraya San, as long as / I live I promise you will not have to perform public service, and you can live comfortably, except for doing your jobs." The men of Pak Phieo volunteered, and caught and killed Phraya Singa and Phraya San. Cao Khòk Si Anocha then took the city, and / sent [to Cambodia] to invite Cao Phraya Cakri and Cao Phraya Surasi to rule—Cao Phraya Cakri, the elder, as the king, with the title of Somdet

---

120 A measure of milled rice, somewhat more than a liter.

121 See, for example, Klaus Wenk, The Restoration of Thailand Under Rama I 1782–1809 (Tucson, 1968), pp. 5–8.

122 In Saraburi province. Sak Rattanachai, "Prawat caoying Si Anocha," in *Prawat Wat Pa Tan Kum Müang* (Lampang, 1986), p. 25.

Phraphutthacao Bòwòn Bòrommakot; and Cao Phraya Surasi, the younger, as Lon Klao Lon Kramòm / Krom Phraratchawang Bòwònsathanmongkhon the Front Palace, in s. 1143, a *luang pao* year (1781/82).¹²³

Cao Kawila Given Charge of Lan Na

As for Cao Kawila, he took troops up to attack the Mæ Luak [valley of] Chiang Sæn¹²⁴ and took families which he brought down to Lakhòn. He stayed to refresh his men, and then he went / down to pay attendance upon the two brother kings and inform them [of what he had done]. The kings were pleased and feasted him, and gave him presents in great profusion, for example, a golden vase, a golden ewer, a golden spittoon, a gold-hilted saber, a lance with /f° 6.43/ a golden handle, arm bracelets, a ring, a belt, gold chains, a jeweled fan, a necklace, implements of ivory, and many rich fabrics; and he appointed Cao Kawila as Phraya Mangra Wachiraprakan Kamphæng Kæo, to be ruler of Chiang Mai. He appointed Cao Thammalangka, his third brother, as *uparaja* of Chiang Mai; / appointed Cao Kham Som, his second brother, as ruler of Lakhòn Lampang; he appointed Cao Duang Thip, his fourth brother, as *uparaja*; appointed Cao Mu La, his fifth brother, as Ratchawong of Lakhòn, and each of them was given insignia of rank befitting ranking persons, higher and lower. / Then, at an auspicious moment, they took leave and returned home by water.

Colophon to Chapter Six

*Sathama nagararājavaṁsa kantho nithitto.*¹²⁵

---

123 This seems a very unusual account of these events, giving a primary role to the Chiang Mai woman, Kavila's sister!

124 The Mæ Luak empties into the Mekong at Sop Luak, about 8 km. north of Chiang Sæn.

125 Pali: "Sixth [Fascicle] of the Royal Chronicle Completed." Notton (p. 209) has misread this as "*Pathama Naggara . . .*," and translated it as "End of the Book on the First Dynasty of Lakhòn."

Chapter 7

Kawila as King of Lan Na, 1782

Tato rājā āggamana maggam patvā rathesi. Tato.[1] At that time, Cao Kawila was in the status of ruler: His Majesty the King had bestowed upon him the land of the state of Chiang Mai. The lord took leave of the king, and accompanied by the / junior royal family members and with his officers and retainers he returned to Lakhòn. There they rested their retainers.

Cao Phraya Mangra Wachiraprakan Kamphæng Kæo was then forty years of age; the Uparaja was thirty-six, and / Cao Rattana Hua Müang Kæo was twenty-seven. The three princely brothers were at their head. The royal scions, the sons of Nai Phò Rüan, were three: Nai Phutthawong, Nai Kham Mun, and Nai Nòi Kawila. There were two sons of Nai Kampha: Nai Nanthasen and Nai Khanan Chumphu. Lady Kom had one child: / Nai Cantharacha. The whole of them, with their officials, military officers, ministers, troops, retainers, and three hundred able-bodied men, left Lakhòn in s. 1144, a *tao yi* year, on Thursday, the full-moon day of the twelfth month (11 August 1782[2]), at an auspicious moment, and traveled by land for eight days. On / Friday, the eighth waning of the twelfth month (19 August 1782), they reached Wang Sakhæng[3] at the mouth of the Mæ Li, which Phraya Ca Ban had founded of old.

---

1 Pali: the meaning approximates that of the translated phrase that follows.
2 Dates this year are off by one month because the chronologers in Chiang Mai failed to intercalate a month. The Ayudhya and Bangkok astrologers sometimes made similar mistakes.
3 Wang Sakhæng: now Ban Wang Sakhæng, Li district, Lamphun.

Policy and Action to Repopulate the North

At that time, all of Lan Na Chiang Mai was in chaos: villages and fields were deserted, all wild and overgrown. To the south there were tigers; to the north were elephants. The land was unstable, as there was no lord /f° 7.02/ or ruler to take charge; there were but few leaders and few followers. The Sovereign King of great merit of the great and glorious capital city of Ayutthiya Dvaravati, considering the state of the country, issued a royal order granting full authority to / a king to come and rule over Chiang Mai. The king lived at Wang Sakhæng village for one month, and requested a list of chiefs, corvéeable males, weapons, and former chiefs, from the time of Phraya Ca Ban. The list of able-bodied men came to [only] seven hundred men, which added to the previous list of young men came to only a thousand.

On / Sunday, the eighth waning of the second month (16 October 1782), in the *kòng ngai* watch, the king established a Velukugāma [temporary capital] called Pa Sang,[4] where he built a small shelter and sleeping chambers, a palace, a palisade and moat and fort, with a large gate; and he built a fort and observation tower for times of warfare. He built the city on the two sides of the Mæ Tha[5] / which passed through its midst. The city on one bank of the river was called Pa Sang Luang and that on the other bank was called Pa Sang Nòi. The king ordered his officers and men to till the fields fully and sufficiently with rice. He built temples to house the / clerics and installed Buddha images to preside over them; and they made merit with alms every day.

Ito pathāya.[6] Thenceforth, the king was endowed with great majesty. He was an expert in warfare, brave and /f° 7.03/ fearless in the face of the enemy, a *sahoviya*;[7] a veritable lion, valorous. He thought, "My country is truly newly founded, and has few people. I should seize those domains which have not submitted / and bring them into the orbit of my power, and put them in my country." Deciding thusly, he sent for the Uparaja and the Cao Rattana Hua Müang Kæo, his younger brothers, and had them assemble their relatives and ministers and officers / and issued a royal

---

4 Pa Sang: see Chiang Mai Region map.
5 Mæ Tha [River]: flows down to Lamphun from the east and northeast to join the Ping.
6 Pali: "Thenceforth."
7 Pali: properly, *siho viya*: roughly, "This lion of a man."

order appointing the Uparaja to command them in accordance with his intentions, as set forth.

The Uparaja received the royal order / and agreed. So the king asked all the old officials from the time of Phraya Ca Ban, "O officials, where are the men who were the subjects of the Uparaja Kòn Kæo?" They replied, "Of the men who were the / *phlang* and red-heads[8] of Uparaja Kòn Kæo, they fled; some to M. Pòn, some to M. Yuam, some to Tha Fang, some to the banks of the Salween, some to Tha Sitò Sitæ, some to Mæ Pa Pha Ku and M. Thalang,[9] where they remain."

In s. 1145, a *ka mao* year (1783/84), the king in concert with his princely brothers issued an order to /f° 7.04/ Phraya Sam Lan who with thirty men was to take forty ornamented bowls to present to the Karen Khang Hua Tat,[10] controlling the frontiers, to win him to their side. The Karen Khang Hua Tat were partisan to Phraya Sam Lan, and stole quietly down to Ban Tòng Phò and brought men and families into the country.[11] This was the first step. /

Next, the king summoned the Uparaja and Cao Rattana Hua Müang Kæo to join him in sending a letter entreating Fa Nòi Mot of M. Thalang and presenting him thirty ornamented bowls and silk clothing. They had him send an important person to take thirty men to go to the Khang Sæn Luang, / the Karen manning the frontiers, and had him take the silk clothing and thirty bowls to the Khang Sæn Luang on the west bank of the Salween. The Khang Sæn Luang were agreeable, and sent the letter on to Fa Nòi Mot. Fa Nòi Mot was pleased with the generosity and friendship, and the important officer persuaded Fa Nòi Mot to put his lands into the country. / This was the second step.[12]

The king used his two younger brothers to cleverly bring [former] enemies within his country, in order to make it grow ever larger. Usually they tried / to collect small

---

8   Probably so termed from the colors of their headdresses; probably Karen.

9   Tha Fang, Tha Sitò Sitæ, Mæ Pu Pha Ku, M. Thalang (or Thrang = Phapun): on the west side of the Salween, in Burma. The *Khlong Mangthra rop Chiang Mai* says that Thrang was between M. Yuam (Mæ Sariang) and Martaban. This passage thus indicates the area around Mæ Sariang and to the west.

10 Paired with the Karen who were "Khang Sæn Luang" in the next paragraph; clearly two different groups of Karen.

11 There continues to be a substantial Karen population in Li district of Lampang.

12 This passage might refer to the area from Mae Hong Son to the west, across the Salween.

villages and larger towns which had been dependent upon Ava, thereby getting more people to enrich his country.

Then the king had Nai Cantharacha command an army to take Ban Tha on the west bank of the Salween and capture the headmen of M. Thu, M. Kitti, M. Yan, and /f° 7.05/ Teacher Nantho; and he swept up people and families into the country.

Then the king ordered Sæn Ratchakot to take a force to attack Ban Mæ Pa. They captured Sæn Khattiya and Mün Chumphu, and swept up people to put into the country.

Then, the king had Nòi China Khao and China Dam and Mò Puk take a letter to recruit / Phraya Mala of M. Sawat.[13] Phraya Mala agreed to submit. The two Nòi China and Mò Puk then returned.

Burmese Invasion, 1784/85

In s. 1146, a *kap si* year (1784/85), Prince Chai Kæo, the royal father, came to visit M. Pa Sang and to see all his royal / sons. On the Mon Wednesday, the full-moon day of the fourth month (1 January 1785), the Burmese Pagân Min-gyi brought troops from Ava to surround Lakhòn. The king handed the domain over to his royal father and the Uparaja, his younger brother, to / take care of, while he himself took a force of a thousand men to fight the Burmese at Lakhòn; and he sent Sæn Sulwa to take a letter down to the king in Ayotthiya asking for troops to help fight the Burmese. Before the South army arrived, the Burmese Pagân / Min-gyi divided his army to go and attack Phræ, Thœn, and Lahæng, which fell and their people fled to the forest. The Burmese captured the rulers of Phræ, Thœn, and Chiang Ngœn, and brought them and their people back.

The king fought the Burmese at Lakhòn for two months and twenty-six days. The king of /f° 7.06/ Ayutthiya called up an army of thirty thousand to go up and fight the Burmese who had surrounded Lakhòn, and defeated them on Tuesday, the sixth waning of the sixth month (18 March 1785?).

The king had a letter put in the hands of a servant to ride urgently on horseback to ask the Uparaja at Pa Sang to go to attack / M. Sawat. Informed of that request, the Uparaja quickly assembled five hundred men and, on Thursday, the sixth waning of the seventh month (17 April 1785?), left. After a journey of seven nights, he reached

---

13   Or Chawat.

M. Sawat on the thirteenth waning of the seventh month. At that time, the ruler of Sawat had gone up with the Burmese to surround / Lakhòn and, defeated, was en route back home. The Uparaja was able to enter and take M. Sawat, and then he attacked M. Næn and rounded up the M. Sawat families, and the M. Næn[14] families, which he took back to settle in his country. When the defeated ruler of Sawat arrived back from Lakhòn and found only an empty town, / he took his men and went in

to follow his wives and children and put himself and them under the governance of Pa Sang.

The king of Ava sent a letter to Ayutthiya on the fifth waning of the fourth month, s. 1146, a *kap si* year (6 January 1785?). Meanwhile, the king [of Lan Na], having restored order in / Lakhòn, took his army and returned to his own country, that is, Pa Sang.

Events in Ava, 1782–1784

Here we will tell of Ava.

In s. 1144, a *tao yi* year (21 September 1782), there was a lunar eclipse from the first waning until the third waning of the first month.[15] Maung Wiang seized the king of Ava and killed him, /fº 7.07/ and ascended the throne as king in that year.[16]

In s. 1145, a *ka mao* year, in the sixth month (January 1784), Maung Wiang was consecrated king. Ai Cat and Ai Kin Thò rebelled in Dagon (Rangoon) for nine days. They were caught and killed.

In s. 1146, a *kap si* year, on the fifth waning of the fourth month (20 December 1784), the king of Ava / sent a letter to Ayutthiya bidding for peace with the king of Ayutthiya. The latter was unreceptive, and sent the letter back.[17]

---

14 M. Næn: now in Burma. The people from Næn were settled near the Chang Phüak Gate.

15 Oppolzer (*Canon*), #4623.

16 Maung Maung (r. 1782) seized the throne from Singu (r. 1776–1782). See Koenig, *The Burmese Polity, 1752–1819*, esp. pp. 204–209. "Since Maung Maung ruled only a week and since this person Maung Wiang was consecrated king in 1784, he can only have been King Bo-daw-hpaya, who in fact killed Maung Maung. Singu died at the hand of an enraged ex-father-in-law, not of Maung Maung." (Lieberman, pers. comm., 3 April 1995.)

17 See "Ceraca khwammüang rawang Thai kap Phama," *Prachum phongsawadan*, pt. 21 (Kaona Edition, 1964, v. 6, pp. 131–133).

Kawila Visits Bangkok, 1785

As for the king, he left Lakhòn and returned [to Pa Sang]. Not much later, he / accompanied the ruler of Sawat to attend upon the king in the golden palace in Ayutthiya. After finishing their public business, the king asked for the people of Lahæng, Ban Tak,[18] Ban Chiang Ngœn,[19] and Thœn, who had fled the Burmese and come down for refuge in Ayutthiya, that they might go up and re-establish their villages and / towns. The Great King bestowed them upon him, as tributary domains of Chiang Mai, reporting to Chiang Mai and dependent upon Chiang Mai's superintendence.

Their public business concluded, the king [Kavila] / took leave and brought away Phraya Mala, Phraya Tak, and the people of Ban Chiang Ngœn, Lahæng, and Thœn to restore their homes, as domains dependent upon Chiang Mai. Phraya Tak returned to his home and domain. He was pleased, and bestowed his daughter, named Lady Khantha, to be a /f° 7.08/ concubine of the king;[20] and, moreover, he bestowed two sons, Nai Nòi Chawana and Nai Nòi Supha, to serve the king at Pa Sang. From s. 1147 (1785/86), M. Tak, Lahæng, and Thœn were in the service of the / king of Chiang Mai at Pa Sang.

Religious Actions in Lamphun, 1786

In s. 1148, a *lwai sanga* year, on the full-moon day of the fourth month (23 December 1786), the king and his two brothers, together with all the royal relatives, erected the great *chatra* on the four corners of the Great Reliquary; and they / erected iron railings and brass railings around the Great Reliquary of Hariphunchai.

---

18 Note that Ban Tak and Rahæng are separately listed. Ban Tak is the old site of the city of Tak, upstream from the modern city, on the west bank; and there is still another old Tak. See Sisak Wanliphodom, *Müang boran nai khet Sukhothai*, pp. 88–89, 239; and Tri Amatyakul, *Müang nüa læ müang tai* (Bangkok, 1970), pp. 298–299.

19 In the Tak region. See Sisak Wanliphodom, *Müang boran nai khet Sukhothai*, pp. 90–91.

20 That is, Kavila (not the Bangkok monarchs).

Military Actions, 1787

Then on Thursday, the second waxing of the eighth month (8 April 1787), the king appointed the Cao Rattana Hua Müang Kæo and the Rear Palace Prince to command a force of five hundred to go and do combat and take M. Pan.[21] They traveled for twenty-five days to get there / and take it, and they captured Cao Fa Nò Kham and his family and subjects. They rounded up the M. Pan and the M. Tòng Khai[22] people and got them for the country.

In the same year, the king appointed the Uparaja, with Nai Kham Mun, Nai Wòn, and Nai Nòi Kawila / to command a force of three hundred to go to recruit the Na Khwa, ruler of Chiang Sæn, and to pursue the rulers of Phræ and Thœn at Chiang Sæn, whom the Burmese had brought there. They got the rulers of Phræ and Thœn, and the Uparaja appointed Nai Kham Mun, Nai Wòn, and Nai Nòi Kawila /f° 7.09/ to take a hundred men to go and persuade the Cao Fa of Chiang Tung to revolt against the Burmese. The Uparaja forcibly brought the rulers of Phræ and Thœn back [to Pa Sang].

A letter was then sent to persuade Phraya Surin of M. Fang to revolt against the Burmese. As for Nai Kham Mun, Nai Wòn, and Nai Nòi Kawila, they went on to try to persuade the ruler of / Chiang Tung to rebel against the Burmese. He did not rebel, however, saying that he feared that the people of his domain would be wiped out.[23] Then [the three] went on to urge the ruler of M. Yòng to rebel. The ruler of Yòng agreed, but he was defeated by the Burmese. Nai Kham Mun, Nai Wòn, Nai Nòi Kawila, and the ruler of Yòng then fled by way of M. Kò, / M. Sai, and M. Luang Phukha and returned to the country.[24]

As for Phraya Surin, he and the rulers of Phrao and Fang sent written promises to the rulers of Chiang Rai, Sat, the ruler of M. Pu Thao Hao, and Thao Sæn Yòt, that they would all revolt against the Burmese and kill Burmese in every domain. At

---

21 M. Pan: in the Shan states. See map.
22 M. Tòng Khai: in the Shan states. Has to be near M. Pan.
23 This is a small glimpse of what may have been involved for the petty rulers of the area.
24 M. Kò, M. Sai, and M. Luang Phukha all are in northwestern Laos. Note that they took a very long route to Chiang Mai, indicating that they were avoiding Chiang Sæn, where the Burmese were still established.

that time, the ruler of Phrao was at / M. Sat with the ruler of Sat; and they revolted against the Burmese in each domain, and brought their families on in.

Burmese Invasion, 1787/88

In s. 1149, a *müang met* year (1787/88), the Burmese Asæ Wun took a force of thirty thousand to go after Phraya Surin, Phraya Phrao, Phraya Sat, Phraya Chiang Rai, and the ruler of M. Pu, all the way down to / Lakhòn. The Burmese Asæ Wun surrounded and besieged Lakhòn.

As for Chiang Mai, the Burmese General Khæng U Min-gyi left Ava with a force of sixteen thousand and came by way of M. Khlang,[25] across the Salween to M. Yuam (Mæ Sariang). The king had Nai Phutthawong take 150 men to inspect the passes of /f° 7.10/ M. Yuam. He met the Burmese vanguard and engaged them, but the Burmese were too numerous. Nai Phutthawong fell back and encamped at Bò Phawæn.[26] They fought. He was fearless, but had to withdraw slowly, fighting all the way. He sent a letter informing the king, who sent the Uparaja and Cao Rattana Hua Müang Kæo, both of them his brothers, as / commanders with a provincial army, e.g., from Kamphængphet and Sawankhalok, to go and meet the Burmese vanguard at Mæ Sòi. They fought, and the Burmese vanguard was beaten and withdrew. Many Burmese died. They were chased to M. Hòt. There they encountered the main Burmese force, which they / fought heavily and fearlessly, but had to withdraw. The Burmese pursued them and invested Pa Sang and Lakhòn, which none could aid.

The king then appointed Thao Kæo to go and pay attendance upon the king in Ayutthiya,[27] / asking for an army to fight the Burmese who had surrounded Lakhòn and Pa Sang. The king raised an army, and had Thao Kæo, the royal messenger, lead the army up. The Burmese had surrounded Pa Sang for two months when the South army arrived, / and fought the Burmese, who were defeated and scattered on Monday, the sixth waning of the sixth month (March 1788).

The king together with his two brother princes and all the royal family welcomed and fêted the commanders and men of the army of the Great king to satiation with

---

25 M. Khlang: probably a mistake for M. Thrang (Papun).
26 Bò Phawæn: presumably between Mæ Sariang (M. Yuam) and M. Thalang (Papun).
27 Whenever the text refers to "Ayutthiya" after 1767, of course Bangkok is meant.

rice and drink and food /f° 7.11/²⁸ for seven days, and then all the officers and armies returned. Nai Kham Mun, Nai Wòn, and Nai Nòi Kawila returned to Nakhòn Pa Sang.

Fatherly Advice, 1789

In s. 1150, a *pœk san* year, on Friday, the seventh waning of the fourth month (5 January 1789), Prince Chai Kæo, the royal father, remembered his children, and feared that they would lose their familial harmony, and so he gave them [the following] royal advice:

"Thenceforth, all my children in Lakhòn and Chiang Mai should heed their father's advice. Don't listen to your subjects, those who would sow discord, but only to those who are well-intentioned. Don't fight among yourselves. All eight of you should love one another, and in all you do, act like one loving individual. Don't consider others as superior to your siblings, younger or elder. You should consider your royal possessions, your property and wealth, not as your own but rather as your common wealth. Whenever any of the eight of you attain to status and happiness, share these. Don't fail to communicate with each other: the elder should help the younger and the younger the elder. Heed carefully your father's advice and you will avert disaster.

"The past calamities of Lamphun, Chiang Mai, Keng Tung, M. Yòng, and Nan, all of them occurred because of discord among siblings and from failure to heed their parents' good advice, and because they vied for the royal /f° 7.12/ wealth of the country, and oppressed and harmed each other. Disaster then followed, and they could no longer be countries as in days of yore. Thus you should carefully consider and understand the fate of those domains. Hear this advice: the swan with a single body and seven / heads will know only discord. Though you have the great good fortune to rule in various domains, you must consider them to be a single domain.

"Those evil ones who steal and flee, the elder seeking out the younger and the younger the elder, you should not harbor, but send back [from whence they came]. Don't consider such persons to be your siblings, elder or younger. / Recognize such actions for what they are. Whichever of you doesn't heed his father's good advice,

---

28 Line-breaks are not indicated on this folio, which was illegible on the microfilm and had to be pieced together from other sources (mainly SN).

and thinks to quarrel and injure his siblings, may that child quickly suffer calamity and die. Though myriad Buddhas may arise, may such a one never know them, even one of them, and may they fall / into the Niriya Hell[29] for a hundred thousand epochs, never to escape, whatever they do. Whatever they do, their country will not prosper: it will be destroyed, day and night, in this life and the next. If you heed your father's / advice, you will prosper and flourish, together with your land, in all you intend.

"Furthermore, Lakhòn is in the hands of three of my sons, headed by the king of Lakhòn; and in Chiang Mai there are two younger sons, /f° 7.13/ headed by the ruler of Chiang Mai. Their six younger siblings should consider the rulers of Lakhòn and Chiang Mai as their parents, and heed this advice of their father.

"Furthermore, all the goods, wealth, elephants, and horses in my sheds should be maintained in accordance with past royal custom, and [on death] pass to the wife, not be divided among / any children, except eighty [units of] gold for the eight children, one *bat* for each child as a gift." So said he.

Pious Donation at Dòi Suthep

In s. 1150, a *pæk san* year (1788/89), the three sibling kings joined in piety to build together a copper *chatra*, beauteous to behold, covered with lacquer, gilt with / gold and beautifully decorated. On the full-moon day, a Mon Thursday,[30] they erected them on the Venerable Reliquary atop Dòi Suthep. They invited 108 monks to chant the *Parittamaṅgalasutta*, the whole of the *Mahāsameyyasutta*, and the Seven Victories chapter of the *Karaniban [sutta]* / to inaugurate it and they joined in a merit-making procession. This was a great occasion, a first there.

Minor Burmese Invasion, 1789/90

Then in s. 1151, a *kat rao* year (1789/90), the Burmese general Yan Khwæng Siri with three thousand men left Ava and established himself at M. Tuan Hua Yòt and M. Cai Mæ Sæn. / With the king as head, and Cao Rattana Hua Müang

---

29 The meaning is "Hell in general."

30 The month of this event is not given. However, there was only one full-moon day that fell on a Thursday in that year, in the second month, 13 November 1788.

Kæo, Cao Phutthawongsa, Cao Cantharacha, Cao Kham Mun, and Cao Nòi Kawila they commanded a thousand men, leaving on Thursday the thirteenth waning of the seventh month (12 April 1789) and traveled for fifteen days. On Thursday the thirteenth waxing of the eighth month (26 April 1789) they /f° 7.14/ battled the Burmese. The Burmese general Yan Khwæng Siri who was holding M. Tuan Hua Yòt was thoroughly defeated. The Thai captured weapons, cannon, guns, and swords to bring back for their country. Moreover, the king had Cao Cantharacha and Cao Kawila Nòi command / a hundred men to cross the Salween to the west bank and take Ban Om Sik, and they captured families to take back to the country.

Then, the king appointed Cao Cantharacha as commander and Thao Sitthi and various titled men to take a force of 150 men to capture Ban Satòi, Ban Wang Lu, and Wang Kat.[31] / They captured the person of Sæn Sri and men, families, and weapons for the country.

A Burmese Royal Impostor

Then there was a Burmese scoundrel named Sakhæng Maung Phung who could not remain at Ava, as they would there have killed or beaten him; so he came to the Shan lands as an impostor, / claiming, "I am a son of the White Elephant King of Ava. Now, Batung of Mokso[32] has come to rule my country, which has displeased me. I am intending to go and see the king of the south Country. When I am king, I will bring troops back to take Badung, most assuredly. If you fear perdition for your land and country, / follow me."[33]

At that time, all nineteen of the Shan *sawbwa*, headed by the *sawbwa* of Hsenwi,[34] followed his every word, and designated officers and men to follow him, from every country. Altogether there were seventy men who went by way of Nan to Krungthep

---

31 Ban Satò, Ban Wang Lu, and Wang Kat: The Ban Satòi people founded a new village with the same name east of Chiang Mai. The Wang Lung people now have a village called Ban Wang Lung in Hòt district of Chiang Mai.

32 Mokso: i.e., Moksobomyo; that is, Shwebo.

33 "Batung is clearly the eater of Badon (the prince of Badon), which was Bo-daw-hpaya's pre-regnal designation. In other words the imposter claimed to be a son of Badon (Min) of the Mokso(bo) dynasty." (Lieberman, pers. comm., 3 April 1995.)

34 Hsenwi is on the maps. Nineteen Shan *sawbwas*?

Mahanakhòn Sri Ayutthiya.[35] /f° 7.15/ He did not think very realistically, and went straight to the king and said, "I am a real son of the king of Ava who is not ruling because Patung has seized the throne. In order to rule, I beg the Royal Indulgence: give me troops to go and fight Patung's country, and I will present [that country] to Your Majesty." / That King of Great Merit was most wise and astute, and realized the real nature of Sakhæng Maung Phung, and knew that all was not as he said. The idea that Burmese and Thai could be friends was not to be; / they were enemies. So the king said to Sakhæng Maung Phung, "Whatever you ask, our country is now disturbed." [Sakhæng Maung Phung] did not know what to say, and he left. /

Tak/Lahæng and Thœn

As for the ruler of Tak Lahæng, he was old and infirm, unable to deal with public affairs. The king went to do battle with the Burmese who were at M. Tuan Hua Yòt and M. Cai Mæ Chæn, and gained victory, and then he returned home. /

Soon, the king took Nai Nòi Supha and Nai Nòi Chawana to attend upon the king in Ayutthiya. After informing him of all public business, he then imposed on the Royal Majesty to ask that Nai Nòi Supha and Nai Nòi Chawana be appointed to rule [Tak Lahæng]. So the /f° 7.16/ Great King appointed Nai Nòi Supha as Phraya Anuchit Chonlathi, to be the governor of M. Tak Lahæng; and Nai Nòi Chawana as Phraya Inthakhiri, deputy governor, to take charge of the government of the domain.

Also, the king [of Lan Na] asked of the Great King, "As for M. Thœn, none can be found to take charge of the domain as governor, / as Phraya Thœn, whom the Burmese seized and took away, came back with them, and is now old and infirm and incompetent; so please appoint a new one."

The Great King asked, "Who pleases the king of Chiang Mai? Who would be appropriate to be the governor of Thœn?" The king / expressed his preference for Thao Chumphu, a royal page, who can be trusted and believed, and also is a Thœn man. The king [of Lan Na] said to him, "Thao Chumphu would be suitable to be the governor of Thœn." So the Great King supported the choice and was pleased to appoint Thao Chumphu as / Phraya Canthapuri Phraya Thœn, and he bestowed insignia of rank on the domains, large and small, and handed over those domains

---

35 This is one instance when Bangkok (Krungthep) is spelled correctly.

to be subject to Chiang Mai. If Lahæng and Thœn had any problems, they were to submit them to the decision of the lord of Chiang Mai.

Moreover, the Great Kings, both of them, / handed over Sakhæng Maung Phung and his seventy followers for the king to take for use in the government of the country. Then the king took leave and brought the governor of /f° 7.17/ Tak, Phraya In, the governor of Thœn, and Sakhæng Maung Phung up to Lahæng and there arranged the government of the domain under the governor of Tak and Phraya In; and in Thœn he did the same for the governor of Thœn. Then he returned to his country.

Royal Merit-Making, 1791/92

In s. 1153, a *luang khai* year (1791/92), the king took two of his younger brothers, his relatives and officials, civil and military, up to the city of Chiang Mai for the / first time. A month later, things were still not yet settled: the time was not right. And so he returned to stay at Pa Sang as before.

Together they built shrine-halls on the four sides of the great reliquary of Lamphun, and they erected the Lawo Buddha Image in the north *vihara* of the Reliquary, in that / *luang khai* year.

Luang Prabang, 1791

In that *luang khai* year, the Vietnamese attacked and failed to take Lan Sang.

The king of Lan Sang rebelled against the king of Ava. On the second waning of the sixth month (8 May 1791) the king of Lan Sang placed himself under the protection of the Great King of Ayutthiya Bang Kòk, and in s. 1153 he presented a lady to him. /

Burmese at Fang, 1792

The Burmese Suraköi Thæng general, with three thousand men, came down to headquarter at Fang. In s. 1154, a *tao cai* year, on Wednesday, the fourth waxing of the ninth month (12 May 1792), the king the eldest brother [Kavila] and Cao Rattana Hua Müang Kæo the Rear Palace, with fifteen hundred men went forth, / traveled for eighteen days, and on Saturday the sixth waning of the ninth month (29 May) did battle with the Burmese Suraköi Thæng general, for a month and four days, but they were unsuccessful and withdrew back.

Sakhæng Maung Phung

As for Sakhæng Maung Phung, he stayed at Pa Sang for a year, and presented himself saying, "I have great merit; more than any other. /f° 7.18/ If anyone tries to kill me, I won't die. Whatever they say, only Indra can come down and kill me, and then I'll die." Moreover, he repeatedly made such claims, that "This country, this land, bamboo and teak, the rulers and men, all this domain is mine." Also, / he expected that all the people there were really in his power, in great numbers. He so boasted of taking the whole country. The three brother princes together decided to seize this Sakhæng Maung Phung and send him to the Great King, and / reported to him what he had been saying, that he would take the whole country. Informed, the Great King was pleased to order the executioners to take and kill him on that day.

Attack on Chiang Sæn, 1793/94

The king took leave and took his men back up / home. He thought, "Chiang Sæn was a dependency of Chiang Mai for a long time, ever since King Thao Sæn Phu founded the subordinate cities, but now it belongs to the Burmese. We should do battle to try to regain it." / The king sent a letter to his younger brother, the ruler of Lakhòn, and [the rulers of] Phræ and Nan asking them to organize a force of troops to go up and take Chiang Sæn.

In s. 1155, a *ka pao* year, on Thursday, the eleventh waning of the third month (17 November 1793), King Mangra Wachiraprakan /f° 7.19/ Kamphæng Kæo, the royal elder brother, had an army of ten thousand men organize a force which traveled for seventeen days. On Monday, the twelfth waxing of the twelfth month (5 December 1793), they encircled Chiang Sæn. After two full months, they failed and returned on the Mon Thursday, full-moon day of the second month (February 1794).

Royal Merit-Making, 1794/95

In s. 1156, a *kap yi* year, on the Mon Sunday, the full-moon day of the eighth month (April 1794), / the First Great Royal Merit-making Ceremony [took place]. The Uparaja built the great *vihara* of Wat Inthakhin, and erected a Buddha image as a focus for worship by the public and the gods, and for the monks and brahmans.

There was a procession and celebration and chanting and great merit-making, with great entertainment for the great inauguration / on the first day in that year.

On the Mon Sunday, the full-moon day of the fifth month (January 1795), the three brother princes presided over the royal family and officials civil and military, and with all the people and religious, all of whom poured the water of consecration / and appointed the abbot of Wat Pha Khao,[36] named Thittamangala, as the Supreme Patriarch over all the monkhood. The king, the royal eldest brother, built an *uposatha* and erected a Buddha image for worship by the people and the gods, / by all religious, and inaugurated and celebrated it, another great happy occasion.

Capital Moved to Chiang Mai, 1794/95

In that s. 1156 (1794/95), the three brother princes organized the country, especially the corvéeable men, to strengthen the domain and make merit, /f° 7.20/ and he quartered in Pa Sang for fourteen years, four months, and twenty days. The city was graced with the presence of all the officials, civil and military, and royal servants and people, all fervent in their faith in the Buddha, resplendent and extensive, until the appropriate moment when the three / princes were appropriately pure; and then announced to the four groups of military—elephantry, horse-cavalry, war-cars, and infantry—that they would go in procession to accompany forth the sovereign. The lord mounted the resplendent howdah, / beauteous and stately.

In s. 1158, a *lwai si* year, on Sunday the eighth waxing of the sixth month (22 March 1797), the two younger royal brothers and the royal family, officers, civil and military, and the people left Pa Sang in procession by land / and traveled for five days. On Thursday the twelfth waxing of the sixth month (26 March), in the *tut chao* watch, the lord came to Wat Buppharam, according to the ancient custom of all past rulers, never neglected, he circumambulated / by the south proceeding to the west to the north of Wat Chiang Yün. The king reverenced the image of Wat Chiang Yün, and then, approaching noon, he led his retainers into the royal city by the White Elephant Gate on the north side, having the Lawa carrying /f° 7.21/ their baskets going ahead. He entered and slept in the Chiang Khwang [area] in front of Wat Chiang Man for one night.

The next morning, after his ablutions, he dressed and ate, and in the *kòng ngai* watch, at an auspicious moment, he entered the auspicious site of the Small Royal Palace, / which had been the home of previous rulers in former times. As for the

---

36 Wat Pha Khao: see Chiang Mai city map.

Uparaja, Cao Rattana Hua Müang Kæo, the royal younger brother, and all the royal relatives and officials, they remained in their appropriate places. / The king entered the royal capital of Chiang Mai for ten months and five days.

Burmese Invasion, 1797/98

In s. 1159, a *müang sai* year, on the second waning of the fourth month (23 December 1797), the Burmese General Ingsek and General Sitsing with an army of ninety-nine thousand men left Ava and surrounded / Chiang Mai and battled them, in a great war.[37] The king appointed the princes, sons and grandsons, to command forces to go out and fight the Burmese. Defeated, the Burmese withdrew and attacked again, and then again.

The three brother princes together / decided, "We and the Burmese will fight. We're not afraid of them. They will not come in and defeat us." The three brother princes [further] decided, "The Burmese may attack, but we're not afraid. However, our city is newly founded, and our food and water supplies are insufficient. We should send down and ask /f° 7.22/ for a Southern army to come up and augment our strength."

So a letter was written, and Sæn Siri-aksòn was appointed to go down with captured Burmese to attend upon the Great King in Ayutthiya and request that the Front Palace king come / as commander, the war-king, with a force of one hundred thousand men. They came up to Thœn and there divided, with Cao Inthapat and Cao Ramnuan, both royal sons, commanding a force of forty thousand to come up by way of M. Li. The Burmese General Ingsœ[38] / sent a force to counter them at M. Li. They fought for three days and three nights. The Burmese army could not withstand them and withdrew back to take up positions at Lamphun.

The Front Palace king was still at M. Thœn, and appointed a force to go up by way of M. Lakhòn to meet them at Lamphun. They fought the Burmese at / Pa Sang city, and defeated them; and then went up to engage the Burmese who were surrounding Chiang Mai city. The Burmese general Ingsæ could not withstand them and was beaten. They captured the Burmese general Uppa Kòng at the Chang

---

37 "*Kon-baung-zet-maha-yazawin-daw-gyi*, vol. II (Rangoon, 1967), 122, identifies the head of this expedition as Nei-myo-kyaw-din-thi-hathu." (Lieberman, pers. comm., 3 April 1995.)

38 There are at least three slightly-different spellings of this general's name.

Khlan Field, together with many Burmese troops. The Burmese had surrounded the city for / two months and eighteen days. When the Burmese had been defeated and withdrew, the South army took leave and withdrew.

Not long afterward, in the same year, the three princes together built the king of Lavo *vihara* at Lamphun, [until] the *pœk sanga* year, s. 1159.[39]

Müang Pu, 1798/99

In s. /f° 7.23/ 1160, a *pœk sanga* year (1798/99), Sæn Si, the ruler of M. Pu,[40] rebelled against the Burmese who had controlled the domain,[41] and migrated with his people and came in to place himself under the protection of Chiang Mai. The king, the eldest brother, took Sæn Si down to attend upon the Great King / in Si Ayutthiya. The Great King received him, and appointed Sæn Si as Phraya Si Puwattisunthòn, and bestowed upon him appropriate insignia of rank, and then had the king take him back up to Chiang Mai. The king then appointed Thao Siri and Thao Bun Rüang to take / three hundred men to attack the Burmese general Siri Nòratha and expel him. They swept up officials great and small, the governor of M. Sat named Sæn Müang Ma, and Nai Nòi Wong of M. Cæt, [together with] Tha Òk, M. Küng, and M. Kun to come within [the kingdom of] Chiang Mai, and captured a male elephant and Lady Mi Khòng to / present to the king in s. 1160.

In s. 1161, a *kat met* year (1799/1800), the king appointed Cao Kham Mun to command an army of three hundred to go and attack Fa Kham Khrüang who had encamped at M. Pu. Fa Kham Khrüang suffered a gunshot wound and died at M. Pu. Then Cao Kham Mun took his army / across the Salween to the west bank to take Ban Ngua Lai,[42] Ban Satòi, Sòi Rai, Tha Chang, Ban Na, and Thong Òk, and captured Mün Khwang of Ngua Lai and the wife of Fa Kham Khrüang and swept up the people to within the country.

In s. 1162, a *kot san* year (1800/1801), the king commanded Thao Maha Yak to command an army /f° 7.24/ of two hundred and take them across the Salween and

---

39 The *pœk sanga* year was 1160, not 1159.

40 M. Pu: in the Keng Tung region; see GUBSS II, pt. 2, pp. 473–476.

41 This last phrase is not in Notton.

42 The people moved from Ngua Lai founded a new village by the same name just to the south of the city walls of Chiang Mai. They have continued to practice silversmithing.

attack Ban Sup Mæ Theng. He captured Mün Khan and Mün Phom, and swept up people to put into the country.

Chiang Mai Renamed; and Merit-Making Works

The three brother princes together bestowed a new name upon the domain, to be victorious over enemies: Ratanatiṁsa Abhinavapuri. / On Saturday the eleventh waxing of the seventh month (March 1801), they built two images of white elephants north of the city.[43] The front one, on the north, was called Prap Cakravala, while the one on the west was called Prap Müang Mara Müang Yaksa. Then they built two images of *Kumbhanda* in front of Wat Chotikaram;[44] and they built an image of / Lord Sudorasi to the west of the Inthakhin Hall in the same year.

Two years later, in the *luang rao* year, s. 1163, on the thirteenth waxing of the fourth month (4 January 1802), an auspicious day, in the *tut chao* watch, an *ukhaṅgarāja* moment, they built two *miggindasiharāja* images[45] / on the Mangala Field north of the city, to be auspicious for the people of the country. The three brother princes had Buddhist temples, images, stupas and *cetiya*s, kuti, *vihara*, and *ubosatha* built for the pleasure of the / monks, for making merit continuously; and they rebuilt the walls, forts, and gates, to be stable and strong; and dug moats to carry water all around the city, strong against the enemy. /f° 7.25/ At that time, all the abandoned places were revived. The king of Ava had taken over many places to be within his control to serve for the provisioning of his troops who came to make war; and M. Ratanatiṁsa Abhinavapuri Chiang Mai took them.

Further Attacks in the Shan Hills

Tato tayo rājā.[46] / As for the three brother princes, they were very skilled in warfare, and they were determined that the enemy should not regain the advantage;

---

43 The white elephant statues are still there, north of the city. These replaced statues made in the time of Sæn Müang Ma (f° 3.30). The names of the elephants translate as "Lord World-Conqueror" and "Lord Conqueror of Demons and Devils."

44 Wat Chotikaram: Wat Chedi Luang, in the center of Chiang Mai city.

45 These are the *khuang sing* images, two images in the form of stylized lions, behind Wat Khuang Sing on the north side of the city.

46 Pali: "The three princes."

so they strengthened the land so they could not injure our country. / They issued a royal ordinance that Thao Inthasiri, a most brave warrior, should take five hundred ferocious warriors as guerrilla troops to go and attack M. Pu. They captured the ruler of Pu and all his men, and swept up all the people and sent them down; and then they continued on / to attack M. Cæt, M. Küng, M. Kun, Tha Òk, and Tha Chæt and take them. Then they went down to attack the Burmese General Siri Nòratha[47] who was encamped at M. Sat. They defeated him, and captured high and low officers and their men for the country.

Shan Lords Submit to Chiang Mai

Then, / the Shan domain lords feared the majesty and power of the king, and they feared losing control of their domains; so they sent tribute and presents, namely, guns and swords and curtains, and had an official, a minister, go down to present them and ask to become a vassal. King Mamra Wachiraprakan /f° 7.26/ Kamphæng Kæo, the royal eldest brother, summoned his two younger brothers to consult with him in the royal palace, and they realized, "The enemy now knows that he cannot seize our country through warfare, and so he now is trying to / win it through stratagems: we know this. To accept this tribute might not be harmful to us. If we were to kill this dignitary, it would be of no use, as he is only the bearer of tribute, / so we should just crimp the guns' muzzles and fold over the knives' points and cut holes in the curtains and have him take them back." Later, the king of Ava learned of this, and had a man bring in the ruler of M. Cit and had his chest split.

Expedition to the Shan Hills Again

Later, the king of Ava again sent Cao Fa Kham Khrüang to come and encamp at M. Pu. / The king [of Chiang Mai] learned of this, and thought, "If I send a large army there, it will become widely known, and I am afraid that Fa Kham Khrüang will become frightened, and will send his people away." Thus he appointed Cao Suwanna Kham Mun, who was his nephew, to command a force of three hundred seasoned warriors to go up and / take M. Pu and imprison Fa Kham Khrüang. He [the latter] had the misfortune to suffer a gunshot wound that killed him.

---

47 Lieberman: General Thi-ri-naw-yahta.

Cao Suwanna Kham Mun swept up all his people and sent them back. Then he went on to attack Ban Satòi, Sòi Rai, Tha Chang, Ban Na, Ban Thong Òk, and Ngua Lai, and took Mün Khwang of Ngua Lai. /f° 7.27/

Then [the king] had Thao Maha Yak command a brave force to attack Ban Sup Theng and took Mün Khantha and Mün Phom and all their people, whom he brought back to settle in the country.

The king then appointed Cao Phutthawongsa, his nephew, to take a force of warriors to go and attack the Burmese army at Tha Pha Pun.[48] The Burmese could not withstand them and were defeated. / He captured three hundred guns and families and goods and silver and gold in great number, which he brought back and presented.

Again, the king had Thao Sitthi command a force of warriors to go up and attack and take M. Mang [and] Ban Khæm.[49] He swept up the ruler of Mang and the people of Khæm and Mang, which he brought back for the country. /

Raja Còm Hong, 1801

Tadā eko rāja haṁsā pabbate nāma. Tadā.[50] At that time, there was a prince, named Hamsaraja, also known as Raja Còm Hong, who had three sons; the eldest named Tu Khun Fu Ta Lao Yæ; the middle one named Sæng Sung Ta Lao Yæ; / and the youngest named Sung Fu Ta Lao Yæ. They lived in M. Nun,[51] on the frontiers of the Hò domain of Videha.[52] When the Burmese Ingsœ was beaten in Chiang Mai, he went to live in Chiang Sæn with his men, and he took M. Chiang Sæn, M. Yòng, and M. Chiang Khæng and [then] returned to stay in Ava for three years. The Great King / of Ava knew that he was a good and honest man, as he was a servant of the Hò and not a servant of the Southerners. Knowing that he himself was a meritful man and brave, he went to the king of Ava and said, "I and the ruler of Chiang Mai

---

48 Tha Pha Pun: Papun, west of Mæ Sariang on the Burma side of the Salween.

49 M. Mang, Ban Khæm: The people taken from M. Mang established a Ban Müang Mang outside the walls of Chiang Mai, in the area of the Khatham fort, near the Lai Khæng Gate.

50 Pali: the meaning is duplicated by the translated phrase which follows.

51 M. Nun: probably Möng Nung in GUBSS, II, pt. 2, 439–440; northern Keng Tung.

52 Videha is the classical name of Yunnan.

are very well known to each other. /f° 7.28/ I can go and persuade him to become a servant of Your Majesty. That is certain, and you need not doubt it."

The king of Ava heard that, and was greatly pleased; so he said, "If that is really so, I will issue a royal order commanding you to take charge of gaining control of the country." / Then he issued an amein-daw ordering, "Among all the Thai who have submitted to the Shans, the Khœn, the Lü, and the Hò, for the past ten generations, you are to take charge of all of them." Moreover, he handed over to him all elephants, male and female, all horses, all / musical instruments and gongs and drums, all gold and silver-handled lances, all the golden umbrellas, all five of the noble's regalia to him, and founded M. Suwanna Selakatasalagi M. Sat.

In the eleventh month (September 1801), he bestowed upon him the title of Cao Maha Suwannahongsa Cakkavatti Cao Fa / Luang Hò Kham of the domain of Chiang Mai, overlord of the 57 Lan Na Thai domains.

Then he bestowed titles on a great many of the generals and ministers, e.g., Phraya Sæn Luang, Phraya Sam Lan, Phraya Ca Ban, and Phraya Dek Chai, to be the greatest of all these lords. Then he / appointed the Phraya Ratchawang, Phraya Cheyyaratchathani, Phraya Cheyyasena Chiang Sæn, Phraya Thepphawong Chiang Khæng, Phraya Prap Chiang Tung, Thao Singkharacha Chamberlain, Thao Wong of Chiang Rai, Sæn Khüan of M. Phayak, Sæn Kæo of M. Len, Racha Tham of M. Yòng—five *phraya*, two *thao*, two *sæn*, and /f° 7.29/ one *raja*; with seventy retainers, to go down and discuss state business and bid for the friendship of the two countries, senior and junior, to engage in friendly commerce, that the waters between them would be always muddied [from travel] and their campfires never be extinguished; and that all their previous enmity might be erased, the graves of all war-dead forgotten.

Chiang Mai Suspicious of Burmese Overtures, 1802

His Majesty the Venerable / King Mangra Wachiraprakan Kamphæng Kæo, the Lord and Chief of his Royal Brothers, presided over a convocation of the generals and ministers to together consider the royal letter. They summoned the royal / astrologers and considered the teachings of the Vedic texts and figured out the *hani* [magical letters] which advised them not to believe what they were hearing. Thus they composed a royal letter of reply, which he had Thao Singkharaja take back on up saying, "If we are to consider the two countries as senior and junior siblings, truly subsisting in royal friendship, / have high-ranking persons come down here together to Chiang Mai, as that is the ancient head of the region." Thao Singkharaja bore the letter up to M. Sat and attended upon Raja Còm Hong, and told him all / that had transpired, in every detail. Raja Còm Hong heard what Thao Singkharaja said, and all that was in the royal letter; and together they composed a letter for Thao Singkharaja to bear back, saying that the ruler of Chiang Mai should proceed up to M. Fang, as the lands and waters of the domain /f° 7.30/ of Chiang Mai extended to M. Fang, as did the frontiers of M. Sat.

Thao Singkharaja bore the letter on down to Chiang Mai and presented the letter in greetings to the king. The king was informed in every detail. The king was clear as to the letter's contents in every detail which the royal envoy had presented, which angered and / offended him. He thought, "Raja Còm Hong wants to take over the country, and this must not be. Perhaps he is dissimulating in order to gain the royal treasure of my country; this is surely so." Therefore he had his two younger brothers fetched to join him, and / then he issued a royal order to all his generals and ministers ordering them to seize all the rulers who were partisans and servants of Raja Còm Hong and imprison them, without exception, allowing none to escape.

In s. 1164, a *tao set* year, on the thirteenth waxing of the seventh month, a Thursday (3 April 1802), in the watch near noon, / an auspicious royal moment (*yam uthaṅgkharāja*), the Cao Uparaja Narathipati Sri Suwanna Fai Na Hò Kham and the Cao Rattana Hua Miiang Kæo Rear Palace, the two younger brothers, together with the generals and ministers and five thousand troops accompanying them, set out from / M. Ratanatiṁsa Phra Nakhòn Chiang Mai and journeyed for sixteen nights, until on the thirteenth waning of the seventh month, a Friday (18 April), in the *kòng ngai* watch, they reached M. Sat and surrounded it. At dark, they had soldiers enter and seize Raja Còm Hong and his middle son and put them into a cage at the main army. /f° 7.31/ As for the eldest son, he encamped at Ban Phan north of Chiang Sæn, while the youngest son remained at Ava, and did not come. They remained there for five days. They sent men to take Raja Còm Hong back to the royal palace of the king's eldest brother at Chiang Mai.

Keng Tung

The prince remained at M. Sat for nineteen days, and then took his army on further for seven days to / Khemarattha Tungkhaburi on Wednesday the tenth waning of the month (30 April 1802). Cao Siri Cheyyachoti Saramphaya, the ruler of Chiang Tung, feared the royal majesty and did not dare attack them: he took the royal princes and generals and officials and men and fled from the domain and went away. / The next day, the king as chief appointed Cao Ratana Hua Müang Kæo, his younger brother, to take a force to suppress and went to M. Ma [La?], M. Lò, M. Phòk, M. Ka, M. Khak, and M. Nung[53] up to the frontiers of the Wa, Khò, and Khui; and then they returned back down to the city of Chiang Tung. /

Burma and Vietnam, 1802

At that time, there was a Burmese named Shwe Lin Mani, whom the king of Ava had sent to bid for friendship with the Vietnamese, but he had reached only to Chiang Tung. He was unable to escape, and our soldiers were able to capture him. They brought him in and interrogated him and learned all, and then imprisoned him. / The prince remained at Chiang Tung for twenty-five days, and left there on the fifth waning of the ninth month, a Sunday (8 June 1802). In a month and nine days they reached Chiang Mai, on the fourteenth waning of the tenth month, a Wednesday (16 July).

Mission to Bangkok, 1802

After seventeen days, on the second waning of the eleventh month, a Sunday (3 August 1802), the royal eldest brother took Raja Còm Hong /f° 7.32/ and his son, and the Burmese Shwe Lin Mani, and sent them by the Suwannanawa [barge] down the currents of the river for twenty days to Ayutthiya Dvaravati Theppha Mahanakhòn. On Friday, the seventh waxing of the twelfth month (22 August), the king accompanied Raja Còm Hong, his son, and the Burmese Shwe Lin Mani, together with presents in / to attend upon the great sovereign king, the lord of great merit, in Ayutthiya. The Great King was much pleased. On Thursday, the fourth waxing of the first month (18 September), the Great King bestowed the *ussarājabhiseka* [coronation] / upon the king, pouring the waters of ablution with the waters of *Muddhābhiseka* upon the bejeweled throne, and had great entertainment for seven

---

53 M. Ma, M. Lò, M. Phòk, M. Ka, M. Khak, and M. Nung (earlier Nun?): on the Laos side of the Mekong.

days and seven nights; a great occasion indeed. He bestowed a new name upon the king as Phra Bòrommaraja Naradhipati Sri Suriyavamsa Ong Inthasurasaktisomya Mahakhattiyaraja Rajatirajachai / Cao Sawan Cao Khüan Khandhasema Phra Nakhòn Chiang Mai Rajadhani Sri Sawatidhighayu Som Utama king of Chiang Mai, lord of the Fifty-Seven domains of Lan Na Thai.

The king remained in the South country for a month and three days. In the first month, on the eleventh waxing, a Thursday (25 September), the king took leave and / ascended back up from Krungthep Mahanakhòn, and traveled for a month and fifteen days before reaching the landing at Wat Ket on the Raming River on the eleventh waning of the second month, a Saturday (8 November).

Welcoming the King Back to Chiang Mai

At that time, the two royal younger brothers, who were caring for the country, ordered the officials, generals, and ministers to sound the drums and /f° 7.33/ announce to the public to decorate the main streets beautifully and smooth them out and erect trees, fronds, mats, sugar-stalks, banners, and flags all along both sides of the road, from the royal pavilion at water's edge to the gates of his royal palace. / The royal generals and ministers, including Phraya Sæn Luang, Phraya Sam Lan, Phraya Ca Ban, Phraya Dek Chai—the four leading officials—were the men who received the royal order, and they had everyone carry it out, in every detail. On the next day, at dawn, / the two royal younger brothers as head of all the royal officials and retainers bore trays of flowers and puffed rice and gold and silver flowers, and gold and silver candles, and went out to invite His Majesty the King / to enter the royal city.

Coronation of Kavila as King, 1802

On the third waxing of the fourth month, a Sunday (14 December 1802), the two royal younger brothers headed up the royal family and officials and ministers and together they consecrated him, administering the waters of *Muddhābhiseka* coronation in front of the / troops for a second time, extending to him their greetings, wishing him "*Jeyyatubhavaṁ, jeyyatubhavaṁ!*" that is, "May the great lord be victorious over all his enemies, and may he be blessed with a long life and be lord over all the land and instruct all the peoples."/f° 7.34/

On the full-moon day of the fifth month, the Mon Sunday (25 January 1803), His Majesty the King listened to the Dhamma Sermon of the Buddha, from the Temiyajātaka through the ten incarnations to the Vessantara, and worshipped and bestowed alms for the Triple Gems in great quantities.

Expedition to Capture Chiang Sæn, 1803

His Majesty the King / reposed in state in the domain for three months, until the eleventh waning of the fifth month, a Thursday (5 February 1803), when he took a great army of about three thousand and proceeded for seventeen days to M. Jeyyasena Rakkhapuri Chiang Sæn / which he reached on the thirteenth waning of the sixth month, a Saturday (7 March).[54] The army encamped surrounding the city in siege to combat [the Burmese]. They were accompanied by Cao In of Vientiane. His Majesty the King stayed to fight with the Chiang Sæn people for two months and eight days, but did not capture Chiang Sæn.

In s. 1165, a *ka / khai* year, on the eighth waning of the eighth month, a Friday (1 May 1803), His Majesty the King withdrew his army from Chiang Sæn back to the mouth of the Mæ Lai. Not long afterwards, on the second waning of the ninth month, a Monday (25 May), His Majesty the King entered the city [of Chiang Mai]. The ruler of Phayak was impressed with the royal majesty, and brought in his children / and wives and men in submission, at the time when His Majesty the King was withdrawing his army from Chiang Sæn. He had remained there for two months and twenty-nine days.

Expedition to Bangkok, 1803/04

On the first waxing of the twelfth month, a Thursday (6 August 1803), the Uparaja of the Front Palace led the ruler of Phayak down by water /f° 7.35/ for twenty days to arrive at Krungthep Mahanakhòn Si Ayutthiya. On the fifth waning of the twelfth month, a Tuesday (25 August), until the fourth waning of the second month, a Thursday (22 October) the Great King of the Front Palace in Krung Si

---

54 Mistake here: Fifth month eleventh waning to Sixth month thirteenth waning is quite a bit more than the seventeen days which the text specifies. The author forgot to include the fifteen days of the waxing half of the Sixth month.

Ayutthiya was ill, and was so for four months and four days until dying on that day.⁵⁵ The prince remained in the / South country for two months and thirteen days. On Thursday, the third waxing of the third month (5 November), he left and traveled for a month and sixteen days and arrived [in Chiang Mai] on the third waning of the fourth month, a Saturday (19 December).

The prince had been back in the city for twenty-seven days when he ordained his royal son named Mahawongsa on the full-moon day of the fifth month, a Mon / Friday (15 January 1804). At nightfall, they reached the time when the moon rose, and Rahu Asurinda eclipsed the moon in the night.⁵⁶ As for the royal son, when he was born there had been lightning, so / he was named for that omen, Nai Fa.

Capture of Chiang Sæn, 1804

The king Maha Uparaja remained in the city for two months and twenty-six days. On the third waning of the seventh month (17 March 1804), the king Maha Uparaja commanded an army of twelve hundred men and set out. While sleeping in the watch before dawn, / he saw an omen most marvelous, dreaming that the Lord Indra bore seven gems and scattered them for any to gather up. He dreamed that the king stretched out his right hand of gold and grabbed a gem that was white and pure and yet radiated many colors, so it was called a "gem that had fallen from the heavens, brilliant in appearance." /f° 7.36/ When the prince awakened, he took this to be a marvelous omen, that he would have great victory and succeed in taking Chiang Sæn. The king moved with his army for twenty-four days.

In s. 1166, a *kap cai* year, on Sunday the thirteenth waxing of the eighth month (10 April 1804), he encamped at Tha Khao P[l]üak, west of Chiang Sæn, full of self-confidence. / He sent an envoy to carry a letter promising to the ruler of Chiang Sæn in accordance with the ancient customs of kings who had conquered the domains. As for the Burmese governor and the Na Khwa, there were rulers and chiefs of many northern places / which had come in to Chiang Sæn, e.g., M. Yòng, Chiang Khæng, B. Yu, M. Luai, M. Wa, Chiang Khang,⁵⁷ all together and unwilling to surrender; and they organized forces to go out and fight at the foot of Dòi Than and Ban

---

55 The death of the Front Palace king is reported in the First Reign Chronicle, pp. 260–261.
56 Oppolzer lists a lunar eclipse on 26 January 1804 (No. 4656).
57 M. Yòng, Chiang Khæng, B. Yu, M. Luai, M. Wa, Chiang Khang: see Map.

Hua Sao. They could not defeat the forces of the king one bit, / as the horoscope of M. Jeyyasen Lakhòn Puri was deficient in that year s. 1166 and [that] month. Everyone, including the high officials, could not withstand them, and they were defeated and scattered in the middle of the first tenth month, the fifth waxing, a Tuesday (1 July 1804), in the *tut chao* watch. As for the Burmese commander / and the *Sitkè,* they died in that city. Some of the city-dwellers who were slaves lost their masters, children lost their parents, husbands lost their wives, and they were sorely hurt and suffering. As for the Na Khwa, he took his children and wives and crossed the Mekong River and fled by way of M. Küang and M. Lü to Dòi Còm Phao / f°7.37/ and Còm Sæo.[58]

At that time, the king Maha Uparaja, who had defeated the enemy, mounted his most glorious elephant-borne royal vehicle, bearing the golden and bejeweled sword Sri Kañjeyya and sat astride an auspicious elephant and waved and bellowed as loud as a lion / echoing like the roar of a lion at the mouth of the Suvannaguha Cave with the following words: "Behold, all ye people of Chiang Sæn: is there any better fitted than I to be your king? Your lives shall be ended this day!" / At that, the Chiang Sæn people, including their officials, generals, and ministers, came in and submitted before the golden feet of the prince, every one of them. They said, "Our lives are yours, Thou Lord; take them!" / At that time, the king was graciously pleased to say, "We are pleased to grant you your lives." All of Chiang Sæn was in chaos, filled with the shrieks and cries of suffering and with the noise of guns that filled the skies. /

Pursuit of the Na Khwa of Chiang Sæn

When the troops of the lord had taken the great city, the king remained at Tha Khao P[l]üak for a month and twenty-one days. He remained in the city of Chiang Sæn for ten days; together two months and one day; and then the king proclaimed an order to his trusted generals, to "Go and catch the Na Khwa, the ruler of /f° 7.38/ Chiang Sæn." The king [then] took all his troops and the people of Chiang Sæn out of Chiang Sæn, on the first waning of the tenth month, a Saturday (11 June 1804). They traveled for seventeen days. On the second waxing of the second tenth month, a Monday (27 June), the king arrived back in the capital.

---

58 M. Küang and M. Lü to Dòi Còm Phao and Còm Sæo: see Map.

As for the trusted officers whom the king had sent / to pursue the Na Khwa, they received their lord's order, and pursued and caught him, together with his children and wives, and returned to the palace in Chiang Mai on the ninth waxing of the eleventh month, a Wednesday (3 August 1804).

About Keng Tung

Here we will tell of Chiang Tung.

After the / two younger-brother kings had captured Raja Còm Hong, their troops took Chiang Tung, and Chiang Tung was deserted. As for Cao Maha Siri Jeyyasaramphaya, i.e., the Cao Hò Kham of Chiang Tung, / and the Cao Sæn Müang and the ruler of M. Lek and the Cao Sam and Cao Phom, these five were the chief among the officials who took their men and slaves and went to M. Luai, M. Yang, and M. Læm. Some fled up to M. Ting and Chiang Khum.[59] As for Cao Maha Khanan, / the fourth brother, he seized men and slaves and hillsmen and went to M. Yang. Later, the Cao Hò Kham of Chiang Tung and the Cao Sæn Müang, the ruler of M. Lek, and the rulers and officials and all the people found their way back to their land as before.

While /fº 7.39/ the king Maha Uparaja was going up to do warfare against Chiang Sæn, His Majesty the King's elder brother had Thao Kham Kæn take a force of 300 men to go up to recruit / the Cao Hò Kham of Chiang Tung. Thao Kham Kæn accepted the royal order, and submitted. The Cao Hò Kham was pleased to enter under the royal umbrella, and brought his officials and relatives and officials / and ministers and men and submitted in Chiang Mai. As for that Cao Maha Khanan, he remained to take care of the land with those men and hillsmen who were at M. Yang. Thao Kham Kæn brought the Cao Hò Kham of Chiang Tung down to M. Chiang Mai in s. 1166, / a *kap cai* year (1804/05).

In the same year, Thao Kham Kæn brought the Cao Hò Kham of Chiang Tung down to the city, and His Majesty the King bestowed upon him a name, and made Thao Kham Kæn to be Phya Khòn Müang Rajasena.

---

59 M. Luai, M. Yang, M. Læm, M. Ting, Chiang Khum: see Map (note Sipsong Panna map).

Mission to Bangkok, 1804

The king Maha Uparaja arrived in the city [Chiang Mai] / and was there for a month and twenty-two days. On the ninth waning of the eleventh month, a Thursday (18 August 1804), the king led the Cao Hò Kham of Chiang Tung and the Na Khwa, father and son, down to attend upon the king His Majesty of Great Merit in Krung Sri Ayutthiya Dvaravati.[60] They traveled for eighteen days. On the twelfth waxing of the twelfth month, a Sunday (4 September), they reached Krung Sri Ayutthiya /f° 7.40/ and the Sovereign King was most pleased. He bestowed the highest ranks upon him. As for the Na Khwa, he was most ill and died in Krungthep Mahanakhòn. The Great King of Great Merit ordered / funerary ceremonies for him.

The king remained in the South country for thirteen days. On the eleventh waning of the first month, a Tuesday (18 October), the king led the ruler of Chiang [Tung] and the son of the Na Khwa out of Krungthep Mahanakhòn. In a month and twenty-six days they came to rest at Tha Wang Tan for one night, and they arrived / on the eighth waning of the third month. The king re-entered the city on that Tuesday (13 December).

Wat Inthakhin, 1805

On the full-moon day of the fifth month, a Mon Thursday (2 February 1805), the king of Chiang Mai took the lead in building the temple of Wat Inthakhin, inaugurating and celebrating and making merit.[61] /

Expedition to M. Yang and M. Ræm, 1805

On the eighth waning of the fifth month, a Friday (10 February 1805), the Cao Ratana Hua Müang Kæo the Rear Palace, who was the royal younger brother, took a force of one thousand men out of the city and went by way of Chiang Tung to take

---

60 In Caophraya Thiphakòrawong's First Reign Chronicle, see under cs 1167

61 When the foundation pillar (lak müang) was moved to be erected at Wat Chedi Luang, Wat Inthakhin and Wat Sadü Müang were abandoned. Thus Wat Inthakhin was founded anew. It was subsequently abandoned, and was restored for the 700th anniversary of the city in 1996.

M. Yang and M. Ræm. They fought the Burmese at M. Nga and Pang Sang / and took them. The Burmese could not withstand them and were defeated and scattered, and they all fled. Many things were captured, such as elephants, horses, gold and silver things, guns, and belongings and people, in great numbers.

The king of the Rear Palace remained at M. Yang until the fifth waxing of the ninth month, a Sunday (21 May 1805), when he took his troops /f° 7.41/ and men out of M. Yang and came back down to Chiang Mai on the eleventh waning of the tenth month, a Sunday (9 July).

Portents of the Uparaja's Future

As for the King Uparaja of the Front Palace, he left the South Country and returned to the city for two months and twenty-six days. On the fourteenth waning of the fifth month, a Thursday (16 February 1805), he took a thousand men and troops out of the city to go up. /

Once, when he was sleeping in the middle of the night he saw an omen in his dreams, that there was a river, flooding somewhat, right up to the level of the islands. He dreamed that he was riding in a boat with two rowers with bamboo paddles floating along near the western bank of the river and moored their boat. Later in his dream, he saw a great crowd of people / who were coming to reverence a reclining Buddha image. The prince went along with those people, and a reclining Buddha was lying with its feet to the east, its head to the west. The prince saw someone take a pair of elephant tusks and *salæng* flowers mounted in them and he went to venerate the Buddha image there. He wanted to obtain those flowers, so he / came in with puffed rice and took the *salæng* flowers in the tusks and the reclining Buddha image, and then he picked up the ivory tusks and the flowers then turned to gold. He dreamed that the Cao Ratana Hua Müang Kæo, his younger brother, interrupted to tell him to take all the flowers. The prince said, "My elder has taken them already; he should take them all." / So he took the ivory tusks and then awakened. The king regarded this as a most auspicious omen, and was most gratified, as he took it to mean that he would take all the fifty-seven domains of Lan Na.

Expedition to M. Yòng, 1805

The king then took his troops up by land, for a month and two days, and /f° 7.42/ attained to M. Mahiyaṅgaratthapuri [M. Yòng]. The king organized the four generals, intending to control and take M. Yòng, taking all within his hands. At that time, the ruler of Yòng at the head of the ruling family and his officers military and civil and his men saw the great army / and elephants and horses of the king, and was greatly afraid, and knew that he could not withstand them; so together they made their submission. He handed over the country, its land and water, to the king.

Then he took the five insignia of rulership, including great male war-elephants, / and golden howdahs, war-horses with saddles, and including Lady Nò Kæo Kiang Kham who was his elder sister by the same father—Thao Nò Cao Müang—and presented them to the king for his use, which he received gratefully. / The king said, "We will not reduce the domain to jungle. We wish to convert the jungle to be a domain. We will develop the land of the fifty-seven domains of Lan Na, as the kings of yore / did." So His Majesty had the people, high and low, gathered in all the north.

Expedition to the Khœn and Lü Regions

As for the Cao Mahawong, the Ratchabut, he took leave of the monkhood to resume being a layman and go with the king, who was /f° 7.43/ his father. The king had the Cao Ratchabut and Cao Suwanna Kham Khrüang, who was his royal nephew, take civil and military officials and troops to go to take cities, e.g., M. Yòng, Ban Yu, M. Luai, Ban Kai, M. Ræm, M. Khan, Chiang Khang, M. Wa, M. Luang, M. Hon, M. Chæ, / M. Rai, M. Cüang, Tha Lò, M. Phan, M. Ma, M. La, M. Khòng, M. Wang, M. Mang, M. Khang, M. Ngat, M. Ò, M. Sò, M. Ngim, M. Siao, M. Sung, and all the Sipsong Panna of Chiang Rung, formerly included within the country of / M. Phing Chiang Mai in the time of Cao Mangrai and ruled through successive reigns, small localities and large domains under the rule of our kings in every respect.[62]

---

62 M. Yòng, Ban Yu, M. Luai, etc., and all the Sipsong Panna of Chiang Rung. Many of these people when moved to Chiang Mai founded new villages with the names of the places from which they had come. Most were to the northeast and east of Chiang Mai.

At that time, the prince and his father, the two of them, headed up the civil and military officials and all the soldiers. / They all received this royal order, and went up. The king stayed at M. Yòng for twenty-three days.

Chiang Khang Expedition, 1805

In s. 1167, a *dap pao* year, on the eleventh waning of the seventh month, a Thursday (13 April 1805), the king took the soldiers and elephantry and cavalry and they advanced out / from Mahiyaṅgkharatthapuri and went up to Ayaratṭha, i.e., M. Chiang Khang, a three-day journey. The king had the troops rest at M. Chiang Khang. He wrote a letter to summon in all the slaves and freemen, and had the Lawa come out and plant dry-rice fields and the Thai come out to plant wet-rice;[63] /fº 7.44/ the religious teachers to come out and perform their religious duties and preach and study and write and read the Scriptures, as the Lord Buddha had instructed.

Te ubbho bhikkhuno sirimahānamo ādiko satabhayo sāmaṇero.[64] At that time, there were two monks, the senior / called Sri Mahanāma and the other called Paña, who lived at Ban Sò in the vicinity of Chiang Khang,[65] who brought out a Buddha image which was named Suwannabimba, of most radiant beauty. They came in to call upon the king and said, "In the generation before ours, it was said that / in the future, there will be a ruler of great majesty and power who will come from Chiang Mai in the south and bring up a great army and defeat the forces of evil, the enemies in all directions in all localities, great and small, from the Lan Na region all the way up to / M. Yòng and Chiang Khæng, Ban Yu, M. Luai, M. Wa, Chiang Khang, and conquer all the way up to the Sipsong Panna, up to the Lü domains of M. Ring and M. La Na Pho, even unto the Iron and Golden Bridges in the north; and he will take charge of the domains and make them right and make Buddhism / prosper and flourish, as they were in the time of King Mangrai. At that time, we were to

---

63 Notton's version of the Chronicle ends exactly here, in mid-sentence (or mid-paragraph), and at the end of the last line of a page, implying that the copy that he used lacked subsequent pages.

A statement of this sort—that the Lawa are to plant upland fields and the Thai to plant paddies—is commonly found in Lan Na historiography. See *Ruam botkhwam sammana rüang Lua nai Lan Na* (Chiang Mai, 1988).

64 Pali: the meaning is duplicated in the translated phrase which follows.

65 In the Sipsong Panna. See map.

bring forth the Thòng Thip Buddha image[66] and present him to you. So we were instructed by the Teacher who died. Now we have come and seen the great power and might of Your Majesty, /f° 7.45/ and we have come to do as our Teacher told us. We therefore have brought this most glorious Buddha image and present it to Your Majesty, for you to reverence. This Buddha image is the image of the ruler of Chiang Mai." The king / received it and raised it up in reverence.

Müang Wa, 1805

At that time, there was a ruler named Nakharat who was the ruler of M. Wa,[67] who was most afraid of dying, so he took his men, families, elephants, horses, children, and wives and fled into the hills and forests in the mountains. The king / wrote a letter [to him] asking that he come out and settle in the country, once and then a second time, but still he did not come. The king then issued a royal command that his five royal sons and the brave generals go and capture the ruler of Wa and bring him in to the king. / The five royal sons and the generals reverenced him and said, "Your Majesty's humble servants agree to do so." So they took an army and went into the forest [Pang Pa] for the ruler of Wa. They captured the ruler of Wa and his people and brought them in to present to the royal palace in M. Chiang Khang. / There, the ruler of Wa led his officers and generals to reverence and most obediently place themselves under the great and Sovereign King; and they led forth an auspicious horse, and a pair of elephants male and female and all the five accouterments /f° 7.46/ of a ruler, together with Lady Nò Kæo Ubonlawanna, who was his daughter, who was in the first blush of adolescence, and presented them to the king on that day.

As for M. Chiang Khang, it had formerly been a major dominion of M. Yòng, and he wanted it to have future prominence, with a *phraya* at its head. / All the officials in M. Chiang Khang together led forth the royal daughter, named Up Kæo, who was of his flesh and blood, to be presented to the king.

---

66 According to the (1990) testimony of Phra Ratchasitthacan, abbot of Wat Phra Sing in Chiang Mai, the Phra Cao Thòng Thip Buddha image, kept in the cell of the abbot of Wat Phra Sing, was the personal image belonging to King Kavila.

67 On M. Wa, to the northeast of Keng Tung, see GUBSS, II, pt. 2, p. 493.

Sipsong Panna

As for M. Luang,[68] it was in the jurisdiction of the Sipsong Panna, and had a ruler named Phraya Luang Kham Lü. Phraya Luang Kæo headed [a group who,] / considering the past, former times, led forth the royal daughter named Lady Kæo Kañña to be presented to the king and placing the country, its lands and waters, under the king, / all of it, every village and town.

As for the Sipsong Panna, the Cao Hò Kham of Chiang Rung led in M. Chæ, M. Hon, M. Rai, M. Cüang,[69] and the [other] seven or eight domains. The king ordered the royal family and the civil and military officers to take control of the domains, every village / and town, large and small, with their rulers and heads of villages and towns and their slaves and freemen all approving and delighted, and they willingly came under the royal protection, every village and town. They were completely unanimous. They considered /f° 7.47/ the former royal customs of yore, of friendship and comity, so they wrote a letter accompanying tribute including a most glorious horse and with Lady Nò Kæo Yòt Còm Müang, of the royal lineage of M. Rai, which all the rulers brought forth / with Phraya Luang Chai of M. Rai, Phraya Khüan of M. Chæ, Phraya Luang the ruler of Chiang Cüang, and Cao Namawong bringing her forth to present, following royal customs of yore.

Upland Peoples

As for the 12 *hua khwæn* of the Kha,[70] headed by the *ròi khwæn* of Ban Ò, and with all the *khun lam* arranging the tribute, / they came forth to pay homage before the royal feet of the king in M. Chiang Khang and presented their tribute.

At that time, the king re-titled the *ròi khwæn* of Ban Ò as Phraya Kamphæng Müang, and then / issued a royal advice as follows: "At this time, Phraya Kamphæng Müang is a good and honest servant of We who am king, and would help Us in expanding our frontiers in the future, so I have asked Phraya Kamphæng / Müang to devise plans for the future state of our domains which are those of a real king; and have issued this forth on a wooden tablet to be preserved in the land to have

---

68 M. Luang is a named domain in the Sipsong Panna; see map.
69 (Correctly) written Chiang Cüang below.
70 Some non-Tai, presumably Austroasiatic, peoples are indicated here.

Phraya Kamphæng Müang hold securely." He then conferred upon him various implements, such as a *nokkok* gun, a gold-handled sword, a silver-decorated /f° 7.48/ dagger, and two *thammarong* rings, to be marks of his status for the future.

Now, as for the Kha Sam Thao, he was reminded of former customs of old times in succession, when he was a vassal of Chiang Mai, and so he came in with tribute and gifts to present in submission to the king / of Chiang Mai. The king conferred upon him letters patent to confirm him in office thenceforth.

As for all the military and civil officers, the king had them go out and summon all the land to come in / and assemble in Chiang Khang.

Return to Chiang Mai

On Thursday, the ninth waxing of the ninth month (25 May 1805), the king took his troops out of Chiang Khang and went back down to M. Yòng on the tenth waxing of the ninth month, a Friday (26 May). The king stayed there for seven days, and then the king left / M. Yòng on the third waning of the ninth month, a Saturday (3 June). He traveled by land for a month and twelve days until reaching the landing at Wat Ket, where he rested for one night; and then the king entered the city [of Chiang Mai], on the twelfth waning of the tenth month, a Friday.

Pious Works, 1806

As for His Majesty the King, / the royal eldest brother, he lived happily and ruled the country. He made meritorious donations and built a *vihara* on the west side of Wat Dòi Ucsupabanphotagiri [Suthep] and erected a parasol at the holy reliquary of Suthep which he inaugurated and consecrated on the full-moon day of the sixth month, a Mon Wednesday (21 February 1806).

On the first waxing of the tenth month, a Thursday (15 June 1806), Phraya /f° 7.49/ Indra and Aisawan battled in the sky causing great thunder to dislodge the finial of the Reliquary of Suthep, in s. 1167, a *dap pao* year (1805/06). The king Uparaja Front Palace Hò Kham entered the royal palace, and remained there for two months and sixteen days.

Mission to Bangkok, 1805

On the second waning of the first month, a Thursday (28 September 1805), the king with the Cao Ratana Rear Palace / and the Cao Hò Kham of Chiang Tung led their domain rulers and village and town heads, including Phraya M. Yòng as head, with Phraya M. Wa, Phraya Chiang Khang, Phraya M. Kai, and Phraya Na Fak of M. Yang, and all went together to attend in audience upon His Majesty the Sovereign Great King of Great / Merit, Lord of the White Elephant, Black Elephant, Speckled Elephant, and Striped Elephant, in Krung Sri Ayutthiya Dvaravati, traveling that long distance for a month and six days and reaching there on the eighth waning of the second month, a Thursday (2 November 1805).

They entered with their tribute and all their gifts / to present to His Majesty the Great King, and reported to him on governmental affairs, in every detail. The Great King expressed his pleasure, and presented them with golden bowls / adorned with seven lions, and ewers of gold, and goblets decorated with gold, swords and daggers, also decorated with gold, to the king Maha Uparaja; a golden bowl and gold ewer for the Cao Ratana Rear Palace and Cao Sri Bun Ma his younger brother; and then /f° 7.50/ silver bowls and silver ewers to Cao Phutthawong and Cao Suwanna Kham Mun the royal nephews. Moreover, he conferred insignia of rank on the domain and village heads, high and low. Then he issued forth a royal command, reverberating like the roar of a lion, "May the Cao Rattana of the Rear Palace and the Cao Sri Bun Ma / of M. Lakhòn the youngest brother rebuild M. Haribhuñjaya." Later, the king Maha Uparaja went in to attend upon the Great king.

His Majesty the royal eldest brother happily ruled the country, and built / an *ubosatha* at Wat Chiang Man, on the tenth waxing of the fourth month in that s. 1167, a *dap pao* year (18 December 1805).

Uparaja Returns from Bangkok, 1806

The king Maha Uparaja remained in the South Country for a month and four days, and on the thirteenth waning of the third month, a Thursday (7 December 1805), he led the officials civil and military / out from Krungthep Mahanakhòn. They traveled for two months and one day, and arrived on the fourteenth waning of the fourth month, a Monday (5 February). The king rested and slept at the Wang Tan Landing for a night, and arrived on the first waxing of the sixth month, a Tuesday (6

February).⁷¹ The king made his entrance into the city with all his followers on that day. The two kings, / elder and younger brothers, made their entry into the country. They remained for a month and four days.

On the fifth waxing of the seventh month, a Tuesday (13 March), the king, the royal eldest brother, and the patriarchs and monks in the city of Ratanatiṁsa Abhinawapuri Phranakhòn /f° 7.51/ Chiang Mai and a chapter of 108 monks led the Cao Ratana Rear Palace and five hundred followers, and Cao Sri Bun Ma of Lakhòn with five hundred followers, together with the ruler of Mahiyangkharatthapuri all four of them, brothers, with their Yòng⁷² followers, slaves and freemen, all who had come by way of / Haribhuñjaya. The chapter of monks was invited to chant the *parittamaṅgala* in nine places, *pa ā te sri mu u ma kā*⁷³ [eight of them] and at Wat Luang Sadü Müang;⁷⁴ the *Sut manta* in full, the *Mahā samayya* in full, and the *Seven Jeyya*.⁷⁵ They made merit until / the eighth waxing of the seventh month, a Mon Thursday (15 March), in the noon watch, when Haribhuñjaya was founded, with Cao Ratana Hua Müang Kæo the Rear Palace as the ruler of the domain and Sri Bun Ma, his youngest brother, as the *uparaja*, in s. 1167, a *dap pao* year. /

Pious Works, 1806

In s. 1168, a *rwai yi* year, on the tenth waning of the seventh month, a Sunday, the *phraya wan* day (New Year, 1 April 1806), there was a consecration with the *Muddhābhiseka* waters, raising up the Venerable Pañya Vajira, lord of the Forest Monks, to be the Supreme Patriarch. Not long afterwards, fourteen days, on / Sunday, the tenth waxing of the eighth month (15 April), the Venerable Cao Nantha

---

71 Clearly the fifth month, not the sixth month, is meant.

72 On M. Yòng, see Thawi Swangpanyangkun, *Tamnan müang Yòng* (Chiang Mai, 1984); and Aroonrut Wichienkeeo, "Tamnan müang Yòng," in *Nangsü pariwat cak khamphi bailan chut tamnan müang læ kotmai* (Chiang Mai, 1988), pp. 1–48.

73 An abbreviated form of the formula "*bòriwan ayu decha sri munla utsaha montri kalakani*" which are the sections of the *thaksa* diagram on which are detailed the eight aspects of the domain's "horoscope."

74 There is a temple by this name in the center of the city of Lamphun, now abandoned.

75 This sutra is chanted especially for state ceremonies.

of Wat Sri Kœt[76] was raised up to be a Patriarch; and the Venerable Cao Gambhīra of Wat Phan Tao[77] was raised up to be a Patriarch. These three venerables were consecrated at Wat Phra Singharam.

Twenty-five days later, on the fifth waxing of the ninth month, /f° 7.52/ a Thursday (10 May 1806), His Majesty the King built the main *vihara* on the east side of Dòi Suthep. The officials, civil and military, decorated the *sanam luang* on that day.[78] Twelve days later, His Majesty the Uparaja of the Front Palace, built the main *ubosatha* of / Wat Phra Sing, in the ninth month, on the second waning, a Tuesday (22 May 1806).

Colophon to Chapter Seven

Naggara niyānika sattama kaṅthaṁ nittitaṁ.[79] The History of the domain, Fascicle Seven, is completed here.

---

76 Wat Sri Kœt: an old temple opposite Wat Phra Sing in Chiang Mai. It is mentioned in the *Khlong nirat Hariphunchai*, which was written around 1500. See also the Jkm.

77 Wat Phan Tao: in Chiang Mai, immediately to the north of Wat Chedi Luang.

78 The *sanam luang* was not a field, like in Bangkok, but rather a building, the center for the administration of the domain. In it assembled the *khao sanam luang*—the chief officials who ran the business of the domain under the presidency of the ruler.

79 Pali: "Seventh [Fascicle] of the History, Here Completed."

Chapter 8

The Revival of Lan Na from 1796/97

Tadā so nagaraṁ puraṁ rammaṁ bahupakā rato rakaṁ janapaddehi khettavudhi khemaṁ devanagaraṁ viya āhosi.[1]

Here we will tell of Ratanatiṁsa Phranakhòn Chiang Mai, which had been deserted and abandoned for twenty years. The whole of the city was overgrown with trees, forest, grass, and vines / slowly growing thickly. It was an abode for animals of all sorts, e.g., tigers, bears, rhinoceros, elephants, cattle, wild oxen, lions, wild boar, *ramang*, deer, and antelope who had come and found abode in the city. The temples and institutions of Buddhism, monasteries, ubosatha, Buddha images, and *cetiya*, were destroyed / and dilapidated and falling down in great number, ever since s. 1138, the *rwai san* year (1776), until s. 1158, a *rwai si* year (1796), when the three brother princes came there to reestablish the city and the domain. The three princes / together rebuilt and renovated the walls, the forts, the city wall on all four sides, the four city forts, and the five gates, and then renovated and rebuilt the reliquaries, temples, and monasteries of the religion and collected all the Buddha images outside the city from deserted and abandoned temples to the west and east, north and south, / their limbs to be the foundations of ones to be established in the temples in the city; to be the foci for worship for people and divinities, monks and brahmans, daily without fail.

Tadā. At that time, *so nagaraṁ*. Rattanatiṁsā Phranakhòn /f° 8.02/ Chiang Mai was now replete with walls, observation towers, fighting towers, and gate towers; and moats wide and deep and formidable with water and filled with profusely spreading white and red lotuses; and it had many temples flourishing; and the city was now replete with officers military / and civil, with chiefs and followers, and with a great

---

1 Pali: the meaning approximates that of the translated phrase which follows.

population; and amply supplied with food and drink, with coconut and sugar palms, with betel and areca, with fruits, with rice in abundance; and in happiness there were entertainments and festivities, celebrations, music, and singing, with all kinds of poetry, with stringed instruments and percussion; / with dancing, the music of orchestras, gongs, oboes, *khæn*, gamelan, *thalò* and *thisò* music, *phia* music, *phin*, *pan dò* drums, and conch-shell trumpets playing loudly and tumultuously day and night, banishing sadness and melancholy, in religious ceremonies.

As for all the officials civil and military, the slaves and freemen, / there were elephantry officers and cavalry officers dressed in fine uniforms, like divinities from the Tāvadiṁsa Heaven, the abode of the gods. As for the building of the ubosatha of Wat Phra Sing, after three months and three days, on the fifth waning of the twelfth month, a Thursday (20 September 1806), the Phra Mahā Swāmī / of Wat Phan Tao died on that day. After another month and fifteen days, in the second month, fifth waxing, Saturday (3 November), His Majesty the Great King the eldest brother, as head; the Cao Maha Uparaja Narādhipatī Sri Suwanna of the Front of the Golden Palace; and /f° 8.03/ the prince of M. Hariphunchai Cao Sri Bun Ma the Front Palace of Lamphun; with all the royal family and civil and military officials organized the fourfold military divisions; and the Buddhist Sangha headed by the Rajaguru; and together they brought forth the implements of alms / and the eight requisites and golden dais for the golden throne for the Ivory Buddha, with the six roof finials and the banners and golden chests and the Buddha banners and the five rulers' implements of *chatra*, fans, cowry shells, parasols, and sunshades / and the wooden insignia of *satta*, *sattā*, *sattu*, and triangular banners and lanterns, small banners, victory pendants, and such were borne out from the capital city at Chiang Mai and proceeded in order for five days to M. Kukkutantaseda Phrahma Khelangkha Nagara Jeyyasukhavati.[2] / They arrived there on the full-moon day of the second month, a Tuesday (13 November), and celebrated and consecrated and inaugurated the finials on the roof of the *vihara*, and bestowed alms on the monks. They included the Jinadhatu of Wat Luang Lampang which sat at the head. This was the first and greatest merit-making occasion there had been, with great

---

2   All these various names refer to Lampang as the city of the cock, which remains the symbol of the city to the present day. See *Tamnan Phrathat Lampang Luang læ Tamnan Phrakæo Mòrakot* (Lampang, 1970).

entertainments and fireworks / and rockets and lights and candles, which was of great and indescribable beauty.

King Kavila's Advice to His Brothers, 1806

When it was done, His Majesty the King and eldest brother convened an assembly of all six of his younger siblings /f° 8.04/ headed by the sovereign lord of the domain of Lakhòn, who heard the royal teachings as follows:

"As from yore and since the time of their royal grandfather and father, when they were subjects of the Burmese and they were vassal domains of the Burmese who oppressed them for a period, happiness was unattainable. Then came the generation of all of us / their descendants, and I became thy king. Facing such distress and sadness, we rebelled against the Burmese and led our younger siblings down to become the subjects of the Great King in Krung Sri Ayutthiya. We all, rulers and ruled, then could live happily. / We could then eat and move freely, as the Great King nourished us and raised us up as king with the silver and gold insignia of rulership as king of the free Tai country in the fifty-seven domains of the Lan Na country.[3]

"From this our own time, forever for ten generations, through our children and grandchildren / and their children and grandchildren and great-grandchildren until the very end of our royal lineage, whoever of our descendants might revolt against the Great King of Ayutthiya, they will become slaves of the Burmese, Hò, / Gulawā,[4] Phāsī,[5] and Vietnamese, whoever; any such person, whatever they do, however successful they may be, may they be destroyed utterly and die, like the banana tree dies when its fruit are picked or the reeds wilt when cut, and fall into Hell for a hundred-thousand eons, never to be reborn or arise again. As for you lords, all my

---

3   I can find no alternative to this translation, which includes both "Tai" and "thai": กรวัด–เมืองไทเปนไทยเปนไทย์. Cf. UR p. 156, which is different, and does not include the two spellings tai/thai; nor despite claims to be checking against HP (cs 1288) does not do so here. I have double-checked the original MS. of HP, and the reading (f° 8.04.3) is unequivocally as given above. The only possibility of reconciling the problem is if the copyist wrote past the first Tai and then realized he had omitted the final consonant, and so simply repeated himself with the proper spelling. But we note that he did not cross out his mistakes, as he might have done.

4   Perhaps the *kula* (Indians) and the Lawa?

5   I think this refers to the "White Turbans" of Yunnan.

younger siblings, /f° 8.05/ you must love one another and live in concord like the strands of a rope. Do not quarrel. Help one another. Don't criticize each other. When the elder knows, he helps; and when the younger knows, he helps. When the enemy invades, help one another. Don't betray the Great King of ours. / Whoever lives in accordance with these my advices, your elder, may you age and prosper and wisely rule, and may you be blessed with majesty and power and extinguish your enemies; may you have long age and long lives. Whoever does not follow these your elder's advices, / may he be destroyed and perish."

His Majesty the Elder Brother gave these royal advices to his six younger siblings and children and grandchildren, his civil and military officials in the three domains [of Chiang Mai, Lamphun, and Lampang], in front of the Jinadhatu / of Lampang in s. 1168, a *rwai yi* year, on the full-moon day of the second month, a Mon Thursday (Tuesday 13 November 1806).[6]

On the fifth waning of the second month, a Sunday (18 November 1806), His Majesty the King set out in a royal procession by land and traveled for five days. He reached the Golden Palace [in Chiang Mai] on the ninth waning of the second month, / a Thursday (22 November).

Expedition into the Shan Region, 1807

Two months and fifteen days later, on the fifth waxing of the fifth month, a Thursday (31 January 1807), His Majesty the King appointed Cao Kham Mun, his nephew, to take an army of five hundred men and travel for seventeen nights. On the sixth waning of the fifth month, a Saturday (1 February 1807), they reached Ta Sai, and all the troops were ordered to fell and trim trees /f° 8.06/ and bind them with rattan to make rafts and link them together and then the troops crossed the Salween River in the middle of the night. Having done so, they advanced by night very rapidly.

When dawn came, they reached Chiang Kham.[7] They broke down the gates and hacked through the palisade and entered like a quick forest-fire of the fifth and sixth

---

6 This date is mentioned above as being a Tuesday, 13 November. I have retained that date.

7 Clearly not the Chiang Kham mentioned in Chapter 1. This place is to the west of the Salween, across the river from M. Pu. It might be identical with the Chiang Thòng mentioned earlier.

months.⁸ / The sound of the gunfire of the vanguard and the din of people crying out was like an earthquake. The Shans of Chiang Kham were defeated and scattered. All the troops came in and surrounded the palace of the prince of Chiang Kham. As for the prince of Chiang Kham, and his mature sons, / they were not taken, but a wife, called Lady Fa, and one son, named Khun Sam, and one daughter, together with some of their relatives and some of their men. These they swept up and brought back across the Salween. Then they came back in orderly march to Chiang Mai. His Majesty the King, / who was clever and brave, saw Cao Khun Sam and Lady Fa Chiang Kham who was his mother, and adopted them as his own.

*Tato param.*⁹ Thenceforth, His Majesty the Supreme King and his two younger brothers, intelligent and / brave, smart and fearless of the enemy's orders, were like royal lions who fear not the lesser animals. They regularly sent troops and called up soldiers to go and attack villages and towns, sweeping up people to bring within the country, filling it / f° 8.07/ so that it became densely settled.

Assistance to Chiang Rung, 1807

In s. 1169, a *müang mao* year (1807/08), Mòm Can the ruler of M. Rung¹⁰ fell out with his nobles and officials. The civil and military officials revolted against Mòm Can, who could not stand against them, and fled with his families and people down and sent asking for an army to go up / and retake his country. His Majesty the King called up troops and sent them up to protect Mòm Can. They captured fifteen Shans and Raja Pha *care* and Ai Kæo whom they brought back. Then Mòm Can took his daughter named Lady In Kham and presented / her to His Majesty the King to live with and serve him. His Majesty the King then received Mòm Can and Raja Pha and his *care* Ai Kæo and sent them down to attend upon the Sovereign Lord King in Ayutthiya. His Majesty the King / bestowed Mòm Can and Raja Pha upon His Majesty the King to serve the government in Chiang Mai.

At that time, the king of Ava learned that Mòm Can had fled down to become a subject of the king of the south. The king of Ava ordered general Shwe Lan Tòng to command an army which encamped at / M. Chiang Rung. Thao Bun Rüang, Thao

---

8   February and March when the rains usually have not fallen since November.
9   Pali: "Then," "Thereupon."
10 The next paragraph makes it clear that Müang Rung is Chiang Rung.

Kham Wang, and Thao Lü Chai Kamphæng, who were taking care of M. Yòng, sent a letter reporting down to His Majesty the King. The king called up Cao Cantharat and Phraya Khòn Müang to command an army to go up and attack them, and told Lamphun, Phræ, and Nan to bring up forces /f° 8.08/ of every province. They went up and fought the Burmese of general Shwe Lan Tòng, who were encamped at Chiang Rung, and they were defeated and scattered. They captured many goods and people and weapons, which they presented to His Majesty the King. His Majesty the King had them sent down and presented to the Great King in the South Country. The king / presented them, and then returned.

Burmese Invasion, 1807/08

In s. 1169, a *mao* year (1807/08), the Burmese general Hon Nò (or Na Nò)[11] with ten thousand men came up to Chiang Rung again. The group taking care of M. Yòng sent a letter reporting this down to the king. The king was informed, / and issued a command to call up the armies of Lamphun, Lakhòn, Phræ, and Nan to go and attack the Burmese general. As for His Majesty the King, he raised up a force of more than five thousand to go up and garrison Chiang Sæn. Then / Cao Cantharaja, Cao Phutthawong, and Cao Nanthasen commanded a force to go. The king ordered the Cao Uparaja of Lamphun and Cao Phimphisan, Cao Nai Nòi Maha Phom, and Cao Nai Nòi Kham Wongsa to command a force to go up. He also commanded Cao Mu La, the Uparaja of Lakhòn and / various Lü princes to command a force to go up and follow them, and also commanded Cao Kham Mun to command a force and Cao Khanan Siwijeyya and Cao Nai Nò Longka of Lamphun to command a force of the two domains of fifteen hundred men to go across the /f° 8.09/ Salween and attack M. Chiang Thòng and block the path of the Burmese general Na Nò. They succeeded in taking M. Chiang Thòng and defeating them, and captured and took some families which they swept up.

As for the army which had gone up to Chiang Thòng, they divided into several small armies. Cao Phutthawong went up by way of M. Luai, / M. Yang, M. Nga, and

---

11 "*Kon-baung-zet*, II, 165, apparently refers to this expedition, but I can't figure out the general's name from the Chiang Mai Chronicle reference." (Lieberman, pers. comm., 3 April 1995.)

Pang Sang.¹² Cao Cantharacha and Cao Nanthasena and the armies of Lamphun, Lakhòn, Phræ, and Nan went and attacked the Burmese general Na Nò at Chiang Rung. They fought for six days. The Burmese general Na Nò was defeated and fled back by way of M. Luai, M. Yang, M. Nga, and Pang Sang, where they met / the army of Cao Phutthawong and fought in a great battle. They went back and forth. The ruler of M. Chün, son of the Cao Hò Kham [of] M. Læm was killed. Mai Hò, son of Raja Còm Hong was killed on that occasion. The Burmese general Na Nò could not withstand them and was defeated and scattered, / and withdrew by way of M. Læm on that day.

Our army pursued him and fought him at M. Læm and defeated him, capturing the royal elephant mount of the Cao Hò Kham of M. Læm, six elbows high. Then they swept up families / and withdrew back to M. Chiang Sæn. His Majesty the King returned first before all the other armies.

Burmese Attack, 1808/09

In s. 1170, a *pæk si* year (1808/09), the Burmese general Nakhan Maung Cha, with 12,000 men came up to attack M. Luai and M. Yang.¹³ Cao Maha Khanan could not withstand them, and took his /f° 8.10/ people off to M. Phang and M. Lòng; and then sent a letter down to ask for an army.

His Majesty the King then commanded Cao Phutthawong to take charge of an army of 500 of Lamphun, and Cao Nai Nòi Kham Wongsa to take charge of an army of 300, to go up to M. Yòng in the midst of the eighth month (April 1808). The king [further] called up a provincial army / from the northern domains, namely M. Yòng, Ban Yu, M. Luai, Chiang Khang, M. Wa, M. Phai, Phayak, M. Len, Chiang Khæng, M. Sing, M. Nò, M. Kang, M. Lòng, M. Kò, and M. Sai altogether 3,500 men;¹⁴ with the forces of Chiang Mai and Lamphun / bringing the total to 4,300 men.

---

12 M. Luai, M. Yang, M. Nga, and Pang Sang: presumably the Luai (Lwe) river valley west of M. Khan, north of Yòng.

13 This has to be immediately west of the Sipsong Panna. See Keng Tung map.

14 See the Keng Tung map. This long list includes localities from both sides of the Mekong.

In the ninth month of s. 1171, a *kot sai* year (May 1809), they came up and attacked the Burmese general Nakhan[15] Maung Cha who was encamped at M. Phiang.[16] They did not succeed in defeating him, and withdrew coming down to encamp at M. Yòng. The Cao Maha Khanan encamped at M. Ma[17] through the rainy season. They remained at M. Yòng / to hold the country there.

Later, Cao Phutthawong came up to M. Yòng. His Majesty the King ordered Cao Phra Wòra Maha Uparaja, his royal younger brother, to take a force of a thousand men, plus five hundred from Lakhòn and three hundred from Lamphun, / and the army was to go up to encamp at M. Yuam.[18]

Then the king the Cao Maha Uparaja ordered Cao Cantharacha, Cao Nai Nòi Kawila, Cao Khanan Mahawong, and Cao Nai Nòi Maha Thep to command a Lamphun force; and commanded Cao Khanan Mahayot and Cao Khanan Siwichai to take charge of a force to go up to attack /f° 8.11/ repeatedly; and appointed Cao Kham Mun, Cao Nanthasena, and Cao Khanan Jeyyawong to command the Lamphun army; appointed Cao Nai Nòi Mahaphom to command the army of Lakhòn; and Cao Kham Lü was to command a force to go up and attack Sò Khi.

As for the army which had gone to attack M. Khateng, it was unsuccessful. Cao Cantharacha / the commander was wounded with a gunshot wound and he could not continue, and came back. As for the army which went to attack M. Sò Khi, it was victorious, and swept up people and weapons and brought them back in the *kat sai* year, s. 1172 (1810/11).[19]

In the hot season (early 1811), / His Majesty the King appointed Thao Sitthi to command a force of 150 to go up and attack a series of domains along the west bank of the Salween. They were victorious and swept up people and weapons and brought them back to present.

---

15 "Nakhan is probably *na-khan*, royal ear or spy; i.e., an administrative post." (Lieberman, pers. comm., 3 April 1995.)

16 M. Phiang: is this the M. Phang earlier?

17 M. Ma: northeast of Keng Tung. See GUBSS, II, pt. 2, pp. 396–397.

18 Not the Yuam identified with Mæ Sariang. Has to be in the Keng Tung region.

19 *kat sai* was 1171; 1172 was kot sanga. 1172 (1810/11) is correct, I think.

Wat Phra Sing, 1811/12

In s. 1173, a *luang met* year (1811/12), His Majesty / the King with His Majesty the Uparaja his younger brother and all the royal family and civil and military officials and all the people together made merit and consecrated and inaugurated the *ubosatha* of Wat Phra Singharam / with great entertainments and festivities.

At that time, the *sæn lam* of M. Yang rebelled against the Cao Khanan, and invited the Burmese Nakhan Maung Cha to come and attack the Cao Maha Khanan, who was defeated and fled with his people across the Mekong to the east bank, going to M. Phang and M. Lòng, and sending a letter down to ask for an army.[20]

When the festivities had completed, /f° 8.12/ at the full-moon of the sixth month (14 February 1812), His Majesty the King appointed the Cao Uparaja as head, with Cao Cantharacha, Cao Nai Nòi Kawila, Khanan Mahawong, Cao Ratchabut, Cao Bun Tha, and Cao Kham Khrüang the ruler of Chiang Tung to command a force of 3,000 men; and M. Lamphun commanded the Cao Uparaja as head, / [and] Cao Phimphisan, Cao Nai Nòi Mahaphom, Cao Nai Nòi Langka, Cao Nai Nòi Kham Wongsa, and Nai Nan Naratha, to command a force of a thousand. They went up on Thursday, fifth waxing of the seventh month, in s. 1173, *ruang met* (March 1812). On the evening of their second day en route, / there was a great fire in the city, from the Si Phum fort down to Wat Dòk Kham.[21] The king took an army up to the Mæ Kham[22] in the region of Chiang Sæn, celebrating the New Year there.[23]

Expedition in the Khœn Area, 1811/12

A royal order was sent up to Cao Phutthawong and / Cao Suriyawong and M. Yòng, and M. Chiang Khang, Chiang Khæng, M. Sing, M. Phang, M. Lòng, M.

---

20 The places for the most part cannot be identified; but the area indicated is in the Upper Mekong region (see map), from Chiang Lap to the east. M. Phang may be M. Sa.

21 Wat Dòk Kham: within the Chiang Mai walls, near the Tha Phæ Gate.

22 Mæ Kham: river; source at Dòi Tum in the Shan states; flows through t. Mæ Kham in Mæ Can district of Chiang Rai; joins the Mæ Can at Chiang Sæn. See Bunchuai Sisawat, *Chiang Mai læ phak nüa*, p. 465.

23 The New Year was on 1 April 1812.

Kò, M. Sai,²⁴ and all the northern cities, for them to hurriedly raise an army and meet the main army of the king at M. Ma.²⁵ The king went up / by way of M. Rai and Sop Yum²⁶ and went straight across Chiang Tung, which was a deserted domain; and they went through the area to M. Ma. The armies of all the northern domains met there. Then there were altogether five thousand men.

The king headquartered at M. Ma, together with the Cao Ratchabut, who was his /f° 8.13/ nephew; and then ordered Cao Cantharacha to command, with Cao Nai Nòi Kawila, and Cao Khanan Mahawong who was his son, to head up, with all the northern armies, to go and attack the Burmese at M. Yang,²⁷ in the course of the eighth month, s. 1174, a *tao san* year (April 1812). They surrounded it, from the eighth month (April 1812) until the / eleventh month (July 1812). They were starved, and could not win, so they left and retreated the army and came down and encamped at M. Yòng. At the end of the Lenten Season, replenished with food supplies, they rounded up all the people of M. Yòng, including especially Cao Suriyawong as head, and Phraya Kai, M. Chiang Khang, Phayak, / and M. Len, which were displaced. Cao Maha Khanan migrated the families down to Chiang Sæn. Cao Maha Khanan also took the people back up to Chiang Tung and M. Yang, to become subjects of the Burmese in s. 1175, a *ka rao* year (1813/14). /

The king the Uparaja took Cao Suriyawong of M. Yòng, Phraya Kai, Phraya Khüan of M. Yang, and the people back to the country. Not long afterwards, they took the officials and relatives and Cao Suriyawong, Phraya Khüan of M. Yang, and Phraya Kai down to / to attend upon His Majesty the King of the south, and informed him. His Majesty the Great King was very pleased, and bestowed presents of gold and silver, cloth and clothes, in great quantities. Then they took leave and came back up.

---

24 M. Chiang Khang, Chiang Khæng, M. Sing, M. Phang, M. Lòng, M. Kò, M. Sai: the Upper Mekong Region again.

25 Far to the north of Keng Tung: see Keng Tung (Khœn) map.

26 The author writes in such a way as to suggest that both he and his "readers" are intimately familiar with the geography of this region.

27 North of Keng Tung. GUBSS II, pt. 2, pp. 497–498.

Môn Refugees Sent to Bangkok, 1815

In s. 1176, a *kap set* year, in the sixth month (February 1815), the Mon Mutu rebelled against the Burmese /f° 8.14/ and came with his people to Chiang Mai; five thousand people into the territory of the Krungthep kingdom. His Majesty the Sovereign King wrote a royal letter to the king in Chiang Mai telling him to send the Mon refugees down. When the king was informed of the royal letter, he ordered / Cao Kham Mun to be head, with royal relatives and officials and organize boats to send them down. They started out in the New Year, s. 1177, a *dap kai* year, tenth waning of the ninth month, a Friday (18 June 1815). The king of Chiang Mai mounted a royal elephant / with surrounding retinue in procession to go out through the Chiang Yün quarter in the *træ* watch to Wang Tan Landing to get in the golden barge (Suwannanawa), with a total of 138 boats including the boats of Cao Maha Suriyawongsa his royal son heading them up, / and they floated down the Raming River.

When they reached M. Læheng, Cao Maha Suriyawong the royal son fell very ill of fever. On Saturday, tenth waning of the first tenth month (17 July 1815), he died. His Majesty the King was very fond of this son, so he / ordered him placed in a coffin, and had people bear him on an elephant back up to be cremated at M. Thœn, on the twelfth waxing of the second tenth month, a Tuesday (3 August).[28]

His Majesty the King left Læheng to continue on down, arriving on the Tuesday, fourth waning of the second tenth month (10 August). In Bangkok, he attended upon His Majesty the Sovereign Great King /f° 8.15/ and presented the Mon refugees to His Majesty the Great King, who was very pleased and bestowed silver and gold and clothes, and feasted him with food and sweets and fruits and entertained him with dances and dramas and fine entertainments, a grand occasion.

On Thursday, the thirteenth waning of the second tenth month (19 August), His Majesty / the King was pleased to have the king [of Chiang Mai] seated in a green warboat with great cannon at its head and tail, and with brightly-dressed soldiers in great numbers. He got in his royal barge, and the boat of the ruler of Lamphun and the boats of his royal relatives and officials, and the boats of the Bangkok nobles / altogether were eleven vessels, each with guns fore and aft, and they all sailed down to the mouth of the river at the sea, where they shot off their guns, each boat firing

---

28 Note that this is a second tenth month—the intercalary month.

two rounds, and then all the boats sailed back up to in front of the royal precincts. The king disembarked to the Pa Sòi Palace. Phraya Thatsayotha invited the king to come back. / His Majesty the King then returned to the city. Phraya Samutthirat [and] the *phraya* then invited the king to return to his home, and they then fêted him with foods and sweets and fruits, for the royals, nobles, and men to be satiated. Then His Majesty the King came / back to the city of Pak Lat at midday, and then came back to Krungthep Phra Nakhòn. He attended upon His Majesty the Great King. The Great King expressed his great satisfaction beyond measure.

On Tuesday, the third waxing of the eleventh month (24 August 1815), His Majesty the King [of Lan Na] was somewhat feverish and ill. His Majesty the /f° 8.16/ King [of Siam] had the royal physicians come to him and care for him until the illness abated. The king had the officials perform soul-tying ceremonies, and bestowed clothing, things of gold and silver, betel, salt, crockery, and various foods to fill each boat of the entourage, together with Thai cloth, parasols, and shoes, a hundred of each, which he gave / to them for bestowal upon Maha Suriyawongsa the royal son.

On the full-moon day of the twelfth month (4 October) they took leave of the king. On Thursday, the third waning of the twelfth month (7 October), in the *phat* watch, the procession went to sleep overnight at Talat Kæo, and then they proceeded in order. In the first month, on the third waning (6 November), they slept at Thap Phui, where they stayed for six / days. On the tenth waning of the first month (13 November), they slept at Mæ Rawan; on the eleventh at Mæ Phik; and on the twelfth at M. Thœn. They were two days at M. Thœn. On the last night of the month (17 November), they slept at Pa Khòng. They continued in order. On the ninth waxing of the second month (26 November), they slept at Lamphun; on the tenth at the Wang Tan Landing; and on the eleventh waxing of the second month, / a Sunday (28 November 1815), in the *kòng ngai* watch His Majesty the King re-entered the city.

Death of King Kavila, 1816

His Majesty the King, having returned, stayed there for two months and three days; and on the first waning of the fourth month, a Sunday (30 January 1816), in the watch near noon, His Majesty the King fell very ill with fever. / On the fourth waning of the fourth month, a Thursday (3 February), he died and attained to the Golden Heaven.

His Majesty the King was born in the *tao set* year, s. 1104 (1742/43). At the age of forty years he established M. Pa Sang. After fourteen years, he went on to re-establish Chiang Mai, where he stayed for twenty years. His age was /f° 8.17/ seventy-four years.

Chronicle of the Reclining Buddha

Here we will speak of former times, of the *Saṅgitikathā* which was chanted forth as the story of the Reclining Buddha,[29] as follows.

After Phra Koṇagamana [the second Buddha] had died, we come to the time of Kassapa. At that time, Chiang Mai was called Kumbhamittanagara. A king named / Kumbhamittarāja was friendly with Phraya Aṅgaraṭṭha. Phraya Aṅgaraṭṭha had a mango tree that bore very sweet and fragrant fruit. So the ruler sent 101 of those mangos to Phraya Kumbhamitta. Phraya Kumbhamitta ate them, and was delighted with their flavor very much, / so he took the seeds from those 101 fruit, and planted them, until they brought forth a single plant. He transplanted it into his royal garden, next to a *makhap thòng* tree. That royal garden was filled with a great many fruits, and delicious and fragrant flowers. The ruler / thus ordered that his gardener, named Dhammapāla, care for it. Dhammapāla and his wife were most honest and faithful to the ruler. From what they sold from that garden, they accumulated four hundred thousand silver and ten thousand of gold, and they told the ruler. / The ruler then told them to "Keep it!" So the gardener put the silver in big jars, ten hundred thousand in each jar, and put the gold in a jar, which he buried between the mango tree and the *makhap thòng* tree. When the ruler died, what he had buried was not dug up.

Later, when the gardener died /f° 8.18/ he was reborn as an ogre, named Kumārayak. He unearthed the things buried by the mango tree. Then Prince Kassappa was born and attained enlightenment, and went about preaching to human beings and other creatures. He came to where the mango tree was, and Kumārayak, who had never previously seen the Buddha, did not allow / Kassappa to rest there. Kassappa puffed himself up full of his Buddhahood, and the Mahāyak was amazed and impressed,

---

29 Now the Reclining Buddha, or the Phra Phutthasaiyat, of Wat Phra Nòn Khòn Muang, Müang district, Chiang Mai; north of the city, near the present provincial offices. This section of the manuscript is omitted in SN.

and reverenced the Buddha. The Buddha Kassappa then preached the Doctrine to the great ogre. Kumārayak heard it, and kept the five precepts, / and three of his tusks, three *kam* (fists) wide and three cubits long, now lengthened to a full *sen* in length. The Buddha Kassappa pulled out a hair a *sen* in length for him to reverence and worship. The Great Ogre took that hair and placed it in a hollow tusk and buried it close / to the jars, and took care of them until the end of the Buddhaṅkara age, the time of the Buddha Kassappa and the age of our own Gotama Buddha.

When our Gotama Buddha was born, and was enlightened, a branch of the mango tree broke off with age, and fell / to earth and crumbled and decayed. Our Buddha was on the verge of entering Nirvana at Kusinara, owing to having eaten pork from a lay follower, so he tried to walk and preach, with five hundred arahats as his followers, in order to enlighten his fellow creatures; and he came to the mango tree /f° 8.19/ and wished to rest under the canopy of that mango tree, as was the custom of the Buddhas of former times. The mango tree branch which had fallen down had completely decayed away. The Buddha arrived tired and thirsty, so he had Maha Anandathera fold up his robes in four layers and spread out on the mango debris; and then the Buddha went to sleep there. At that time, the Mahāyak appeared / and asked, "What's your name? Aren't you brave to be lying down here under my mango tree? Get up!" When he said that, the Buddha replied, "I am called the Tathāgatha, the greatest in all the Three Worlds; and I have never fled from anyone. Whatever you / will do, go ahead and do it!" The Mahāyak said, "In former times, in the time of the Buddha Kassappa, I saw him and reverenced him, and he was not small, like you!" The Buddha then puffed himself up with his Buddha-nature, as large as Kassapa, and radiated his rays / over all the world. The Mahāyak recognized him as a Buddha and paid his respects to the Buddha, and the Buddha preached his Doctrine to the Mahāyak. He heard the Doctrine of the Buddha, and accepted the five precepts and the three / Basic Truths. He was most delighted, and brought forth a tree from the forest to shelter him, with lotus bamboo to serve as a parasol for the Buddha.

At that time, the Buddha felt warm and thirsty, so asked Mahā Anandathera, "Ananda, the Tathāgata is thirsty, and wishes you to go and /f° 8.20/ bring some water for me." Anandathera took an alms-bowl to the river for drinking-water. At that time, merchants' carts were resting there, their animals unhitched to go down and drink and lie down there, and they muddied the water. The thera went along the banks of the river, and saw two pigs on the edge of the river. / The Mahathera called those two pigs and asked them to dig a well. The two pigs dug a well, enough so that water came out, and the Mahathera used the lid of the almsbowl to scoop out the water. It was still not clear enough, and the Buddha was waiting for water, so the Mahathera quickly scooped some up and brought it to the Buddha. The Buddha drank it anyway, though it was not clean. Thus the / river was called the Disgusting River.

The Buddha Prophesies the Future of Lan Na

The Buddha drank the water, and prophesied, "In the future, when I have attained Nirvana, in eight hundred years the arahats will take my ashes and put them in a place for people and divinities to reverence in / this place. The Mahāyak, this person, will be reborn as a ruler in this domain, and will uphold the Religion of the Tathāgatha, and will erect a Buddha image as a focus for worship. Later, my Teachings will disappear after more than two thousand years. The Devasukkarori, the two pigs, / will be reborn as rulers of Ayutthiya at the end of the river. The Mahāyak will be reborn as the ruler of this domain. There will be children born of the same womb, seven male. They will become friends and confidants of the ruler of La Nam (the end of the river).[30] The Lord Mahāyak will be a ruler of great majesty and power, conquering all the way up to the Hò regions. He will exalt the /f° 8.21/ Teachings and will renovate and rebuild the images and reliquaries of the Tathāgatha, for certain. He ordered the Lord Indra, "In future, Mahāyak will become a ruler and exalt the Teachings of the Tathāgatha: forget this not!" Having said this, he raised his hand to his head and pulled a single hair and gave it to the Mahāyak for him to preserve / and venerate and respect.

The Buddha and the Lawa

The Mahāyak listened to the Teachings, and maintained the five precepts and maintained the hair-relic. One of the tusks of the Mahāyak remained, while the other he removed and placed in it the hair-relic and placed it in the jar. / The Lord Buddha took all the arahats to the foot of the mountains on the southwest, and sat above a mountain-peak and all the Lawa prepared food and drink and presented it as

---

30 An oblique reference to the name of the kingdom, Lan Na!

alms to the Lord Buddha and all the arahats. The Buddha received / these alms and ate and gave blessings, and then four Lawa (Thammila)[31] asked to be ordained with the Buddha. The Lord Buddha ordained those four with an *ehibhikkhu* ordination,[32] as new monks; and then He preached the Doctrine to all the Lawa.

At that time, there was a divinity Indrabrahma, who released golden rain which fell down / in veneration of the Doctrine of the Buddha. The Lord Buddha prophesied, "Because of the newly-ordained Thammila, in the future this domain will be called Müang Chī Mai ("New Monks"); this mountain will be called Golden Mountain (Dòi Kham[33])."

Having so prophesied, the Lord Buddha asked all the Thammila, "Why has this city no inhabitants?" The Thammila /fº 8.22/ then replied to the Buddha, "Sire, we your servants have two demons, husband and wife, who constantly eat and oppress people, and that is why the city is empty and deserted." The Lord Buddha then called forth the two demons and preached to them the Doctrine and called upon them to abandon their evil ways, and not to eat people. The demons replied / to the Lord Buddha, "In order to sustain our bodies we have to do this. If we are forbidden to do so, we will have nothing to eat. Let us just eat a person a month." The Lord Buddha forbade it. Then they asked to eat a person a year. The Lord Buddha again forbade it. Then they asked to eat a water-buffalo a year. "If the people / will give us a buffalo a year, we will sustain them and the Teachings of the Buddha for five thousand rainy-seasons."

The Lord Buddha then reflected, "It is in the nature of all demons to have flesh and blood as food, and they cannot live without it." He silently consented, and said nothing; but he spoke / a sermon instructing all the demons not to disturb people.

The demons Pu Sæ and Ya Sæ[34] reverently asked the Buddha and the arahats to have mercy on them each year. When they had said this, the Lord Buddha took all the

---

31 Note the equivalency established here between the Tamila and the Lawa ethnic group. This is uncommon in Northern Thai historical writings. See *Doi Tung*, p. 76 and fn. 4; and pp. 80–81.

32 Pali: *ehibhikkhu*: "come bhikkhu!" "the oldest formula of admission to the order" (PTS).

33 Dòi Kham: small mountain south of Dòi Suthep. It is surmounted by a reliquary called the Phrathat Dòi Kham.

34 Pu Sæ and Ya Sæ: There is a shrine to these two spirits in a village at the foot of Dòi Kham, Hang Dong district. On the annual ceremony to propitiate them, see Sawat Khemakapasit, *Tamnan müang Chiang Mai, Pu Sæ Ya Sæ, Sao Inthakhin, Phra Bot, Chang Phüak Kumphan* (Chiang Mai, 1977), pp. 1–4.

arahats off to Kusinārāi. / From then on, everyone made sacrifices and offerings and spread forth banners,[35] and had newly-ordained *bhikkhu* teach Buddhists every year.

Indra Recalls the Prophecy

Seven hundred and fifty years after the Buddha had attained Nirvana, there was a city named Kururatthanagara and Kumārayak was born as its ruler. /f° 8.23/ After he had attained to this royal status, the Lord Indra remembered the instructions of the Buddha, when he was still alive, and he took incarnation as a brahman and came to the court of the ruler of Kururattha. He revealed himself as Indra to the ruler, and the ruler invited / Indra to ascend and sit upon his throne. Then he asked him from whence he had come to be Indra.

The Lord Indra said, "Sire, in your former existence you were the gardener to King Kumbhamitta and you buried things. When you died, you were Kumārayak, and watched over those goods. / When the Lord Kassappa came he preached and gave you a hair-relic, and you preserved it inside a hollow tusk of yours, which you buried with the things. When the Gautama Buddha came to teach, you arranged a shelter in which the Buddha could stay. That Lord gave you a hair-relic, for you / to preserve, and you took that hair-relic and placed it in the tusk casket and buried it there with the jars of things. The Lord Buddha then asked me, Indra, to take care of them and not let them disappear, and I have come to tell you this.

"When the Teachings are aged eight hundred years, the arahats / will bring the ashes of the Buddha forth, and you will exalt the Teachings, and you will dig up all those things, including the hair-relics, and bring them forth and will construct an Image of a Reclining Buddha in the place where the mango tree limb decayed, and in it you will place the hair-relics and the ashes, to be worshipped and venerated; and this will be called /f° 8.24/ the Reclining Buddha of the Fallen Branch. Later, you will be reborn as the ruler of this city, and again you will exalt the Teachings. There will be seven sons born from the same womb, who will erect a Buddha Image, a second time. Then the Teachings will last for a full two thousand years." Then he ascended to Heaven, his home. /

---

35 Special banners (*phra bot*) on which are drawn representations of the Buddha. A half-century ago these were kept at Wat Fai Hin, near what is now Chiang Mai University. They are now at Wat Pa Ci, Hang Dong district.

So rājā sakkassa vaccanaṁ sutvā abhirammāmiti.[36] The ruler of Kururattha heard these words of Indra, and was greatly delighted. He thought, "I must exalt the Teachings of the Lord Buddha, which are His legacy." / He awaited upon the *mahāthera* who would bring the ashes of the Lord Buddha. The ruler and his civil and military officials, his advisers and scholars, together newly named this town, Müang Inthasaket,[37] in accordance with the omen of the Lord Indra having come down to relate these circumstances which would / include the ashes and hair-relics of the Lord Buddha.

The Buddha's Ashes Come from Pegu

When the era of the Teachings had attained to eight hundred years, four *mahābhikkhu* brought the [ash]-relics of the Lord Buddha from Hamsavati. When the mahāthera / had come, they preached to the ruler, and told him what the Lord Buddha had prophesied, in every detail. The ruler was greatly delighted, and arranged for them to be given food alms; and then asked them, "When will I know /f° 8.25/ where the things and the holy hair-relics are buried?" The mahāthera replied, "I know." Then the ruler sent the mahāthera to a place where he might stay and rest.

Punadiparo.[38] The next morning, after the morning meal, the ruler had civil and military officials surround him / as his servants and invited the four mahāthera to accompany him north of the city, to the place where the mango branch had broken off and fallen down. The mahāthera who was the guru examined the site with his arahantish eyes, and knew that this was the place, and they dug there, and brought up the ogre's tusks / into which had been placed the hair-relics, both of them. Then the thera had them dig further, and brought forth the four jars of silver and the one jar of gold. Brought forth, they revealed three hundred thousand[39] of silver and ten thousand of gold. The ruler and his officials, as well as the villagers and townsmen, were all greatly pleased. They brought forth / the hair-relic of the Lord Buddha into their city, above their heads, and they lustrated and bathed it, and worshipped it for seven days and seven nights with great festivities. Then the ruler assembled his

---

36 Pali: the meaning approximates that of the translated sentence which follows.
37 M. Inthasaket: "the domain where Indra came down."
38 Pali: perhaps *Punadivaso,* "The next morning."
39 Have one hundred thousand pieces of silver disappeared?

officials and people, headed by the mahāthera, and they took the / holy hair-relic back to the place where it had been, and then they erected a Buddha image of earth, bricks, cement, sand, and lime, into which they placed the hair-relic of the Buddha and his ashes, to be venerated and worshipped. It was given the name, Reclining Buddha of the Fallen Branch.

Kawila and His Brothers Fulfill the Prophecy

In due course, in [the year] /f° 8.26/ 1140 (1778), the Lord Indra took birth in M. Lakhòn; eight brothers all born of the same womb. In the year c.s. 1158 (1796/97), Mahāsakkarat 11240,[40] the city was founded; its name was Phra Pavarapurājā Narādhipatī Srī Suriyavaṁsa Aṅga-indāsurasakti Samayāmahākhattiyarājā / Jātirājājai Svarga Cao Khüan Khanthasemā Phranakhòn Chiang Mai. The Reclining Buddha was 897 fathoms from the gate of the city.

White Elephant Captured, 1816

In s. 1178, a *rwai cai* year (1816/17), Doctor Nò Kæo went to catch elephants in the Nòng Sakün district, and in the districts of Chiang Rai, Phayao and / M. Phan. He caught a white elephant, nine cubits and one *khüp* high, with long tusks an elbow and 3 *niu* long. He brought it back to the city on the tenth waxing of the ninth month, a Wednesday (24 May 1816). On the twelfth waxing, a Friday (26 May), all the princes and officials handed the domain over to the / Uparaja, the royal younger brother, whom they consecrated as the ruler to perpetuate the ruling dynasty, named Setahatthi Suwaṇṇapatumarājā, Lord of the White Elephant; and then they invited the ruler of Lamphun, the sixth brother, / to be the Uparaja. Cao Sri Bun Ma, who was the seventh brother, ruled Lamphun.

On the sixth waning of the eleventh month, a Mon Wednesday, a Thai *kat khai* day (2 August 1816), Cao Setahatthirājā as head and Cao Maha Uparaja of the Front Palace issued a command ordering Cao Phuttawong and Cao Suwanna Kham Mun to command /f°8.27/ an army to take the White Elephant down to present to the Great King.

---

40 1796 is indicated. But what is the Mahasakarat Era year? This could be Buddhist Era 2240, which -544 would be 1796/97.

On the fifth waxing of the second month, a Mon Thursday (12 October 1816), the King Lord of the White Elephant went in procession with many retainers mounted in the Golden Barge (*suvannanāwā*) gaily decorated, a total of fifty boats, and went in procession floating down / led by Cao Phutthawong and Cao Kham Mun and took the lord white elephant to present to the Great King in Krung Sri Ayutthiya. The Great King was greatly pleased and bestowed rewards of white parasols, a royal crown, a robe, a belt, necklace, the five insignia of kingship, a golden tray, a royal sword, / a royal dagger, things of gold and silver, cloth, and clothing beyond measure.

Lesbians Quarrel, 1816

The king was still in the South when an inauspicious thing[41] occurred in his country. Villagers of the Ban Hon-Mæ Sa-Mæ Lim region,[42] two women jealously were contesting the same woman and spread the lie that the Burmese were coming and would catch them. On the / eleventh waxing of the ninth month, a Saturday (?22 July 1816), in the midnight watch, a commotion arose throughout the domain.

Return and Re-Coronation of the King, and Pious Works, 1817

On the full-moon day of the sixth month (18 February 1817), the king arrived back from the South to the capital. The Cao Maha Uparaja led the nobles and royalty and civil and military officials and / all the people of the domain together to consecrate the ruler for a second time. They invited him to return to dwell in the golden palace, the royal palace. The king resumed his rule of the domain, and issued an order that everyone should make merit /f° 8.28/ and hear the Dhamma and observe the precepts and heed the preaching, and build temples and monasteries, kuti, *vihara*, stupa and *cetiya*, in great glory.

The king noticed that the precincts of Wat Phra Singharam which had been there since ancient times in the time of Phra Müang Kæo who had built it as a place for public worship and veneration, had become dilapidated and in ruins; so he ordered

---

41 Called *hani*; something out of the ordinary that presages the decline of the domain, according to the teachings of King Mangrai. See Sommai Premcit, *Khamsòn Phraya Mangrai* (Chiang Mai, 1976), pp. 25–26.

42 In Mæ Rim district, Chiang Mai province.

the Sæn Wat / to head up all the parishioners to dig up earth and gather up all the bricks which had fallen down. They discovered a brass box and in that box there were 22 silver Buddha images, 17 images, and 21 bronze Buddha images, one jade Buddha image, twelve white crystal images, 1 black crystal image, 85 other / crystal images, 18 ruby images, 1 white crystal bottle, 1 gold bottle, 9 gold boxes, a gold nugget and 5 silver ingots, a betel container of gold and niello, and 3 three-faced Brahma figures topped with Buddha figures on their heads. The king had them reburied in their old place; and then he renovated and rebuilt it / to be beautiful and complete for the religion. Then he prepared and organized the inauguration and consecration and made meritorious offerings.

Miraculous Events in 1817

In s. 1179, a *müang pao* year, on the second waxing of the eighth month, a Mon Thursday, a Thai *dap sai* day (5 April 1817), the Karen Old Man Tong, of Mæ Ngao, found the Sri Kan Chai sword[43] in the hollow of a tree and presented / it to the king.

On the fifth waxing of the second tenth month, a Mon Friday, Thai day *müang pao* (6 July 1817), there was a banana tree, two elbows high, which arose northeast of the city, on the banks of the Laming. Its roots were like a *nuan* banana, while its peak was a yellow flower with a complexion like a golden frangipani flower; and it had seven leaves spreading straight out /f° 8.29/ and their midst was like a lotus flower 2 *khüp* in circumference with a color like gold. His Majesty the King of the White Elephant was informed, and ordered that the tree should be decorated with flowers, candles, puffed rice, and incense on a golden tray, and officials civil and military should surround it as its servants, and various kinds of music / be brought there to the banana tree which had given birth to a lotus. Then there was worship and veneration of the flower with candles, incense, music, and offerings. Then it was dug up, roots and soil, and moved to be planted in a big pot set upon a palanquin and then it was paraded into the city to in front of the royal palace. / Then a shrine was built for it, and the banana/lotus tree was set up in the center of the shrine. It was honored and worshipped with music, drums, gongs, and singing for seven days and seven nights, without cease; and then it was set up in front of / the Golden Palace within the Royal Palace, as an auspicious thing.

---

43 Referred to above, f° 2.30.

The Còm Thòng Reliquary

Later in s. 1179, the King Maha Setahatthi Suwannapathumā Lord of the White Elephant and the Golden Lotus formed the intention to perform a great merit-making, and beheld the great *vihara* / of Còm Thòng which was much dilapidated and crumbling down, and resolved to renovate and rebuild it. So His Majesty the King ordered the royalty, relatives, officials civil and military, and the people to cut timber for the pillars and beams; and then on the thirteenth waxing of the sixth month, a Mon Thursday, Thai *ruang sai* day (7 March 1818), in the morning watch, *lagna* attaining /f° 8.30/ *mīna-āpo rasi* they raised the great *vihara* of Còm Thòng, and at the same time built the shrine of Inthakhin and first built the Great Reliquary of Wat Phra Sing, built next to the Bhikkhuni Ordination Hall[44] on that same day.

Canals Dug in Chiang Mai, 1818

On the ninth waning of the sixth month, a Wednesday (March 1818), the king again ordered the officials civil and military and all the people to dig a three- or four– / *sen* canal from the Hua Rin corner of the city to the Sri Phum corner circling around to the Katham corner[45] Sena Sanao flowing along the main road in front of Wat Dap Phai[46] and Wat Phra Sing straight past them, for one *sen*; another canal extending along the foot of the city on the west for a *sen*, north of the royal palace circling around / the swamp in front of the plaza cutting through the middle of the city to the Chiang Yün Gate[47] on the east; the Katham corner in front of Wat Sai Mun;[48] every canal built with earth and brick on both banks.

---

44 At Wat Phra Sing, there is an uposot behind the main *vihara*, next to the *cetiya*, which has two entrances, on the north and the south. This uposot is used for Sangha ceremonies involving both *bhikkhu* and *bhikkhuni* (male and female monks), the north side being for the women.

45 The southeast corner of the city.

46 Wat Dap Phai: in Chiang Mai city, north of Wat Phra Sing.

47 In front of Wat Chiang Yün.

48 Wat Sai Mun: by the southeast corner of the city there are two "Wat Sai Mun," namely Wat Sai Mun Müang and Wat Sai Mun Man (the "Burmese" Wat Sai Mun).

Miracles and Pious Works, 1818/19

In s. 1180, a *pæk yi* year (1818/19), the king enshrined the Jinadhātu Relic in the new *cetiya* / at Wat Phra Sing. On Thursday, the tenth waxing of the eighth month (2 May 1818), in the midday watch, until the full-moon day of the eighth month, a Mon Tuesday, a Thai *tao sanga* day (7 May), the king made merit and inaugurated and consecrated the *vihara* of Wat Pa Dæng Suthep.

On the tenth waxing of the twelfth month, a Mon Thursday, Thai *rwai cai* day (29 August 1818), / an eel as thick as a knife-handle was found in the well of Grandmother Li Hui in the village in front of Wat Jotikaram Ceti Luang.

On the third waning of the fourth month, a Mon Thursday, Thai *tao sanga* day (2 January 1819), a person of M. Kæn[49] caught two albino pigeons in the same nest, and presented them to the king.

On the full-moon day of the sixth month, a Mon Thursday, /f° 8.31/ a Thai *pæk yi* day (27 February 1819), the king again made merit in the inauguration and celebration of four temples, i.e., Wat Umong,[50] Wat Duang Di, Wat Saphao,[51] and Wat Phan Thao; and on the same day bestowed alms of the eight requisites and curtained golden preaching thrones and other utensils / presented for the Three Gems, all in great festivities with fireworks, rockets, candles, and illuminations; there were 114 rockets in the weight of a hundred-thousand; and of others, with weight less than a thousand, there were / ten.

Attack on M. Pan, 1818

In s. 1180, *pæk yi*, on the sixth waxing of the fourth month, a Friday (20 December 1818), the king of the White Elephant appointed Cao Suwanna Kham Mun, his nephew, to take a force of ten thousand men up to attack M. Pan. They captured people there to bring back to populate the domain.

---

49 M. Kæn: now Ban Müang Kæn, t. Inthakhin, Mæ Tæng district, Chiang Mai.

50 There are two temples by this name, the other being at the foot of Dòi Suthep. Since the latter was built in the time of King Kü Na, the one meant is in the city, on Ratchaphakhinai Road.

51 Wat Saphao: now Wat Samphao, Ratchadamnœn Road, Chiang Mai city.

City Moat

On the fourth waning of the fourth month, / a Thursday (2 January 1819), they began digging the outer moat of the city.[52] They built from the Ku Rüang corner to the Hai Ya Gate, a length of 606 fathoms.

More Pious Works, 1819/20

In s. 1181, a *kat mao* year, on the full-moon day of the eighth month, a Mon Saturday (26 April 1819), Maha Thep, who was a royal nephew, was the leading pious layman who built the *vihara* of Wat Phan Ong.[53] / As a leading layman, the king renovated the *vihara* of Wat Pan Phing,[54] Wat Dòk Kham, and Wat Chiang Yün, and the preaching hall *vihara* of Wat Buppha, the one on the east side.

On the first waxing of the tenth month, a Thursday (12 June), the king lord of the white elephant went with many retainers to gild the pillars of the *vihara* of Còm Thòng and its walls, and then they returned /fº 8.32/ to the city.

On the fourteenth waxing of the twelfth month (22 August), an elephant doctor caught by hand a red *kambalahatthi* elephant with mango-colored complexion. The king came out to receive this *kambalahatthi*, and altogether received five hundred elephants, which he brought in to the royal stables.

On the eighth waxing of the sixth month, a Sunday (8 February 1820), the king of the white elephant / with a thousand retainers surrounding him went to venerate the four Buddha footprints,[55] and then built a *vihara* sheltering them. He worshipped and lustrated them.

On the eighth waning of the sixth month (23 February 1820), he went to venerate the Khuang Phlao Buddha footprint,[56] and then returned into the / city.

---

52 Note that the text here indicates the outer earthen wall.
53 Wat Phan Ong: probably Wat Phan On; next to Wat Samphao
54 Wat Pan Phing: now Wat Pan Ping, next to Wat Umong in the city of Chiang Mai.
55 At the base of Dòi Suthep, t. Saluang, Mæ Rim district.
56 On a hill in Khuang Pao village, Mæ Tæng district, Chiang Mai province.

Pious Works, 1821/22

In s. 1183, a *kat si* year (1821/22),⁵⁷ that same year, the king built the main Buddha image in the *vihara* of Wat Phra Singha. The king first constructed the outer wall of the city: / in the dawn watch, they fired a salute of cannon inside, the *khruba* of Wat Pha Khao⁵⁸ being at the head, with the *khruba* Cantharangsi of Wat Phra Singha, and *khruba* Kesalapañño of Wat Phathanu Dong Di⁵⁹ at the head of a chapter of nineteen monks. They chanted the *Parittamangala sutta*, one chapter of the *Suttamanta*, the *Mahasameyya* in full, / and the Seven *Jaiya*.

More City Construction

They sprinkled the waters, and began the construction of the Sri Phum Fort; and then proceeded in order to the south. In that first night of constructing the outer city wall, rain fell as hail, thunder roared, and lightning fired bricks, the heavens forecasting that these reconstructed fortifications would be auspicious. / fº 8.33/

Death of the King, 1822

In s. 1184, a *tao sanga* year, on the fourteenth waxing of the eighth month, a Tuesday (June 1822), the king of the white elephant and the golden lotus fell ill, coughing up phlegm. On the full moon day of the eighth month, a Wednesday, a Thai *dap met* day (28 June 1822),⁶⁰ in the *kòng ngai* watch, the king died. He was seventy years of age when he began to rule the city, and ruled for seven years, so he was seventy-seven years old on his death. / The Cao Uparaja, his royal younger brother, appointed Cao Mahawong, who was his son, as Lord of the White Elephant to bear a letter with the news to inform His Majesty the great and glorious king in Krung Si Ayutthiya / that His Majesty the King of the White Elephant had died. His

---

57 1181 was *kat mao*; 1182 was *kot si*; 1183 was *ruang san*. I have to choose *kot si*.
58 Wat Pha Khao, Ratchamankha Road, t. Phra Sing, Chiang Mai city.
59 Wat Duang Di.
60 These dates in this part of the chapter are very confused, probably owing to misintercalation. I use the *dap met* day to choose Wednesday, seventh waning of the tenth month, 28 June 1822.

Majesty the Great king was pleased to have his officials arrange the requisites for bestowal on the monks, namely, iron alms bowls, robes, sandals, parasols, sugar, cloth for wrapping the corpse, candles, joss sticks, and a golden urn in which to enshrine the royal corpse / and had a royal commissioner bear them back up with Cao Mahawong.

When they reached the country, together they built a great and beautifully-decorated palace, with five spires nine fathoms and two elbows high; and then they installed the royal corpse in the golden urn into the tiered palace, and made / merit and bestowed alms and played entertainments for seven days and seven nights. On the third waxing of the second month, a Sunday (October 1822), they moved the catafalque off to be cremated.

King Maha Suphathrarat

All the royalty and officials, headed by Cao Phutthawong, together /f° 8.34/ handed over the country to the Cao Maha Uparaja to rule as king over all the people and country, under the name of Cao Maha Suphathrarat. The gods signaled in many ways, namely: the sun appeared as two; the moon appeared as two; and / hog-deer entered the city. The king sought out the physicians and philosophers to venerate the cardinal directions and Indra, and invited the Sangha to chant the *parittamaṅgala*, a thousand chapters of the *karaṇi*, and the Seven Jaiya in all twenty-eight places, namely the horoscopes of the city and the city gates / all ten navels of the city at the Inthakhin Pillar and the two white elephants north of the city. The monks who chanted at each place were nineteen to worship and do ceremonies to the horoscopes, and they venerated the *süa müang*,[61] namely the Inthakhin, for seven days and seven nights.

Bangkok Installs the New King, 1823

On the third waxing of the sixth month (January 1823), the Great King of Ayutthiya / bestowed insignia of rank for the royal commissioner to come and had the king of Lakhòn Cao Phutthawong go and receive his status as Uparaja in the *tao sanga* year 1184, on the third waxing of the sixth month (31 January 1823). The Cao Maha Khanan had monks come down to bear the official word / in the same year. A month later, on the third waxing of the seventh month (2 March), the king

---

61 The guardian spirit of the city.

with many retainers went in procession down to pay attendance upon the Great King in Ayutthiya. The Great King bestowed the five insignia of kingship, a crown, necklace, /f° 8.35/ gold and silver things, and many items of apparel, plus two large *labu* guns. Then he took leave and returned back up to his country.

He attained to his palace on the banks of the Ping on the fourteenth waxing of the first month (6 October), and rested at his palace for three nights. On Thursday, the third waning of the first month (11 October), the Cao Maha Uparaja Phutthawong headed up the princes of the royal blood, the officials civil and military, and all together with flowers / and puffed rice went to invite him to enter the White Elephant Gate and reside in the royal palace. / On the full-moon day of the fifth month (2 February 1824), the king went to inaugurate the ordination-hall of Wat Jotikārām on the west side of the Chedi Luang, with great benefactions, e.g., the eight monastic requisites, a golden preaching throne, nine images of elephants and 133 images of horses, and necklaces on which these were strung, 122 of each, / together all weighing 13,550; five cloth palaces, presenting these as alms to the Buddha, the Dhamma, and the Sangha [represented by] 101 monks.

Royal Dissension in Chiang Mai, 1823

King Maha Suphathra saw that this was not enough, and consulted with King Rattanaraja the Cao Hò Kham of Lakhòn. The king of / Lakhòn was informed, and came with two thousand retainers, with the ruler of Lamphun, his youngest brother with a thousand retainers. On the thirteenth waxing of the eighth month (22 February 1823), he came and was established in the palace north of the bridge over the Mæ Raming, coming to forbid quarrels between the two princes.

King Suphathra Ordained a Monk, 1823

On the /f° 8.36/ first waning of the eighth month (24 April 1823), the King Hò Kham as head, and the ruler of Lamphun, sat as heads of the royal family in assembly. The King Maha Suphathra, the sovereign lord of Ratanatiṁsa Nagara Chiang Mai, went to be ordained at Wat Sangkharam Chiang Man. There were twenty-one monks. On the / Monday, the fifth waning of the eighth month (28 April 1823), the king the Hò Kham of Lakhòn released malefactors who had killed elephants and taken the ivory, and six men were reprieved from death on that day.

On the sixth waning of the eighth month (29 April 1823), the ordained king went to live his ordained life with the *mahārāja guru* / Cao Paññajira of Wat Bupphakāraārām of Suan Dòk city.

A New King is Needed, 1823

At that time, the Cao Maha Uparaja Phutthawong as head, the Cao Ratchawong Suwanna Kham Mun presiding / over the royal family, rulers, and civil and military officials together said, "Our country is deserted and empty, without a lord; so we should take puffed rice and flowers and go to invite / the four relics of Còm Thòng to come up to take mercy on us. Then the king had goldsmiths fashion a golden casket, weighing 222 units of gold, and had a silver casket weighing eight hundred of gold to present as alms in which the relics might reside; and then invited all the people /f° 8.37/ of the domain to venerate the relics, and make a great deal of merit and make gifts to it, amounting to 8,700 of *thòk* silver[62] and 250 silver strips, and all the eight monastic requisites and a great many robes, and then they invited the relics to reside at Còm Thòng as before, in the season at the beginning of the year / in the eighth month, the *ka met* year s. 1185 (April 1823). As for Cao Ratchawong Suwanna Kham Mun, he built five pavilions in the Si Phum area to the east of the Mæ Kha; and built them of teak floors, walls, and roof, on Tuesday, the fifteenth waning of the seventh month;[63] and he offered forth the / five pavilions and erected banners twenty fathoms high. That was a grand celebration, with seven cloth elephants, nine cloth elephants, six cloth palaces, and the eight requisites for the Sangha and other utensils were numerous.

An Age of Misfortune

At that time, a misfortune arose to portend the calamity of a Kali Age. / The two princes, namely the king Maha Suphathra and the Ratchawong Suwanna Kham Mun, quarreled, and threatened to fight each other. The civil and military officers of

---

62 Thòk silver: "lump" or "bullet" money, traditionally used for weddings and for buying land. See Songphan Wannamat, Photcananukrom phap læ sinlapawatthanatham Lan Na (Bangkok, 1993), p. 20.

63 The last day of the seventh (Northern) month must be the fourteenth waning.

our country wanted a prince who lived by the eight royal precepts to rule the country to be the / lord and master of all of us, who would be worthy of all our respect and obedience, past and future. So the Cao Hò Kham was pleased to say that we should sacrifice to the city spirits and spirits, and /f° 8.38/ to Indra and Brahma and take an oath and release a royal chariot to seek a lord who had merit and mercy.

At that time, the Cao Maha Uparaja as head and the royalty and princes and lords, all of them, came back to the city, and together prepared a royal chariot, an auspicious one, and sacrificed to Indra and Brahma and the spirits of the city, / all of them; and then took an oath together that whoever was found by the royal chariot, that prince should rule our domain and country. Having done so, they released it; and all the royal pundits, antiquarians, teachers, and priests sounded music and drums to accompany the chariot's progress /

The horse went by the south around the royal city, thrice, and then went straight to the west and came to the city of Suan Dòk, and there thrice circumambulated around a prince of merit, and then stopped. At that time, the royal family / and all the rulers and civil and military officials together prayed to invite the Phra Maha Samanathera Cao the ordained prince, to leave the monkhood and then they invited him to become king, to mount the royally-caparisoned elephant.

They sounded musical instruments, drums and gongs, and the prince came to the Hua Rin.[64] / There he took the water from the seven bejeweled fountains in which to bathe and wash his hair; and then he came to the White Elephant Gate. Then he went to reverence the Buddha image at Wat Chiang Yün and the relics; and then he entered the White Elephant Gate and had the Lawa lead their dogs and carry baskets and chickens and lead him.[65] He stopped to reverence the reliquary of /f° 8.39/ Wat Chiang Man, and then he proceeded to in front of the royal palace. Within, there were 108 monks, and outside were the seculars. His Majesty the King Hò Kham of Lakhòn was head, with the ruler of Lamphun, the Cao Maha Uparaja, and the Cao Ratchawong were leading, and they led the prince in to the Hò Düa and the Hò Chai for the administration of the waters of the *Muddhābhiseka* / in sixteen dippers; and then they led him into the Golden Palace and handed over the rule of the country to him. The monks chanted the *parittamaṅgala* and the various

---

64 The area of the "seven fountains" just north of Chiang Mai University.

65 This ceremonial role of the Lawa has long since ended in Chiang Mai, but it was performed in living memory in Keng Tung. See *Rüang müang Chiang Tung*, pp. 16–17.

chants and the *mahāsameyya* in full, the *jeyyabāhum*, the *jeyyabengjara, jeyyapathawi samuttakatha / unhassavijai pariputta* in full; and then the king resided in the bespired golden palace for three days and three nights.

The king was a bit ill; so all the royal sons and daughters brought him / to ascend the royal couch and go to the rear palace of the south, as before; and then they assembled all the royal physicians to come in and take care of his illness. The physicians administered him medicine, and his illness abated.

On Tuesday, the thirteenth waxing of the ninth month (9 June 1824), / His Majesty the King of the Golden Palace of Lakhòn and the ruler of Lamphun with a retinue of retainers visited his domain, in s. 1186, a *kap san* year (1824/25), on that day.[66]

News of the Death of King Rama II of Siam, 1824

On Friday, the first waning of the ninth month (30 May 1824), in the same year, Luang Can and Luang Thippharaksa and Nai Kham Wang, the royal commissioner, brought in a /f° 8.40/ letter with the Rajasi seal to say that His Majesty the King of Krungthep Pha Mahanakhòn Sri Ayutthiya had been very ill and had died,[67] and that his royal remains had been taken in procession to a room in the royal palace and Prince Kromma Cetsadabòdin had been raised up to rule the country / as King Somdet Phraphutthachao,[68] and had raised Caofa Krommasak up to be the Front Palace king,[69] in the manner of former kings of times gone by.

On Tuesday, the eighth waxing of the twelfth month (19 August 1824), the king / Maha Suphathra had alms bestowed on 120 monks to make merit for His Majesty the Great King of Ayutthiya.

---

66 TM (f° 39) is somewhat clearer, though less-detailed on dates: "In s. 1186, on the thirteenth waxing of the ninth month, His Majesty the King of the Golden Palace of Müang Chaisakhawadi with two thousand troops and the ruler of Lamphun with one thousand troops stationed themselves by the head of the Ping River bridge. On the fifth waning of the ninth month, the ruler of Chiang Mai was ordained [a monk] at Wat Chiang Man and went to stay at Wat Suan Dòk." That is, they staged a coup and forced the king to abdicate.

67 The death of Rama II occurred on 22 July 1824, according to the Second Reign Chronicle of Prince Damrong. It is impossible that Chiang Mai could have heard of the death on 30 May!

68 King Rama III, r. 1824–1851.

69 The Second King (*uparaja*) of the Third Reign (Rama III) was Prince Sakdiphonlasep (1785–1832).

Floods in Chiang Mai, 1824

In s. 1186, when it came to the Tuesday, the full-moon day of the twelfth month (26 August 1824), the waters greatly flooded, sinking boats belonging to the king. / The king had ordered boats to be built by the banks of the Ping, and two boats survived, but three sank.

In s. 1186, on Tuesday, the thirteenth waxing of the first month (23 September), the Cao Maha Uparaja Phutthawong the Front Palace led forth the royal family and relatives, and the rulers and civil and military officials down by water to / attend upon the Great King in Krung Si Ayutthiya. Later, the Cao Maha Uparaja and the King Maha Suphathra fell ill. The Cao Ratchawong was head, Cao Phimmaphisan the Ratchabut and the royal family, rulers, and officials civil and military had a letter /f° 8.41/ going down by water to the Great King so informing him. The Great King had Mün Kham Wang take a party of royal physicians, seven of them, and they arrived on Friday, fifth waxing of the fourth month (12 December 1824), to care for the king. He was not cured, improving only slightly. On the seventh waxing of the fourth month (14 December), they propitiated the city's *khrò* / and propitiated the city spirits and worshipped the city's horoscope in twenty-eight places, e.g., Inthakhin, and the horoscope of the king. On the Wednesday, the full-moon day of the fifth month (21 January 1825), the Cao Uparaja left the South, and returned to the domain.

Death of King Maha Suphathra, 1825

When it came to the Sunday, / the eleventh waning of the fifth month (1 February 1825), in the evening, at two strokes of the afternoon gong, plus 5 *pada* of water, King Maha Suphatra died. He had ruled for three years, and he was seventy-one years old. /

At that time, the Cao Mahawong, the son of the King of the White Elephant, and Cao Kæo Müang Ma, son of the Cao Ratchawong, had taken five hundred men to attack the Burmese Maung Pæ in the region of Martaban, and had not yet returned. The Cao Maha Uparaja, and the Cao Ratchawong / sent a letter reporting the death of the king to the Somdet Phra Cao Hò Kham of Lakhòn. So informed, with more than nine hundred men, and the ruler of Lamphun, the youngest son, with six hundred he came in on Sunday the fourth waxing of the sixth month (8 February

1825). Then together they worked daily to erect a funerary pyre /f° 8.42/ in which to place the royal remains; and then together they wrote a letter for Cao Jeyyalangkā to bear down to the Great King.

Sibling Greed

As for the Hò Kham ruler of Lakhòn and the ruler of Lamphun, they hurried to arrange the collection of gold and silver things, and the families and property of the king who had died, in great quantities. Cao Phimphisan, the royal son, / was offended, and left the corpse of his royal father and went with Cao Thammakitti Suriya Meghanarin, his younger brother, down to attend upon the royal mercy of His Majesty the Great King in Ayutthiya for / a period.[70]

Ill Omens, 1825/26

In s. 1187, a *dap rao* year, in the waning half of the seventh month, approaching the New Year,[71] circumstances arose in the country with foxes, frogs, and toads stealthily entering by the Chang Mòi Gate,[72] completely covering the ground, such that one could not walk without treading on them. Herons fought in the air by the swamp at the Si Phum Fort. Moreover, / *nok tung tung* and vultures and crows flocked over the whole city in innumerable numbers, darkening the sun.

At that time, the Cao Mahawong and Cao Kæo Müang Ma, who had gone to fight the Burmese Maung Pæ were victorious, and swept up families and returned to the domain. / Dysentery descended upon the city, and people were ill with diarrhea and vomiting, and many died. In all the kingdom, more than ten thousand people died.

The Accumulated Merit which had been erected to illuminate the Teachings had not yet been completed. On the Saturday, the fourteenth waxing of the eighth month (18 April 1825), a barking deer came to the foot of the city walls outside the Tha Phæ Gate.[73] /f° 8.43/

---

70 The import of this paragraph is that the "fatherly advice" of Chai Kæo was ignored.
71 Last week of March 1825. New Year's Day was on 1 April that year.
72 Modern gate on the east side of Chiang Mai, north of the Tha Phæ Gate.
73 Not the modern gate by this name, but the gate in the earthen walls somewhat east of that.

Attempts to Ward Off Misfortune

They sacrificed to Indra, and sacrificed to the *khrò* of the city, and invited 108 monks to chant the *parittamaṅgalasutta* throughout the city for seven days, and they gave alms in great quantity.

On Sunday, the full-moon day of the eighth month (19 April 1825), the Cao Maha Uparaja, the Cao Ratchawong, the royalty and rulers and their relatives, and the whole population together erected *chatra* at the Great *Cetiya* / of Wat Bupphakarām Suan Dòk Mai.

On Saturday, the eleventh waning of the eighth month (2 May), the Cao Maha Uparaja as head, Cao Ratchawong presiding, and all the royal relatives together built the great *vihara* at Wat Sangkharam Chiang Man. For this *vihara*, the Cao Ratchawong flattened the old palace of / the king of the White Elephant.

On Wednesday, the second waxing of the ninth month (6 May), they invited the royal remains of King Suphatra to come down to repose in the funeral pyre, and they had entertainments and made merit and bestowed alms in great number.

On Sunday, the sixth waxing of the ninth month (10 May 1825), / they invited the remains to go out to the cremation grounds and cremated them.

On Monday, the seventh waxing of the ninth month (11 May), His Majesty the Hò Kham of Lakhòn and the ruler of Lamphun performed their deeds and led out their retainers to return to their domains. /

Funerals, Further Deaths, and Missions to Bangkok

Not long after the King Hò Kham had returned to Lakhòn he became very ill. On Saturday,[74] near noon, he died. He was seventy-eight years of age.

In s. 1187, a *dap rao* year (1825/26), the country was unstable and disturbed, for the rulers and ruled alike, /f° 8.44/ in great measure. On the eleventh waxing of the twelfth month (10 September 1825), the Great King of Ayutthiya bestowed 4 *chang* of seal silver, 50 monastic robes, 70 bolts of imported white cloth, 700 parasols, 350,000 of refined sugar, and had Phraya Sisapha and Phra Surenratchasena / go

---

74 We have to assume, lacking further details, that this occurred in the same week as the previous reference; therefore 16 May.

with seventy men as royal commissioners to present them as alms in honor of King Maha Suphathra, the ruler of Chiang Mai.

In the same year, on Thursday, the third waxing of the first month (1 October 1825), the Cao Ratchawong went down and attended upon the Great King / in Krung Si Ayutthiya.

On the third waning of the first month (16 October), in the watch near midnight, there were three halos around the moon, and the clouds disappeared.

On Monday, the fourth waning of the first month, they sacrificed to the *khrò* of the city and consulted the city horoscope / in all twenty-eight places, e.g., the Inthakhin pillar. Lightning struck the Great Reliquary of Wat Lok[moli] on the seventh waning of the first month, a Tuesday (20 October).

As for the Cao Ratchawong, who had gone down to attend upon the Great King, he fell ill, and took leave and returned to Ban Sæn Tò, where he / died, on Thursday, the eleventh waxing of the fifth month (4 February 1826), in the *kòng dük* watch at the second striking of the gong in s. 1187, a *dap rao* year (1825/26). He was aged sixty-six years. The royals and relatives brought his remains back to Ban Müt Ka. Cao Suriyawongsa, the deputy of Lakhòn, who was his youngest /f° 8.45/ brother, had been the assistant of Cao Maha Uparaja, who was his elder brother, in Chiang Mai for a short time.

In s. 1188, a *rwai set* year, on the twelfth waxing of the ninth month, a Wednesday (June 1826), the Cao Ratchawong was cremated at Ban Müt Ka.[75]

As for the leading officials and ministers, they went down to attend upon / the Great King accompanied by the new Cao Ratchawong. When they returned to the domain, he took ill and died.

Together they built a funerary pyre in which to place his remains. On the fourth waning of the ninth month (12 June 1826), they invited his remains to enter the pyre and cremated him on that day. His age was / sixty-six years when he died.

In s. 1188, a *rwai set* year (1826/27), on the eighth waxing of the second tenth month,[76] a hog-deer came in to the White Elephant Gate to the east.

On the ninth waxing of the second tenth month, there was a drum-beating ghost.

---

75 Ban Müt Ka, Hòt district, Chiang Mai province.

76 Here is a good example of bad intercalation: there was no intercalary second tenth month that year.

On the eleventh waxing of the second [tenth] month, the ghosts / fought at Dòi Ang Song at Chiang Dao. It was most fearsome.

On the eighth waning of the second tenth month of Ashadha,[77] a Saturday (14 August 1826),[78] the Great King had Luang Phom of M. Kamphængphet take 30 monastic robes, 30 bolts of imported white cloth, 6 *chang* of seal silver, 300 parasols, / 300 pairs of sandals, and 16 scarlet bags to present for the Cao Ratchawong.

On the twelfth waning of the second tenth month (18 August 1826), in the noon watch, the chief-queen of His Majesty the White Elephant King, whose name was Fòng Samut Rajadevi, died. She was seventy-five years old. /f° 8.46/

King Phutthawong of Chiang Mai

When the King Maha Suphathra had died, in s. 1187, a *dap rao* year, on Wednesday the full-moon day of the ninth month (20 May 1825), the royal family, rulers, and officials civil and military handed the government over to the Cao Maha Uparaja Phutthawong as sovereign ruler, as lord and master over all the people, and had him take up / residence in his old palace, west of Wat Si Kœt, in front of Wat Phra Sing, for three years.

In s. 1188, *rwai set* (1826/27), the Cao Mahawong and Cao Maha Thom sailed down to attend upon the Great King in Krungthep Mahanakhòn. The king / was pleased to have the ruler of Lamphun promoted to be king of Lamphun, appointed the Cao Mahawong to be the Maha Uparaja, and appointed Cao Maha Phom to be the Ratchawang.

Later, the two princes, younger and elder, were returning but had not yet arrived. In s. 1188, a *rwai set* year, on a Monday, in the second tenth month, / on the twelfth waning (16 August 1826), in the midday watch, the queen of the king of the White Elephant, named Fòng Samut Ratchathewi, died at the age of seventy-five years.[79] The royal descendants all together took her remains and placed them in a casket to await Cao Mahawong Uparaja / who was her son. On the Monday,

---

77 This information tells us that the tenth month in the North was the month of Ashadha, which was the eighth month in Siam.

78 The weekday gives us enough information to make a reasonable guess as to the date.

79 This repeats an entry that is just above.

the tenth waning of the eleventh month (13 September), the Maha Akkharamahesi Ratchathewi of His Majesty the King of Chiang Mai, who was the senior of all, named Cantharatchathewi died, at the age of seventy-eight years. /f° 8.47/

All the royal family, the rulers and civil and military officials together constructed a funerary pyre north of the funeral cart of Her Majesty the Queen, and then they made merit and had great entertainments made, and on the third waxing of the second month (?20 November 1826) they invited the remains to enter the funerary pyre of Canthrathewi to be cremated on that day. / On Sunday, the twelfth waxing of the third month (?28 December), in the *kòng ngai* watch, they inaugurated a new governing council.

On Monday, the full-moon day of the sixth month (?28 March 1827), the king who was lord and superior over the great ruling family, the rulers and civil and military officials and all the country, together / made merit to inaugurate and consecrate the great *vihara* of Wat Phra Sing, which the royal younger brother the Cao Ratchawong had constructed. They bestowed the eight monastic requisites, 50 preaching thrones, 21 sets of monastic robes, 42 cloth elephants, 31 cloth horses, 6 cotton elephants, 3 cotton horses, 4 horses made of betel, 3 cloth *mondok*, 3 cloth junks, / 1 paddle (?), 52 cloth *prasada*, 1 figure of an ox, 1 *mondot* of betel, altogether 166 pieces. There were redwood gunpowder rockets of more than 5,000 weight totaling 64; fireworks called *bòk fai thap* of greater than 5,000 weight totaling 46 units; altogether 110. Small fireworks of less than 5,000 units were innumerable. It was a grand occasion / this time.

On Friday, the third waxing of the seventh month, the Cao Mahawong Maha Uparaja, and Cao Ratchawong left the South Country to come back and reached Chiang Mai on that day.

On Thursday, the ninth waxing of the seventh month, they made merit and invited the remains of Queen Mother Cao Fòng Samut /f° 8.48/ to be taken out to be cremated on that day.

Rebellion of Cao Anu of Vientiane, 1827

At that time, Cao Anu of Vientiane went into rebellion against the Great King. His Majesty Krommaphra Ratchawang Bòwòn the Front Palace commanded an army of one hundred thousand who went up by way of Nakhòn Ratchasima, Champassak, and Lomphu Nòng Bua. / Then a Ratchasi sealed order came up ordering the conscription of an army of all the provinces. At that time, Cao Mahawongsa Maha Uparaja came up and was there for fifteen days. His Majesty was very brave and very skilled in warfare, so he arranged a force of / five thousand troops.

On Friday, the twelfth waning of the seventh month, in the *kòng ngai* watch, the prince led the fourfold army out of the city by the Chiang Rüak and Tha Phæ gates to the east, going to the Nòng Chang Khlan Field,[80] mounted on a royal mount named / Phap Müang Ma Kariya, who had been victorious, who knelt in three stages and bellowed loudly, and the prince led the army to Hua Fai Fon Sæn Ra, at the mouth of the Luang Lamphun Canal. He rested there for a night. That was the *nao* day of New Year's.[81] On the next day, which was the full New Year's Day, a Saturday, / the year incremented by one to be s. 1189, a *müang kai* day, and he led the army out by land to Vientiane to meet with the main royal army of the [front palace] commander and joined the great battle to capture Vientiane, which was defeated and broken. They captured Cao Anu the king of Vientiane, and weapons /f° 8.49/ and families in great number, more than three hundred thousand. The Front Palace King took Cao Anu, the Ratchabut, and the Ratchawong, and imprisoned them in Krung Si Ayutthiya to the ends of their lives.

Expedition to M. Leng, 1827/28

When the Cao Maha Uparaja went to Vientiane, Cao Kæo Müang Ma, Cao Suya, and Cao Mahawong the son of the old Cao Ratchawong, / these three brothers took an army of three hundred men, and on the fifth waxing of the eighth month, a Tuesday, in s. 1189, a *müang kai* year (19 April 1827), they went up to attack M. Leng, but did not take it, and withdrew back down. Ai Kæo Kang Wiang[82] missed the group that went to M. Leng, and was sent to Ava. Later, he was released to return, and returned to his country as before. /

---

80 Nòng Chang Khan Field: area of Chang Khlan Road, Chiang Mai city.

81 The *nao* day of the New Year period is the day immediately preceding the first full day of the new year "proper."

82 His name indicates that this was a young man (Ai) whose personal name was Kæo and lived in the midst of the city (Klang Wiang).

On the twelfth waning of the eighth month (10 May), the king lord of the country went to set up large *chatra* in reverence to the Great Reliquary atop Dòi Suthep, one on each of the four corners.

On Thursday, the sixth waning of the first month, in s. / 1189, a *müang kai* year (29 September), the Cao Maha Uparaja left the Vientiane army and returned home.

On the seventh waning of the fifth month, a *müang kai* year (26 January 1828), the Cao Phra Waramaha Uparaja was overcome with piety, and built the earth bridge, namely Phanang Mæ Kha,[83] / laying a water conduit under it, 179 fathoms in length. He built two floating pavilions, taking out five pavilions which the old Cao Ratchawong had built there, and beautifying the area close to the head of the bridge crossing the Ping to the west; and then he built a reliquary for the ashes of the venerable king of Chiang Mai,[84] which was octagonal, 12 elbows in height. He built /f° 8.50/ the walls around the city on all four sides, and the moat on all four sides.

A New Royal Palace

The Cao Maha Uparaja as head, the Cao Ratchawong, and the Cao Rattana Müang Kæo presiding over the royal family, rulers, officials civil and military, together invited the Cao Phutthawangsa Phummipalat to come in and reside in the royal palace. He was the king, and he / exalted the ranks of the first concubine, niece and aunts, elders of the ones who had died before, but who had not come to live in the grand palace. So he built a palace near the royal palace to the south. On Saturday, the third waxing of the seventh month (March 1828), he invited them to come and move the (bad) fortunes and go and live at Huai Kæo and Wiang 7 Rin for a space; and on the Thursday, the [first] waxing of the seventh month, the Cao Maha Uparaja / as head, the royalty, rulers, civil and military officials, ministers, priests, and teachers all came out to invite him to be king and come in by the White Elephant Gate by the customs of elephant-riding rulers of yore, and come mount elephants and rule the city and reside in the palace in front of the royal palace. /

Seven days later, on the full moon day of the seventh month, a Mon Thursday, of the [city-dwelling monks] there were the Phra Mahāthera Cantharangsi of Wat Phra Singharam and the Phra Mahāthera Kesalapañño of Wat Phanthanu Duang Di

---

83 Now the bridge by which Tha Phæ Road crosses the Mæ Kha in front of Wat Sæn Fang.

84 Later, all such reliquaries for the remains of former kings were moved to Wat Suan Dòk.

who presided over a chapter of 108 monks; and of the [secular] there were the Cao Maha Uparaja as head, the rulers and royalty / and officials civil and military who led the lord to enter the royal palace and led him up into the Hò Düa and Hò Chai, lustrated him with the holy water of consecration, in sixteen dippers, and then he was led into the Hò Thiam that had been newly built; and they handed over to him the government and treasures for the second time. He took the name Phummibāla Raṭṭhādhipati. The monks chanted the *parittamaṅgala*, and /f° 8.51/ the brahmans, priests, and teachers bestowed blessings on him, with the words "*Jayatubhavaṁ*" three times; and saying "May our Lord Mahārāja be victorious over Māra and all his enemies." That was a *müang* year, s. 1189 (1827/28).

Final Colophons

The history *naggaranidānakathā* fascicle 8 is here completed.

Completed on Wednesday, the third waxing of the fourth month, a dap met day, in the kap set year s. 1356, in the twenty-second lunar mansion; far above Cayuga's waters.

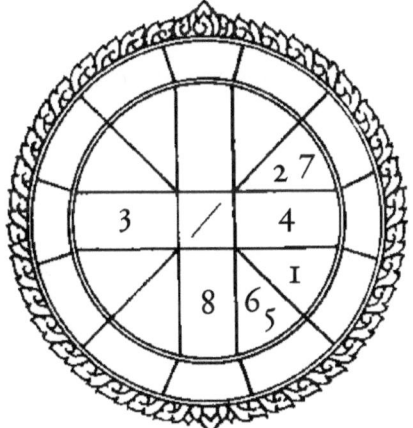

INDEX

12 hua khwæn of the Kha, 256
Abhayagamani, 144, 196, 197, 198, 199, 210, 211
Achap Nòi Tha, 206
Acsima, 20
Adit, 24
adultery, 51
Ai, Han, 126, 127
Ai, Mün, 127, 157, 165, 167, 168
Ai, Nai, 205, 210
Ai, Thao, 56, 120, 153
Ai Cat, 227
Ai Chang Market, 106
Ai Fa, 42, 43, 47, 53, 54, 55, 56, 60, 61, 62, 160
Ai Hang Chang, Mün, 127
Ai Hò, 61
Ai Kæo, 265
Ai Kæo Kang Wiang, 297
Ai Kin Thò, 227
Ai Nakhòn, Mün, 157
Ai Op, 109
Ai Phian, 44
Ai Ratchakuman, Nai, 205
Ai Sam Pi, 190
Ajātasatthu, 22
Ajātasattu, 23
alarm drums, 118
Albino Crow Prince, 186, 187
albino buffalo, 112, 129
albino chicken, 129
albino deer, 77
albino hog-deer, 74, 75, 77
albino monitor-lizard, 64
albino mouse, 76, 77, 78
albino pigeons, 283
Amaradevi, Lady, 33
Amaradevi, Queen, 32, 34
ambassador, 149, 150, 157, 178
amein-daw, 243
Amitatā, 21
Amittattodhana, 21
Ammat, Phraya, 219

amulets, 81
Anandathera, 23, 274
Ang Song, Dòi, 77, 295
Angels, 71
Añjana Era, 23
Añjana, 21, 23
Anu of Vientiane, Cao, 8, 296
Anuchit Chonlathi, Phraya, 234
Anuruddha, 22
Anuruddha Dhammikarāja, 24, 25
Anuruddha Era, 28, 37
Ao, Thao, 120
Aphintha Luk Khrüa Khròng, 181
Araññavasi Sect, 142
archer, 44, 153
armor, 118
arrows, 83, 118, 132, 140, 153, 177, 203
arts and sciences, 88, 105, 146
Asa River, 65, 66
Asæ Wun, 198, 230
Asæ Wun-gyi, 216
ascetic, 21, 23, 143, 145, 146, 148, 194
Asoka, King, 24, 119, 146, 148
Asoka Dhammarāja, 23
Asoka Dhammikarāja, 24
assassination, 167
astrologers, 119, 145, 146, 223, 243
At, Mün, 159, 160
Athit, King, 164
Athura, 196
Atthika, Khanan, 195
Atura, 177
Atya, Sæn, 188
Ava, 68, 69, 178, 188, 189, 190, 191, 193, 194, 196, 197, 198, 199, 200, 201, 205, 207, 209, 210, 211, 215, 218, 226, 227, 230, 232, 233, 234, 235, 238, 240, 241, 242, 243, 244, 245, 265, 297

Ava, King of, 69, 191, 194, 195, 197, 198, 199, 200, 207, 211, 215, 227, 233, 234, 235, 240, 241, 242, 243, 245, 265
Ayarattha, 254
Ayotthiya, 108, 137, 195, 196, 197, 201, 210, 211, 212, 226; see also Ayudhya
Ayudhya, 1, 130, 139, 180, 184, 186, 211, 223
Ayutthiya Bang Kòk, 235
Ayutthiya Dvaravati, 224, 245, 251, 258
Ayutthiya Dvaravati Theppha Mahanakhòn, 245
Ayutthiya, 51, 184, 199, 209, 211, 226, 227, 228, 239, 245, 275, 287
Aṇṇjanasakka, 21
Aṅgaraṭṭha, Phraya, 273

Ba, King of Hariphunchai, 53, 54, 55, 56, 59, 60, 61, 62, 79, 80, 81, 82
Ba [of Hariphunchai], Phraya, 100
Ba, Mount, 135
Ba Hai, Dòi, 135
Badung, 233
bamboo stakes, 117
Ban Fòn, Wat, 201, 203
Bang, Han, 49, 50
Bang Kòk, 215, 216
Bang Thok, 151
Bangkok, 1, 2, 8, 9, 271
banyan, 77, 91, 109, 133, 145, 147, 193
barking deer, 292
Bathing Bowl Mountain, 77
Batung, 233
bears, 102, 217, 261
Beauty City, 72
beehives, 98

Bejjabala, 81
Benares, 20
beñcangapradiṣṭha, 214
Bhattiraso, 20
Bhikkhuni Ordination Hall, 282
Bimbisāra, 22
Bindusāra, 23
Black Back, General, 207, 215, 216
black magic, 143
blunderbusses, 153
Bò Phawæn, 230
Bò Sæng [Mogok], 178
Bò Thòng, 161
boats, 63, 99, 153, 170, 172, 210, 211, 212, 271, 272, 280, 291
Bodhi tree, 109, 110
Bodhisamphāra, Mahāthera, 142
Bœk, Phraya, 61, 79, 80, 81, 82, 83, 85, 86, 205
Bòn Bang Khun Phom Sæn, 106
Bòn [Bòrommatrailokanat], King, 125, 126, 127
border imposts, 163
Bòrommaracha, King, 125, 126, 135, 136, 142, 149
Bòrommatraicak, King, 168, 169
Bòrommatrailok, King of Siam, 130, 133, 135, 136
borānasakkarāja, 21
Bòwòn, 195, 220, 296
Brahma, 281, 289
Brahmadesa, 148
brahmans, 205, 236, 261, 299
bricks, 162, 279, 281, 285
bridges, 126
bronzesmiths, 69
Bua Sam, Cao, 153, 154
buak, 97
Buddha, 23, 25, 70, 237, 246, 273, 274, 275, 276, 277, 279, 289
Buddha footprints, 284
Buddha Gotama, 20
Buddha images, 65, 66, 110, 224, 261, 281
Buddha Kassappa, 274
Buddhaṅkara age, 274
Buddhañāna, Mahāsvāmī, 110
Buddhasihiṅga [Image], 104
Buddhism, 10, 254, 261
Buddhist Era, 24, 28
Bun Hüang, Cao Phò Thao, 135
Bun Hüang, Thao, 136, 138
Bun Kian, Wat, 166
Bun Ma, Cao, 209

Bun Rüang, Cao Phò Thao, 148, 159; see also Bun Hüang
Bun Rüang, Mün, 151
Bun Rüang, Thao, 150, 239, 265
Bun Som, Lady, 219
Bun Tha, Cao, 269
Bun Tin Chiang, Mün, 150
Buppha, Wat, 192, 201, 284
Bupphakarām Suan Dòk Mai, Wat, 293
Bupphakāraārām, Wat, 288
Buppharam, 160
Buppharam, Wat, 237
Burma, Burmese, 8, 9, 10, 12, 29, 65, 109, 124, 143, 145, 146, 148, 149, 150, 186, 191, 192, 193, 195, 197, 198, 199, 200, 201, 205, 207, 208, 210, 211, 212, 213, 214, 216, 218, 225, 226, 227, 229, 230, 233, 234, 235, 236, 238, 239, 242, 247, 251, 263, 270, 271, 280
Burmese ascetic, 145, 146, 148, 149, 150
Burmese cloth, 156

Ca Ban, Cao, 201
Ca Ban, Cao Phraya, 201, 207, 216, 217, 218
Ca Ban, Phraya, 186, 211, 212, 214, 219, 220, 221, 224, 225, 243, 246
Ca Ban Bunma, Cao Phraya, 201, 207
Ca Ban Ròng, 161
Ca Kæo, Phan, 158
Ca Kham Nòi, Mün, 156, 157, 158
Ca Sòi, Mün, 136
ca ban, 88, 90, 134, 178
Ca, Mün, 156, 159
Ca, Mün, the judge, 156
Cæm, Mün, 134
Cæm, Phan, 150
Cæt, M., 239, 240
Cai Mæ Chæn, M., 234
Cai Mæ Sæn, M., 232
cakkavati, 23
Cakri, Caophraya, 212, 213, 215, 216
Callus (kæo) Canal, 55
Cam Kha, M., 151
Cam Klup, 124
Camadevi, Queen, 9, 62, 87, 205
Cāmadevi, Lady, 61

Cānakkhaphām, 23
Cambodia, 220
Can, Cao, 195, 196, 197
Can, Phraya, 210, 211
canal, 55, 118, 282
Candagutta, 23
Candama, 21
Candamukkhasivirāja, 21
Cang, M., 151, 203
cangue, 150
cannon, 112, 129, 151, 215, 218, 233, 271, 285
Canthapuri Phraya Thœn, Phraya, 234
Cantharacha, Cao, 233, 267, 268, 269, 270
Cantharacha, Nai, 210, 223, 226
Cantharaja, Cao, 266
Cantharangsi, khruba, 285
Cantharangsi, Phra Mahāthera, 298
Cantharat, Cao, 266
Cantharatchathewi, 296
Canthra, Queen, 209
Canthrathewi, 296
Cao Khanan, Cao Maha, 250, 267, 268, 269, 270, 286
Cao Sikkhi Buddha image, 109
cao nüa hua, 39
cao sæn, 122
care, 208, 265
cattulokapāla, 120
catulokavāla, 119
Catupari Nò Kham, 183
cavalry, 82, 83, 86, 118, 132, 137, 138, 156, 162, 237, 254, 262
cavalrymen, 133
Cephutrai Müang, King, 189
Cet, Thao, 120
Cet Chang, Mün, 158
Cetiya, 20, 24, 112, 293
Cetsadabòdin, Prince Kromma, 290
Chæ, Ban, 133
Chæ, M., 135, 253, 256
Chæ Chang, 63, 71, 168
Chæ Chang district, 123
Chæ Hæng, 181
Chæ Hom, 152
Chæ Lao, Ban, 133
Chæ Nòng Reliquary, 199
Chæ Phran, Ban, 112
Chæ Phran, Mün, 128
Chæ Sak, 59, 89, 105, 181
Chæ Sak, Cao, 136

Chæ Sak, M., 135
Chæ Sak, Phraya, 136
Chæ Ta, 182
Chai, Cao Phò Thao, 167
Chai, Phraya, 219
Chai, Thao, 167
Chai Kæo, Cao, 206, 207
Chai Kæo, Cao Fa, 207
Chai Kæo, Prince (chaofa), 198, 201, 207, 208, 209, 210, 211, 212, 213, 214, 215, 218, 226, 231
Chai Prakian Rattanapañña, Supreme Patriarch, 179
Chai Prap Sattru, Cao Sæn, 117
Chai Songkhram, 136
Chaiyasongkhram, Cao Phraya, 205
Chaiyasongkhram, Phraya, 205
Chakhrao, 132
Chaliang, 131, 140, 141, 142, 161
Chaliang-Sukhothai, 127, 140
chamberlain, 88, 243
Champassak, 296
Chan River, 45
Chana Chang, 39
Chang Khlan Field, 297
Chang Kò Kham Cet Yòi Nüa, 176
Chang Kum Kam, Mün, 146, 147
Chang Kum, Dòi, 114
Chang Mòi Gate, 292
Chang Phap, 179
Chang Phüak, 134
Chaptha, 208
charcoal-burners, 98
Chare Nòi, 203, 204
Chawa, 130, 132, 133, 152, 176, 177, 181, 182
Chawa (Luang Prabang), M., 152
Chawa Bridge, 182
Chedi Luang, 112, 173, 287
Chen Phò, 81
chess, 204
Chetawan, Wat, 188
Chettharat Phra Müang Ket, King, 167
cheyyabhumi, 73
Cheyyaratchathani, Phraya, 243
Cheyyasena Chiang Sæn, Phraya, 243
Cheyyasongkhram, 87, 88, 90, 94, 95
Cheyyasongkhram, Cao Phraya, 87, 88, 89, 90, 91, 92, 94, 95
Cheyyasongkhram, Phraya, 88

Chiang Chang, 39
Chiang Chi, Dòi, 97
Chiang Chün, 152
Chiang Cüang, 256
Chiang Dao, 87, 88, 89, 92, 179, 295
Chiang Dao, Sæn, 177
Chiang Khæng, M., 242, 248, 254, 267, 269
Chiang Kham, 39, 101, 102, 103, 264, 265
Chiang Kham River, 103
Chiang Khang, M., 254, 255, 256, 269, 270
Chiang Khòm, Wat, 169
Chiang Khong, Phò Thao, 164, 165, 167, 168
Chiang Khong, Thao, 165
Chiang Khòng, 41, 83, 91, 97, 104, 117, 118, 126, 187, 190
Chiang Khòng, Mün, 85
Chiang Khrœng, 171
Chiang Khrüng, 82
Chiang Khum, 250
Chiang Khwa, Mün, 164
Chiang Khwang [ward], 107, 113, 237
Chiang Lan, 72
Chiang Lan, Cao, 120
Chiang Lao Ngœn Yang, 34
Chiang Lap, 180, 191, 195
Chiang Lü, Mün, 158
Chiang Lüa, 56,
Chiang Lüa, Mün, 158, 168
Chiang Lüak, Phraya, 183
Chiang Mai, 1–5, 8, 11, 14, 17, 19, 71, 79–82, 86, 87, 90–95, 98, 99, 103–109, 112–114, 118, 119, 121–123, 125–127, 130–135, 138, 139, 141–143, 145–151, 153–158, 161, 162, 164, 167, 168–171, 173–181, 183–195, 197–202, 206, 207, 210–218, 221, 223, 224, 228–241, 243–248, 250–255, 257, 259, 261, 262, 264, 265, 267, 271, 273, 279, 294, 296, 298
Chiang Mai Gate, 91
Chiang Mai market, 79, 81, 90, 91, 175
Chiang Man, 75
Chiang Man, Wat, 237, 258, 289
Chiang Ngœn, 226
Chiang Ngœn, Ban, 228
Chiang Phlu Island, 200
Chiang Phum, Wat, 107

Chiang Rai, 40, 43, 44, 45, 47, 52, 53, 54, 55, 80, 87, 88, 90, 92, 94, 95, 96, 99, 100, 105, 112, 114, 117, 119, 172, 176, 182, 186, 219, 279
Chiang Rai, Mün, 158
Chiang Rai, Phò Thao, 140
Chiang Rai, Phraya, 230
Chiang Rao, M., 25, 28
Chiang Rüa, 55, 62, 113, 114, 123, 152
Chiang Rüa district, 63, 120
Chiang Rüak, 165, 168
Chiang Rüak Gate, 134, 174
Chiang Rüak Market, 112
Chiang Rüang Plaza, 93
Chiang Rung, M., 113, 157, 187, 253, 265, 266, 267
Chiang Sæn, M., 182, 242, 267
Chiang Sæn, Phraya, 186, 188
Chiang Sæn Gate, 96
Chiang Sæn walls, 117
Chiang Som, 72, 92, 109, 134, 169
Chiang Sum, 49, 50
Chiang Thang, 75
Chiang Thòng, M., 82, 176, 266
Chiang Thum, 72
Chiang Tin Khròng Nòi Khròng Luang, 132
Chiang Tung (Keng Tung), 69, 96, 245, 250, 251, 270
Chiang Yün, 271, 282
Chiang Yün, Wat, 110, 172, 237, 284, 289
Chiang Yün Gate, 282
chicken-bone oracle, 99
chief of a thousand, 129
China Dam, 226
Chinese Muslim, 149, 150
Chinnawong, 194
Chiraprapha, Queen, 168
Chit, Mün, 204
Chœng Upali, Phan, 158
Chotikaram, Wat, 240
Chronicle of the Sihiṅga Buddha, 9, 108
chronicles, 2, 95
Chum Sæng, Thao, 46
Chumphu, Mün, 226
Chumphu, Nai Khanan, 223
Chumphu, Thao, 234
Chumphu, Wat, 203
Chün, M., 267
Chī Mai, Müang, 276
Cintrathewi, 104

302   INDEX

Cit, M., 152, 241
Cit, Mün, 161, 172
city gates, 78, 91, 150, 158, 286
city horoscope, 294
city moat, 79, 81, 107, 133, 169
city spirits, 289, 291
city walls, 78, 107, 162, 167, 292
city-boon, 77
cloth, 63, 87, 125, 126, 133, 169, 213, 219, 225, 270, 271, 280, 286, 288, 296
cockfight, 140
Còm Hong, Raja, 242, 244, 245, 250, 267
Còm Pha Rüang, 31, 34
Còm Pha Rüang, Cao, 31
Còm Pha Rüang Mæn Kham Kha, Thao, 34
Còm Phao, Dòi, 247
Còm Ratchamonthianban, Khun, 172
Còm Sæo, 249
Còm Thòng, 206, 282, 284, 288
Còm Thòng, Dòi, 40
comedians, 102
comet, 177, 199
consecrated, 23, 33, 38, 46, 51, 66, 89, 91, 94, 95, 104, 107, 111, 122, 148, 180, 205, 227, 246, 257, 260, 262, 269, 279, 283
cook, 134, 150
coronation, 38, 45, 46, 147, 159, 163, 165, 173, 245, 246
corvée, 97
councilors, 86, 90, 98, 99, 101, 103, 104, 107
cowries, 52, 71, 80, 109, 156, 210
cremation, 293
crow's-wing defense [formation], 118, 136
crown, 50, 129, 147, 148, 159, 280, 287
Cu, Sæn, 159
Cüang, Cao Phraya, 32, 33
Cüang, Khun, 31, 34, 35
Cüang, King, 31, 32, 33, 34, 35, 45, 46
Cüang, M., 253, 256
Cumpa, Nai, 209
customs of rulers, 159

Dagon, 199, 200, 227
Dai, Ban, 47
Dam Phra Ai, Mün, 150, 156, 157, 158, 161

Dam Phra Han Tæ Thòng, Mün, 135, 147
Dam Phra Khot, Mün, 152, 156
Dam Phra Sai Na, 139
Dan Patu Hò, Mün, 172
Dang Lan, Mün, 170, 171
Dang Nung Khrai, 174
Dang Patu Hò, Sæn, 174
Dang Tao Kham, Mün, 162, 163
dang sip, 151
Dang, Mün, 162, 163, 170, 171
Dang, Phan, 168
Dang, Sæn, 174
Dap Nòi, Phan, 165
Dap Phai, Wat, 282
Deer City, 73
Dek Chai, Phraya, 243, 246
deposed, 9, 159, 167, 187
Devadahanagara, 21
Devadahasakka, 21
devaloka, 109
Devasukkarori, 275
devata, 71, 79, 119
Devila, 23
Dhamma, 23, 64, 76, 145, 206, 280, 287
Dhammapāla, 273
Dhammapaño, 193
Dharaṇi, Lady, 70
dharmaśāstra, 105
Din Khò Gate, 96
diplomats, 157
Disgusting River, 275
distilleries, 98
divinities, 98
Doctor Nò Kæo, 279
Dòi Ucsupabanphotagiri [Suthep], Wat, 257
Dòk Düa, King, 211
Dòk Kham, Wat, 269, 284
Dòn Fai, 211
Dòn Mun [island], 197
Dòn Thæn [island in the Mekong], 98, 99
Dòn Thæn, Wat, 119
donation, 71, 121, 160, 257
Dong Nakhòn, Mün, 136, 138, 139
Dong, Mün, 136, 137, 138, 139, 140, 141, 142, 152
dreams, 36, 113, 252
drum towers, 164
drum-beating ghost, 294
drummers, 136, 150
drums, 59, 82, 83, 98, 118, 137 243, 246, 262, 281, 289

drum smiths, 97
du, 147
düa kiang, 71
Duang Di, Wat, 283, 298
Duang Thip, Cao, 209, 213, 221
Duang, Cao, 195
ducks, 129, 216
dueling, 113
dysentery, 292

earlobe cutting, 219
ears pierced, 200
earthquake, 160, 169, 198, 200, 265
eclipse, planetary, 218
eclipse, solar, 196, 198, 227
eel, 283
ehibhikkhu ordination, 276
elephant combat, 161, 162
elephant doctor, 284
elephant-bells, 137
elephant-combat, 162
elephantry, 83, 85, 109, 128, 132, 137, 156, 162, 164, 168, 237, 254, 262
elephants, 28, 38, 42, 48, 49, 60, 61, 62, 66, 67, 69, 75, 78, 80, 81, 82, 83, 85, 87, 91, 92, 97, 98, 105, 107, 108, 113, 118, 124, 126, 127, 131, 133, 136, 152, 153, 158, 162, 163, 171, 172, 174, 176, 178, 181, 186, 216, 217, 224, 232, 240, 243, 251, 252, 253, 255, 261, 279, 284, 286, 287, 288, 296, 298
embassy, 164
Emerald Buddha, 173
envoys, 105, 142, 154, 155, 157, 168, 178, 179, 203, 206
exile, 42
Eyyara, 162

Fa, Lady, 265
Fa, Nai, 248
Fa Chiang Kham, Lady, 265
Fa Fün, Han, 203
Fa Kham Khrüang, 239, 241
Fa Kham Læp, 164
Fa Mæp, Han, 203
Fa Ngam, Han, 203
Fa Nòi Mot, 225
Fa Sang Kung, 189
Fa Yieo, 178
Fa Yòng Hui, 169
Fai Fa, Cao, 117, 154

Fang Kæn, 124, 168
Fang Kæn, Mün, 90
Fang Kæn Panna, 110, 111
Fang, M., 91, 96, 229, 244
Fang, Sæn, 163
fifty-seven domains, 19, 246, 252, 253, 263
fire, 118, 121, 129, 166, 200, 205, 214, 269
fire-flints, 141
firearms, 200
fireworks, 263, 283, 296
First Great Royal Merit-making Ceremony, 236
floods, 88
Flower Garden [Suan Dòk], 163
Fœi Rai, 181, 193
Fòm, M., 107
Fòng Samut Rajadevi, 295
Fòng Samut Ratchathewi, 295
Fòng Samut, Cao, 296
foreign affairs, 97
Forest Monks, 259
Fortune, Majesty, and Age gods of the domain, 119
foster-father, 195
Fountain-Water, Mount, 114
four poses, 155
Front Palace, 217, 220, 247, 252, 257, 260, 262, 279, 291, 296
Front Palace king of the South, 217
funeral, 35, 44, 103, 107, 163, 206, 293, 296
funerary rites, 94, 105

gajjaśāstra, 105
Gambhīra, Cao, 260
Gandhakuti, 68
gatekeeper, 93, 102, 134
Gates: city, 78, 91, 150, 158, 286. See also named gates: Chang Mòi, 292; Chiang Mai, 91; Chiang Rüak, 134, 174; Chiang Yün, 282; Din Khò, 96; Hai Ya, 284; Lai Khæng, 200; Mahawan, 171; Nòng Mut, 96; northern, 167, 175; Pæn, 148; Rai Ya, 191; Sæng Phung [i.e. Suan Prung] 171; Si Phum, 147; Sri Phum, 176; Suan Dòk, 91, 103; Suan Hè, 111; Tha Man, 96; Tha Nang, 162, 171; Tha Phæ, 211, 292, 297; White Elephant, i.e. Chang Phüak,

172, 191, 214, 237, 287, 289, 294, 298; Yang Thœn, 96
Gautama Buddha, 277
gemstones, 69
Glory of Two Cities, Phraya, 187–88
gold and silver, 43, 62, 92, 97, 99, 172, 175, 178, 213, 243, 246, 251, 270, 272, 280, 287, 292
gold, 32, 36, 109, 112, 145, 149, 187, 221, 232, 248, 252, 258, 263, 273, 278, 281, 288
Golden Mountain (Dòi Kham), 276
Golden Palace (Rong Kham), 53, 79, 119, 122, 125, 262, 264, 281, 289
Golden Pavilion, 154, 155
golden plates, 180
goldsmiths, 69, 288
gongs, 83, 87, 93, 102, 137, 243, 262, 281, 289
Gotama Buddha, 274
granaries, 88, 97, 199
Great Bodhi tree in Lanka, 70
Great Bodhi tree, 70, 71, 146, 160
Great Lampang Reliquary, 177
Great Reliquary of Hariphunchai, 228
Great Reliquary of Lamphun, 166, 235
Great Reliquary, 42, 166, 228, 282, 294, 298
groom, 102
guardian spirit-tree, 77
guardian spirits, 42, 78, 119, 120, 204, 205, 206
Gulawā, 263
guns, 118, 140, 191, 201, 203, 205, 218, 233, 241, 242, 249, 251, 271, 287
gunshot, 80, 206, 211, 239, 241, 268

Hæm, Ban, 72
Hæn, Ban, 72
Hai Ya Gate, 284
Hamsaraja, 242
Hamsavati, 65, 66, 71, 278
Han Nakhòn, Mün, 131
han dek chai, 135, 150
Hang, M., 141, 152, 163
Hang Dòn Mun, 97
Hang Ruang, 179
hani [magical letters], 243

Hao, Thao, 229
Hard (khæng) Canal, 55
Haribhuñjaya, M., 41, 42, 45, 47, 53, 258, 259
Hariphunchai, 43, 53, 54, 60, 61, 62, 80, 81, 100, 104, 228, 262
hasip ca La, 150
Hat Luang customs post, 97
headman, 134
Hin, M., 157
Hin, Mün, 157
Hin, Phraya, 164, 165
History of the Hò Attack, 120
history, 12, 13, 105, 299
Hò, 8, 33, 46, 96, 117, 118, 120, 153, 154, 155, 156, 159, 190, 198, 199, 210, 242, 263, 275
Hò Chai, 289, 299
hò cia kham lüang, 154
Hò domain, 210, 242
Hò Düa, 289, 299
Hò flutes, 87
Hò Kham, Cao, 1250, 251, 258, 267, 287, 289
Hò Kham, Somdet Phra Cao, 291
Hò language, 155
Hò Lum Fa Phao Phiman, Phraya, 33
Hò Muk, Cao Mæ Thao, 148, 151
Hò Phrakan, M., 32
hog-deer, 73, 74, 75, 77, 215, 286, 294
Holy Reliquary of Hariphunchai, 81
Holy Reliquary of Suthep, 173, 257
Hon, Ban, 280
Hon, M., 253, 256
Hon Nò, 266
horns, 137, 156, 215
horoscopes, 119, 286
horsemeat, 165
Hòt, M., 201, 212, 230
howdah, 187, 198, 214, 237, 253
Hsenwi, 233
Hua Fai Fon Sæn Ra, 297
Hua Khian, 161
Hua Khian, Mün, 168
Hua Khian, Phraya, 185
Hua Khian of Sæn Wi, Mün, 168
Hua Lin, 113
Hua Pong customs post, 97
Hua Rin, 171, 194, 289
Hua Rin corner, 282

Hua Sao, Ban, 248
Hua Süa, Ban, 211
Hua Wiang, Phraya, 175
Hua Wiang quarter, 166
Huai Hat, 171, 172
Huai Hok, 59
Huai Kæo, 298
Huai Som, 183

In, Cao, 247
In Kham, Lady, 265
In Müang, Cao, 191
Indadhipatiraja, 148
Indapatti, 24
Indavara, 24
Indavatti Dhammikarāja, 24
Indra, 25, 70, 119, 120, 236, 257, 277, 278, 286, 289, 293
Indrabrahma, 276
infantry, 156, 172, 176, 237
Ing, M., 133
Ing River, 52, 53, 54
Ing Sæ Min [Ein-she-min, the uparaja], King, 189
Ingsæ, 238
Ingsæ, King, 189
Ingsek, 238
Ingsœ, 238, 242
interpreter, 146, 147, 150, 155
Intha, *Sitkè*, 197
Inthakhin, 282, 286, 291
Inthakhin, Wat, 236, 251
Inthakhin Hall, 240
Inthakhin Pillar, 286, 294
Inthakhiri, Phraya, 234
Inthapat, Cao, 238
Intharacha, 135, 136, 138, 139, 142
Inthasaket, Müang, 278
Inthasiri, Thao, 241
intoxication, 93
Iron and Golden Bridges, 254
iron forges, 98
iron, 118
ironsmiths, 69
irrevocable gift, 124
Isananerajapuri, 77
Ivory Buddha, 262
ivory, 36, 83, 97, 156, 221, 252, 262, 287

Jālanandāla, 23
Jālī, 21, 22
Jambu Continent, 23, 25, 146, 147

Jayasena, 21
Jayavaranagara, 25, 26
jewelers, 69
jewels, 66, 148
Jeyyalangkā, Cao, 292
Jeyyanagara, 73
Jeyyasen Lakhòn Puri, M., 249
Jeyyasena Rakkhapuri Chiang Sæn, M., 247
Jeyyawong, Cao Khanan, 268
Jinadhātu Relic, 283
Jotikāram, Wat, 287
Jotikaram Ceti Luang, Wat, 283
judges, 97, 123
Jupiter, 177, 198, 218
Jyestha, 91

Ka, M., 245
Kaccāyanā, 21
Kachin, 113
Kæ, Mün, 176
Kæn, M., 283
Kæn Phongsa, King, 45, 46
Kæn Phongsa, Thao, 45
Kæn Thao, King, 129, 140
Kæn Thao, Phraya, 128
Kæo, 31, 32, 33, 34, 35, 45, 46, 123
Kæo, King, 160, 161, 162, 163, 164, 165
Kæo, M., 172
Kæo, Mün, 126, 168
Kæo, Mün, of Chiang Khòng, 82
Kæo, Phraya, 164
Kæo, Sæn, 243
Kæo, Thao, 230
Kæo Kañña, Lady, 256
Kæo Kling, Dòi, 176
Kæo Mano, Mün, 173
Kæo Müang Ma, Cao, 291, 292, 297
Kæo Nakhòn, Mün, 127
Kæo Phrakan, 35, 46
Kæo Phutadipatiraja, King, 160
kæsan, 180
Kæt Læng, 132
Kai, Ban, 253
Kai, M., 191, 258
Kai, Phraya, 163, 270
Kai Dam banyan tree, 193
Kai Sam Thao, M., 96
Kakkattha'apo, 74
kalakini, 159
Kāladevila, 21
Kālasoka, 23, 24

Kālāsoka, 23
Kali Age, 288
Kali Epoch, 174
Kalinga, King, 119
Kalyāṇa, 20
Kam Mæng Khrüa, 179
Kam Mæng Phrom, 178
kambalahatthi, 284
kamnak, 112
Kampha, Nai, 223
Kamphæng Müang, Phraya, 256, 257
Kamphængphet, 135, 161, 162, 230, 295
Kamphængphet, Mün, 171, 172
Kamphængphet, Phraya, 214
Kamphon, Phraya, 180, 182
Kan, Phraya, 163
Kan Thom, 64, 66, 67, 68, 100
Kan Thom [officiant], 100
Kan Thom, Wat, 68, 69, 71, 109
Kan Thom *vihara*, 68
Kang, 114
Kang, M., 267
Kangli, 48
Kannika Well, 179
Kao [people of Nan], 100, 101
Kao, Thao, 31, 32, 46
Kao Cha, Thao, 31, 32
Kao Chòng [Nine Passes] district, 163
Kapilavatta, 23
Kapilavatthu, 21
Kapilavātthu, 21
Karaniban [*sutta*], 232
Karen, 225
Karen Khang Hua Tat, 225
Karādaranandārājacakapatti, 21
Kasæ, 197
Kassapa, 20, 273, 274
Kassappa, Prince, 273
Kat Du, 182
Kat Thom, Wat, 71
Kat Thuam, Wat, 64
Katham corner, 282
Kawila, Cao Khanan, 209
Kawila, Cao, 201, 210, 211, 212, 213, 214, 215, 216, 219, 220, 221, 222, 223
Kawila Nòi, Cao, 233
Keng Tung, 10, 164, 205, 231; *see also* Chiang Tung
Kesalapañño, *khruba*, 285
Kesalapañño, Phra Mahāthera, 298

Ket, King, 165, 166, 167
Ket, Wat, 192, 246, 257
Ket Chettharat, King, 168, 169
Ket Landing, Wat, 192
Kha, Ban, 27
Kha Kan, Thao, 152, 153, 154, 155
Kha Sam Thao, 257
Kha Thap, Mün, 153
Khachāng, 60
Khæk Cheyyamongkhon, Sæn, 173
Khæk Phuttima, Cao Phraya, 179
Khæk Sai, Mün, 178
Khæm, Ban, 242
Khæn, 60
Khæn, M., 60
Khæng U Min-gyi, 230
Khæng, *Sitkè*, 214
Khak, M., 245
Khalaho, 161
Kham, Dòi, 80, 81, 82, 276
Kham, Lady, 205, 209
Kham Chang, 60
Kham Fan, Cao, 209
Kham Fu, 95, 99, 100, 101, 103
Kham Fu, Cao Phraya, 101
Kham Fu, Cao Thao, 95
Kham Fu, Phraya, 99, 100, 101, 102, 103
Kham Kæn, Thao, 250
Kham Khai, Mün, 161
Kham Khrüang, Cao Fa, 241
Kham Khün, 82
Kham Lòt, 150
Kham Lü, Cao, 268
Kham Lü, Nai, 210
Kham Mu, 184
Kham Mun, Cao, 233, 239, 264, 266, 268, 271, 280
Kham Mun, Nai, 210, 223, 229, 231
Kham Pha, 205
Kham Pha, Mün, 164
Kham Pha, Nai, 209
Kham Phuak, Müang, 150
Kham Ròng, 41
Kham Rüang, Cao Sæn, 117
Kham Som, Cao, 209, 210, 212, 213, 221
Kham Sòn, Nai, 209
Kham Wang, Mün, 291
Kham Wang, Nai, 290
Kham Wang, Thao, 265–66
Kham Yat, Mün, 126

Kham Yòt Fa, 164
Khamani, 207, 210
Khamani, Prince, Nemyo 199
Khan district, 122
Khan, 126, 165, 168
Khan, M., 253
Khan, Mün, 240
Khan, Mün, who ruled Fang Kæn district, 124
Khan, Sæn, 122
Khang Sæn Luang, 225
Khang, M., 253
Khantha, Lady, 228
Khantha, Mün, 242
Khao Hò, Sæn, 61
Khao Khæn Lan, Mün, 170
Khao San Plain, 91
Khap Phræ, Mün, 176
Khateng, M., 268
Khattiya, Nai, 209
Khattiya, Sæn, 226
Khattiyawong, 191
Khelang, 61, 81, 85
Khelang Lakhòn, 79
Khem, M., 94, 164, 165
Khem, Mün, 114
Khem people, 164
Khemarattha Tungkhaburi [Keng Tung], 164, 244
Khi Hut, Cao, 196
Khi Lek [Stream], 206
Khi Ya Fa, 56
Khlang, M., 230
Khò, 245
Khœn, 194, 243
Khòk Müang Hò Kham, Mün, 174
Khòk Si Anocha, Cao, 220
Khòm, Mün, 125
Khòn Müang Rajasena, Phya, 250
Khòn Müang, Phraya, 266
Khòng, M., 253
Khrai, Mün, 170, 174
Khrai Mòng Yian, Mün, 170
Khram, Cao Khun, 41
Khram, Cao Phraya, 86, 87, 88, 89
Khram, Khun, 43, 88
Khram, Phraya, 85, 86
Khram, Prince, 80, 81, 82, 83
Khrao, Sæn, 167, 168, 173
Khrao Ai, Phan, 145, 146
Khrao Nanthakhiri, Cao Sæn, 172
Khrao Pheri, Sæn, 173
Khrao Ton Hua, 183
khrò, 291, 293, 294
Khròk Ngua, 205

Khròm, Mün, 172
Khròng, M., 163
Khrüa, Cao Khun, 41, 89, 90, 91, 94, 175
Khrüa, Khun, 44, 89, 90, 92, 93
Khrüa, Phraya, 91, 92, 93
Khruan, Mün, 172
Khrüang, Cao Khun, 43
Khrüang, Khun, 40, 43, 44, 88, 89
khruba, 131, 285
Khüa, Mün, 114
Khüan, Phraya, 256, 270
Khüan, Sæn, 243
Khuang Phlao Buddha footprint, 284
Khui, 123, 245
khum, 97
khun, 28, 42, 53, 173
Khun Fa, 53, 55, 62
khun lam, 256
Khun Luang Nakhòn, Mün, 174
Khun Phu beach, 52
Khun Phu River, 52
Khuppasiha, General, 199
Khuppha Thihapate, General, 201
Khwa, Mün, 132, 161
Khwa Dong Phalæo, 97
Khwa Sük, Mün, 132
Khwa Yan, 176
Khwæn, Mün, 152
Khwan of the Elephant Stables, Sæn, 197
Khwang, Mün, 239, 242
Kiang, Ban, 208
Kin, 29
King, M., 151
king, 296
Kip, M., 157
Kip, Mün, 157
Kitti, M., 226
Kiu Khang Wai Nòng Ngua, 97
Kiu Khò Ma, 96
Kimnavasanti, 21
Kīnavasanti, 23
Klai Rüang, 181
Klamphængphekphon, 127
Klang, Ban, 178
Klang, Phraya, 170
Klang Chiang, 159
Klük Kla, 197
Ko Thao, 136
kò, 97
Kò, M., 229, 267
Kœng Tin Chiang, Mün, 132, 135, 142, 147

Kok River, 40
Koleyya, 23
Kom, Lady, 215, 220, 223
Kòm, Ban, 211
Kòn Kæo, Nai, 209
Kòng, Mün, 152
Kòng Cò, 211
Kòng Lom, 195
Krom Phraratchawang Bòwònsathanmongkhon, 220
Krommasak, Caofa, 290
Krungthep Mahanakhòn Si Ayutthiya, 247
Ku Kham [area], 171
Ku Kham *cetiya*, 63
Ku [i.e. Chedi] Luang, Wat, 119
Ku Rüang, 194
Ku Rüang corner, 284
Ku Rüang Fort, 169
Kü, M., 168
Kü (or Khüi), M., 123
Kü Han Tæ Thòng, Mün, 123, 124
Kü Na, 105, 109
Kü Na, Cao Phò Thao, 103
Kü Na, Cao Phraya, 104, 105
Kü Na, Cao Thao, 105
Kü Na, King, 55, 107, 109, 117
Kü Na, Phò Thao, 104
Kü Na, Thao, 104
Kuai, Cao, 194
Kuai, Phraya, 197
Kuang River, 55
Küang, M., 249
Kuei Siang, 208
Kuei Siang Muk, 208
Kukkutantaseda Phrahma Khelangkha Nagara Jeyyasukhavati, M., 262
Kum Kam, 16, 62, 63, 64, 68, 69, 71, 72, 77, 80, 81, 82, 83, 87, 89, 91, 95, 106, 110, 171
Kum Kam Bridge, 67
Kum Kam Market, 63
Kumbhamitta, King, 277
Kumbhamitta, Phraya, 273
Kumbhamittanagara, 273
Kumbhamittarāja, 273
Kumbhanda, 240
Kumārayak, 273, 274, 277
Kun, M., 239, 241
Küng, M., 239, 241
Kup, M., 151
Kururattha, 277, 278
Kururatthanagara, 277

Kusinara, 174
Kusinārāi, 277
Kusāvatti, 20
kuti, 105, 146, 240, 280
Kwa, Mün, 176
Kwan Phayao, 52

La, *hasip ca*, 150
La, M., 253, 254, 266
La Na Pho, M., 254
La Nam, 275
La-hta, 212
Lacquer Palace, 198
lacquers, 98
Læ Nara, Min, 191
Læm, M., 250, 267
Lagna, 74, 79, 96, 169, 282
Lahæng, M., 218, 271
Lai, M., 39, 151
Lai Hka, 198
Lai Kha, M., 151
Lai Khæng Gate, 200
Laka, 150
Lakhòn [Lampang], M., 238, 258, 279
Lam Bun, 158
Lam, Mün, 147
Lam Khæk, Mün, 177, 179
Lam Khæk, Phan, 158
Lam Khæk Kassapa, Phan, 158
Lam Khæk Sai, Mün, 179
Lam Kham Nòi, 158
Lam Mün Sai Phrao, 162
Lam Mün Sai Udom, 162
Lam Na Pan Songkhram, Phan, 129
Lam Pan Songkhram, Phan, 129
Laming, 281
Lampang Luang, 208
Lampang, M., 186, 187, 194, 198, 201, 202, 206, 208, 214, 215, 264; *see also* Lakhòn
Lampang, Ban, 215
Lampang, Wat, 204
Lamphun, M., 10, 24, 59, 62, 76, 80, 81, 87, 125, 168, 170, 171, 183, 185, 194, 196, 197, 198, 202, 206, 210, 219, 231, 235, 238, 264, 266, 267, 268, 269
Lamphun, Mün,170
Lamphun, Phraya, 185
Lamphun, Sæn, 173
Lamphun Reliquary, 199
Lan Chang, 34, 46, 153, 154, 168, 170, 172, 174, 175, 182, 185, 186, 192, 211

Lan Na, 1, 7, 9, 65, 66, 69, 70, 120, 153, 154, 155, 156, 186, 190, 211, 227, 252, 253, 254, 263, 272
Lan Na Chiang Mai, 224
Lan Na Thai, 11, 25, 180, 198, 202, 207, 211, 243, 246
Lan Sang, *see* Lan Chang
Lan Sapo, 207
lan palm, 218
lances, 140, 171, 172, 243
Langka, 70
Langka, Khanan, 208
language, 1, 10, 153
Lao, 27, 31, 32, 45, 46, 62, 186, 190, 195, 197, 208, 210, 211
Lao Cakkrarat, 27, 46
Lao Chang, 26, 28, 38
Lao Chang, Cao, Grandfather, 39
Lao Chün, 31, 32, 35
Lao Chün, Khun, 31
Lao Cong, 30, 31
Lao Cong [Cangkaracha], Grandfather, 38, 40
Lao domain, 208, 210, 211
Lao Kao, 27, 28
Lao Kao, Grandfather, 40
Lao Kao, King, 28
Lao Kao Kæo Ma Müang, 27, 28
Lao Kap, 28, 29
Lao Khiang, 29
Lao Khòp, 27, 28
Lao Khòp, Cao, 38
Lao Khriang, Grandfather, 40
Lao Khriu, 29
Lao Khròp, 26, 41
Lao Kin, 29
Lao Kom, 28
Lao Kòp, 38
Lao Kuak, 29, 30
Lao Kün, 29
Lao Kwin, 30
Lao Læ, 28
Lao Meng, 36
Lao Meng, Cao, 36, 38
Lao Meng, King, 37
Lao Ming, 35
Lao Mœng, 36
Lao Mœng, Cao, 36
Lao Ngœn Bun Rüang, 32
Lao Ngœn Rüang, 33, 35
Lao Sao, 28
Lao Som, 29
Lao Tang, 28
Lao Thœng, 29

Lao Thüng, 29
Lao Ton, 29
laterite, 112
Lavaraṭṭha, 46
Lavo, 24
Lavo *vihara*, King of, 239
Lawa, 113, 157, 218, 237, 254, 275, 276, 289
Lawacakkradevaputta, 25
Lawacangkara, 25
Lawacangkarat, 19, 90
Lawacangkarat, King, 26, 38, 82
Lawacangkarattharacha, 26
Lawacangkraracha, 28
Lawarāja, 45
Lawo, Mün, 170
Lawo Buddha Image, 235
lawsuits, 51
Laṅka, 24
Lek, M., 250
Len, M., 97, 191, 243, 267, 270
Len Nüa, M., 97
Len Tai, M., 97
Leng, M., 297
Lesser Era, 26, 38, 40
letter, 125, 148, 229, 238, 290, 291
letters, anonymous, 148
Li, M., 89, 212, 238
Li, Mün, 161
Li Chiang Phra [i.e., Wat Phra Sing], Wat, 104
Li Chiang Phra, 104
Li Gate [of Lamphun], 171
Li Hui, Grandmother, 283
life-extending techniques, 146
lightning, 120, 248, 285
Lin Kan, Thao, 203, 204, 206, 207, 208
Lingka, Khanan, 208
lion characteristics, 147
lion, 113, 224, 249, 258
Lisisivivāhana, 21
Lò, 128
Lò, M., 219, 245
Lok Nakhòn, Mün, 122, 123
Lok Sam Lan, Cao Mün, 126
Lok Sam Lan, Mün, 123, 124, 125
Lòk Còk, M., 151
Lok, Cao Phraya, 112
Lok, Cao Thao, 124
Lok, Mün, 107, 122, 123
Lok, Thao, 120, 121, 124
Lokamoli, Wat, 166, 167, 169
Lom Phu Nòng Bua, 219
Lomphu Nòng Bua, 296

Lòng, M., 133, 203, 211, 267, 269
Lord Albino Mouse Spirit, 78
Lord Kassappa, 277
Lord Sudorasi, 240
Lü, 130, 180, 194, 195, 243, 266
Lü, M., 249
Lü Chai, Chao Phraya, 174
Lü Chai, Phraya, 173, 176
Lü Chai Kamphæng, Thao, 266
Lü Chai Sena, Phraya, 176
Lü domains, 139, 254
Luai, M., 180, 248, 250, 253, 254, 266, 267
Lüak, M., 132
Luang, M., 189, 253, 256
Luang, Mün, 156, 176
Luang, Phraya, 256
Luang Bò Ræ, M., 96
Luang Ca Ban, Cao Mün, 172
Luang Ca Ban, Mün, 163
Luang Can, 290
Luang Chai, Phraya, 256
Luang Chan Nòk, Mün, 166
Luang Chiang, Mün, 156
Luang Kæo, Phraya, 256
Luang Kham Lü, Phraya, 256
Luang Lam Khæk Ñanakitti, Cao Mün, 172
Luang Lam Khæk, Mün, 172, 173
Luang Lampang, Wat, 202, 203, 262
Luang Lamphun Canal, 297
Luang Man Than, 100
Luang Mit, 170
Luang Phom, 295
Luang Phran, Cao Mün, 173
Luang Phran, Mün, 172
Luang Phukha, M., 229
Luang Phuttha, Cao Mün, 172
Luang Prabang, 130, 152
Luang Sadü Müang, Wat, 259
Luang Thippharaksa, 290
luk panna, 157
Lum Fa, Cao, 46, 117, 118, 153, 154, 155, 156
Lum Fa Phao Phiman, Cao, 32, 33, 46, 117
lunar eclipse, 227

Ma [La?], M., 245
Ma, M., 253, 270
Ma, Mün, 122, 138, 141, 148, 176
Ma Ho, Dòi, 164
Ma Kham Wæng, Mün, 132
Ma Thao, Dòi, 150

Mæ Cæm, 71
Mæ Chan, 45
Mæ Chok, 160
Mæ Kha, 77, 288
Mæ Kham, 269
Mæ Khua Dæng, 218
Mæ Khun Phu, 52
Mæ Ki, Wat, 179
Mæ Ku, Cao Thao, 175, 183
Mæ Ku, King, 15, 175, 176, 177, 178, 179, 180, 181, 183
Mæ Lai, 247
Mæ Laming, 215
Mæ Lawa, 29
Mæ Li, 219, 223
Mæ Lim, 280
Mæ Ngao, 281
Mæ Pa, Ban, 226
Mæ Pa Pha Ku, 225
Mæ Phik, 272
Mæ Phlao, 182
Mæ Phra, 196
Mæ Ping, 77, 114
Mæ Raming, 62, 77, 287
Mæ Rawan, 272
Mæ Ròng Chang, 48
Mæ Sa, 280
Mæ Sæo, 62
Mæ Sai, 25, 29
Mæ Saklit, 215
Mæ Sòi, 230
Mæ Ta, 170
Mæ Tha, 224
Mæ Thao Hò Muk, 148, 151
Mæ Thu, 77, 95, 150
Mæ Tœm, 96
Mæ Yuak, 73
Mæn, 195
Mæn Kham, Thao, 128
Mæn Khun, Thao, 128, 129
Mæn Ta Thòk, 35, 46
Mæn Ta Thòk Khòk Fa Ta Yün, 34, 46
Mæng Rong Po, 195
Māghadevacakkavatti, 20
magical arts, 49, 52, 119, 143, 146
magical pillar, 148
magical power, 50, 147
magical sciences, 49
Maha Akkharamahesi Ratchathewi, 296
Maha Anandathera, 274
Maha Chedi Luang, 152, 156
Maha Pa Dòn Thæn, 188
Maha Phrom, Cao Phò Thao, 107

Maha Phrom, Cao Thao, 106, 108
Maha Phrom, Phò Thao, 104, 105, 107
Maha Phrom, Thao, 106, 107, 108
Maha Setahatthi Suwannapathumā Lord of the White Elephant and the Golden Lotus, King, 282
Maha Suphathra, King, 286, 287, 288, 290, 291, 294, 295
Maha Suriyawongsa, 272
Maha Thep, 284
Maha Uparaja, 295
Maha Yak, Thao, 239, 242
Mahadhamma, 190
Mahadhamma Phukam, 189
Mahantayasa, 24
Mahantayot, 87
Mahaphon, Wat, 165
Maharishi, 87
mahathewi, 110
Mahawan Gate, 171
Mahawong, Cao, 253, 285, 286, 291, 292, 295, 297
Mahawong, Cao Khanan, 268, 270
Mahawong, Khanan, 269
Mahawong Maha Uparaja, Cao, 296
Mahawong Uparaja, Cao, 295
Mahawongsa Maha Uparaja, Cao, 297
Mahawongsa, 248
Mahayot, Cao Khanan, 268
Mahayot, Thao, 203, 204
Mahayot Luang, Cao, 202
Mahin, Mün, 158, 167
Mahindathera, 23
Mahiyangkharatthapuri, 259
Mahiyaṅgaratthapuri [M. Yòng], M., 252
Mahā Abhayaculathera, 104
Mahā Anandathera, 23, 274
Mahā Chedi Luang, 169
Mahā Chedi Luang, Wat, 160
Mahā Chiraprapha, Queen, 168
Mahā Mæ Mak Lœk, Mün, 179
Mahā Mongkhon, Ban, 163
Mahā Ñāṇathera, 158
Mahā Phutthima, 179
Mahā Sangharaja Pussadeva, 160
Mahā Sri Sadhammarāja, 122
Mahā That, Mün, 170
Mahā-acsimarāja, 20
Mahākassapa, 64, 66, 68

Mahākassapathera Temple, 66
Mahākassapathera, 68
Mahākassappa, 23
Mahāmeru, 20
Mahāmucalin, 20
Mahāpanāda, 20
Mahāpattāpa, 20
Mahārāja, 66
Mahāsakkarat, 279
Mahāsamantarāja, 20, 21
Mahāsameyyasutta, 232
Mahāsra, 77
Mahāsuddassana, 20
Mahāswāmī, 111
Mahāthan Landing, 167
Mahāthera, 64, 70, 119, 120, 121, 131, 142, 158
Mahāyak, 273, 274, 275
Mai Hò, 267
Mai, Sæn, 101
mai du fine timber, 98
mai düa kiang—a Burmese word for a large saphan tree, 64
Mak Kham, Mün, 114
Mak San, 215
Mala, Mün, 161, 162
Mala, Phraya, 226, 228
Man of Merit, 202, 203
Mandhātu, 20
Mang, M., 242, 253
Mangala Field, 240
Manglai, Cao, 37
Mangra Wachiraprakan Kamphæng Kæo, Cao Phraya, 223
Mangrai, Cao, 59, 62, 63, 86, 253
Mangrai, King, 12, 19, 38, 39, 40, 41, 42, 43, 44, 45, 46, 47, 51, 52, 53, 55, 56, 59, 60, 61, 62, 63, 64, 65, 66, 67, 68, 69, 70, 71, 72, 73, 74, 75, 76, 77, 78, 79, 80, 81, 86, 87, 88, 89, 90, 91, 100, 119, 147, 159, 175, 179, 180
Mano, Mün, 168
Mano, Phraya, 208, 209
Māra, 299
mārapakkha, 214
market, 63, 90, 100, 104, 113, 134, 151, 165
market landing, 99
Mars, 200
Martaban, 199, 215, 216, 291
marvel, 70, 71, 73, 77
Mat City, 72

matchlocks, 151
mattress, 155
Maung Cha, Nakhan, 267, 268, 269
Maung Myo, 205
Maung Pæ, 291, 292
Maung Wiang, 227
Maung, Nai, 201
mayang churawa, 75
Mekong River, 45, 95, 120, 161, 249
Meng, 36, 37, 71
Meng Garuda, 127
merchants, 109, 274
Meru, 20
messenger, 97, 102, 158
messenger for the judiciary, 97
Metta-āsana-natiyasutta, 120
Mi Khòng, Lady, 239
miggindasiharāja images, 240
military arts, 87
military commander, 159
Min Sala, King, 190
Min Taya, King, 181, 188
Mina-apo *rasi*, 74
mīna-āpo rasi, 282
Ming, Khun, 35
miracle, 70
Mit, M., 178
Mithilā, 20
Mittabhubabha, 23
Mò, M., 203
Mò Ban Lòng, 149
Mò Chuang Na, 149
Mò Khæn, 149
Mò Puk, 226
Mò Yi, M., 181
moat, 62, 63, 75, 78, 79, 81, 95, 107, 133, 146, 147, 169, 170, 192, 224, 240, 261, 284, 298
Mœng, Khun, 35
Mòk Lòng, Mün, 125, 127
Mòk Lòng, Mün, of Phayao, 127
Mokkhalāna, 70
Mokso, 233
Moksobo, 197
Moksobomyo, 233
Mòm Can, 265
Mon, Mün, 158
Mòn, Phan, 177
Mon Chiang Rai, Mün, 158
Mon Country, 65, 66
monastic requisites, 142, 287, 288, 296
Mòng, Nai, 211

Mongkhon, 125, 136
monkey, 102
monkhood, 121, 196, 203, 237, 253, 289
monks, 71, 103, 142, 160, 172, 205, 210, 232, 236, 240, 259, 261, 262, 276, 286, 289, 298, 299
Mons, 71, 210
moon, 74, 96, 128, 131, 152, 162, 198, 218, 248, 286, 294
Mòp, M., 38
Moraya, 23
mother, 73, 74, 77, 110, 111, 137, 217
Moulmein, 216
mountain people, 218
Mu La, Cao, 209, 221, 266
Müang, Cao Sæn, 250
Müang, Mün, who ruled Tha Kan, 124
Müang Kham Khai Fa, Thao, 160
Müang Ma, Sæn, 110, 239
Müang Mahin, Cao, 163
Müang Sai, Cao, 97
Mucalin, 20
Mucalinda, 20
Mukkha, 22
Mukkharāja, 22
Mün, 123, 126, 152, 161
Mün San, Wat, 164
Mung, Thao, 49, 50
munitions, 97
music, 262, 281
muskets, 214
Müt Ka, Ban, 294
Mutu, 271
myowun, 210

Na, Ban, 239, 242
Na Fak, Phraya, 258
Na Khwa, 191, 229, 248, 249, 251
Na Khwa, Cao, 195
Na Nò, 266
Na Sai, 191
Na Yang, 202
Na Yang, Wat, 202
Nabbapuri Sri Nagara Chiang Mai, 79
Nabbapurī Srī Biṅgajaiya Chiang Mai, 19
Næn, M., 227
Nagadāsaka, 22
nagaraguṇa, 77
Nai, M., 90, 91, 150, 151, 163, 164, 168, 169, 175, 176, 177, 178

Nakharat, 255
Nakhòn [Lampang], 107, 141, 183
Nakhòn, Mün, 132
Nakhòn, Phraya, 175
Nakhòn Khelang [Lampang], 85, 107
Nakhòn Khun Luang, Cao, 164
Nakhòn Pa Sang, 231
Nakhòn Ratchasima, 296
Nakhòn Si Fa, Phraya, 177
Nam Bò Kæng Hòi, 162
Nam Khan, 165
Nam Lüm, 131
Nam Mæ Phathang, 216
Nam Mò, 183
Nam Ram, 151
Nam Ta, 183
Nam Thuam, 94
Nam Thuam, Cao Phò, 92
Nam Thuam, Cao Phò Thao, 92, 93, 94
Nam Thuam, Phò Thao, 88, 91, 92, 93, 94
Nam Thuam, Thao, 88, 92
Nam Un, 182
Nam Yang, 182
Namawong, Cao, 256
Nan Kao, 100
Nan Naratha, Nai, 269
Nan River, 128
Nan, M., 100, 152, 153, 157
Nan, Phraya, 187
Nandapuri [Nan], 34, 46
Nang Hæng, Mün, 142
Nangsü, Cao Mün, 170
Nangsü, Mün, 171
Nangsü, Sæn, 203
Nangsü Luang, Mün, 168, 170
Nantha, Cao, 259, 266, 267, 268
Nantha Kòi Tò, 185
Nanthachit, 179
Nantharam, Wat, 145
Nanthasen, Cao, 266, 267, 268
Nanthasen, Nai, 209, 223
Nanthasena, Cao, 267, 268
Naret, King, 185
navels of the city, 286
Ne Tæk, *Care*, 192
Ne Thæk, *Care*, 192
Merañjarā River, 22
Net-Fence City, 72
New Village (Ban Mai), 62
New Year, 71, 74, 88, 179, 259, 269, 271, 292, 297
new era, 21, 23, 24, 25

Nga, M., 251, 266, 267
ngæ, 147
Ngæ, M., 101
Ngæ district, 123
Ngæ Ngao, 114
Ngam Müang, King, 47, 48, 49, 50, 51, 52, 75, 76, 79
Ngao, M., 181
Ngao Kao, M., 138
Ngao Kao, Mün, 128
Ngat, M., 253
Ngim, M., 253
Ngœn, Mün, 130
Ngœn Pòng Fa, 151
Ngœn Rüang, Cao Khun, 34
Ngœn Rüang, Cao, 33
Ngœn Rüang, Khun, 31
Ngœn Rüang, King, 35
Ngœn Yang, M., 26, 38, 40
Ngua, Cao Phò Thao, 94
Ngua, Khun, 100
Ngua, Phò Thao, 91, 105
Ngua, Thao, 88, 94, 120
Ngua Hong, 101, 102, 103
Ngua Lai, 239, 242
Ngua Lai, Ban, 239
Ngua Thœng, Cao, 104
Ngua Thœng, Phò Thao, 105
Ni Wun, 190
Niriya Hell, 232
Nò, M., 267
Nò Cao Müang, Thao, 253
Nò Kæo Kiang Kham, Lady, 253
Nò Kæo Ubonlawanna, Lady, 255
Nò Kæo Yòt Còm Müang, Lady, 256
Nò Kham, Cao Fa, 229
Nò Kham Fa, 187
Nò Longka, Cao Nai, 266
Nò Müang, Cao, 190
Nò Sai, 190
Nœk, Ban, 85
Nòi, *Care*, 203
Nòi, M., 148, 165, 167
Nòi, Mün, 139, 172, 177
Nòi Chawana, Nai, 228, 234
Nòi Chiang Rüak, Mün, 172
Nòi China Khao, 226
Nòi Chumphu, Nai, 211
Nòi Cumphu, Nai, 211
Nòi Kæo, Mün, 177
Nòi Kawila, Cao, 233
Nòi Kawila, Cao Nai, 268, 269, 270
Nòi Kawila, Nai, 210, 223, 229, 231

Nòi Kham Wongsa, Cao Nai, 266, 267, 269
Nòi Khòn Thòng, Nai, 215
Nòi Kòn Kæo, Nai, 214
Nòi Langka, Cao Nai, 269
Nòi Maha Phom, Cao Nai, 266
Nòi Maha Thep, Cao Nai, 268
Nòi Mahaphom, Cao Nai, 268, 269
Nòi Mano, Phraya, 208
Nòi Phom, *Sitkè*, 199, 211
Nòi Phung, 194
Nòi Somtamit, 214
Nòi Supha, Nai, 228, 234
Nòi Tha, 204, 206
Nòi Tham, 206, 207
Nòi Tham, Nai, 203
Nòi Thammalangka, Cao, 209
Nòi Tòn Tò, Nai, 215
Nòi Wisut, 195
Nòi Withun, Nai, 214
Nòi Wong, Nai, 239
nokkok gun, 257
Nòng An, 114
Nòng Bòn, 182
Nòng Bòn, M., 151
Nòng Chang Khlan Field, 297
Nòng Khwang, 193
Nòng Khwang, M., 166
Nòng Lom, Ban, 123
Nòng Lòng, 206, 208, 210, 211, 218
Nòng Muan, 193
Nòng Muan field, 171
Nòng Mut Gate, 96
Nòng Pha Chi, 106
Nòng Pha Di, 106
Nòng Pha Tæp field, 168
Nòng Phai, 114
Nòng Phak Wun Min Taya, King, 186, 187
Nòng Ram, 184
Nòng Sæn Thòn, 114
Nòng Sæn Thòn Sòn, 114
Nòng Sæn Tò Plain, 92
Nòng Sakün district, 279
Nòng Tang, 63
Nòng Tao, 112
Nòng Ya, 171
Nòng Yai, 77
Nopburi Si Chiang Mai, 90
North Gate, 92
northern gate, 167, 175
novices ordained, 188
nuan banana, 281

Nun, 132
Nun, M., 242
Nung, M., 245

Ò, Ban, 256
Ò, M., 253
oath, 51, 178, 201, 289
oath of loyalty, 178
oath-taking, 52
observation tower, 78, 112, 164, 224, 261
offerings, 52, 78, 129, 204, 277, 281
ogress, aquatic, 102
Òi, Mün, 128
Okākamukkha, 21
Okākarāja, 21
Old Era, 21
Old Man Tong, 281
Om Sik, Ban, 233
Omens, 166, 177, 199, 292
Òng, Khun, 44
Ong Kham, Cao, 192, 193, 194, 195, 197, 202, 207
Ong Khwan Kham, 100, 101
Ong Nok, 192
Ong Nok, Cao, 192
Ong Thip, Lady, 194
Òng Cheyya, Phraya, 196, 197
Òng Cheyya Nòng Tò, Phraya, 197
oracle, chicken-bone, 99
orchestra, 262
ordeal by water, 208
ordination, 163, 172, 176
ordination rafts, 160

Pa Dæng Suthep, Wat, 283
Pa Kæo, 205
Pa Khet, Wat, 169
Pa Khòng, 272
Pa Kò, Dòi, 127
Pa Lao, 182
Pa Mòk, 196
Pa Sang, M., 226, 273
Pa Sieo, 182
Pa Sòi Palace, 272
Pa Tan, Wat, 169
Pa Than Khum Müang, 202
Pa Yai, 181
Pæn Gate, 148
pæng, 134
Pæt, Thao, 120
Pagân, 109, 143, 145
Pagân Min-gyi, 226

Pagân monk Mang Lung Lwang, 146, 147, 148
Pagân Temple, 146
page, 135, 136
painter, 155
Pajāpattīgotamī, 21
Pak Lat, 272
Pak Phieo, 220
Pak Yom, 131
Pak Yom, M., 131
palace, 32, 53, 56, 62, 76, 78, 79, 88, 93, 98, 141, 147, 166, 173, 201, 224, 286, 287, 290, 298
palace elephant corps, 167
palace elephantry, 168
Pan, M., 89. 151, 178, 229, 283
Pan Chomphu, 136
Pan Phing, Wat, 284
Pan Phon Sæn, Phan, 85
Pan Songkhram, 129
Paña, 254
Pang Chang, 151
Pang Pa, 255
Pang Sang, 251, 267
panna, 71, 80, 97, 110, 151, 168, 199, 211
Paññajira, Cao, 288
Panāda, 20
parittamaṅgala, 259, 286, 289, 299
Parittamaṅgalasutta, 293
Pat, Cao, 196
paternal grandmother, 166
Pathum, Dòi, 176
Pattāpa, 20
Patu Hò, Mün, 170
Patu Sop Sai, 50
Patu Suk Sai, 50
Patung, 234
Pegu, 65, 145, 177, 178, 179, 180, 181, 183, 184, 185, 186, 187, 188, 194
Pha, Raja, 265
Pha Dæng Chiang Khòng, M., 41
Pha Khao, Wat, 237, 285
Pha Khao ("White Turban") *panna*, 199, 211
Pha Lai, Dòi, 124
Pha Lao, 27
Pha Lat Luang, 115
Pha Lat Luang, Dòi, 113
Pha Nòng, Cao Sæn, 106, 107, 113
Pha Nòng, Sæn, 100, 101, 106, 107
Pha Rao, Ban, 28

INDEX   311

Pha Rao, Mount, 40
Pha Rüang, Thao, 33, 45, 46
Pha Rüang Mæn Kham Kha, Cao, 33
Pha Rüang Mæn Kham Kha, Thao, 45, 46
Pha Sæng, Thao, 129
Pha Ta Læo, 96
pha si, 149
Phæng [of] Phayao, Mün, 128, 140
Phai, M., 267
Phai Kho, Lady, 65, 66, 71
Phala E, 190
Phalæo, 191
phan, 124, 136
Phan, Ban, 244
Phan, M., 219, 253, 267, 269, 279
Phan Ong, Wat, 284
Phan Phrao, M., 219
Phan Tao, Wat, 260, 262
Phanang Mæ Kha, 298
Phang, M., 267, 269
Phanthanu Duang Di, Wat, 298
Phantu, Phò Thao, 104
Phao Nòi, 181
Phap Müang Ma Kariya, 297
Phathanu Dong Di, Wat, 285
Phawa Min Taya Suddhodhammaraja, Prince, 188
Phawa Min Taya, Prince, 186, 188
Phayak, M., 39, 191, 243, 247, 267, 270
Phayao, 47, 48, 50, 51, 101, 112, 117, 118, 127, 128, 132, 182, 186, 193, 279
Phayu, Cao Phò Thao, 103, 104
Phayu, Cao Phraya, 103, 104
Phayu, Cao Thao, 99
Phayu, Cao, 104
Phek Chai, Mün, 162
Phek Chot, 137
Phek Chot, Khun, 135, 136, 137, 138
Phek Maha Phinai, 136
Phek Yot, 113
Phet Fa, Thao, 208
Phet Maha Phinai, 136
Phetchaphon, 81
Phia Narak, 194, 195
Phia Saphæk, 194
Phia Sarak, 194
Phiang, M., 268
Phimmaphisan the Ratchabut, Cao, 291

Phimmara, 205
Phimmara, Queen, 205
Phimphisan, Cao, 266, 269, 292
phin yòng, 77
Phing [Chiang Mai], M., 178
Phing Chai Kæo, Cao Sæn, 171, 172
Phing Chai Kæo, Sæn, 173
Phing Chai, Sæn, 173, 174
Phing Chiang Mai, M., 117, 134, 177, 178, 179, 180, 253
Phing [River Basin] domains, 156
Phing Yi, Mün, 161, 162, 163, 173
Phitsanulok, 216
Phitsanulok, Phraya, 86
phlang, 225
Phlao Nòi, 181
Phò Rüan, Nai, 205, 206, 210, 223
Phœng, Wat, 111
Phœng Müang, 181
Phòk, M., 245
Phom, Cao Maha, 295
Phom, Cao, 250
Phom, Mün, 240, 242
Phom Sathan, Han, 135
Phòng domain, 89
Phòng people, 89
Phòng Tai, 91
Phòng Tai Shan, 90
Phra Athit, 162
Phra Hin landing, 99
Phra Kosa (Pan), 200
Phra Koṇagamana, 273
Phra Luang, Wat, 98, 99
Phra Maha Samanathera Cao, 289
Phra Müang Chai, 198, 210
Phra Müang Kæo, 280
Phra Müang Kæo, King, 166
Phra Müang Ket Chettharat, 167
Phra Ok, 162
Phra Ratcha-uppayo, 173
Phra Rom Prang, 152
Phra Sæng Müang, 188
Phra Salœm Müang, 189
Phra Sing, Wat, 104, 160, 169, 179, 260, 262, 282, 283, 285, 295, 296
Phra Singha, Wat, 285
Phra Singharam, Wat, 260, 269, 280, 298
Phra Surenratchasena, 293
Phra Ton Kham, 173
Phra Ton Thip, 173
Phra Wanañjeyya, 188
Phrabat Plain, 200

Phræ, 139, 160, 161, 175, 182, 183, 188, 189, 194, 206, 207, 219, 226, 229, 236, 266, 267
Phrakan, M., 45
Phram, Wat, 105, 107, 147
Phran, 168
Phran, M., 173
Phran, Mün, 132, 133
Phran, Phraya, 194, 219
Phran Dong, Mün, 132, 133
Phrao, 59, 89, 125, 163, 229, 230
Phrao, M., 89, 120, 121, 130, 151
Phrao, Mün, 158, 170, 171
Phrao, Phraya, 230
Phrao Salang, 159
Phrao Wang Hin, M., 121
Phraphutthacao Bòwòn Bòrommakot, Somdet 220
phraya of the golden-bowl rank, 173
Phrom Sathan, Han, 133, 134, 135, 145
Phrong, M., 139
Phu, Sæn, 68, 91, 95, 99
Phu Hœt, 32, 46
Phu Kha, 168
Phu Phiang, 169
Phuak Han, Mün, 138
Phuak Na Rüan, 170
Phuang Tu Ma, Phan, 157
Phuban, 136
Phukâm Mang Lung Lwang, 149
Phukâm-Ava, 68, 69,
Phukha, 97
Phukha district, 132
phum and *phai* spirits, 202
phum tasæng, 136
Phum, 126
Phummibāla Raṭṭhādhipati, 299
Phün, Sæn, 206, 207, 208
Phung, Ban, 130
Phuripañña Thao, Khun, 172
Phutadhipatiraja, 159
Phutrai, King, 189
Phutthawangsa Phummipalat, Cao, 298
Phutthawong, Cao, 233, 242, 258, 266, 267, 268, 269, 280, 286
Phutthawong, Nai, 210, 223, 230
Phutthawongsa, 191
Phutthawongsa, Cao, 233, 242
Phutthawongsa, Nai, 210
physician, 98
Phāsī, 263
pig, 190

Ping Chiang Mai, M., 105, 146
Ping Mountains, 139
Ping River, 54, 55, 63, 67, 77, 80, 81, 126, 131, 160, 171, 212
Plan Thæng Cò Swa, *Sitkè*, 198
Plang Phon, M., 140
plaza, 93, 164, 176, 191, 282
Po Læ Thò Khabæhuan, 218
Pœng Phawa Min Taya, 180
Pœng Phawa Min Taya, Cao, 183
Pœng Phawa Min Taya, King, 178, 180
poetry, 262
poison, 149
poisoned arrows, 44, 132
Pòk Rapids, 150
Pòm, M., 171
Pòn, M., 225
Pong, M., 161
Pong Nòi, Nang, 159
Porcupine Village, 85
Prap Cakravala, 240
Prap Chiang Tung, Phraya, 243
Prap Kamlang, 178
Prap Müang Mara Müang Yaksa, 240
Prap Traicak, 148
pregnancy, 33, 110, 205
processional implements, 172
Pu Sæ and Ya Sæ, 276
Pu, M., 230, 239, 241
pu cao cannon, 129
Pukkawut, Phraya, 181
Pundit Nòi, 158
Punnabasu, 74
Puṇṇa, 21

queen, 21, 22, 36, 37, 66, 95, 128, 129, 130, 159, 173, 175, 205, 215, 295
Queen Mother, 110, 111, 118, 128, 166, 296

Racha Tham, 243
Ræ, Min, 187, 208
Ræ Nara, Min, 190, 191, 192, 202
Ræ Thip, Min, 187
Ræ Thippha[net], Min, 187
Ræm, M., 251, 253
raft ordination, 163
rafts, 98, 264
Rai, Ban, 182
Rai, M., 97, 190, 191, 253, 256, 270
Rai Dòi Chang, M., 96

Rai Ya Gate, 191
rainstorm, 120
Rajagaha, 20
Rajaguru, 262
Rajamoli, 170
Rajamuli, 170
Rajapañña, 93
Rajasi seal, 290
rajaśāstra, 105
Rak Phaya Cesu, 190
Rak Samœ Cai, 90
Ram, Khun, 137, 138
ramang, 261
Ramaññadesa, 65
Raming, 192
Raming River, 264, 271
Rammasen, 190
Ramnuan, Cao, 238
Rang Sat, 204
Rangoon, 215, 217
Rao Phu Tao Ròi, M., 39
Rat Ban, 47
Rata, 20
Ratana Hua Müang Kæo the Rear Palace, Cao, 251, 259
Ratana Hua Müang Kæo, Cao, 245, 251, 252, 259
Ratana Rear Palace, Cao, 258, 259
Ratanatiṁsa Abhinavapuri Chiang Mai, M., 240
Ratanatiṁsa Phra Nakhòn Chiang Mai, M., 244
Ratcha-asa, Khun, 135, 136
Ratchabut, 103, 104, 253, 291, 297
Ratchabut, Cao, 253, 269, 270
Ratchakot, Sæn, 226
Ratchasing Khòi Thang, 200
Ratchathani River, 135, 138
Ratchawang, 295
Ratchawang, Phraya, 243
Ratchawong, 297
Ratchawong, Cao, 289, 291, 293, 294, 295, 296, 297, 298
Ratchawong Suwanna Kham Mun, 288
Ratchawong Suwanna Kham Mun, Cao, 288
rattan, 67, 117, 264
Rattana, Cao, 159, 258
Rattana Hua Müang Kæo, Cao, 223, 224, 225, 229, 230, 235, 238
Rattana Hua Müang Kæo Rear Palace, Cao, 244
Rattana Krung Sri Ayutthiya, 211

Rattana Müang Kæo, Cao, 298
Rattana Panya, 178
Rattana Prai, Phan, 178
Rattanaprāsāda, Mahāthera, 142
Rattanaraja, King, 287
Rattanasutta, 120
Rear Palace Prince, 229
rebellion, 8, 214, 296
Reclining Buddha of the Fallen Branch, 277, 279
Reclining Buddha, 200, 273, 277, 279
Red Forest monks, 167
Red Forest [Sect], 158
Red Forest Temple, 163
red *kambalahatthi* elephant, 284
red-heads, 225
refugees, 40, 271
relics of the Lord Buddha, 70, 278
Reliquary of Dagon, 200
rhinoceros, 217, 261
rhinoceros horns, 156
rice, 33, 45, 56, 67, 77, 78, 88, 109, 117, 128, 129, 172, 175, 214, 224, 231, 246, 262
rice-land tax (*kha na*), 71
Ring, M., 254
robes, 70, 145, 274, 286, 288, 293, 295, 296
Ròi, M., 68, 95
Ròi Ngua, 148
ròi khwæn, 256
Rok Nakhòn, Mün, 106
Rong, Nai, 100, 101
Ròng, Khun, 41
Ròng Li, 208
Ròng Lü, 206
Roofed Bridge, 85
Rose Garden (Suan Dòk), 160
Rot Sang Lam, 189
royal advice, 151, 231, 256, 264
royal blood, 204, 287
royal family, 210, 230, 237, 246, 256, 262, 269, 287, 288, 289, 291, 295, 296, 298
royal kitchens, 134
royal palace, 32, 33, 74, 79, 88, 97, 121, 147, 148, 166, 173, 175, 241, 244, 246, 255, 257, 280, 281, 282, 287, 289, 290, 298, 299
Royal Plaza (Khuang Luang), 163–4
royal pundits, 158, 289
royal teachings, 263

royal treasury, 156
royal ways, 94
Rüan, Nai, 203
Ruang, King, 48, 49, 50, 51, 52, 75, 76, 77, 78, 79
Rüang, Mün, 93
Ruciya, 20
rukkhadevata, 109
Run, 50
Rung, M., 265
Rung, Thao, 37
Rung Kæn Chai, King, 37
Rung Kæn Chai, Thao, 36, 37
Rājagaha, 22, 23

Sa, Min, 189
Sabat Chai drum, 93
sacrifice, 35, 112, 119, 277, 289, 293, 294
sacrificial stands, 120
Sæ, M., 117, 154
Sæ Lo, 136
Sæ Nò Kham, Mün, 172
Sæn, Phraya, 174
Sæn Chai, Cao Phraya, 174
Sæn Luang, Phraya, 243, 246
Sæn Müang Ma, Cao, 105, 107, 108, 109, 110, 111
Sæn Müang Ma, Cao Phò Thao, 105
Sæn Müang Ma, Cao Phraya, 108, 111
Sæn Müang Ma, Khun, 106
Sæn Phòk, Wat, 167
Sæn Phu, Cao, 88, 91, 92, 94, 95, 98, 99
Sæn Phu, Cao Phò Thao, 94
Sæn Phu, Cao Phraya, 98
Sæn Phu, Phraya, 91, 98
Sæn Phu, Thao, 88, 91
Sæn Thòng, Wat, 171
Sæn Tò, Ban, 294
Sæn Yòt, Thao, 229
Sæng Phung [i.e. Suan Prung] Gate, 171
Sæng Sung Ta Lao Yæ, 242
Sāgara, 20
Sahatsachai, 162
Sai, M., 229, 267, 270
Sai, Mün, 161, 162
Sai, *Sitkè*, 200
Sai, Thao, 120
Sai Lü, Phraya, 112, 113, 114, 117
Sai Mun, Wat, 282
Sai Riang, Khun, 44

Sai Sung, Han, 133
Sak, 114
Sakhæng Maung Phung, 233, 234, 235, 236
Sakhæng Phaya, 193
Sakhæng Phia, 194
Sakkanüng, Phraya, 215
Sākya, 21, 23
Sākyarāja, 21
Salao, M., 101
Saliang, 199
Salit, 215
Salween River, 65, 177, 178, 264
Sam, Cao Khun, 265
Sam, Cao, 162, 250
Sam, Han, 126
Sam, Khun, 265
Sam, Thao, 120
Sam Chang, 165
Sam Dek Yòi, 121, 122, 123
Sam Fang Kæn, 110
Sam Fang Kæn, Cao, 111, 112
Sam Fang Kæn, King, 113, 114, 117
Sam Fang Kæn, Prince, 111
Sam Fang Kæn, Thao, 110
Sam Kha, Wat, 202
Sam Kham Chiang Rai, Cao, 162
Sam Khrai Han, 126
Sam Khrai Han, Mün, 125
Sam Khrao, 168
Sam Lan, 163
Sam Lan, Cao Mün, 125
Sam Lan, Mün, 123, 124, 125, 126, 127, 159, 161, 166
Sam Lan, Phraya, 175, 219, 225, 243, 246
Sam Lan Ai, Cao Mün, 171, 172
Sam Lan Ai, Mün, 168
Sam Lan Kham Lòm, Mün, 163
Sam Lan Lü Chai, Mün, 173
Sam Mak Pu, Mün, 114
Sam Praya Fang Kæn, Cao Phraya, 117
Sam Praya Fang Kæn, King, 114, 117, 119, 121, 123
Sam Praya Mæ Nai, Cao, 124
Sam Praya, Cao, 124
Sam Praya, King, 119, 120, 121
Sam Yi Phing Chai, 164
Samat, M., 160
Samutthirat, Phraya, 272
San, Ban, 196, 206, 208, 209
San, Phraya, 220
San Tawan, 218

sanam luang, 260
Sanam, 203
Sang Kòi La Khya Saphæk, 191
Sang Yiap, M., 181
Sangha, 23, 142, 175, 218, 286, 287, 288
Sangharaja, 99, 169
Sangkhan, Wat, 191
Sangkharam Chiang Man, Wat, 287, 293
Sañjeyya, 21
Santha, Lady, 210
Santhakan, Ban, 197
Saphao, Wat, 283
Sappabuddha, 21
Sappanwood Pavilion, 164
Sapung, 206
Sāradeva, 20
Sāriputta, 70
Sat, M., 96, 122, 124, 164, 186, 194, 230, 239, 241, 243, 244
Sat, Phraya, 230
Sat Kæo Khang Mum, Mün, 165
Sathira-amat, Phraya, 173
Satòi, Ban, 233, 239, 242
sattrujeyyasenā, 87
Sawankhalok, 215, 216, 218, 230
Sawat, 227, 228
Sawat, M., 226, 227
Sawat Thaman, M., 163
sawbwa, 233
Saṅgitikathā, 273
scholars, 1, 2, 5, 15, 119, 145, 278
scout forces, 118
sealed rescript, 154, 155
Sena Sanao, 282
Setahatthi Suwaṇṇapatumarājā, 279
Setahatthirāja, Cao, 279
Seven Fountains, 114, 169
Seven Fountains City, 115
Seven Fountains Mountain, 113, 114
Seyya, 162
Shan army, 164
Shan domains, 92, 150, 151, 152, 163
Shan rulers, 151
Shan, 90, 92, 150, 151, 152, 163, 164, 195, 198, 211, 212, 213, 233, 241
Shans, 150, 151, 161, 163, 164, 169, 170, 184, 209, 243, 265
shooting stars, 166
Shwe Lan Tòng, 265, 266

314   INDEX

Shwe Lin Mani, 245
Si, Sæn, 239
Si Bun Rüang, Phò Thao, 159
Si Kœt, Wat, 295
Si Phan, 178
Si Phlan Sai, M., 177
Si Phò, M., 151
Si Phra Mun, 178
Si Phum, 147, 148, 165
Si Phum area, 288
Si Phum Bridge, 147
Si Phum fort, 216, 269, 292
Si Phum Gate, 147
Si Phum Ward, 148
Si Puwattisunthòn, Phraya, 239
si lam cing plan, 155
Siao, M., 253
Siddhattha, 22
Siddhattharājakummān, 22
Sihassara, 21
Sihatanu, 21, 23
Sihiṅga Buddha [image], 108
silver, 36, 43, 62, 69, 70, 80, 81, 92, 92, 97, 99, 100, 109, 125, 134, 145, 153, 156, 160, 207, 213, 219, 242, 251, 263, 271, 273, 280, 287, 288, 292
silver Buddha image, 160, 281
Sim, Mün, 122
Sing, M., 267, 269
Sing, Phraya, 220
Sing Khòi Thang, 198
Singharatchathani, Cao Fa, 207
Singkharacha, Thao, 243
Singkharaja, Thao, 243, 244
Siṅhala, 70
Sip, Thao, 120
Sip Kham, Lady, 95
Sip Kham Bridge, 95, 150
Sipsòng Panna, 110, 253, 254, 256
Siri, 208, 213,
Siri, Thao, 239
Siri Cheyyachoti Saramphaya, Cao, 244
Siri Cò Su, *Sitkè*, 213
Siri Jeyyasaramphaya, Cao Maha, 250
Siri Nòratha, 239, 241
Siri-aksòn, Sæn, 238
Sirivaṁso, Mahāthera, 119
Sisapha, Phraya, 293
Sisota, 178
Sitkè, 190, 194, 197, 198, 199, 200, 208, 211, 213, 214, 249
Sitsing, 238

Sitthi, Thao, 233, 242, 268
Sitthiratchaprakian, Phraya Sæn Luang, 173
Sivakaya golden palanquin, 148
Sivivāhana, 21
Siwichai, Cao Khanan, 268
Siwijeyya, Cao Khanan, 266
smallpox, 161
Sò, Ban, 254
Sò, M., 253
Sò Khi, M., 268
Sœm, Mün, 138, 141, 167, 168
Sœn, 164
Sœng, 41, 118, 160, 182
Sœng, M., 41, 83, 124, 182
Sœng, Mün, 85, 128
Sœng Khrai Han, Mün, 125
Sœng Sam Khrai Han, Mün, 124, 125
Sœng Ta Ngam, Mün, 128
Sòi Nakhòn, Mün, 163
Sòi, Cao Thao, 120, 124
Sòi, Thao, 124
Sòi Rai, 239, 242
Sòi Sam Lan, Mün, 164, 165, 167
sok sawat sylvan sprite (tree spirit), 64
Somdet Phraphutthachao, King, 290
somdet, rank, 188
Sòng, M., 182
Sòng Khwæ, 86, 127, 130, 131, 132, 137, 138
Sòng Khwæ, Cao Phraya, 135
Sòng Khwæ, M., 140
Sòng Khwæ, Phraya, 132, 135, 136
Sop Khuang, 169
Sop Pap, 211
Sop Pap [rapids], 211
Sop Yum, 270
sorcerers, 149
soul-tying [*su khwan*] ceremony, 45, 272
South Country, 133, 210, 233, 252, 258, 266, 296
South, 67, 68, 107, 108, 114, 125, 126, 127, 129, 132, 133, 134, 135, 137, 138, 139, 142, 143, 149, 150, 164, 168, 169, 170, 171, 185, 186, 210, 213, 215, 216, 217, 219, 220, 226, 230, 233, 239, 246, 248, 251, 252, 258, 266, 280, 290, 291, 296
Southern Court, 164

Southern Domain, 50
Southern, 107, 108, 112, 113, 114, 126, 137, 149, 162, 164, 166, 168, 169, 171, 200, 212, 213, 214, 216, 238
Southerners, 67, 107, 113, 114, 126, 127, 132, 136, 137, 138, 139, 147, 157, 160, 161, 162, 168, 171, 172, 189, 200, 212, 213, 214, 219, 242
sparrow, 110
spirit of King Mangrai, 119
spirits, 202
spy, 79, 80, 133, 135, 194
Sri, Mün, 164
Sri, Sæn, 233
Sri Anocha, 209
Sri Anocha, Lady, 215
Sri Ayutthiya, 26
Sri Bun Ma, 259
Sri Bun Ma, Cao, 258, 259, 262, 279
Sri Bun Than, 209
Sri Kan Chai sword, 281
Sri Kañjeyya sword, 82
Sri Kañjeyya, 249
Sri Kœt, Wat, 260
Sri Mahanāma, 254
Sri Mahā Thet, Mün, 171
Sri Nantha, Somdet Cao, 179
Sri Phum, *See also* Si Phum
Sri Phum corner, 192, 282
Sri Phum Fort, 285
Sri Phum Gate, 176
Sri Sòng Müang, Phraya, 188
Sri Sudhammarājanagara Luang, 51
Sri Wanna, Lady, 209
Srīmahāmayā, Lady, 22
starving, 193, 216, 220
Su, M., 151
Süa, Caophraya, 215
Suan Dòk, 160, 169, 170, 289
Suan Dòk city, 288
Suan Dòk Gate, 91, 103
Suan Hè Gate, 111
Suan Hè, Ban, 111
Suan Lan, 168
Suddassana, 20
Suddho, King, 187
Suddhodhammaraja, King, 188
Suddhodhammaraja Min Ræ Cò Swa, King, 187
Suddhodhammaraja Min Taya, King, 188

Suddhodhana, 21
Suddhodhanarāja, 21
Sudhammarattana, Mahāthera, 142
Sudorasi, 76, 240
Sukhothai, 48, 51, 108, 114, 135, 152, 160, 161, 162, 216
Sukhothai, Mün, 170, 171
Sukkadandarasi, 76
Sukodhana, 21
Sulva Lü Chai, King, 205
Sulva Lü Chaiyasongkhram, Cao Phraya, 206
Sulwa, Sæn, 226
Sum Sæng, Thao, 34
Sum Sai, M., 177, 178
Sumongkhon, Mün, 158
Sung, M., 253
Sung Fu Ta Lao Yæ, 242
Sungsi Mountain, 199
Sunāga, 23
Sup Mæ Theng, Ban, 240
Sup Theng, Ban, 242
Suphathrarat, Cao Maha, 286
Suphatra, King, 293
Supreme Patriarch, 160, 179, 237, 259
Sura, Phraya, 160
Surakòi Thæng, 235
Surasi, Caophraya, 215, 216
Surasi, Phraya, 212, 213, 215, 220
Surawong, Phraya, 215
Surayotha, 178, 181
Surin, Phraya, 229, 230
Suriya, *Sitkè*, 211
Suriyawong, Cao, 269, 270
Suriyawong, Cao Maha, 271
Suriyawongsa, Cao, 294
Suriyawongsa, Cao Maha, 271, 272
Suruciya, 20
Suthep, 257
Suthep, Dòi, 72, 77, 113, 232, 257, 260, 298
Suthon, Sæn, 211
Suttasoma, 65
Suttasomarāja, 66
Sutthasana, Phraya, 167, 173, 174
Sutthasana-amat, Phraya, 173
Suttodhana, 21
Suvejeyyanta Palace, 148
Suwanna Kham Khrüang, Cao, 253
Suwanna Kham Mun, Cao, 241, 242, 258, 279, 283

Suwanna Selakatasalagi M. Sat, M., 243
Suwannabimba, 254
Suwannahongsa Cakkavatti Cao Fa Luang Hò Kham, Cao Maha, 243
Suwannanawa [barge], 245
Suya, Cao, 297
Suya, *Sitkè*, 211
sweets manufactories, 98
swords, 118, 141, 171, 172, 201, 233, 241, 258
swordsmen, 124, 140, 148, 150

Ta, M., 203
Ta Chuai, Sæn, 101
Ta Dam ("Black Eyes"), Lady, 210
Ta Sæng, 168
Ta Sæng Phò Nòi, Mün, 168
Ta Sai, 264
Tæng River, 55
Tak, Ban, 228
Tak, M., 228, 234
Tak, Phraya, 228
Tak Lahæng, M., 228, 234
Taksin, King, 212, 214, 215, 216, 219, 220
tala [secretary], 178
Talaban, 197
Talat Kæo, 271
Tam, Mün, 122
Tan, Cao Khun, 205
Tan, M., 117, 183
Tan, Mün, 138, 141
Tan River, 86
Tang ("Window") Pond, 63
Tao Ròi, 40
Tao Ròi Yam Di, 40
Tathāgatha, 274, 275
Tāvadiṁsa Heaven, 25, 262
Tavoy, 195
tax collection, 156
tax-collectors, 123
taxes, 53, 54, 156, 203
Taya, Min, 177, 178, 180, 184, 185
Teacher Nantho, 226
Temiyajātaka, 247
Temple of the Brave Women, 106
temple of the Reclining Buddha, 200
temple slaves, 194
ten royal precepts, 159, 167
Tenasserim, 143

Tha, 195
Tha, Ban, 226
Tha, Dòi, 40
Tha, Mün, 127
Tha Chæt, 241
Tha Chang, 239, 242
Tha Din Dæng, 215, 216
Tha Fang, 225
Tha Kan, 124, 151, 168, 206
Tha Kan district (panna), 71, 126, 163
Tha Kham Mæ Khrao, 181
Tha Khandai, 127
Tha Khao P[l]üak, 248, 249
Tha Lò, 253
Tha Man Gate, 96
Tha Nang, 99
Tha Nang Gate, 162, 171
Tha Ngua, 125
Tha Òi, 197
Tha Òk, 239, 241
Tha Pha Pun, 242
Tha Phæ, 166
Tha Phæ Bridge, 192
Tha Phæ neighborhood, 166
Tha Sai customs posts, 97
Tha Sitò Sitæ, 225
Tha Than, 182
Tha Wang customs post, 97
Tha Wang Phrao, 217
Tha Wang Tan, 212, 214, 251
Thado Khòi, 186
Thai, 13, 14, 16, 17, 52, 73, 74, 91, 93. 96, 108, 111, 112, 159, 166, 168, 169, 170, 172, 173, 174, 179, 181, 191, 193, 211, 212, 220, 233, 234, 254, 272, 279, 281, 282, 283, 285
Thai cloth, 156, 272
Thai words, 16, 52
Thakan, 196
Thalang, M., 225
Tham, Ban, 27
Tham Nòng Khwang, Mün, 162
Tham Phra, Dòi, 114
Thammakitti Suriya Meghanarin, Cao, 292
Thammalangka, Cao, 215, 221
Thammila, 276
Thamong Plik Sai, 178
Than, Dòi, 248
Thao Theppha Kham Khrai, Lady, 36, 37
Thap Mak customs post, 97
Thap Mu Kam, 208

Thap Mu Kham, 208
Thap Muang Khan, 162
Thap Pa Khia, 176
Thap Phœng customs post, 97
Thap Phui, 182, 272
Thap Puai, 183
Thap Salit, 108
Thap Siri, 208
Thap Som Pòi, 130
Thap Tao Pun, 176
Thap Yang, 97
Tharrawaddy Nòratha Min Khòi, Prince, 184, 186
Tharrawaddy, Prince, 184
Thatsayotha, Phraya, 272
Thep, Nang, 207
Thep, Sæn, 203
Thep Kham Khrai, 71
Thep Monthian, Phan, 171
Thep Sing, 202
Theppha Kham Khrai, Lady, 36
Thepphakhun, Phan, 146, 147
Thepphasing, 191, 192, 193
Thepphawong Chiang Khæng, Phraya, 243
Thera Devakula, 142
Thipphacak, 203, 204, 205
Thipphacak the Vagabond, 204
Thipphalòng, 149
Thipphanet, Phraya, 187, 188
Thittamangala, 237
Tho, 193
Tho River, 85, 95
Thò Po, 218
Thœn, 211, 212, 215, 226, 228, 229, 234, 235
Thœng, 194, 219
Thom, Cao Maha, 295
Thòn, M., 178
Thong Iang, 194
Thong Òk, 239
Thong Òk, Ban, 242
Thong San, 206
Thòng Thip Buddha image, 254
Thra, Mün, 174
Thrang, M., 145
three-complexioned ladies, 199
Throw-Away City, 72
Thu, M., 226
Thuan, Mün, 123, 124
Thuan district, 123
Thuan [district 2,000], 123
Thuan Ñanasathian, Cao Sæn, 179
Thuan Phukha, 54

Thum, Mün, 153
Thum Tum, 168
Thung, Dòi, 40
Thung Yang, 131
tiger cubs, 217
tigers, 217, 224, 261
Tilok, Cao Phraya, 111, 112
Tilok, King, 7, 112, 122, 123, 124, 125, 129, 134, 135, 136, 142, 149, 150, 152, 156
Tilok, Thao, 122
Tilokacukthewi, 111
Tilokarat, 138
Tilokarat, King, 11, 123, 125, 127, 128, 133, 134, 135, 136, 138, 139, 142, 145, 146, 147, 148, 149, 150, 151, 152, 153, 154, 155, 156, 157, 158, 159
Tin Chiang, Mün, 156
Ting, M., 250
tò, 97
Tœk, Phraya, 164, 165
Tœn, M., 157
Ton Rai Ton Luang [area], 171
Ton Thip, Cao, 195
Tòng Khai, M., 229
Tòng Phò, Ban, 225
tonic herbs for elephant, 127
Trailok, King of Siam, 130, 131, 136, 137, 145
translator, 142, 143
tree spirit, 64, 109
tribute, 156, 205, 213, 241, 256
Tricakkhu Anuruddha Dhammikarāja, 24
Trœn, Mün, 167, 168
Tu Khun Fu Ta Lao Yæ, 242
Tuan Hua Yòt, M., 232, 233, 234
Tui, 158
Tuk Tu, M., 150, 151
Tun, M., 133
Tün, Phraya, 191, 196
Tung, Dòi, 25

U, M., 180
Ua Chiang Sæn, Lady, 48, 49
Ua Kham Chiang Sæn, Lady, 49
Ua Kham Khòn Müang, Lady, 31, 32
Ua Ming Còm Müang, Lady, 36
Üai Cai, Lady, 33
ukhaṅgarāja moment, 240
Umong, Wat, 283
Un Müang drum, 86, 87
Up Kæo, Lady, 32, 33

Upadaya, 22
uparaja, 87, 130, 214, 215, 216, 221, 259
Uparaja, Cao, 269, 285, 291
Uparaja, Cao Maha, 268, 279, 280, 286, 289, 291, 293, 294, 297, 298, 299
Uparaja, Cao Phra Waramaha, 298
Uparaja, Cao Phra Wòra Maha, 268
Uparaja Kòn Kæo, 225
Uparaja Kòn Kæo, Cao, 218
Uparaja Narathipati Sri Suwanna Fai Na Hò Kham, Cao, 244
Uparaja Narādhipatī Sri Suwanna of the Front of the Golden Palace, Cao Maha, 262
Uparaja of the Front Palace, Cao Maha, 279
Uparaja Phutthawong the Front Palace, Cao Maha, 291
Uparaja Phutthawong, Cao Maha, 287, 288, 291, 295
Uposatha, 20
Uppa Kòng, 238
Uppayo, 172, 175, 182
Uppayowarat, King, 173, 174, 175
Ussupabatta, 77
Ussupabatta, Mount, 72
uṭṭaracayasaya, 51

Vajira, Pañya, 259
Varakalyāṇa, 20
Varamandhātu, 20
Varatāja, 20
Varoja, 20
Varābosatha, 20
Vaṭṭhakuli, King, 64
Vedic texts, 243
Velukugāma [temporary capital], 224
Venerable Reliquary, 215, 232
Venus, 36, 200
Vesa Phu, Phò Thao, 104
Vessantara, 247
Vesantarāja, 21
Vesāntara Dhammikarāja, 21
Victory Drum, 101, 106
Videha, M., 155, 242
Vientiane, 219, 220, 297, 298
Vietnam, 153
Vietnamese, 128, 129, 152, 154, 235, 245, 263

INDEX 317

Wa, 245, 255
Wa, M., 248, 253, 254, 255, 258, 267
Wachira-amat, Phraya, 173, 174
Wachirapraya, 179
walls, 261, 268, 288, 298
Wan day, *Phraya*, 74
Wang, M., 193, 253
Wang Kam, 53
Wang Kat, 233
Wang Kham, 182
Wang Kœng, 219
Wang Lu, Ban, 233
Wang Phrao, 196, 206, 218
Wang River, 206, 211
Wang Sakhæng, 219, 223, 224
Wang Tan Landing, 258, 271, 272
war boats, 171
war elephants, 81, 87, 253
war horses, 81, 87, 253
washing their hair, 140
Wat, Phraya, 194
Wat, Sæn, 281
Watchare-amat, Phraya, 173
water of allegiance, 134
water ogress, 103
water-buffalo, 34, 149, 276
waters of allegiance, 129
wax, 98
Weluwan Ku Tao, Wat, 197
White Crow Prince, 187
White Crow, Lady Princess, 188
White Head, General, 199, 201, 211, 212, 213, 214, 215, 216
white elephant, 71, 279, 280, 284, 285
white elephant statues, 109
white-robed ascetic, 143, 194
Wi, Sæn, 168
wiang, 72
Wiang 7 Rin, 298
Wiang Can, 201
Wiang Cet Lin, 120, 121
Wiang Chiang Mai, 81
Wiang Chiang Thòng, 82
Wiang Din, Müang, 138
Wiang Din, Mün, 141, 158
Wiang Fan, 73
Wiang Kum Kam, 16, 62, 63, 64, 81, 82, 89, 90, 91, 95, 106, 110
Wiang Lò, 182
Wiang Pa Sang, 193
Wiang Rua Nang, 169
Wiang Sœng, 182
Wiang Suan Dòk, 169

wife, 232, 265
wild ogres, 102
wild tigers, 102
windstorm, 198
Wisutthathewi, Lady, 184
Wisutthithewi, Lady, 184
wolves, 73, 74, 77
women, 66, 106, 131, 160, 163, 203, 280
Wòn, Nai, 229, 231
Wong, Thao, 243
Wòng, Mün, 158
Wongsa, Nai, 210
writing, 145
writing-palm (lan) tree, 72
wun, 186

Ya the blacksmith, Grandfather, 192
ya mung khatai, 73
Ya Thao, Dòi, 40
Yai Thala Siang, Phraya, 215, 216
Yan, M., 226
Yan Khwæng Siri, 232, 233
Yanasakhòn, 178
Yang, M., 178, 250, 251, 252, 258, 266, 267, 269, 270
Yang Field, 182
Yang Grove, 70
Yang Khok, 208
Yang Khun Sayiap, 182
Yang Ngœn, M., 26, 29
Yang Phak, 72
Yang Phrak, 179
Yang Sieo, Ban, 29
Yasodharā, Lady, 22
Yasuntharathewi, Lady, 105
Yi, Han, 126
Yi, Mün, 168
Yi, Sæn, 163
Yi, Thao, 120
Yi Ai, Mün, 164, 167
Yi Ba, King, 43, 53, 54, 55, 56, 59, 60, 61, 62, 79, 80, 86, 87
Yi Ca Ban Lam Khæk, 178
Yi Kham Hao, 33, 34, 46
Yi Kham Müang, 178
Yi Kum Kam, Cao Phò Thao, 112, 114
Yi Kum Kam, Cao Thao, 114
Yi Kum Kam, Phò Cao Phò Thao, 111
Yi Kum Kam, Phò Thao, 112, 113, 114
Yi Kum Kam, Thao, 110, 113

Yi Lò, Mün, 126
Yi Lok, Mün, 128
Yi Mongkhon, 172
Yi Phing Chai, 164, 165
Yi Phing Chai, Mün, 165
Yi Phing Chai, Sæn, 164
Yi Ra, 109
Yi Thara, Mün, 131, 132
Yian, Ban, 181
Ying, M., 44, 88
Yodhiya, 42, 81
yokkrabat, 181
Yòn Nguak, 101
yong gong, 106
Yòng, M., 130, 151, 157, 180, 229, 231, 242, 243, 248, 252, 253, 254, 255, 257, 258, 266, 267, 268, 269, 270
Yòng Hui, M., 151
Yot, Mün, 204
Yòt, King, 159, 160
Yòt Cai Phek, Han, 113
Yòt Chiang Rai, Cao Phò Thao, 150
Yòt Chiang Rai, King, 159, 165
Yòt Chiang Rai, Phò Thao, 159
Yòt Chiang Rai, Thao, 150, 160
Yòt Müang, Cao, 135
Yòt Nakhòn Tower, 164
Yotsarat, Phraya, 157
Yotthiya, 169
Yu, Ban, 16, 180, 253, 254, 267
Yuam (Mæ Sariang), M., 191, 230
Yuam Tai, M., 121, 156
yung muai, 73
Yuttha, 162
Yutthisathiang, 130, 131
Yutthisathiang, Phraya, 130, 132

www.ingramcontent.com/pod-product-compliance
Lightning Source LLC
Chambersburg PA
CBHW040929240426
43667CB00027B/2995